HOLT *Traditio...*

Introductory Course

Language and Sentence Skills
Practice
Support for *Warriner's Handbook*

► **Lesson Worksheets**
► **Chapter Reviews**
► **"Choices" Activities**
► **Literary Models**
► **Proofreading Applications**

FOR
■ **Grammar**
■ **Usage**
■ **Mechanics**
■ **Sentences**

HOLT, RINEHART AND WINSTON

ISBN 978-0-03-099700-6
ISBN 0-03-099700-3

18 19 20 21 22 0304 22 21 20 19 18
4500725962

Contents

Contents

Contents

Chapter 8

USING PRONOUNS CORRECTLY

Chapter 9

USING MODIFIERS CORRECTLY

Chapter 10

A GLOSSARY OF USAGE

Contents

Chapter 11
CAPITAL LETTERS

Chapter 12
PUNCTUATION:
END MARKS, SEMICOLONS, COLONS, COMMAS

Chapter 13
PUNCTUATION:
UNDERLINING (ITALICS), QUOTATION MARKS,
APOSTROPHES, HYPHENS

Contents

Chapter 14
SPELLING

Chapter 15
CORRECTING COMMON ERRORS

Contents

Chapter 16
WRITING EFFECTIVE SENTENCES

Using This Workbook

The worksheets in this workbook provide practice, reinforcement, and extension for *Warriner's Handbook.*

Most of the worksheets you will find in this workbook are **traditional worksheets** providing practice and reinforcement activities on every rule and on all major instructional topics in the grammar, usage, and mechanics chapters in *Warriner's Handbook.*

You will also find in the workbook several kinds of **Language in Context worksheets**, which have been developed to expand the exploration and study of grammar, usage, and mechanics. The Language in Context worksheets include Choices worksheets, Proofreading Applications, Literary Model worksheets, and Writing Applications.

- **Choices** worksheets offer up to ten activities that provide new ways of approaching grammar, usage, and mechanics. Students can choose and complete one independent or group activity per worksheet. Choices activities stimulate learning through research, creative writing, nonfiction writing, discussion, drama, art, games, interviews, music, cross-curricular activities, technology, and other kinds of projects, including some designed entirely by students.

- **Proofreading Application** worksheets help students apply what they learn in class to contexts in the real world. Students use proofreading symbols to correct errors in grammar, usage, and mechanics in practical documents such as letters, applications, brochures, and reports. A chart of proofreading symbols is provided on page 348 of this workbook.

- **Literary Model** worksheets provide literary models that demonstrate how published authors use various grammatical forms to create style or meaning. Students identify and analyze each author's linguistic choices and then use grammatical forms to create style or meaning in their own literary creations. Students are asked to reflect on their own linguistic choices and to draw connections between the choices they make and the style or meaning of their work.

- **Writing Application** worksheets are similar to the Writing Application activities in the grammar, usage, and mechanics chapters in *Warriner's Handbook.* Following the writing process, students use specific grammatical forms as they create a publishable document such as a letter, report, script, or pamphlet.

The Teaching Resources include the **Answer Key** in a separate booklet titled *Language and Sentence Skills Practice Answer Key.*

for **CHAPTER 1: THE SENTENCE** *pages 2–14*

Choices: Using Your Sentence Sense

Here's your chance to step out of the grammar book and into the real world. You may not notice parts of sentences, but you and the people around you use them every day. The following activities challenge you to find a connection between sentences and the world around you. Do the activity below that suits your personality best, and then share your discoveries with your class. Have fun!

REPRESENTING

Bigger and Bigger

Help your classmates see how a complete subject can grow from a single letter (*I*) to a dozen words or more. Write a series of sentences, each one with a complete subject that is just a bit longer than the last. Then, prepare a poster. At the top of the poster, write the sentence with the smallest complete subject. As you move down the poster, write sentences with increasingly longer complete subjects. Center the sentences so that they form a pyramid. Write the simple subject of each sentence in a different color.

WRITING

The Nitty-Gritty

Subjects and verbs are the core, the nitty-gritty, of sentences. Write a poem using only subjects and verbs. That's right—no adverbs, adjectives, articles, complements, or prepositional phrases.

DEBATE

Show Me

Can you write a sentence in which an adverb, an adjective, or a preposition functions as the subject of a sentence? Try it! Then, ask your classmates to try, and lead them in a discussion of whether or not it is possible.

DEMONSTRATION

Bare Bones

The subject and verb carry the essential meaning of a sentence. But just how much meaning can subjects and verbs carry? Take a paragraph or two of published writing that you like. Identify each subject and verb in every sentence. Then, cross everything else out. What do you have left? Read the paragraph made up of only subjects and verbs. Does it make sense? If so, why? If not, why not? Have answers to these questions ready

when you demonstrate this process to the class. Prepare "before and after" posters, or write your paragraphs on the chalkboard so that you can erase everything except the subject and verb.

MUSIC

As Fast as You Can

You probably know several traditional handclap routines and the raps and rhymes that go with them. Many of them are made up of imperative sentences. Get together with a friend and create a handclap routine with a rap to go with it. Be sure you use complete imperative sentences. When you're satisfied with your routine, perform it for your classmates. Maybe they'll remember it for at least as long as you have remembered "Pat-a-Cake."

DISCUSSION

Natural Habitats

Some places are natural habitats for certain types of sentences. For instance, you can hear plenty of imperative sentences, such as "Salute your officers," on any military base. You can hear interrogative sentences—such as "What seems to be bothering you?"—at a doctor's office. Write down at least two natural habitats for each sentence type; then, come up with at least two example sentences for each habitat. Share copies of your list with your classmates.

DRAMA

Communication Gap

Write a dialogue for four characters. One character speaks in only declarative sentences, one in only interrogative sentences, one in only imperative sentences, and one in only exclamatory sentences. Find three or four friends and stage your skit for the class.

Language and Sentence Skills Practice

Sentences and Sentence Fragments A

1a. A *sentence* is a word group that contains a subject and a verb and that expresses a complete thought.

> EXAMPLE   The American bison is brown and black.

A *sentence fragment* is a word group that looks like a sentence but either does not contain both a subject and a verb or does not express a complete thought.

SENTENCE FRAGMENT   Graze on the plain.

SENTENCE   The bison graze on the plain.

EXERCISE   Decide whether each group of words is a sentence or a sentence fragment. Write *S* for *sentence* or *SF* for *sentence fragment* on the line provided.

Example ___*SF*___ **1.** Has a large head and shoulders.

_____ **1.** Zoologists call the American buffalo a bison.

_____ **2.** May weigh up to three thousand pounds.

_____ **3.** Live in herds and feed on grass.

_____ **4.** Once roamed across North America.

_____ **5.** In 1850, there were still about twenty million bison.

_____ **6.** By 1890, bison were almost extinct.

_____ **7.** Didn't kill all those bison.

_____ **8.** Now, more than thirty thousand.

_____ **9.** Bison were difficult to hunt on foot.

_____ **10.** The horse and the gun changed Plains Indian life.

_____ **11.** Moved from camp to camp.

_____ **12.** Plains Indians began to use horses about 1600.

_____ **13.** Brought to America by the Spanish.

_____ **14.** Wild herds of mustangs in the American West.

_____ **15.** *Mustang* may come from a Spanish word meaning "ownerless horses."

_____ **16.** *Bronco* another Spanish word.

_____ **17.** Some people call any bad-tempered horse a bronco.

_____ **18.** Also another word for mustang.

_____ **19.** Descendants of wild mustangs are still used to herd cattle.

_____ **20.** Broncos, or broncs, in rodeo competitions.

Sentences and Sentence Fragments B

1a. A *sentence* is a word group that contains a subject and a verb and that expresses a complete thought.

> **EXAMPLES** Didn't a picture of that headdress appear on a United States stamp?
> What a beautiful arrangement of feathers it is!

A *sentence fragment* is a word group that looks like a sentence but either does not contain both a subject and a verb or does not express a complete thought.

SENTENCE FRAGMENT Brown feathers of the golden eagle.

SENTENCE Brown feathers of the golden eagle adorn the headdress.

EXERCISE A Decide whether each group of words is a sentence or a sentence fragment. Write *S* for *sentence* or *SF* for *sentence fragment* on the line provided.

Example ___SF___ **1.** When we entered the museum's exhibit area.

_____ **1.** No two headdresses of the Plains Indians.

_____ **2.** The feathers of the male golden eagle are a sign of bravery and speed.

_____ **3.** Have you ever seen a real Plains Indian headdress?

_____ **4.** At the famous Battle of the Little Bighorn, General George Custer!

_____ **5.** What a fierce battle that was!

_____ **6.** Lived in earth lodges or tepees.

_____ **7.** Villages along rivers and streams.

_____ **8.** As they followed herds of buffalo across the vast plains.

_____ **9.** Buffalo meat a main part of their diet.

_____ **10.** The skins of the buffalo were used for bedding, clothing, and tepees.

EXERCISE B On each line below, write a sentence that includes each sentence fragment. Add punctuation and change capitalization as needed for your sentence.

Example 1. Hissing, the cat ___Hissing, the cat swatted at the unfamiliar dog.___

11. After the football game _____

12. Gave the school a donation _____

13. Standing by the mailbox _____

14. Will become a firefighter _____

15. Jumping up and down _____

Sentences and Sentence Fragments C

| **1a.** | A *sentence* is a word group that contains a subject and a verb and that expresses a complete thought. |

A *sentence fragment* is a word group that looks like a sentence but either does not contain both a subject and a verb or does not express a complete thought.

SENTENCE FRAGMENT Because we were tired.

SENTENCE We left early because we were tired.

EXERCISE Each item below shows one way a sentence fragment can be corrected. Study each correction. Then, on the line provided, show another way each fragment can be corrected.

Example 1. Fragment: Studying the solar system. Correction: Kim is studying the solar system.

 The class was studying the solar system.

1. Fragment: My neighbor Flo. Correction: My neighbor Flo is a dancer.

_____

2. Fragment: Waiting for the bus. Correction: Mr. Bossio is waiting for the bus.

_____

3. Fragment: Cutting the apple into four pieces. Correction: Cut the apple into four pieces.

_____

4. Fragment: Len's new puppy. Correction: Have you seen Len's new puppy?

_____

5. Fragment: After the soccer match. Correction: I spoke to Kara after the soccer match.

_____

6. Fragment: Sent the postcards yesterday. Correction: Walt sent the postcards yesterday.

_____

7. Fragment: Both hamsters. Correction: Both hamsters seem sick.

_____

8. Fragment: Jogging in the park. Correction: The sisters were jogging in the park.

_____

9. Fragment: Beneath the surface. Correction: What mysteries lie beneath the surface?

_____

10. Fragment: Before she left. Correction: Janet called me before she left.

_____

Simple Subjects and Complete Subjects

1b.	The *subject* tells *whom* or *what* the sentence is about.

The *complete subject* consists of all the words needed to tell *whom* or *what* the sentence is about.

1c.	The *simple subject* is the main word or word group that tells *whom* or *what* the sentence is about.

COMPLETE SUBJECT   **The English reports** are due on Tuesday.

SIMPLE SUBJECT   The English **reports** are due on Tuesday.

EXERCISE A   The complete subject is underlined in the following sentences. Circle the simple subject.

Example 1. Has ⟨anyone⟩ in the class seen *The Miracle Worker*?

1. Young Helen Keller could not see, hear, or speak.

2. Didn't a serious illness cause her disabilities?

3. Helen's father hired Anne Sullivan, a teacher from Boston.

4. Ms. Sullivan used the sense of touch to communicate with Helen.

5. *The Miracle Worker* was a play and movie about Anne Sullivan and Helen Keller.

6. In 1904, Keller graduated from Radcliffe College.

7. Her college classes were interpreted for her by Anne Sullivan.

8. The problems of sightless people were a concern to Keller.

9. After college she worked for the American Foundation for the Blind.

10. Many people with disabilities have been inspired by Helen Keller's achievements.

EXERCISE B   Underline the complete subject in the following sentences. Then, circle the simple subject.

Example 1. In the 1820s, ⟨Louis Braille⟩ devised a way for sightless people to read.

11. At first Louis Braille's dot system was not officially accepted.

12. Eventually Braille's system won acceptance all over the world.

13. Braille is a code of raised dots on paper.

14. Different arrangements of dots stand for the alphabet, punctuation marks, and numbers.

15. Sightless people can run their fingers along the dots.

16. Since the early 1960s, the process of making braille books has been improved with computers.

17. First, the text is typed into a computer.

18. The computer automatically translates the words into braille.

19. Then the raised braille figures are transferred onto metal plates or paper.

20. Have you ever seen a braille book?

Language and Sentence Skills Practice

GRAMMAR

Simple Predicates and Complete Predicates

1d.   The *predicate* of a sentence tells something about the subject.

The *complete predicate* consists of a verb and all the words that describe the verb and complete its meaning.

1e.   The *simple predicate,* or *verb,* is the main word or word group in the complete predicate.

EXERCISE A   The complete predicate is underlined in each of the following sentences. Circle the verb (simple predicate).

Example 1. Their nests (are) usually (found) along the southeast coast of the United States.

1. Sea turtles face many dangers.

2. They can't withdraw into their shells for protection.

3. Size and swimming speed are their only defenses.

4. Shrimp boats can snag turtles in nets.

5. Sometimes other animals dig up the turtles' eggs for food.

6. People have also used turtle meat and eggs for food.

7. Volunteers are protecting the fragile eggs of the sea turtle.

8. The efforts of the volunteers may save the sea turtle from destruction.

9. Turtle preserves have been established in certain areas.

10. Do some countries protect rare turtle species?

EXERCISE B   Underline the complete predicate in each of the following sentences. Then, circle the verb (simple predicate).

Example 1. Because of the efforts of Ida B. Wells, several cultural and educational services (were established).

11. Ida B. Wells was born into slavery in 1862 in Holly Springs, Mississippi.

12. She participated in the establishment of the National Association for the Advancement of Colored People.

13. She had taught school to her younger brothers and sisters after her parents' death.

14. As a journalist, Ms. Wells raised public awareness of African American issues.

15. Ida B. Wells was active in the women's suffrage movement.

Verb Phrases

A simple predicate that consists of a main verb and one or more helping verbs is called a
verb phrase.

> **EXAMPLES** Elie **was born** in Alexandria, Egypt.
> He **has lived** in Cairo, Egypt's capital.
> **Have** you not **seen** the photographs of his home?

EXERCISE A Underline the verb phrase in each of the following sentences.

Example 1. Elie's family <u>didn't move</u> to the United States until last year.

1. We have traveled to Elie's home in Cairo, Egypt.

2. Egypt is situated in the northeastern section of Africa.

3. We couldn't wait for our first tour of the country.

4. The ancient wonders of Egypt have been preserved.

5. Elie has been teaching us Egyptian history.

6. Tomorrow we will go to Pharaonic Village.

7. Daily life in ancient Egypt is reenacted there.

8. You can dress in the clothing of an Egyptian pharaoh.

9. Perhaps someone will take your picture.

10. Don't forget your camera.

EXERCISE B Underline the complete predicate in each of the following sentences. Then, circle each verb
or verb phrase.

Example 1. During the reign of Ramses II, <u>many great temples (were built)</u>

11. From about 1290 to 1224 B.C., Ramses II was pharaoh of Egypt.

12. Ramses II is known as Ramses the Great.

13. The preparation of Ramses' body for burial may have taken seventy days.

14. Scientists have conducted tests on the mummy of Ramses.

15. What did the scientists learn?

16. The pharaoh's health couldn't have been too poor.

17. The reign of Ramses lasted more than sixty years.

18. For three thousand years his mummy has survived.

19. Some ancient mummies can be found in museums.

20. New airtight cases have been developed for their protection.

Simple and Complete Subjects and Predicates A

| **1c.** | The **simple subject** is the main word or word group that tells *whom* or *what* the sentence is about. |

The *complete subject* consists of all the words needed to tell *whom* or *what* the sentence is about. The *simple subject* is part of the complete subject.

| **1e.** | The **simple predicate,** or **verb,** is the main word or word group in the complete predicate. |

The *complete predicate* consists of a verb and all the words that describe the verb and complete its meaning.

EXERCISE A In each of the following sentences, underline the complete subject once. Then, underline the simple subject a second time.

Example 1. Did your family go downtown to see the parade?

1. Thousands of people went to the parade last night.

2. Those amazing acrobats are members of the same family.

3. Have you ever seen so many beautiful horses?

4. On my seat lay a pamphlet about the history of our city.

5. Who was your favorite performer?

EXERCISE B In each sentence, underline the complete predicate once. Then, underline the simple predicate, or verb, a second time.

Example 1. Have you ever entered a project in the science fair?

6. My younger brothers are always working on some kind of project.

7. They both hope for a career in chemistry.

8. Sometimes my brothers go into the basement and shut the door.

9. They stay busy for hours.

10. Most of the time their projects are really messy.

11. For example, one time they mixed butter and ink.

12. They have never done anything dangerous.

13. They can clean the basement themselves.

14. My mother once hosed them off in the front yard.

15. How dirty their clothes get!

for **CHAPTER 1: THE SENTENCE**   *pages 8–12*

Simple and Complete Subjects and Predicates B

1c. The *simple subject* is the main word or word group that tells *whom* or *what* the sentence is about.

The *complete subject* consists of all the words needed to tell *whom* or *what* the sentence is about. The *simple subject* is part of the complete subject.

1e. The *simple predicate,* or *verb,* is the main word or word group in the complete predicate.

The *complete predicate* consists of a verb and all the words that describe the verb and complete its meaning.

EXERCISE A   In each of the following sentences, underline the simple subject once, and underline the simple predicate twice.

Example 1. Have you seen my favorite sweater?

1. Are your friends coming with us tomorrow?

2. Those swimmers practice for hours every day.

3. Next year, my uncle will be driving his truck to Alaska.

4. The rainy weather must have caused floods in the city.

5. The biology class finally finished the experiment.

EXERCISE B   In each of the following sentences, underline the complete subject once, and underline the complete predicate twice.

Examples 1. Did a little brown dog run past your house?

2. The most amazing thing happened!

6. Would you join us for lunch tomorrow?

7. Inside the birdhouse were two speckled eggs.

8. James usually makes his bed before breakfast.

9. You will find your coat behind that door.

10. The light of the moon shone through the clouds.

11. During the campaign, we worked hard for our candidate.

12. Has your brother seen the dinosaur bones at the museum?

13. In one room we saw several complete skeletons.

14. The man in the blue baseball cap is my father.

15. We listened to scary stories at the campout.

Language and Sentence Skills Practice

Compound Subjects

1f. A *compound subject* consists of two or more subjects that are joined by a conjunction and that have the same verb.

> **EXAMPLE** Do **oranges, grapefruit,** or **lemons** make the best fruit drink?

EXERCISE A Underline the compound subject in each of the following sentences.

Example 1. Did <u>Cameron</u>, <u>Jared</u>, or <u>Mitch</u> win the award?

1. Moose and elk are the largest members of the deer family.

2. Before dinner, Michael or Pierre will set the table.

3. Blue, green, and violet are cool colors.

4. Tigers and cheetahs belong to the cat family.

5. Mr. Itoh and Mr. Evans plan to climb Mount Everest next year.

6. Edward, Christy, and Chang won prizes in the science fair.

7. Either Tanya or Cam will play the part of Dorothy.

8. During Hurricane Hugo, rain and wind battered the coast.

9. Did Beethoven or Haydn write the *Moonlight Sonata*?

10. Cardinals and bluebirds have bright, colorful feathers.

EXERCISE B Combine each group of sentences to create one sentence with a compound subject. Make sure that the other words in the new sentence agree in number with the compound subject.

Example 1. Ceres is an asteroid. Eros is an asteroid, too.

Ceres and Eros are asteroids.

11. Cork is used to make baseballs. Rubber is used, too. Yarn is also used.

_____

12. The flapping shutter frightened the dog. The howling wind did, too.

_____

13. Jasmine may win the race. On the other hand, Anna may win it.

_____

14. Baseball is a favorite sport of mine. I like tennis, too.

_____

15. Copper is mined in the Andes. Tin is mined there, too. Also, nitrates are mined there.

_____

for **CHAPTER 1: THE SENTENCE** *page 14*

Compound Verbs

| **1g.** | A *compound verb* consists of two or more verbs that are joined by a conjunction and that have the same subject. |

> **EXAMPLES** Dogs **are owned** and **loved** for many reasons.
> Some adult dogs **appear** mean but **can be** quite gentle.

EXERCISE A Underline the compound verb in each of the following sentences.

Example 1. Police dogs can track or even capture suspects.

1. On the job, police dogs obey and react quickly.

2. In the Swiss Alps, Saint Bernards locate and assist people in snowstorms.

3. German shepherds serve as guide dogs and help sightless people.

4. Dogs can offer companionship and provide protection.

5. A dog's bark may frighten burglars or awaken families in case of fire.

6. Pets can raise the spirits of people in hospitals and can improve attitudes.

7. Puppies thrill and delight many young children.

8. Dog obedience classes are starting tomorrow and will continue for six weeks.

9. In time, you will handle and guide your dog with confidence.

10. Dog ownership is a big responsibility and should be taken seriously.

EXERCISE B Add verbs to complete the following sentences. You may need to add other words to complete the meanings of your sentences.

Example 1. Jon rode an elephant and _____ *saw a newborn giraffe* _____ at the wildlife park.

11. The two clowns _____ and amused the crowd.

12. This trail winds down the mountain and _____.

13. Milton will rake the leaves or _____.

14. After school, Dwayne will _____ or do his homework.

15. Cheryl peeled the orange but _____.

GRAMMAR

Compound Subjects and Compound Verbs

1f. A *compound subject* consists of two or more subjects that are joined by a conjunction and that have the same verb.

1g. A *compound verb* consists of two or more verbs that are joined by a conjunction and that have the same subject.

EXERCISE For each of the following sentences, underline the parts of compound subjects once and underline the parts of compound verbs twice. Some sentences contain both a compound subject and a compound verb.

Example 1. Modern city planners create and draw maps with the help of computers.

1. City planners predict and guide the development of towns and cities.

2. Local governments and citizen groups often employ city planners.

3. Recreational areas and transportation are important to many communities.

4. Ancient people changed and improved their cities, too.

5. The public buildings and monuments of ancient Rome and Athens are evidence of planning.

6. Water and garbage were always problems in ancient cities.

7. People often threw garbage into the streets or piled it up outside the city walls.

8. Diseases spread quickly and killed many people.

9. The Roman water supply system and sewer system are still admired today.

10. With better roads and vehicles, merchants could transport and sell their goods.

11. The people of Teotihuacán, in Mexico, planned a street system and built apartment buildings.

12. During the Middle Ages, some overcrowded towns and cities knocked down their walls.

13. Churches often stood in the center of a town and were the most expensive buildings.

14. Italy and France have examples of beautiful plazas from the Renaissance.

15. The palace and gardens at Versailles, in France, still amaze and delight visitors today.

16. Colonial American cities and towns were designed or planned, too.

17. Charleston and Philadelphia, for example, are among the early planned cities in America.

18. George Washington hired and then fired Pierre L'Enfant, the planner of Washington, D.C.

19. L'Enfant's plan was still followed and used during the development of the city.

20. His plan included parks and wide streets and provided for many grand public buildings.

HOLT HANDBOOK | Introductory Course

for **CHAPTER 1: THE SENTENCE** *pages 7–16*

Subjects and Verbs A

1c.	The *simple subject* is the main word or word group that tells *whom* or *what* the sentence is about.
1e.	The *simple predicate,* or *verb,* is the main word or word group in the complete predicate.
1f.	A *compound subject* consists of two or more subjects that are joined by a conjunction and that have the same verb.
1g.	A *compound verb* consists of two or more verbs that are joined by a conjunction and that have the same subject.

EXERCISE For each of the following sentences, underline the subject once and the verb twice. Be sure to underline both the main verb and any helping verbs. Underline all parts of a compound subject or verb.

Example 1. Haven't cats been pets for thousands of years?

1. Cats may have been tamed about five thousand years ago.

2. According to some scientists, members of the cat family first appeared about forty million years ago.

3. The ancient Egyptians considered cats sacred.

4. Cats were brought to Europe and the Middle East about 1000 B.C.

5. Artists in China and Japan often included cats in their paintings.

6. Cats have long been valued for their skills as hunters.

7. Many people are not familiar with the different breeds of cats.

8. Shorthaired breeds and longhaired breeds are the two major groups of cats.

9. Two of the most popular breeds are the Siamese and the Persian.

10. The Siamese has a beautiful coat and a loud, mournful meow.

11. Have you ever noticed the blue eyes on that Siamese cat?

12. The Persian has long, fluffy fur.

13. Cats use their tails for balance.

14. A Manx, however, can balance without a tail.

15. Another unusual breed is called the ragdoll.

16. This cat relaxes completely and becomes as limp as a ragdoll.

17. Cat lovers have formed many clubs and associations.

18. The Cat Fanciers' Association has clubs in the United States, Japan, and Canada.

19. Didn't you see the information about the cat show next Saturday?

20. My brother and I will go after soccer practice.

Language and Sentence Skills Practice

13

for **CHAPTER 1: THE SENTENCE** *pages 7–16*

Subjects and Verbs B

1c. The *simple subject* is the main word or word group that tells *whom* or *what* the sentence is about.

1e. The *simple predicate,* or *verb,* is the main word or word group in the complete predicate.

1f. A *compound subject* consists of two or more subjects that are joined by a conjunction and that have the same verb.

1g. A *compound verb* consists of two or more verbs that are joined by a conjunction and that have the same subject.

EXERCISE For each of the following sentences, underline the subject once and the verb twice. Be sure to underline both the main verb and any helping verbs. Some sentences may contain a compound subject, a compound verb, or both.

Example 1. The Tigris River and the Euphrates River define the ancient land of Mesopotamia.

1. *Mesopotamia* means "the land between two rivers."

2. The area of Mesopotamia is dry and hot but floods annually.

3. Cities first appeared in Mesopotamia about 3500 B.C.

4. The Sumerians, the Babylonians, and the Assyrians dominated the region at different times.

5. Around 3000 B.C., the Sumerians invented writing and used it for business.

6. The Sumerian writing was inscribed on clay tablets.

7. Later an Assyrian king founded the first national library.

8. Ancient Mesopotamians also named constellations and recorded the position of the stars.

9. Weren't the signs of the zodiac originally named by the Mesopotamians?

10. The wheel and the arch were also first used in Mesopotamia.

11. Mesopotamian farmers grew wheat and raised livestock outside the cities.

12. The sixty-minute hour and the twelve-month year are credited to the Babylonians.

13. Nebuchadnezzar II restored Babylon and built the Hanging Gardens of Babylon.

14. He also conquered Jerusalem and destroyed the Temple there.

15. The first famous author may have been Enheduanna, daughter of the Sumerian king Sargon.

16. Enheduanna's poems are not as famous as the epic of *Gilgamesh.*

17. In one of the stories, Gilgamesh seeks immortality but must remain a mortal man.

18. Ancient Greek histories and the Old Testament tell us about Babylon and Assyria.

19. Sumer, however, died out long before those civilizations.

20. In 1835, a British soldier compared Sumerian writing to other writings and broke its code.

Sentences Classified by Purpose A

1h.	A *declarative sentence* makes a statement and ends with a period.
1i.	An *imperative sentence* gives a command or makes a request. Most imperative sentences end with a period. A strong command ends with an exclamation point.
1j.	An *interrogative sentence* asks a question and ends with a question mark.
1k.	An *exclamatory sentence* shows excitement or expresses strong feeling and ends with an exclamation point.

DECLARATIVE	Shel Silverstein's poetry makes me laugh.
IMPERATIVE	Please hand me that book of poetry.
INTERROGATIVE	Have you ever read *Where the Sidewalk Ends*?
EXCLAMATORY	What a wonderful collection of poems that is!

EXERCISE A Identify each sentence by writing *DEC* for *declarative*, *IMP* for *imperative*, *INT* for *interrogative*, or *EXC* for *exclamatory*. Then, insert the punctuation mark that should follow the sentence.

Example _____*IMP*_____ **1.** Read his poems when you get a chance.

_____ **1.** My mother once met Shel Silverstein in a bookstore

_____ **2.** Did she say anything to him

_____ **3.** How exciting it must have been

_____ **4.** She bought this book as a present

_____ **5.** Please be careful when you read it

EXERCISE B Rewrite each of the following sentences as an interrogative sentence or an exclamatory sentence. You may have to change or add some words. Be sure to use correct end punctuation.

Example 1. You made a mess in the kitchen. *What a mess you made in the kitchen!*

6. He didn't want to go to the movies with us. _____

_____

7. That is a wonderful book. _____

_____

8. We should be there already. _____

_____

9. You are coming on the field trip next week. _____

_____

10. The game must have been very exciting. _____

_____

Language and Sentence Skills Practice

Sentences Classified by Purpose B

1h. A *declarative sentence* makes a statement and ends with a period.

1i. An *imperative sentence* gives a command or makes a request. Most imperative sentences end with a period. A strong command ends with an exclamation point.

1j. An *interrogative sentence* asks a question and ends with a question mark.

1k. An *exclamatory sentence* shows excitement or expresses strong feeling and ends with an exclamation point.

EXERCISE A Identify each sentence by writing *DEC* for *declarative*, *IMP* for *imperative*, *INT* for *interrogative*, or *EXC* for *exclamatory*. Then, insert the punctuation mark that should follow the sentence.

Example _____*INT*_____ **1.** Did you buy kite-making supplies yesterday?

_____ **1.** I want to make a kite this week

_____ **2.** What time does the kite festival start on Saturday

_____ **3.** Don't let the paper get too wrinkled

_____ **4.** What a perfect breeze this is

_____ **5.** Watch out for that tree

EXERCISE B Following the instructions in parentheses, rewrite each of the following sentences on the line provided. Be sure to use correct end punctuation.

Example 1. She didn't remember the book. *(Rewrite as an interrogative sentence.)*

_____*Didn't she remember the book?*_____

6. The stars are brilliant tonight. *(Rewrite as an exclamatory sentence.)*

_____

7. The bread tasted salty to her. *(Rewrite as an interrogative sentence.)*

_____

8. Would your aunt like a glass of lemonade? *(Rewrite as a declarative sentence.)*

_____

9. You should dry that vase carefully. *(Rewrite as an imperative sentence.)*

_____

10. How exciting that concert was! *(Rewrite as a declarative sentence.)*

_____

for **CHAPTER 1: THE SENTENCE** *pages 4–5*

Review A: Sentences and Sentence Fragments

EXERCISE A Decide whether each group of words is a sentence or a sentence fragment. Then, on the line provided, write *S* if the group of words is a sentence or *SF* if the group of words is a sentence fragment.

Example ___*SF*___ **1.** At my aunt's cabin in Tennessee.

_____ **1.** Long conversations about nothing.

_____ **2.** Please arrive on time for the meeting.

_____ **3.** In the jungles of South America.

_____ **4.** Those flowers bloom twice a year, in the spring and the fall.

_____ **5.** Left his books on the bus.

_____ **6.** In gymnastics, on the trampoline.

_____ **7.** Lois won the election by just three votes.

_____ **8.** When the firefighters reached the blaze.

_____ **9.** My brother constantly talks on the telephone.

_____ **10.** At the post office, Mr. Acuno.

EXERCISE B Some of the following word groups are sentences, and some are sentence fragments. If a word group is a complete sentence, rewrite it, adding a capital letter and end punctuation. If a word group is a sentence fragment, add a subject or a verb, a capital letter, and end punctuation to make it a complete sentence.

Example 1. wear shorts in the winter   *I usually don't wear shorts in the winter.*

11. had a sore throat and a runny nose _____

_____

12. tell me your reasons _____

_____

13. barked all night long _____

_____

14. the neighbors all up and down the block _____

_____

15. what a lot of noise he made _____

_____

Review B: Sentence Parts

EXERCISE A In each of the following sentences, underline the complete subject once and the complete predicate twice. Then, circle the simple subject and the simple predicate, or verb.

Example 1. This morning my parents told us about a mysterious theft.

1. A valuable stamp collection is missing from the library.

2. One stamp is worth ten thousand dollars.

3. Part of the image on the stamp had been printed upside down.

4. The librarian has called the police.

5. Two representatives from the police department have arrived.

6. Detective Durand is questioning people.

7. His partner will look for clues.

8. Unfortunately we had no information for the police.

9. The insurance company will be called.

10. Of course, money can never replace those stamps.

EXERCISE B In each of the following sentences, underline the complete subject once and the complete predicate twice. Then, circle the simple subject and the simple predicate, or verb.

Example 1. In your history book you will find the story of Ponce de León.

11. Throughout the centuries many legends have been told about the Fountain of Youth.

12. The waters of the Fountain of Youth had special powers.

13. They could make old people young again.

14. Illnesses could be cured.

15. However, most people don't believe the legends.

16. Some people have searched for the Fountain of Youth.

17. Ponce de León may have believed the legends.

18. His search for new lands brought him to Florida.

19. A spring in St. Augustine, Florida, was discovered by Ponce de León.

20. Its youth-giving powers were never proven.

HOLT HANDBOOK | Introductory Course

for **CHAPTER 1: THE SENTENCE**   pages 13–16

Review C: Sentence Parts

EXERCISE A Underline any compound subjects or compound verbs that appear in the following sentences. Then, if the sentence contains a compound subject, write *CS* on the line provided. If the sentence contains a compound verb, write *CV* on the line provided. Write *CS, CV* if the sentence contains both a compound subject and a compound verb.

Example ___*CS*___ **1.** Swing and boogie-woogie are my favorite kinds of jazz.

_____ **1.** Ella Fitzgerald and Louis Armstrong were great American jazz musicians.

_____ **2.** Ella Fitzgerald worked as a solo singer and also performed with vocal groups.

_____ **3.** Louis Armstrong played the trumpet and sang in a low, gruff voice.

_____ **4.** He and Fitzgerald both sang scat, a type of music full of meaningless syllables.

_____ **5.** Duke Ellington and his band played in Harlem and soon achieved fame.

_____ **6.** Later, in the 1960s, Ellington wrote film scores and composed sacred music.

_____ **7.** Charlie Parker and Thelonious Monk contributed to the jazz style bebop.

_____ **8.** Bebop musicians played complicated melodies and improvised during performances.

_____ **9.** By the 1950s, more audiences accepted jazz and attended jazz concerts.

_____ **10.** My father and my uncle think highly of Miles Davis.

EXERCISE B Underline any compound subjects or compound verbs that appear in the following sentences. Then, if the sentence contains a compound subject, write *CS* on the line provided. If the sentence contains a compound verb, write *CV* on the line provided. Write *CS, CV* if the sentence contains both a compound subject and a compound verb.

Example ___*CV*___ **1.** A country inn underliningoffers fresh air and pretty views and can be enjoyed for days.

_____ **11.** Mrs. Fernandez and her husband run a hotel in Mexico.

_____ **12.** People from all over the world travel to Mexico and stay at their hotel.

_____ **13.** The mealtime fruits and vegetables are grown and prepared on the property.

_____ **14.** Mrs. Fernandez inherited the land and stopped further development of it.

_____ **15.** Neither condominiums nor golf courses will be built there.

_____ **16.** Guests enjoy home-cooked meals and take walks on the property.

_____ **17.** The guest rooms and dining areas are bright and colorful.

_____ **18.** The chef and his assistants make traditional Mexican dishes.

_____ **19.** Nearby, guests can visit a spa or take a horseback ride.

_____ **20.** Mrs. Fernandez and her staff welcome guests and make them comfortable.

Review D: **Kinds of Sentences**

EXERCISE A   Decide what kind of sentence each of the following sentences is. On the line provided, write *DEC* for *declarative,* *IMP* for *imperative,* *INT* for *interrogative,* or *EXC* for *exclamatory.* Then, insert the punctuation mark that should follow the sentence.

Example   *EXC*   **1.** What a talented man James Weldon Johnson was *!*

_____ **1.** Research the life of James Weldon Johnson, an activist and writer in the early 1900s

_____ **2.** In his early years he worked as a school principal, a newspaper editor, and a lawyer

_____ **3.** How inspiring his life was

_____ **4.** Did you know that he wrote songs for musicals with his brother

_____ **5.** One of his songs, "Lift Every Voice and Sing," is sometimes called the unofficial African

American national anthem

_____ **6.** Don't miss the choir's performance of that magnificent song

_____ **7.** Wasn't Johnson one of the major writers of the Harlem Renaissance literary movement

_____ **8.** Some of the others were Zora Neale Hurston, Langston Hughes, and Countee Cullen

_____ **9.** Zora Neale Hurston collected African American folk tales and wrote novels

_____ **10.** What an amazing amount of writing they all did during the 1920s

EXERCISE B   On the line provided, write *DEC* for *declarative,* *IMP* for *imperative,* *INT* for *interrogative,* or *EXC* for *exclamatory.* Then, insert the punctuation mark that should end the sentence.

Example   *INT*   **1.** What caused the French Revolution *?*

_____ **11.** In 1789, the people of France revolted against Louis XVI

_____ **12.** France was almost bankrupt from paying for wars

_____ **13.** Read about the abuses the French people suffered under this cruel ruler

_____ **14.** How courageous the people were to go against the powerful king

_____ **15.** What was Marie Antoinette supposed to have said when the people had no bread

_____ **16.** Let them eat cake

_____ **17.** Don't confuse Louis XVI with Louis XIV, who was called the Sun King

_____ **18.** Did you know that the French Revolution was inspired by the American Revolution

_____ **19.** Many people in the United States supported the French Revolution

_____ **20.** What exciting times those were

Literary Model: Compound Verbs in Narration

> I reached over and shut off the insistent buzzing of my bedside alarm clock. I sat up, swung my feet over the edge of the bed, and felt for my slippers on the floor. Yawning, I walked toward the bathroom. As I walked by the corner of my room, where my computer table was set up, I pressed the *on* button, slid a diskette into the floppy drive, then went to brush my teeth. By the time I got back, the computer's screen was glowing greenly, displaying the message: *Good Morning, Kevin.*
>
> I sat down before the computer table, addressed the keyboard, and typed: *Good Morning, Louis.* The computer immediately began to whir and promptly displayed a list of items on its green screen.
>
> —from "User Friendly" by T. Ernesto Bethancourt

EXERCISE A

1. Of the seven sentences in the above excerpt, how many contain compound verbs? (Hint: *Buzzing, yawning, to brush, displaying,* and *to whir* are not used as main verbs.)

_____

2. Write the verbs that make up the compound verb in each of those sentences.

_____

_____

_____

_____

EXERCISE B

1. Rewrite the first two sentences to eliminate all compound verbs. Create as many sentences as necessary. _____

_____

_____

_____

2. What makes the original version more interesting than the version with no compound verbs?

_____

_____

From "User Friendly" by T. Ernesto Bethancourt from *Connections: Short Stories*, edited by Donald R. Gallo. Copyright © 1989 by T. Ernesto Bethancourt. Reprinted by permission of *Delacorte Press, a division of Random House, Inc.*

Literary Model (continued)

EXERCISE C The passage on page 21 is from a short story set in the future in which a computer suddenly begins to act like a human. Using the excerpt above Exercise A as a model, write two paragraphs that could be part of a longer story. Use the first-person point of view, and set your story in the future. Include several compound verbs. _____

_____

_____

_____

_____

_____

_____

_____

_____

_____

_____

_____

_____

_____

_____

_____

_____

_____

_____

EXERCISE D How does using compound verbs affect the style of your paragraphs? How would your paragraphs sound if they contained no compound verbs? _____

_____

_____

_____

_____

Writing Application: Advertising

It's no wonder that writers sometimes have trouble writing complete sentences. Every day they see information presented in fragments: on TV, in magazines, even on the packaging of foods they eat.

FRAGMENTS New and Improved!

Packed with the vitamins and minerals you need!

Tastes better than the leading competitor's brand!

Each of these bits of information is a fragment, missing either a subject, a verb, or both. Advertisers and package designers use fragments because they deliver information quickly, take up less space, and cost less than complete sentences. In your writing, you don't have to consider space and cost. Writing complete, clear sentences will help readers grasp your meaning.

WRITING ACTIVITY

Your teacher has asked you to bring the packaging or label from a favorite food to school with you so that you can write a paragraph about the ingredients in this food. At the end of your paragraph, you will decide how good (or bad) for your body the food is. As you write, you will need to take information presented in fragments and rewrite it in complete sentences.

PREWRITING First, gather your writing materials, including the package or label that has information about ingredients, calories, and so on. Remember that the ingredients are listed in order from the greatest to least amounts. Read all claims that the label makes about the food's taste and healthfulness. Then, decide how accurate these claims are. Make a list of all the main points you will use to demonstrate your opinion.

WRITING You might open your paragraph with a sentence about why you like the food you chose. Does the food live up to the claims on the packaging? List some of the package's claims, and tell your readers why these claims are or are not correct. End your paragraph with your opinion of the food and its packaging.

REVISING Consider the paragraph's organization. Can you use the prewriting list to order your paragraph? Check the paragraph's content against your prewriting and the label of your food item. Did you discuss all the important ingredients? Did you give solid reasons why the product does or does not meet the claims of its packaging? Did you use complete sentences to explain what you learned?

PUBLISHING Check your paragraph for mistakes in spelling or punctuation. With your teacher's permission, work with other students to create a bulletin board on which you post the labels or packages along with the paragraphs that discuss them. Read other students' paragraphs, too, and think about what people can do to pay attention to what they buy.

EXTENDING YOUR WRITING

This exercise could lead to a more developed writing project. You could write, for a few weeks, a food column for your student newspaper in which you review foods both for their taste and for their health value.

GRAMMAR | Language in Context: Choices

Choices: Exploring Parts of Speech

Here's your chance to step out of the grammar book and into the real world. You may not notice nouns, pronouns, and adjectives, but you and the people around you use them every day. The following activities challenge you to find a connection between parts of speech and the world around you. Do the activity below that suits your personality best, and then share your discoveries with your class. Have fun!

SCIENCE

Sedimentary, Metamorphic, Volcanic

Could science be scientific without adjectives? Probably not. Science uses adjectives to categorize qualities of just about everything from rocks to clouds. What are some of these adjectival categories? Look through a science textbook to find some of these groupings, and organize a list. Make handouts of your list for your class.

DEBATE

Looking Out for Number One

Choose performers to play each part of speech. Then, have a debate among the parts of speech. Each one claims to be the most important. Don't be shy! Tell why you are number one!

LINGUISTICS

Like, Cool, Man

Adjectives rule slang. Haven't you noticed? Brainstorm a list of slang adjectives. Don't limit yourself to the twenty-first century! Interview people born in the early and middle twentieth century, and find out what adjectives they used way back when. Check out a slang dictionary, and find out what the cool adjectives of 1850 were. Then, give your fellow explorers of English the lowdown.

ANALYSIS

Dangerous Intersection

Sometimes, deciding whether a noun is concrete or abstract can tie a person's brain in a knot. Use Venn diagrams to show how some nouns are clearly abstract or concrete and how other nouns could be categorized as either. Provide at least five examples for each of the three parts of your diagram. Then, present your diagram to the class. Be ready for arguments!

TECHNOLOGY

Bugs and Viruses

Computer bugs don't have six legs or even eight! Computer viruses don't make you sick, but they can be a real headache! *Bugs* and *viruses* are two old nouns that computer technology has given new meanings. Brainstorm a list of other old nouns that have new meanings. Try to find a few that no one in the class has heard yet! You may want to flip through a computer magazine to get yourself going. In fact, you could cut out pictures from the magazine to illustrate a poster of the list that you make. With your teacher's permission, hang your poster in the classroom.

SURVEY

Flavor of the Month

There's not much that advertising people like more than adjectives. Cut out a few ads from magazines and newspapers. Then, highlight the adjectives. After you're done, make a list of all these adjectives. What seems to be the favorite this month? Since you've already got a bunch of ads cut out, make them into a collage and paste your list of adjectives in the middle of it.

INDEPENDENT PROJECTS

Suit Yourself

If you don't like to be told what to do, tell yourself! Create a project of your own that would answer some question you have about the parts of speech or be of use or interest to your classmates. For instance, does sign language use parts of speech? When did grammar get started? Make a one-page list of every definition in this chapter. Write a poem using only nouns. Be sure to get your teacher's approval before you start the project you decide on.

The Noun

2a. A *noun* is a word or word group that is used to name a person, place, thing, or idea.

EXAMPLES Charles Drew, officer, Perkins Middle School, town, pencil, holiday, democracy, guilt

EXERCISE A Underline all the nouns in the following sentences.

Example 1. <u>Sumatra</u> is a large <u>island</u> in <u>Indonesia</u>.

1. Unusual plants and animals live in this part of the world.

2. Orangutans live in Sumatra and Borneo.

3. This area of Asia contains many jungles.

4. The rafflesia is the largest flower in the world.

5. The blossom may be as wide as a yard.

6. The plants have huge flowers but no leaves or stems.

7. This giant plant needs the hot climate of Indonesia.

8. Aunt Pearl took a picture of a rafflesia.

9. Each flower has five wide lobes.

10. Most people think the rafflesia has a terrible smell.

EXERCISE B Supply nouns to fill in the blanks in the following sentences.

Example 1. Did the _____*cat*_____ and the _____*dog*_____ make this _____*mess*_____?

11. _____ is the strongest _____ in our _____.

12. He tries always to tell the _____.

13. Are they visiting _____ or _____?

14. _____ and _____ are both _____.

15. Will you bring your _____ to the _____?

EXERCISE C The paragraph below contains twenty nouns. Underline each noun.

Example <u>Delaware</u> is a small <u>state</u> in the eastern <u>United States</u>.

During the summer, Mike visited his grandparents at Coin Beach in Delaware. The boy wondered about the name of the beach. A lifeguard provided an explanation: Apparently, coins often wash up on the shore of the Atlantic Ocean. People think the money comes from a sunken ship, the *Faithful Steward,* which is a ship that sank off the coast in the eighteenth century.

Proper and Common Nouns A

A *proper noun* names a particular person, place, thing, or idea and begins with a capital letter. A *common noun* names any one of a group of persons, places, things, or ideas. A common noun is not capitalized unless it begins a sentence or is part of a title.

PROPER NOUNS	COMMON NOUNS
Branford Marsalis	musician
Peru	country
Washington Monument	monument
the Industrial Revolution	industry

EXERCISE A For each of the following sentences, decide whether the underlined noun is common or proper. Above each underlined noun, write *C* for *common* or *P* for *proper*.

Example 1. James Madison was president of the United States.
              _P_

1. Thomas Jefferson was one of his friends.

2. In 1787, Madison took part in the Constitutional Convention.

3. He helped create the system of checks and balances in the United States government.

4. His wife was Dolley Madison.

5. Dolley Madison was younger than her husband.

6. The people of Washington loved her parties.

7. She liked to surprise her guests with unusual dishes.

8. Mrs. Madison welcomed many important leaders to the White House.

9. During the War of 1812, the White House was burned.

10. The Madisons moved to a different house.

EXERCISE B Fill in the blanks in the following sentences with the type of noun indicated in parentheses.

Example 1. ____Sheila____ (*proper*) wants a ____bicycle____ (*common*) for her birthday.

11. _____ (*common*) make good pets.

12. _____ (*common*) and _____ (*common*) are ingredients in my favorite dish.

13. Have you ever visited _____ (*proper*)?

14. _____ (*proper*) and _____ (*proper*) are planets in our solar system.

15. All of the _____ (*common*) downtown are decorated for the holidays.

for **CHAPTER 2: PARTS OF SPEECH OVERVIEW** `page 26`

Proper and Common Nouns B

A *proper noun* names a particular person, place, thing, or idea and begins with a capital letter. A *common noun* names any one of a group of persons, places, things, or ideas. A common noun is not capitalized unless it begins a sentence or is part of a title.

PROPER NOUNS	COMMON NOUNS
Robert Frost	poet
Shiloh	dog
Taoism	religion

EXERCISE A For each of the following sentences, decide whether the underlined noun is common or proper. Above each underlined noun, write *C* for *common* or *P* for *proper*.

                 P

Example 1. *The Grizzwells* is still my favorite comic strip.

1. Mr. Garza and Ms. Francis will be chaperones at the dance.

2. Are books or tapes on sale this week?

3. Thursday is the busiest day of the week for our family.

4. Is Russia one of the world's largest countries?

5. The backhoe rumbled into the construction site.

EXERCISE B In the following sentences, fill in the blanks with the type of noun indicated in parentheses.

Example 1. ____*Mrs. Davis*____ (proper) assigns ____*nicknames*____ (common) to her students every year.

6. _____ (common) and _____ (common) live in the sea.

7. I always enjoy having _____ (common) and _____ (common) for dinner.

8. _____ (proper) and I are working on a _____ (common) for our social studies class.

9. The _____ (common) scampered across the yard and disappeared into the _____ (common).

10. Diane lived in _____ (proper) before she moved here.

11. My older brother is trying to learn _____ (proper) before he visits _____ (proper).

12. Did you turn in your _____ (common) on time?

13. The radio station just played the latest song by _____ (proper)!

14. _____ (proper) plays _____ (common) in the school orchestra.

15. When is _____ (common) supposed to arrive?

Pronouns and Antecedents

2b. | A *pronoun* is a word that is used in place of one or more nouns or pronouns.

The word or word group that a pronoun stands for is called its *antecedent*. Sometimes the antecedent is not stated.

> **EXAMPLES** After **he** hit the home run, **Joe Thundercloud** trotted around the bases and waved to the crowd. [*Joe Thundercloud* is the antecedent of the pronoun *he*.]
>
> The doctor said **your** test results were all normal. [The pronoun *your* has no antecedent in this sentence.]

EXERCISE A Underline each of the pronouns in the following sentences.

Example 1. My paper blew away just before I could catch it.

1. When you finish your part of the project, proofread it carefully.

2. After she finished her homework, Jane read two chapters of a novel.

3. Did Manuel paint the set by himself?

4. The three of us always sit at the same table for lunch.

5. Replace the tape in its case when you finish listening to it.

EXERCISE B Each of the following sentences contains an underlined pronoun. Circle the antecedent of each underlined pronoun.

Example 1. Ms. Griffith offers (help) when we need it.

6. Salmon are born in freshwater streams, but most salmon spend part of their lives in the ocean.

7. Mother called to the twins and told them dinner was on the table.

8. The ball flew by Mr. LaPorte and just missed him.

9. Kara tapped on the door, but nobody heard her.

10. Whales can't breathe underwater, so they must come to the surface for air.

11. How long has Angela been saving her money?

12. The sea horse wrapped its tail around a piece of seaweed.

13. The players were tired, but they had won the game.

14. Cora found a new lightbulb and installed it.

15. Rachel, please show me your painting.

Personal, Reflexive, and Intensive Pronouns

A *personal pronoun* refers to the one speaking (*first person*), the one spoken to (*second person*), or the one spoken about (*third person*).

> EXAMPLE   **I** can give **you** the telephone number **she** left.

A *reflexive pronoun* refers to the subject and is necessary to the basic meaning of the sentence. An *intensive pronoun* emphasizes its antecedent and is unnecessary to the basic meaning of the sentence.

> REFLEXIVE PRONOUN   Mavis reminded **herself** to speak slowly and clearly.
> INTENSIVE PRONOUN   Mr. Hogan **himself** supplied the decorations.

EXERCISE A   Underline each of the pronouns in the following sentences.

Example   1. Jessica wrote a reminder to <u>herself</u> about the due date.

1. If you give it a cracker, the parrot might speak for you.

2. The cat washed itself carefully after it finished eating.

3. The principal herself will be speaking to us today.

4. Justin thanked me for returning the book to him.

5. After she left the astronaut program, Sally Ride became a professor of physics.

6. The director himself said the book was better than the movie.

7. Kevin said he thought the cloud looked like a rocking horse, but I thought it looked like an old

oak tree.

8. The sparrow has just finished building a nest for itself.

9. Would you give the message to Marie when you see her?

10. Sharon wanted tamales, but by the time she reached the front of the line, they were gone.

EXERCISE B   For each of the following sentences, decide whether the underlined pronoun is a personal pronoun, a reflexive pronoun, or an intensive pronoun. Above the word, write *PER* for *personal,* *REF* for *reflexive,* or *INT* for *intensive.*

Example   1. Toni Morrison <u>herself</u> will be the speaker.   *INT*

11. Cesar said <u>he</u> liked that kind of music.

12. Two weeks later, Sarah found <u>herself</u> in Nigeria.

13. Mike's cat likes to give <u>itself</u> dust baths.

14. Kim Chun recopied the paper and handed <u>it</u> in.

15. The banquet will be attended by the gold medalists <u>themselves</u>.

GRAMMAR

Demonstrative Pronouns and Relative Pronouns

A *demonstrative pronoun* points out a specific person, place, thing, or idea.

EXAMPLE   **That** is the best idea I've heard!

A *relative pronoun* introduces a subordinate clause.

EXAMPLE   Mr. Chang, **who** coaches volleyball, is admired by his players.

EXERCISE A   Underline each of the demonstrative and relative pronouns in the following sentences.

Example 1. Are you going to wear these shoes or <u>those</u>?

1. These are wonderful, ripe, juicy grapes.

2. Mrs. Deets is the person to whom you must give the permission slip.

3. The experiment that we conducted in chemistry class was fascinating.

4. Did you hear that?

5. This has been an interesting conversation, but I have to leave now.

6. My aunt Mikki, who is a substitute teacher, worked at my school Monday.

7. The rain, which had been falling all morning, began to let up.

8. That was definitely the best book of the series.

9. The guide, whose eyesight and hearing were very sharp, motioned for the group to halt.

10. The noise that had started so suddenly ended just as quickly.

EXERCISE B   For each of the following sentences, decide whether the underlined pronoun is a demonstrative pronoun or a relative pronoun. Above the word, write *DEM* for *demonstrative* or *REL* for *relative*.

                    DEM
Example 1. Are <u>those</u> Julio's tennis shoes?

11. <u>This</u> is a wonderful book with clear illustrations.

12. Cynthia, <u>who</u> plays center on the basketball team, is over five feet tall.

13. Isn't <u>that</u> a great song?

14. The snow <u>that</u> fell last night has already melted.

15. Orchids, <u>which</u> come in a variety of colors, can be speckled or streaked.

16. When the governor said <u>this</u>, the secretary laughed.

17. <u>These</u> are beautiful Zuni earrings.

18. The boy <u>whose</u> dog is chasing Sam has gone to get a leash.

19. Leave <u>those</u> on the table for now.

20. Ms. Jackson is a teacher <u>whom</u> the students admire.

for **CHAPTER 2: PARTS OF SPEECH OVERVIEW** **pages 34–36**

Indefinite Pronouns and Interrogative Pronouns

An *indefinite pronoun* refers to a person, place, thing, or idea that may or may not be specifically named.

> **EXAMPLES** **Nobody** noticed the sign.
>
> Does **anyone** here speak Mandarin?

An *interrogative pronoun* introduces a question.

> **EXAMPLES** **What** are your plans?
>
> **Who** will design the flyers?

EXERCISE A Underline the indefinite pronouns and interrogative pronouns in the following sentences. Then, identify the pronouns by writing *IND* for *indefinite* or *ITR* for *interrogative* above them.

                    IND
Example 1. <u>Neither</u> of the glasses had spilled.

1. Someone has been sitting in my chair!

2. Couldn't you find anybody?

3. Whose are those shoes?

4. Anyone may enter the essay contest.

5. Many of the contestants have finished.

6. No one in the class selected that subject for a research report.

7. Which of your cousins haven't you talked to yet?

8. I think either of the girls could do the job.

9. What is the title of the next school play?

10. To whom did you address the letter?

EXERCISE B For each blank in the following sentences, write an appropriate indefinite pronoun or interrogative pronoun. Use a different pronoun for each sentence.

Example 1. _____*Which*_____ of the frogs jumped the farthest?

11. Give one copy to _____ of your classmates.

12. Can _____ tell me how to get to Madison Street?

13. _____ of the leaves have already fallen off the tree.

14. _____ did you find under the desk?

15. _____ was that new student's name?

Identifying Kinds of Pronouns

EXERCISE Each of the following sentences has an underlined pronoun. Decide what kind of pronoun the underlined word is. Above it, write *PER* for *personal*, *REF* for *reflexive*, *ITN* for *intensive*, *DEM* for *demonstrative*, *IND* for *indefinite*, *ITR* for *interrogative*, or *REL* for *relative*.

> REF
Example 1. Tom Sawyer was always getting himself into trouble.

1. In the book by Mark Twain, Tom is like some other boys you may have met.

2. Who hasn't woken up on a Monday morning and dreaded going to school?

3. Tom decides that he can stay home if he makes himself sick.

4. First, he imagines a pain in his stomach, but that goes away.

5. One of his teeth is loose, but Tom knows Aunt Polly would just pull it out.

6. Next, Tom remembers that he heard a doctor talking about something that takes two weeks to heal.

7. Tom wakes up his half brother, Sid, and convinces him that Tom's sore toe will lead to death.

8. Sid, who should know about Tom's tricks by now, believes him anyway.

9. Sid runs downstairs calling Aunt Polly and tells her that Tom is dying.

10. Aunt Polly herself is worried about Tom until she finds out that he is dying from a sore toe.

11. Aunt Polly laughs and cries, and Tom is embarrassed about all of the noise he has made over a sore toe.

12. Tom then tells Aunt Polly about his tooth, which she decides to pull.

13. Tom tells her that he would rather go to school than have his tooth pulled.

14. Anyone who has had a tooth pulled knows why Tom said so.

15. What do you think Aunt Polly did?

16. She tied a thread around Tom's tooth and then scared him so that he pulled the tooth out himself.

17. Tom couldn't think of anything to help him stall further and ended up going to school.

18. Most of the boys at school thought that the gap in Tom's teeth was cool.

19. Another boy, whose cut finger had been the center of attention, said a missing tooth wasn't such a big deal.

20. Tom and the others knew that the boy was just jealous.

The Adjective

2c. An *adjective* is a word that is used to modify a noun or a pronoun.

EXAMPLES The explorers searched for **fresh** water.

Its blossoms are **pink** and **red.**

EXERCISE A Underline all the adjectives in the following sentences. Do not include *a, an,* or *the.*

Example 1. The climate of surrounding areas is affected by the huge body of water.

1. Lake Baikal is in southeast Siberia.

2. It is the deepest lake in the entire world.

3. It is also one of the oldest lakes on earth.

4. The lake freezes for five months of every year.

5. Many scientists study the unique plants and animals that live nearby.

6. Hundreds of animals are found only in Lake Baikal or the nearby area.

7. The lake is so large that the nearby area stays cool in the summer and warm in the winter.

8. Also in Russia is the Caspian Sea, which is the largest inland body of water in the world.

9. The Caspian Sea is a saltwater lake.

10. There are many lakes in Russia.

EXERCISE B In each of the following sentences, underline all the adjectives except *a, an,* and *the.* Then, draw an arrow from each adjective to the word that it modifies.

Example 1. The house was old but sturdy.

11. The flowers in the front yard are purple and yellow.

12. Twelve clowns squeezed into the tiny car.

13. Many fires are caused by careless campers.

14. Do not feed any bear in the park.

15. Several children played on the grassy slope.

16. The stinger on the scorpion is poisonous.

17. The puppy loved to chew leather shoes.

18. Bright lightning lit up the dark sky.

19. Weird noises filled the old house.

20. Fruits and vegetables contain many important vitamins.

Proper Adjectives

A *proper adjective* is formed from a proper noun and begins with a capital letter.

> **PROPER NOUNS** Vietnam, Arab, January
> **PROPER ADJECTIVES** **Vietnamese** food, **Arabian** horses, **January** weather

EXERCISE A Underline the adjectives in each sentence below. Then, underline the proper adjectives a second time. Do not underline *a, an,* or *the.*

Example 1. The costumes of the <u>African</u> dancers were <u>colorful</u>.

1. The meal began with a clear French soup.

2. Do you enjoy spicy Chinese food?

3. Margaret Atwood is a Canadian novelist and poet.

4. Seoul is the largest South Korean city.

5. We ate small Greek salads for the first course.

6. Emma speaks with a lovely British accent.

7. Did you enjoy the Southern hospitality?

8. The graduation gift was a Mexican blanket.

9. The local museum showcased American Indian pottery.

10. That's an Irish lullaby.

EXERCISE B Underline the proper adjectives in each sentence below. Then, draw an arrow to the word each proper adjective modifies.

Example 1. I saw a beautiful painting by a <u>Japanese</u> artist.

11. They will be traveling along the Irish coast.

12. Can you imagine what it would have been like to ride in a Roman chariot?

13. The speaker was a Buddhist priest.

14. The float was almost ready for the Independence Day parade.

15. The review said the author used Dickensian language.

16. On what date is the February meeting?

17. Sean listens to Celtic music.

18. The Martian soil was stored in isolation.

19. He sent a postcard showing the Egyptian pyramids.

20. The Aztec empire rose in Mexico during the 1400s.

for **CHAPTER 2: PARTS OF SPEECH OVERVIEW** page 41

Demonstrative Adjectives

The words *this, that, these,* and *those* can be used as adjectives or as pronouns. When they modify nouns or pronouns, they are called *demonstrative adjectives.* When they are used alone, they are called *demonstrative pronouns.*

DEMONSTRATIVE ADJECTIVE   I will buy **these** tapes.
DEMONSTRATIVE PRONOUN   I will buy **these.**

EXERCISE A For each of the following sentences, decide whether the underlined word is a demonstrative adjective or a demonstrative pronoun. Above the word, write *DA* for *demonstrative adjective* or *DP* for *demonstrative pronoun.*

                                    DA
Example 1. How long have those sweaters been at the cleaners?

1. Then the cook served this Mediterranean dish.

2. Most people love these tiny Japanese paintings.

3. Is that the Winstons' cat?

4. These Japanese woodcuts were made during the eighteenth century.

5. This little picture was painted by an unknown artist.

6. That is a brilliant idea!

7. Will those candles burn for more than five hours?

8. This is a mixture of fresh fish and several vegetables.

9. Please take these to the post office.

10. Nathan bought those puzzles for his little sister.

EXERCISE B Underline the demonstrative adjectives in the following sentences. If a sentence does not contain a demonstrative adjective, write *none* after the sentence.

Example 1. This tree is over one hundred years old.

11. Please hand me those tapes.

12. These clouds are called cumulonimbus.

13. Does this bus stop at Pine Street?

14. That was one of the funniest books I've read.

15. This Sunday, we are having a family picnic.

Noun, Pronoun, or Adjective? A

The way a word is used in a sentence determines what part of speech it is.
The same word may be used as different parts of speech.

NOUN	We get our water from a **well** in the backyard.
ADJECTIVE	Aren't you feeling **well**?
PRONOUN	**This** is the next book I want to read.
ADJECTIVE	**This** book has received terrific reviews.

EXERCISE Identify the underlined word in each of the following sentences by writing above it *N* for *noun*, *PRO* for *pronoun*, or *ADJ* for *adjective*.

Example 1. That must be the <u>tallest</u> building in the city! *(ADJ)*

1. Three tall <u>trees</u> shaded the backyard.

2. When are <u>you</u> going to visit your grandmother?

3. The last step is to trim <u>those</u> edges.

4. <u>This</u> is the best apple juice I've tasted in a long time.

5. The crowd was quiet as the <u>Australian</u> flag was raised.

6. <u>Another</u> reason to do it that way is to save money.

7. Jason didn't see <u>anyone</u> that he knew.

8. That species is commonly found in <u>Asia</u>.

9. <u>Both</u> of the squirrels disappeared behind a tree.

10. The stars were bright and clear in the <u>Nebraska</u> sky.

11. He was hungry, so he asked for <u>more</u>.

12. Have you read *Oliver Twist* by Charles <u>Dickens</u>?

13. <u>Those</u> goats are very curious.

14. The flowers could use <u>more</u> rain.

15. The <u>chicken</u> coop is at the back of the garden.

16. Samantha had studied <u>Buddhism</u>.

17. <u>Each</u> wanted something different.

18. It drizzled all day, but my cousins and I managed to find <u>something</u> to do.

19. <u>Roosters</u> make great alarm clocks.

20. <u>Chinese</u> food is my favorite.

Noun, Pronoun, or Adjective? B

The way a word is used in a sentence determines what part of speech the word is.
The same word may be used as different parts of speech.

NOUN	The **French** are very proud of their foods.
ADJECTIVE	Have you ever eaten at a **French** restaurant?
PRONOUN	**Which** will be the last team to perform?
ADJECTIVE	**Which** play will they be performing?

EXERCISE Write ten original sentences according to the instructions below.

Examples 1. Use *baseball* as a noun. _They spent the entire afternoon throwing a baseball to each other._

2. Use *baseball* as an adjective. _Baseball season starts in two weeks._

1. Use *those* as an adjective. _____

_____

2. Use *those* as a pronoun. _____

_____

3. Use *each* as an adjective. _____

_____

4. Use *each* as a pronoun. _____

_____

5. Use *chicken* as a noun. _____

_____

6. Use *chicken* as an adjective. _____

_____

7. Use *which* as an adjective. _____

_____

8. Use *which* as a pronoun. _____

_____

9. Use *Easter* as an adjective. _____

_____

10. Use *Easter* as a noun. _____

_____

GRAMMAR

Review A: Nouns

EXERCISE A Underline all the nouns in each of the following sentences.

Example 1. Mother looks forward to the Sunday paper.

1. People in North America are usually eager for news.

2. Newspapers often cover the news in more detail than television does.

3. An early Chinese paper was printed from carved wooden blocks.

4. Some of the first newspapers were published in Germany.

5. One early paper was called the *Boston News-Letter.*

6. It was the first paper published regularly in the American colonies.

7. It was first published by John Campbell, the postmaster of Boston.

8. Today, large daily newspapers cover politics, sports, business, and many other topics.

9. They include editorial pages and regular columns.

10. Comics, puzzles, and humorous columns entertain readers.

EXERCISE B In each of the following sentences, underline each common noun and circle each proper noun.

Example 1. According to this article, Georgia is sometimes called the Peach State.

11. Peaches are tasty fruits.

12. Currently, the United States produces more peaches than any other country.

13. Actually, China was their original home.

14. It is still one of the leading producers of peaches, along with Italy, France, and Spain.

15. Some painters made portraits of the fruit.

16. The people in ancient Rome spread the trees throughout Europe.

17. Peaches could be found in Mexico as early as the seventeenth century.

18. Spanish explorers brought them to America.

19. Large orchards are generally located in areas with few late frosts.

20. Insects, diseases, and severe cold can damage the trees.

Review B: Pronouns

EXERCISE A   In each of the following sentences, underline the pronoun and draw an arrow to its antecedent.

Example 1. Many visitors make a small donation as they enter the museum.

1. Most band members rent their instruments.

2. Mayor Martinez gave his speech before the Women's Club.

3. People filed into the hall, and soon most were seated.

4. The armadillo curled itself into a tiny ball.

5. That silly dog has hidden its bones under the couch!

6. Eating well is one way Lono keeps himself healthy.

7. A redbird built its nest in the maple tree.

8. Carmen said she was ready to begin.

9. People in the audience can help themselves to some popcorn.

10. Carrie and Jack asked if they could start a school newspaper.

EXERCISE B   Underline all the pronouns in the following sentences.

Example 1. Would someone help me clean up this mess?

11. Everyone finished the test before the end of class.

12. These plants will not thrive if they are watered too often.

13. Can you imagine yourself as an astronaut?

14. Alma bought the red boots and returned those.

15. The president herself presented the award to me.

16. Who will play the lead in this year's play?

17. The announcer asked the question, but no one answered.

18. The batteries in my tape player are dead.

19. "Put these on next," said the costume designer.

20. She read the list of books and recognized several immediately.

Language and Sentence Skills Practice

Review C: Nouns, Pronouns, and Adjectives

EXERCISE A Underline the adjectives in each of the following sentences. Do not include *a, an,* or *the.* Then, draw an arrow from each underlined adjective to the word it modifies.

Example 1. These vegetarian burritos are delicious.

1. The old car may not make the long trip.

2. On the coldest day in winter, Grandmother built a fire.

3. This winter is supposed to be cold and damp.

4. That beautiful vase is made from Venetian glass.

5. The late movie was about Martian invaders.

6. We took an early train to avoid large crowds.

7. The hikers made it to the top of the mountain in two hours.

8. This movie should be funny.

9. The early settlers caught many terrible diseases.

10. Notice the beautiful collar made from delicate Belgian lace.

EXERCISE B For each of the following sentences, decide what part of speech the underlined word is. Above the word, write *N* for *noun, PRO* for *pronoun,* or *ADJ* for *adjective.*

Example 1. Several explorers visited the Indonesian islands. *(ADJ)*

11. They returned with many interesting stories.

12. Some explorers told about huge monsters they had seen.

13. What could these creatures be?

14. They were Komodo dragons.

15. These enormous reptiles are found on certain Indonesian islands.

16. These animals are giant lizards.

17. Each one can weigh more than three hundred pounds!

18. Komodo dragons are the largest lizards in the world.

19. These dangerous animals have long, sharp claws.

20. These unusual creatures are an endangered species.

for **CHAPTER 2: PARTS OF SPEECH OVERVIEW**   *pages 38–41*

Literary Model: The Adjective

> When I think of the home town of my youth, all that I seem to remember is dust—the brown, crumbly dust of late summer—arid, sterile dust that gets into the eyes and makes them water, gets into the throat and between the toes of bare brown feet. I don't know why I should remember only the dust. Surely there must have been lush green lawns and paved streets under leafy shade trees somewhere in town; but memory is an abstract painting—it does not present things as they are, but rather as they *feel*. And so, when I think of that time and that place, I remember only the dry September of the dirt roads and grassless yards of the shanty-town where I lived. And one other thing I remember, another incongruency of memory—a brilliant splash of sunny yellow against the dust—Miss Lottie's marigolds.
>
> —from "Marigolds" by Eugenia Collier

EXERCISE A   Underline the adjectives that appear in the above excerpt. Then, circle the noun each adjective modifies. (Do not include articles. Hints: *Paved* is used as an adjective. *Home town* is a compound noun.)

EXERCISE B

1. In this excerpt, the author is describing (1) her memories of the town where she lived, (2) the same town as it "surely" must have been, and (3) flowers called marigolds. On the lines below, write the adjectives you underlined in Exercise A. (Hint: Not every adjective in the passage will fit in one of these three categories.)

Author's Memories of Town _____

_____

_____

Town as It Must Have Been _____

_____

_____

Marigolds _____

_____

_____

From *"Marigolds"* by Eugenia W. Collier from *Negro Digest,* November 1969. Copyright © 1969 by Johnson Publishing Company, Inc. Reprinted by permission of *Eugenia W. Collier.*

for **CHAPTER 2: PARTS OF SPEECH OVERVIEW** *pages 38–41*

Literary Model (continued)

2. Compare the adjectives used to describe the marigolds with those used to describe the author's memories of her town and then with those used to describe the town as it must have been. Use the lists of adjectives to answer the following: Why do you think the author calls the marigolds an "incongruency [something that is not appropriate or fitting] of memory"?

_____

_____

_____

EXERCISE C Write a paragraph in which you compare two places. As Eugenia Collier did, use many descriptive adjectives to reinforce the comparison.

_____

_____

_____

_____

_____

_____

_____

_____

_____

_____

EXERCISE D Describe how the adjectives you used reinforce your comparison of the two places.

_____

_____

_____

_____

_____

_____

for **CHAPTER 2: PARTS OF SPEECH OVERVIEW**   **pages 38–41**

Writing Application: Using Adjectives in a Poem

Writers can use adjectives as powerful tools to describe the writers' experiences, thoughts, and the world around them. Not all adjectives are equally descriptive, however. Writers must choose adjectives that show readers the world through words.

> **LESS INTERESTING**   The little toddler stared at the big dog.
>
> **MORE INTERESTING**   The pint-sized, wobbly toddler stared at the pony-sized, panting dog.

Both sentences use adjectives to describe the toddler and the dog, but which scene can you imagine more clearly? Help your readers see the scene by describing it to them.

WRITING ACTIVITY

Writers don't just describe the world around them; they also describe themselves. For your homeroom class, students are writing name poems to display on the bulletin board. Each student will write the letters of his or her name down the left side of the page. Then students will choose descriptive adjectives to go with each letter and write a sentence using these adjectives beside the letter. Look at the brief example below.

> *T   I'm terrific at soccer but terrible at cleaning up my room.*
>
> *I   I'm interested in everything about the oceans, and I'm never irritating!*
>
> *M   I'm a magnificent and marvelous friend to have around.*

PREWRITING   List the letters of your name on paper. Then, for each letter, brainstorm a list of adjectives that describe you. List as many as you can for each letter so that you can choose the most interesting.

WRITING   After you have chosen one or two adjectives for each letter of your name, write a sentence about yourself that uses the adjectives you've chosen. You may have to write several sentences for each letter before you produce one you really like. That's fine—play with the sentences until you are pleased with how they sound and what they say.

REVISING   If you get stuck on a letter and have trouble coming up with good adjectives, ask a good friend to suggest something positive about you that starts with that letter. You can help that friend in return. Finally, read your sentences out loud and listen to them. Do they make sense? Is each a complete sentence?

PUBLISHING   Check your poem for mistakes in spelling and punctuation. On colored paper, copy the poem in your best handwriting. With your teacher's permission, display your poem with the other students' poems in the room. Read your classmates' poems, and enjoy getting to know each other better.

EXTENDING YOUR WRITING

This exercise could lead to a more extended writing project. You could write name poems as gifts for important people in your life—family, friends, teachers. Accompany your gift with a brief letter that tells the person what he or she means to you.

Choices: Investigating Parts of Speech

Here's your chance to step out of the grammar book and into the real world. You may not notice the parts of speech, but you and the people around you use them every day. The following activities challenge you to find a connection between the parts of speech and the world around you. Do the activity below that suits your personality best, and then share your discoveries with your class. Have fun!

CRITICAL THINKING

Face It

Adverbs that modify adverbs can be confusing. Face the problem head-on. First, make a list of adverbs that can modify other adverbs. Start with *so* and *quite*. Write ten sentences showing adverbs modifying other adverbs. Share your list with your classmates. They just might appreciate it.

ANALYSIS

Alike and Different

Adverbs and adjectives that have the same form can twist a person's brain until it feels like a bowl of spaghetti. Straighten everybody out. Make a chart titled "Adverbs and Adjectives." Then, draw a line to divide the chart into two columns. Label one column "Adjective" and the other "Adverb." Create a list of adjectives and adverbs that are identical in form (you can use your textbook to get started). Then, write phrases or sentences that demonstrate how these identical words function as adjectives and adverbs. Write your sentences or phrases in the correct column. Give copies of your chart to your classmates.

MATHEMATICS

By the Numbers

Now that you know all the parts of speech, take a look at your own writing. Choose a page or two of your writing. Then, count the number of each part of speech that you use. If you can't identify a word's part of speech, make a note to discuss it with your friends. Transfer your tallies to a bar graph. Then, compare your graph to the graphs made by your classmates who picked this choice. What parts of speech do you favor? Which do you seem to avoid? How does your usage compare with your classmates' usage? with your textbook's? with your favorite writer's?

MUSIC

Take Notes

Compose lyrics and music for a song about one or more parts of speech. You can write any kind of song—rap, rock, children's song, ballad, or some other kind. Your lyrics should include information about or references to the functions of the part or parts of speech.

VIEWING AND REPRESENTING

The Ins and Outs

Help your classmates understand verbs. Create two Venn diagrams—one showing the relationship between transitive and intransitive verbs, the other showing the relationship between action and linking verbs. Include example sentences for each section of each diagram. Distribute copies to your class. Explain the diagrams so that everyone understands them. Have several extra examples of specific verbs in specific sentences ready to plug into your diagrams.

BUILDING FLUENCY

Chameleon Conjunctions

Have a contest. Who can find a word that can function as the most parts of speech? The winner must have complete sentences appropriately using his or her word as each part of speech. Winners must present and defend each entry. First, though, decide on the prize. Make it good!

ORIGINAL STUDY

Blaze Your Own Trail

What? None of these choices appeal to you? Well, make up a project of your own. Write a poem using only verbs and interjections. Make a poster of all the types of conjunctions. Illustrate a transitive verb, or, better yet, illustrate a linking verb. The choice is yours. Be sure to get your teacher's approval before you begin your project.

The Verb

3a.	A *verb* is a word that expresses action or a state of being.

> **EXAMPLES**   We **rode** on that Ferris wheel last night.
>
>   John **seemed** happy to be with us.

Every complete sentence has a verb. The verb says something about the subject.

EXERCISE A   Underline the verb in each of the following sentences.

Example   1. The alligator <u>snapped</u> its jaws shut.

1. We all jumped about three feet into the air.

2. Is that alligator hungry?

3. Look at that beautiful heron!

4. Alligators and crocodiles appear somewhat alike to me.

5. How are they different?

6. I saw hundreds of alligators in Florida.

7. Were you near St. Augustine?

8. They made me really nervous.

9. The boat sat very low in the water.

10. My brother took pictures during the boat ride.

EXERCISE B   Complete each of the following sentences by writing a verb on the line provided.

Example   1. Sarah and Keadra _____*jumped*_____ into the pool.

11. I _____ the names of all fifty states.

12. John _____ an advertisement in today's newspaper.

13. The juice _____ a little too warm.

14. The dog _____ wildly in circles.

15. The marching band _____ in the middle of the field.

16. Alia's family _____ two mountain bikes.

17. Which tangerine _____ better?

18. Julio _____ the violin, not the cello.

19. My grandmother _____ me a letter at least twice a month.

20. The milk _____ all over the table.

Main Verbs and Helping Verbs

In many sentences a single word is all that is needed to express action or state of being. In other sentences the verb consists of a main verb and one or more helping verbs. A *helping verb* (also called an *auxiliary verb*) helps the *main verb* to express action or a state of being.

EXAMPLES   The kitten **curled** up in his lap.

The kitten **has curled** up in his lap. [*Has* is the helping verb. *Curled* is the main verb.]

EXERCISE A   For each of the following sentences, underline each main verb once and each helping verb twice. Some sentences have more than one helping verb, and some sentences do not have any.

Example 1. Farmers in that region may have already harvested their wheat.

1. My grandfather has traveled to Europe many times.

2. You must have heard all that noise last night!

3. Those children are wearing their seat belts.

4. The moon had risen early that evening.

5. Does Simon play the trumpet in the band?

6. Broccoli, carrots, and squash are all vegetables.

7. Which way did he run?

8. The cat should not be sitting on the kitchen counter.

9. Do you want some of these carrots?

10. Would you please call me first thing in the morning?

EXERCISE B   Complete each of the sentences by writing one or more helping verbs on the line provided.

Example 1. David _____*should*_____ be doing his homework right now.

11. He _____ been sleeping instead of studying.

12. We _____ practice our skit at my house tonight.

13. _____ you come over after dinner for about an hour?

14. We probably _____ not drive very far in this snow.

15. My brother _____ take four people in his car.

16. _____ you know how to sew on a button?

17. My sister taught me to do that, but I _____ not remember.

18. _____ you planning to do anything special during the winter holidays?

19. We certainly _____ arrived early if we had known the theater would be so crowded.

20. By the time we found our seats, the curtain _____ already risen.

Verb Phrases

Together, the main verb and its helping verb or verbs are called a *verb phrase*.

> **EXAMPLES** We **will study** Brazil.
>
> Forest tribes **have been living** in Brazil for thousands of years.

Sometimes a verb phrase is interrupted by another part of speech.

> **EXAMPLE** **Did** you **learn** about the Portuguese settlers in Brazil? [The verb phrase *Did learn* is separated by the pronoun *you*.]

EXERCISE A Underline the verb phrase in each of the following sentences. Then, underline the helping verb or verbs a second time.

Example 1. What role did the Portuguese play in Brazil's history?

1. Portugal had claimed possession of Brazil in the year 1500.

2. The Portuguese settlers must have arrived soon after.

3. They may have been looking for gold.

4. Was gold ever discovered?

5. Cacao beans and sugar cane could be harvested.

6. Large plantations were established by the Portuguese settlers.

7. The settlers and the native tribes did not remain friendly.

8. Some Indians may have been enslaved as plantation workers.

9. Brazil has become a leader in agriculture.

10. Coffee may be one of the most important crops in Brazil.

EXERCISE B Underline all the verb phrases that appear in the following paragraph. Be sure to include all the helping verbs.

Example [1] People have relied on rubber products for many decades.

[11] Latex, a milky-white substance that is used in the production of rubber, is produced by the rubber trees of the Amazon rain forest. [12] Diagonal cuts are made in the trees by rubber tappers. [13] Then a small cup is carefully placed beneath each cut. [14] Rubber tappers must cut all the trees on a rubber tree trail before the latex is flowing too freely. [15] Rubber trees can often be spaced one hundred yards apart, and a rubber tapper may walk several miles before dawn; later that same day, the rubber tapper will repeat the journey through the forest so that he may collect the cups of latex.

Action Verbs

An *action verb* expresses either physical or mental activity.

EXAMPLES   Maple sap **drips** from the tree.

I **carry** the bucket to the cottage.

Santos **is dreaming** about a delicious breakfast.

EXERCISE A   Underline the action verbs in the following sentences.

Example 1. For breakfast Victor enjoys whole-wheat pancakes.

1. Vermont leads the nation in maple syrup production.

2. Maple syrup comes from the sap of sugar maple trees.

3. In the late winter and early spring, the maple sap flows from the trees.

4. Some people drill holes into the trees.

5. They insert metal tubes or spouts into the holes.

6. They hang buckets from the spouts.

7. The buckets fill with the maple sap.

8. Workers collect the buckets of sap.

9. Other workers boil the sap.

10. This process turns the sap into maple syrup.

EXERCISE B   Two words are underlined in each of the following sentences. Identify and circle the word that is an action verb.

Example 1. (Select) your pet carefully.

11. Some people own dogs or cats.

12. I prefer a ferret for a pet.

13. Ferrets often play tricks on their owners.

14. They get into everything.

15. Sometimes they hide things like socks.

16. Some ferrets walk on a leash.

17. Randall bathes his ferret every few weeks.

18. He washes it with mild shampoo.

19. Ferrets possess one bad habit.

20. They sometimes bite people.

Linking Verbs

A *linking verb* connects, or links, the subject to a word or word group that identifies or describes the subject.

> **EXAMPLE**   The headlights on the car **became** dim. [The linking verb *became* connects the subject *headlights* with the adjective *dim*.]

EXERCISE A   Underline the linking verbs in the following sentences.

Example 1. The bark on the tree <u>feels</u> dry and rough.

  1. Bradley's mother is an air-traffic controller.

  2. Warren was sick several times this year.

  3. I have grown weary of television.

  4. The Wilsons are our nearest neighbors.

  5. Jamie looked uncomfortable on the stage.

  6. She has been late every day this week.

  7. The sky remained cloudy until late afternoon.

  8. This carton of milk smells sour.

  9. You should be hungry after all that work.

 10. The top-ranked player in the tennis tournament is Venus Williams.

EXERCISE B   Underline the verb in each of the following sentences. Then, above the verb, write *AV* for *action verb* or *LV* for *linking verb*.

                           AV

Example 1. Derrick <u>stays</u> with his grandparents during the summer.

 11. My grandfather received the Congressional Medal of Honor.

 12. I am the only female grandchild in my family.

 13. My grandmother seems young to me.

 14. Jeanette found a picture of her grandparents as teenagers.

 15. They looked odd in the old-fashioned clothing of the 1950s.

 16. Tony's great-grandfather will be eighty years old on Sunday.

 17. Alexa's grandparents once lived in Indonesia and in the Netherlands.

 18. Mrs. Shuman cooks great Indonesian and Dutch food.

 19. Joseph never knew his grandparents.

 20. He feels sad about that.

NAME _____ CLASS _____ DATE _____

for **CHAPTER 3: PARTS OF SPEECH OVERVIEW** *pages 55–56*

Transitive and Intransitive Verbs

A *transitive verb* is a verb that expresses an action directed toward a person, place, thing, or idea.

EXAMPLE The tourists **explored** the city. [The action of *explored* is directed toward *city*.]

An *intransitive verb* tells something about the subject or expresses action without the action passing to a receiver, or object.

EXAMPLE The tour bus **arrived** on time. [The action of *arrived* is not passed to a receiver.]

EXERCISE A In each of the following sentences, decide whether the underlined verb is transitive or intransitive. Above the verb, write *TR* for *transitive* or *INT* for *intransitive*.

Example 1. The Thames River winds *INT* through the heart of London.

1. Restaurants and shops line the banks of the Thames River in London.

2. Most shops open early during tourist season.

3. A tour bus company offers several tours.

4. Our bus driver spoke clearly and intelligently.

5. She provided a great deal of information about London and its famous river.

6. The depth of the Thames River changes with the tides every day.

7. Ancient Romans built the first bridge across the river.

8. In ancient times, traders from other countries sailed up the river.

9. Terrible slums and poverty existed along the riverbanks.

10. Charles Dickens described the slums of London in his novels.

EXERCISE B In one sentence in each of the following pairs, the verb is transitive. In the other sentence, the verb is intransitive. Underline the verb in each sentence. Then, on the line provided, write *TR* if the verb is *transitive* or *INT* if it is *intransitive*.

Example 1. *INT* We met last year at a basketball game. *TR* I met Tomás for lunch.

11. _____ Cynthia plays the piano well. _____ Roger plays in the school band.

12. _____ The townspeople survived the flood. _____ The entire crew of the sunken ship survived.

13. _____ Alberto writes in his journal each evening. _____ Mishi often writes letters to her grandmother.

14. _____ The pilot landed the plane. _____ The plane landed on time.

15. _____ Please do not leave your coat there. _____ Please leave as soon as possible.

Kinds of Verbs

Some action verbs may be either transitive or intransitive, depending on how they are used in a sentence.

TRANSITIVE Eduardo **practices** piano at least once every day.

INTRANSITIVE He usually **practices** for two hours at a time.

Linking verbs are intransitive.

EXAMPLE Martina **will become** a certified diver next month.

EXERCISE Underline the verb in each of the following sentences. Be sure to include any helping verbs. Determine whether each verb is an action verb or a linking verb and whether the verb is transitive or intransitive. On the line provided, write *ACT* for *action verb* or *LINK* for *linking verb;* on the same line, write *TRAN* for *transitive verb* or *INT* for *intransitive verb.*

Example _ACT, INT_ **1.** Martha doesn't sleep very well.

_____ **1.** Her sister always studies late into the night.

_____ **2.** Martha is sometimes very sleepy in the morning.

_____ **3.** Martha's sister could have read in the kitchen.

_____ **4.** She could also have taken her books into the living room.

_____ **5.** The light there is better for my eyes.

_____ **6.** Sometimes Martha's sister studies at the library.

_____ **7.** Most of the time, Martha and her sister have fun together.

_____ **8.** They share clothes and school supplies.

_____ **9.** Martha and her sister both like the same music.

_____ **10.** Martha is also different from her sister in some ways.

_____ **11.** She is much messier, for one thing.

_____ **12.** Her sister always hangs clothes up neatly.

_____ **13.** Martha leaves things all over the floor and the beds.

_____ **14.** Martha likes fresh air in the room, even in the winter.

_____ **15.** Martha's sister complains about the cold air.

_____ **16.** The noise from the traffic bothers her, too.

_____ **17.** Every night, she closes the window.

_____ **18.** Then the room becomes hot and stuffy.

_____ **19.** Martha is always the first one up in the morning.

_____ **20.** She doesn't even wait for the alarm.

GRAMMAR

The Adverb A

| **3b.** | An *adverb* is a word that modifies a verb, an adjective, or another adverb. |

> **EXAMPLES** Timothy **often** goes to the library. [The adverb *often* modifies the verb *goes*.]
>
> He began reading when he was **very** young. [The adverb *very* modifies the adjective *young*.]
>
> He can finish a book **very quickly.** [The adverb *very* modifies the adverb *quickly*. The adverb *quickly* modifies the verb phrase *can finish*.]

Adverbs answer the following questions: *Where? When? How? How often? How long? To what extent? How much?*
Adverbs may come before, after, or between the words they modify.

EXERCISE A In the following sentences, underline each adverb. Then, draw an arrow from each adverb to the word or words it modifies.

Example 1. Did you already know that Americans throw away 195 million tons of garbage in a year?

1. Open garbage dumps sometimes pose serious health hazards.

2. Most trash is now buried in sanitary landfills.

3. Methane gas from garbage can easily catch fire.

4. Pipes safely bring the gas to the surface.

5. People seldom want landfills near their homes.

6. Scientists and engineers are always looking for new ways to reuse recyclable materials.

7. Many of us thoughtlessly discard possibly useful items daily.

8. Some people willingly reuse bottles and jars.

9. Throughout the country, many cities efficiently separate garbage from easily recyclable items.

10. Some of the largest landfills will very soon be full.

EXERCISE B Complete each of the following sentences by filling in the blank with an appropriate adverb.

Example 1. _____*Yesterday*_____ the rain flooded our garden.

11. Two white swans glided _____ across the pond.

12. Close the door _____!

13. The workers will finish the bridge _____.

14. _____, LuAnn made her way up the steep staircase.

15. Mom and Sally _____ go fishing on Saturday mornings.

GRAMMAR

The Adverb B

3b.   An *adverb* is a word that modifies a verb, an adjective, or another adverb.

> **EXAMPLES**   Did you see the meteor shower **tonight**? [The adverb *tonight* modifies the verb phrase *Did see.*]
>
> That state park has an **extremely** popular swimming area. [The adverb *extremely* modifies the adjective *popular.*]
>
> The parking lot fills **so rapidly.** [The adverb *so* modifies the adverb *rapidly*. The adverb *rapidly* modifies the verb *fills.*]

EXERCISE   Circle each adverb in the following sentences. Then, draw an arrow from each adverb to the word or words that the adverb modifies.

Example 1. The book is entirely too long to finish in one day.

1. *Stuart Little* has always been my favorite book.

2. George quietly asked the librarian for help.

3. I finally finished the report.

4. On the table lies a very old bookmark.

5. Trisha's library books are usually returned on time.

6. You should not fold any pages in a library book.

7. I have never read an entire book of poetry.

8. Lately, I have been reading more nonfiction books.

9. During the week Mom is entirely too busy to read.

10. She frequently reads novels on the weekends.

11. She finishes a book easily in one or two days.

12. She recommends especially enjoyable books to all her friends.

13. In addition, her reading list always includes new biographies.

14. She thinks stories about inventors and explorers are exceptionally good choices.

15. Now she is reading both a new mystery and a book about Mount Everest.

16. Our librarian works hard to make the displays interesting.

17. I usually learn something new from the displays.

18. Old books must be handled quite carefully.

19. The paper in this old book is particularly fragile.

20. Yesterday I saw an exhibit of extremely rare books at the museum.

Language and Sentence Skills Practice   **53**

Adverb or Adjective?

Remember that not all adverbs end in *–ly* and not all words that end in *–ly* are adverbs. The same word may be used as different parts of speech. You cannot tell what part of speech a word is until you know how it is used in a particular sentence.

EXAMPLES I was **only** trying to help. [*Only* is used as an adverb to modify the verb phrase *was trying*.]

Her father was an **only** child. [*Only* is used as an adjective to modify the noun *child*.]

EXERCISE Write *ADJ* above each underlined word you identify as an *adjective* and *ADV* above each underlined word you identify as an *adverb*. Then, draw an arrow from each underlined word to the word or words it modifies.

Example 1. The coach will soon decide on a practice schedule.

1. Joaquín runs three miles daily.

2. That is certainly the better opportunity for her.

3. I know we will arrive later than they will.

4. We had just stopped by the house for a few minutes.

5. Would you like to have time for a leisurely walk through the town?

6. Kai is always an early riser.

7. The judge made a reasonable and just decision in the case.

8. May the best candidate win!

9. Susan's sister lost the bright red ball.

10. Why did he take the only book about that subject?

11. His job pays a higher hourly wage than mine does.

12. Put the water into the pan first.

13. My mother said she had found a very scholarly book on the subject.

14. Do you think he plays the tuba well?

15. He has been taking weekly swimming lessons for years.

16. She really seems well today.

17. Sarah can still remember when her best friend moved away.

18. Those oranges were very sour.

19. He will most likely want to come with us to the movies.

20. He is always late, unfortunately.

The Preposition

3c. A **preposition** is a word that shows the relationship between a noun or a pronoun and another word in the sentence.

> **EXAMPLE** They traveled **on** foot. [The preposition *on* shows the relationship of *foot* to *traveled*.]

Prepositions that are made up of more than one word are called *compound prepositions*.

> **EXAMPLE** **According to** some historians, the explorers Lewis and Clark traveled more than eight thousand miles.

EXERCISE A Underline all the prepositions in the following sentences.

Example 1. The explorers were successful on their mission in spite of many challenges.

1. Meriwether Lewis and William Clark were officers in the United States Army.

2. President Thomas Jefferson suggested that Lewis find a northwest passage to the Pacific Ocean.

3. The Lewis and Clark expedition was one of the most important in United States history.

4. On account of their exploration, territories recently acquired by the United States could be mapped.

5. Lewis and Clark began their journey in 1804.

6. They left from St. Louis and traveled to the Pacific coast.

7. Lewis and Clark endured many hardships during their long journey.

8. They traveled with horses and a large amount of supplies.

9. In spite of a severe winter in the Rocky Mountains, they survived.

10. The expansion and settlement of the West was easier because of Lewis and Clark.

EXERCISE B Underline the preposition in each of the following sentences. Then, on the line provided, rewrite the sentence using a different preposition in place of the one you underlined.

Example 1. The puppy crawled behind the bed. *The puppy crawled under the bed.*

11. Lay the magazines on the sofa. _____

12. We walked down the garden path. _____

13. Martha is sitting next to Keith. _____

14. The ball landed between Jennifer and Tamika. _____

15. We found the toy underneath the chair. _____

The Prepositional Phrase

A preposition always has at least one noun or pronoun as an object. This noun or pronoun is called the *object of the preposition*. The preposition, its object, and any modifiers of the object make up a *prepositional phrase*. A preposition may have more than one object.

> **EXAMPLES** The most valuable pearls are found **in tropical seas.** [*Seas* is the object of the preposition *in*. *Tropical* is an adjective modifying the object *seas*.]
>
> Here is a picture **of Mick and Yoshi.** [The preposition *of* has the two objects *Mick* and *Yoshi*.]

EXERCISE A For each underlined prepositional phrase, write *P* above the preposition and *OP* above its object.

 Example 1. Beneath the water lay rich pearl beds.

1. Pearls are formed when sand or other debris gets trapped inside the oyster shell.

2. The oyster begins covering the piece of debris with a special substance.

3. After several years, a pearl is formed.

4. In the early 1900s, a Japanese man discovered a way to fool oysters.

5. This process involves shoving a small bead into the oyster.

6. The oyster mistakes the bead for debris and starts making a pearl.

7. The layers of a pearl can be seen under a microscope.

8. On a string of pearls, each pearl must look like the others.

9. A large, perfectly round pearl is one of the most valuable gems in the world.

10. Pearls with irregular shapes are not as valuable.

EXERCISE B Add prepositional phrases to the following sentences. Write your new sentences on the lines provided.

 Example 1. The woman described the accident. *The woman across the street described the*
 accident to the police.

11. Milo rode his horse. _____

12. Una drove home. _____

13. The carpenter repaired the roof. _____

14. The ship sank. _____

15. The coach explained the play. _____

for **CHAPTER 3: PARTS OF SPEECH OVERVIEW**   `page 65`

Preposition or Adverb?

Some words may be used as both prepositions and adverbs. Remember that a preposition always has at least one noun or pronoun as an object. An adverb never does.

> **ADVERB**   You might get cold if you stay **outside** too long.
>
> **PREPOSITION**   I could see a flock of geese **outside** the window.

EXERCISE   Identify the underlined words in the following sentences as either adverbs or prepositions. If the word is an adverb, write *ADV* above it. If the word is a preposition, write *PREP* above it. Then, if the word is a preposition, write *OP* above its object.

Example 1.   The sailors could see the faint outlines of an island <u>across</u> the water. *(PREP across, OP water)*

 1. Please place your books <u>beneath</u> your desk.

 2. She had never smelled anything like that <u>before</u>.

 3. Threatening storm clouds were gathering <u>above</u>.

 4. You can always find a jar of peanut butter <u>inside</u> that cupboard.

 5. I'm sure the dog came <u>in</u> last night.

 6. We could hear the band playing as it marched <u>down</u> the street.

 7. The weather was certainly miserable <u>outside</u>.

 8. If the gate won't open, climb <u>over</u> the fence.

 9. The balloons floated far <u>above</u> our heads.

10. The goats are <u>in</u> the far pasture.

11. Let's get popcorn <u>before</u> the movie.

12. You might have to wade <u>across</u> the creek to find the trail again.

13. The bus drove <u>past</u> the people.

14. Don't turn that log <u>over</u> so quickly!

15. Meet me <u>outside</u> the front door after you've finished shopping.

16. A fire blazed <u>inside</u>, welcoming the weary travelers.

17. High <u>above</u> the mountain, the hawks wheeled in lazy circles.

18. What do you think you'd find <u>over</u> the rainbow?

19. The boy clasped the money tightly <u>in</u> his hand.

20. Bring your skates <u>in</u> before the rain starts.

The Conjunction A

3d. A *conjunction* is a word that joins words or groups of words.

EXAMPLES You **and** I have been invited to the wildlife park.

We waited for an hour **but** then left without the two boys.

I am reading about canaries, **for** I want one as a pet.

Heather will **either** walk home **or** call her brother.

EXERCISE Underline each conjunction in the following sentences.

Example 1. Both Africa and Asia have many kinds of butterflies.

1. The insect order Lepidoptera includes not only moths but also butterflies.

2. Powdery scales cover the wings of both butterflies and moths.

3. Moths usually have plump, furry bodies, but butterflies have slender, hairless bodies.

4. Most butterflies fly during the daytime and rest with their wings folded upright.

5. There are between 15,000 and 20,000 species of butterflies.

6. Butterflies live almost everywhere, but tropical rain forests have the most different kinds.

7. Both other insects and birds are among butterflies' enemies.

8. Butterflies appear fragile to us, yet they have powerful defenses.

9. Butterflies may blend with their surroundings or mimic distasteful species.

10. Predators avoid the viceroy butterfly, for it resembles the bad-tasting monarch butterfly.

11. To make themselves taste bad, some butterflies eat plants that are either poisonous or bitter.

12. The bright or striking colors on some butterflies are actually a warning to predators.

13. The skin of a caterpillar neither grows nor stretches.

14. Adult butterflies usually feed only on nectar, but caterpillars can do a lot of crop damage.

15. The caterpillar of the cabbage butterfly, for example, feeds on cabbage and cauliflower plants.

16. The transformation of a caterpillar into a butterfly is both amazing and interesting.

17. Butterflies cannot live actively in cold weather, so many of them migrate to warmer climates for the winter.

18. The monarch must be the long-distance champion of the butterfly world, for it travels up to two thousand miles to escape cold weather.

19. Other butterflies produce a substance like antifreeze, so they can survive the cold.

20. The word *butterfly* comes from *buterfleoge,* an Old English word meaning "butter" and "fly."

The Conjunction B

3d. A *conjunction* is a word that joins words or groups of words.

EXAMPLES Keisha **and** Jack were the winners.

Noel remembered her notebook **yet** forgot her pen.

We hurried down the hall, **for** we didn't want to be late.

Neither rain **nor** snow bothers my dog.

EXERCISE In the following sentences, write an appropriate conjunction in the blank or blanks provided.

Example 1. _____*Either*_____ Jeff _____*or*_____ Jared can throw the ball that far.

1. I'm taking a full class load this term, including biology _____ chemistry.

2. We could _____ take a bus _____ walk to the museum.

3. You'll have to choose one _____ the other.

4. Jessamyn wanted to be at school early, _____ her alarm clock didn't go off.

5. Aaron, Alex, _____ Andy are always the first names on the class list.

6. She had to decide _____ to take a walk _____ read a book.

7. My sister is in tonight's performance, _____ we have bought front-row seats.

8. He hasn't written, _____ has he called.

9. _____ cold water _____ lemonade are refreshing on a hot day.

10. We stopped to rest after hiking only three miles, _____ we were already weary.

11. _____ our team makes the playoffs _____ the season is over.

12. Make sure the cats are in tonight, _____ the weather service is predicting rain.

13. If I can take only one friend on the trip, I'll pick Jessie, Maria, _____ Daniela.

14. I'm supposed to finish the book today, _____ I haven't even begun to read it.

15. I'll _____ have to stay up late tonight _____ get up early tomorrow.

16. _____ Nate _____ Sandy will be our representative on the committee.

17. I was hungry when I got home, _____ I hadn't eaten anything since breakfast.

18. This project requires _____ tape _____ glue.

19. The bell had not rung, _____ the door was already closed.

20. Turn right at the next corner, _____ look for a blue house on your left.

GRAMMAR

The Interjection

3e. An *interjection* is a word that expresses emotion.

    EXAMPLES   **Hurray!** Here comes the parade!

                   Oh, I made a mistake.

                   Raising a puppy is, **well,** challenging.

EXERCISE A In each of the following sentences, underline the interjection.

Example 1. <u>Ouch</u>! That hurt!

1. Aha! There you are!

2. Oh, no! I stubbed that same toe again!

3. It must be a hundred degrees in the shade. Whew!

4. Do you think you could, well, work my shift tonight?

5. Our team made it to the playoffs! Hooray!

6. Oops, I didn't mean to lose your place in the book.

7. We'll be on time if we leave here about, oh, nine o'clock.

8. Hey! That's a stop sign, not a yield sign!

9. Yikes! Is that pan hot!

10. It looks as though the pipes froze last night. Oh dear!

EXERCISE B In each of the following sentences, fill in the blank with an appropriate interjection. Try not to use the same interjection more than once.

Example 1. _____*Hey*_____! Look out for that fence!

11. _____! You certainly took your time.

12. _____! That hammer just missed my foot.

13. Rosita sat down, _____, just before the bell rang.

14. I forgot my bus pass again, _____.

15. _____, I guess the movie should be over by now.

16. _____, did I tell you what happened to me at the mall?

17. Here comes Daniel with, _____, the biggest Great Dane I have ever seen.

18. _____, I didn't think you would mind if I brought my friend.

19. I scraped my knee. _____!

20. _____! That squirrel can fly!

HOLT HANDBOOK | Introductory Course

for **CHAPTER 3: PARTS OF SPEECH OVERVIEW**   *page 70*

Determining Parts of Speech

3f.	The way a word is used in a sentence determines what part of speech it is.

VERB	We **walk** in the woods.	**ADVERB**	A small, furry animal ran **by.**
NOUN	We will take a **walk** in the woods.	**PREPOSITION**	They will arrive **by** noon.

EXERCISE A   Decide what part of speech each underlined word in the following sentences is. Above the word, write *V* for *verb*, *ADV* for *adverb*, *PREP* for *preposition*, *CON* for *conjunction*, or *I* for *interjection*.

                       ADV
Example 1. Tigers <u>rarely</u> attack humans.

1. The huge elephant <u>sensed</u> danger.

2. "She must be hungry," <u>thought</u> the elephant's handler.

3. He climbed <u>down</u> and fed her some leaves.

4. Then he scrambled back <u>to</u> his perch.

5. <u>Suddenly</u> a tiger sprang from the bushes.

6. The tiger's claw <u>then</u> scraped the handler's leg.

7. Man <u>and</u> tiger tumbled to the jungle floor.

8. The elephant lifted the handler <u>with</u> her trunk.

9. The handler was badly hurt <u>but</u> recovered from his wounds.

10. <u>Alas!</u> He refused to enter the jungle again.

EXERCISE B   For each sentence, underline the word that is the part of speech named in parentheses.

Example 1. The birds flew <u>up</u> into the sky. *(adverb)*

11. My grandparents planned a trip to Alaska. *(verb)*

12. We played well, but we lost the game. *(adverb)*

13. Barbara lives with her parents. *(preposition)*

14. The hikers took off their packs and sat under the tree. *(conjunction)*

15. Did you climb aboard the bus? *(preposition)*

16. Jamal arrived early for dress rehearsal. *(verb)*

17. Those clouds look awfully dark to me. *(adverb)*

18. Did Teresa or Joseph make this birdhouse? *(conjunction)*

19. Well, wish us luck in the game! *(interjection)*

20. The puppy lay down on the examination table. *(preposition)*

Language and Sentence Skills Practice

Review A: **Parts of Speech**

EXERCISE A In each of the following sentences, underline all parts of each verb phrase. Then, underline any helping verbs a second time.

Example 1. Have the suspects finally been arrested?

1. Has the lawn been mowed this week?

2. The chorus will sing a medley of Beatles hits.

3. Mr. Wauneka may be elected to the state legislature.

4. You should have phoned first.

5. Their main offices have been moved downtown.

6. The writer will proofread his latest article.

7. I have been jogging five miles a day.

8. Can you ever forgive me for that?

9. The baby is sleeping in his mother's arms.

10. Lupe would have never found her wallet without your help.

EXERCISE B Decide whether each underlined verb is an action verb or a linking verb. On the line provided, write *AV* for *action verb* or *LV* for *linking verb*. On the same line, write *TRAN* for *transitive verb* or *INT* for *intransitive verb*.

Example ___*LV, INT*___ **1.** Did that fish taste strange to you?

_____ **11.** I found that information in the telephone book.

_____ **12.** Eddie must be the fastest runner on the team.

_____ **13.** That bread looks moldy.

_____ **14.** Most birds migrate at night.

_____ **15.** We built a shelter near the edge of the forest.

_____ **16.** The contestants appear confident.

_____ **17.** They rescued the passengers from the capsized ferry.

_____ **18.** My throat feels scratchy this morning.

_____ **19.** We were the largest class in the history of the school.

_____ **20.** Do raccoons hibernate in the winter?

Review B: **Parts of Speech**

EXERCISE A In each of the following sentences, underline the adverb once. Then, draw an arrow from each adverb to the word or words the adverb modifies.

Example 1. Will you soon clean the kitchen?

1. Some kinds of opals are extremely beautiful.

2. I often go to the movies.

3. The ocean appears especially beautiful at sunrise.

4. The store window elegantly displayed coats and shoes.

5. The last grapefruit disappeared mysteriously.

6. She is particularly interested in sports.

7. Have you ever climbed a mountain?

8. Which part of this assignment would you do next?

9. No room remained at the end of the row, so everyone moved over.

10. On Sunday, the dogs in my neighborhood barked early.

EXERCISE B In each of the following sentences, write *P* above the preposition and *OP* above its object or objects. Also, write *C* above any conjunction and *I* above any interjection.

Example 1. They swam slowly and patiently toward shore and safety.

11. There were only a few flowers among the weeds.

12. Ouch! That waiter crashed into the swinging door!

13. The food splattered onto the wall and floor.

14. After the game, the MVP award will be announced.

15. I am doing my science project with Julio and Karen.

16. The forecast calls for rain, so bring your umbrella.

17. Watch for speeding cars and trucks.

18. Do you ride a bus or walk to school?

19. Well, I found my slippers under the couch, but I still can't find my socks.

20. Not only did Lisa hit the ball past the shortstop, but she also helped win the game.

Review C: **Parts of Speech**

EXERCISE A Identify the part of speech of each underlined word or word group in the following sentences. Above the word or word group, write *V* for *verb*, *ADV* for *adverb*, *PREP* for *preposition*, *C* for *conjunction*, or *I* for *interjection*.

　　　　　　　　　　　　　　　　　　　　　　　　　　V　ADV
Example 1. The achievements of Leonardo da Vinci were quite remarkable.

1. Leonardo da Vinci was an Italian artist and scientist.

2. Wow! Did you know that da Vinci designed a flying machine?

3. He studied a bird's wing and modeled the flying machine on it.

4. Many of da Vinci's paintings can be viewed today in museums around the world.

5. For many years Galileo Galilei was a mathematics professor, but he left teaching to pursue

   scientific research.

6. Some people disagreed with his ideas and sought other explanations.

7. They believed the sun moved around the earth, but Galileo believed that the earth moved

   around the sun.

8. Would you have agreed with Galileo or with his opponents?

9. Galileo made his most sensational discovery when he discovered the moons of Jupiter.

10. Oh, I wasn't aware of that fact.

EXERCISE B In each of the following sentences, underline each word or word group that is the part of speech indicated in parentheses.

Example 1. Selina's pet rabbit has scampered underneath the front porch. *(verb)*

11. Joyce will mow the lawn either Saturday or Sunday. *(conjunction)*

12. Chinese is a language with a long history. *(verb)*

13. The room looks bare without curtains. *(preposition)*

14. Carefully he jumped over the deep puddle. *(adverb)*

15. Hey! Who wants to play softball? *(interjection)*

16. These apples should not taste so tart. *(verb)*

17. They are arguing about rules and regulations again. *(adverb)*

18. The planet Venus seems more like Earth in appearance than any other planet does. *(verb)*

19. India and Pakistan became independent states in 1947. *(conjunction)*

20. Lightning streaked across the night sky. *(preposition)*

Literary Model: Poetry

Foul Shot
by Edwin A. Hoey

With two 60's stuck on the scoreboard
And two seconds hanging on the clock,
The solemn boy in the center of eyes,
Squeezed by silence,
Seeks out the line with his feet,
Soothes his hands along his uniform,
Gently drums the ball against the floor,
Then measures the waiting net,
Raises the ball on his right hand,
Balances it with his left,
Calms it with his fingertips,
Breathes,
Crouches,
Waits,
And then through a stretching of stillness,
Nudges it upward.
The ball
Slides up and out,
Lands,
Leans,
Wobbles,
Wavers,
Hesitates,
Exasperates,
Plays it coy
Until every face begs with unsounding
    screams—
And then
    And then
        And then,
Right before ROAR–UP,
Dives down and through.

EXERCISE A Write each verb that appears in the poem "Foul Shot". Do not include *stuck, hanging, squeezed, waiting, stretching,* and *unsounding*. These words are verb forms used as other parts of speech.

_____

_____

_____

_____

_____

_____

_____

_____

_____

_____

_____

_____

_____

_____

_____

_____

_____

_____

_____

_____

_____

_____

_____

_____

Literary Model (continued)

EXERCISE B How does the poet's use of verbs contribute to the feeling of tension that you, the reader, experience as the last seconds of a tied basketball game are being described?

_____

_____

_____

_____

EXERCISE C Using Hoey's writing as a model, write a poem describing a topic related to an athletic competition. As Hoey did, use verbs to create a feeling of excitement or tension.

_____

_____

_____

_____

_____

_____

_____

_____

_____

_____

_____

_____

EXERCISE D

1. Read your poem critically, and replace the linking verbs that you used with active, descriptive verbs such as those Hoey used in the poem "Foul Shot." For each verb that you replace, write the original verb, followed by the replacement, on the lines below.

_____

_____

2. How does your use of verbs contribute to your poem?

_____

_____

Writing Application: Skit

Interjections bring a sense of the spoken—or yelled—word to writing. Writers set them off either with a comma or an exclamation point to tell readers how strong the interjection is. Read the sentences below out loud.

    MILD INTERJECTION   Well, I was a bit surprised at his sky-blue hair coloring.

    STRONG INTERJECTION   Well! I never had such a shock as when I saw his blue hair!

Notice how the tone of the interjection—mildly surprised in the first sentence and shocked in the second—sets the tone for the sentence that follows, too.

WRITING ACTIVITY

For a drama class, you are writing a short, humorous skit in which a group of people your age hosts a surprise birthday party for a friend. Unfortunately, the friend really does not like surprise parties. Write the dialogue between the hosts and the friend from the time the friend comes through the door. Use interjections to express the feelings of the characters in the skit.

PREWRITING   You could work this scene out in various ways. Brainstorm endings for the unwanted surprise, keeping them funny. Which possibility seems more real to you? Which provides the best chance for comedy? After you have sketched out several endings, choose the one you like best.

WRITING   With the skit's ending in mind, you can now write the lines for the characters to say. The first line is a giveaway: "Surprise!" the hosts will yell as their friend comes through the door. What happens after that is up to you. As you write lines, try to make them sound like spoken English. You will probably use some slang and a few sentence fragments.

REVISING   The best way to test the lines you have written is to gather up a few friends and read the lines out loud together, as you would if you were performing the skit. Listen for awkward pauses. Ask your friends whether any lines leave them with questions about meaning. Have you used interjections that help the audience understand how each character is feeling?

PUBLISHING   Check your skit for mistakes in spelling and punctuation. Make enough copies for all the players. Then, with your teacher's permission, perform your skit for the class. Watch as other versions of the scene are played out. Discuss the different endings that you and your classmates wrote.

EXTENDING YOUR WRITING

This exercise could lead to a more developed writing project. You could expand your skit by writing several different endings, some positive and some negative. Then, you and your classmates could role-play these endings and lead a class discussion on how to turn a bad situation into a good one.

Language and Sentence Skills Practice

Choices: Exploring Phrases and Clauses

Here's your chance to step out of the grammar book and into the real world. You may not notice phrases and clauses, but you and the people around you use them every day. The following activities challenge you to find a connection between phrases and clauses and the world around you. Do the activity below that suits your personality best, and then share your discoveries with your class. Have fun!

MUSIC

On Top of Old Smokey

Adverb phrases make great introductory lines for songs. How many songs can you recall that begin with an adverb phrase? Write down the first line of at least four songs. Then, underline each adverb phrase.

BUILDING BACKGROUND KNOWLEDGE

Over, Under, Up, Down

Show your classmates how useful prepositions can be. First, make a list of ten prepositions that can be used to express location. Then, find or create illustrations that show what each preposition means.

WRITING

Something out of Nothing

Most people have plenty to say but have trouble putting their thoughts into words. Prepare a visual presentation that shows how one word can become the building block for a whole sentence. You will need four different colors for writing—one for each of the following steps. Begin by writing one word. Then, add a word or two and create a phrase. Next, turn that phrase into a clause. The final step is to turn your clause into a sentence.

LINGUISTICS

By the By

Pick a preposition, and make a list of every common phrase or expression you can think of that uses that preposition. For *by,* you could start with *by the by, by the way,* and *by hook or by crook.* Begin by brainstorming, and finish by checking in a dictionary of common expressions (usually known as a dictionary of idioms). When you've completed your list, pass out copies to your classmates.

CREATIVE WRITING

Sauce for the Goose

Not only could Mother Goose rhyme, but she also could use prepositional phrases. Write a few of your own nursery rhymes. Be sure to use at least three prepositional phrases in each rhyme. Be ready to identify each phrase as either an adverb phrase or an adjective phrase.

CONTEST

School for Thought

Challenge your classmates to a contest. Pick a noun, and write as many adjective phrases as you can about it. For instance, if you choose *school* you might write *school of thought* or *school for boys.* Pick a common, general noun so that you'll be able to generate a lot of phrases. The person or team with the most adjective phrases wins.

MOVIES

At the Theater

Have you ever noticed that many movie titles contain prepositional phrases? There are also plenty of movie titles that *are* prepositional phrases. With a partner, brainstorm at least ten of these movie titles—five that contain prepositional phrases and five that are prepositional phrases. Put your list on a poster, and get permission to hang it in the classroom.

WORD ORDER

Mix and Match

Write a sentence that has a subject, a verb, and two phrases. Then, get your scissors and cut out each phrase. Next, see how many ways you can combine the pieces of your sentence. (Don't forget that punctuation often changes with word order.) Put the versions of your sentence on a poster, and ask to post it in the classroom.

Identifying Phrases

4a. A *phrase* is a group of related words that is used as a single part of speech and that does not contain both a verb and its subject.

> **EXAMPLES** should have been studying [no subject]
>
> behind the large boxes [no subject or verb]

A word group that has both a subject and a verb is called a *clause*.

> **EXAMPLE** although I should have been studying [*I* is the subject of the verb phrase *should have been studying*.]

Phrases cannot stand alone as sentences. They must be used with other words to make a complete sentence.

> **PHRASE** with a special cane
>
> **SENTENCE** Shawn walks with a special cane.

EXERCISE A Identify each word group by writing *P* for *phrase* or *NP* for *not a phrase* on the line provided.

Examples __*P*__ **1.** with every student

__*NP*__ **2.** while the plane landed

_____ **1.** with long white curtains

_____ **2.** had been swimming

_____ **3.** as a baby sitter

_____ **4.** after the bell rang

_____ **5.** is running

_____ **6.** The cat sat.

_____ **7.** over the fence

_____ **8.** in the middle

_____ **9.** under the car

_____ **10.** where her books are

EXERCISE B Each of the following sentences contains an underlined word group. On the line provided, write *P* if the word group is a phrase or *NP* if the word group is not a phrase.

Examples __*P*__ **1.** Arachnids are members of a class <u>of small, insectlike animals</u>.

__*NP*__ **2.** Unlike insects, however, <u>arachnids do not have wings</u>.

_____**11.** The names of many arachnids <u>have caused</u> people to shudder in fear.

_____**12.** The black widow spider, <u>for instance</u>, is the most dangerous spider in the United States.

_____**13.** However, <u>while the bite of a black widow can cause severe pain</u>, it usually does not

cause serious harm.

_____**14.** Many people also fear tarantulas, but the bite of tarantulas found <u>in the United States</u> is

no more dangerous than the sting of a bee.

_____**15.** Spiders, <u>while they may look frightening</u>, can be helpful because they eat harmful

insects.

Language and Sentence Skills Practice

Prepositional Phrases A

4b. A *prepositional phrase* includes a preposition, the object of the preposition, and any modifiers of that object.

> **EXAMPLES** They will picnic **by the river.** [*By* is the preposition, *river* is the object, and *the* modifies *river*.]
>
> The mantel was decorated **with twelve candles.** [*With* is the preposition, *candles* is the object, and *twelve* modifies *candles*.]
>
> A preposition may have more than one object.
>
> **EXAMPLE** The shuttle traveled **to Mars and Venus.** [The preposition *to* has the two objects *Mars* and *Venus*.]

EXERCISE A Underline each prepositional phrase in the following sentences. Hint: Some sentences contain more than one prepositional phrase.

Example 1. What are the differences between moths and butterflies?

1. He read about butterflies and moths.

2. Butterflies and moths belong to the same insect group.

3. However, butterflies are different from moths.

4. Butterflies are some of the most beautiful creatures in the insect world.

5. Some giant moths can send shivers down your spine.

6. Most butterflies fly only during the day, but moths usually fly at night.

7. Many butterflies' antennae have ends that are shaped like bulbs.

8. The moth's antennae, however, do not end in knobs.

9. Like a butterfly, a moth takes different forms throughout its life cycle.

10. The caterpillars of some moths can cause damage to trees and plants.

EXERCISE B Complete each of the following sentences by writing an appropriate prepositional phrase on the line provided.

Example 1. The store ___*on the corner*___ was robbed last night.

11. I heard the report about the robbery _____.

12. The reporter said the robbery occurred _____.

13. _____, thousands of dollars were stolen.

14. A few _____ said they heard the report, too.

15. Police arrested a suspect _____ this morning.

Prepositional Phrases B

4b. A *prepositional phrase* includes a preposition, the object of the preposition, and any modifiers of that object.

EXAMPLES The man **from Chicago** is here. [*From* is the preposition, and *Chicago* is the object.]
In spite of the rain, the class enjoyed the field trip. [*In spite of* is the preposition, *rain* is the object, and *the* is a modifier of *rain*.]

A preposition may have more than one object.

EXAMPLE I have already looked **in** the **closet,** the **car,** and my **bedroom.** [The preposition *in* has the three objects *closet, car,* and *bedroom*.]

EXERCISE Underline the prepositional phrases in the following sentences. Then, circle the object or objects of each preposition.

Example 1. According to this checklist, the final project is due next Friday.

1. Swimming in the lake was our favorite summer activity.

2. Birds chirped noisily among the branches.

3. The missing puzzle piece was hidden beneath the sofa.

4. The rain finally stopped, leaving puddles on the sidewalk.

5. The ball hit the ground just inches in front of the outfielder's glove.

6. During the concert the audience listened attentively.

7. The new highway will not be completed until next spring.

8. The cat was curled up underneath the window.

9. Nothing smells quite like a new car.

10. Above the mantelpiece was a large portrait.

11. Who is that new student sitting next to Marcia?

12. How lucky it is that we are on the same team again!

13. For my report, I studied Thomas Nast.

14. The wind was blowing steadily from the west.

15. The nest had been built with twigs and grass.

16. No one may enter without a ticket.

17. The picnic will be sponsored by the drama club.

18. The snowstorm was slowly drifting toward our city.

19. After dinner, we finally felt content.

20. Throughout the night, noises kept him awake.

for **CHAPTER 4: THE PHRASE AND THE CLAUSE** | pages 79–80

Adjective Phrases

| **4c.** | A prepositional phrase that modifies a noun or pronoun is called an **adjective phrase**. |

EXAMPLE The plot **of the story** is simple. [The adjective phrase *of the story* modifies the noun *plot*.]

More than one adjective phrase may modify the same noun or pronoun.

EXAMPLE The letter **from my sister about the puppy** is cute. [The adjective phrases *from my sister* and *about the puppy* both modify the noun *letter*.]

An adjective phrase may modify the object of another adjective phrase.

EXAMPLE Several **of the sculptures by that artist** have already been sold. [The adjective phrase *of the sculptures* modifies the pronoun *Several*. The adjective phrase *by that artist* modifies the noun *sculptures*.]

EXERCISE A Circle the adjective phrases in the following sentences. Draw an arrow from each adjective phrase to the noun or pronoun it modifies.

Example 1. The sounds of chipping and scraping reached our ears.

1. One of my sisters saw that famous Mexican woodcarver.

2. Her favorite carvings are small statues of fire dragons and other fantasy creatures.

3. Collectors around the world enjoy these imaginative Mexican woodcarvings.

4. The colors of the carvings are bright and bold.

5. Animal figures in bright green, yellow, blue, and red are common.

6. Wooden carousel animals are still a specialty of some Mexican woodcarvers.

7. Many of the carvings are exported.

8. The style of the animals, though, is clearly Mexican.

9. New generations of woodcarvers have kept the craft and the tradition alive.

10. Oaxaca was my sister's favorite part of our vacation.

EXERCISE B Each of the following sentences contains two adjective phrases. Underline each adjective phrase separately. Then, draw an arrow from each adjective phrase to the word it modifies.

Example 1. The sound of the laughter of the children pleased him.

11. He studied each of the pictures by John James Audubon.

12. The collection of rare photographs from the Civil War has great historical value.

13. There are many different kinds of folk remedies for hiccups.

14. The painting of sunflowers by van Gogh is a masterpiece.

15. Is the woman in this picture your grandmother from Italy?

Adverb Phrases

| **4d.** | A prepositional phrase that is used to modify a verb, an adjective, or an adverb is called an *adverb phrase*. |

EXAMPLES   Ruben ran **to the store.** [The adverb phrase *to the store* modifies the verb *ran*.]

The captain is aware **of the situation.** [The adverb phrase *of the situation* modifies the adjective *aware*.]

Early **in the morning** she heard a knock on the door. [The adverb phrase *in the morning* modifies the adverb *Early*.]

More than one adverb phrase may modify the same word.

EXAMPLE   We rode **for three hours on the reservation.** [The adverb phrases *for three hours* and *on the reservation* modify the verb *rode*.]

EXERCISE A   Underline the adverb phrases in the following sentences.

Example 1. The city of Katmandu has been inhabited <u>for many centuries</u>.

1. We traveled to Nepal's capital city.

2. In Katmandu are many Buddhist shrines.

3. The city lies between Himalayan mountain peaks.

4. During our visit we saw many interesting shops and restaurants.

5. We walked slowly through narrow, crowded city streets.

6. Most people in Nepal survive by farming.

7. Extra crops are traded for kerosene, salt, and other important items.

8. In the Himalayas live the Sherpas.

9. The Sherpas are known for their special mountaineering skills.

10. During mountain-climbing trips, they guide the climbers and help carry supplies.

EXERCISE B   In the following sentences, circle each adverb phrase and draw an arrow to the word or word group it modifies.

Example 1. (In 1998,) Eduardo traveled (throughout Spain.)

11. He shopped in Madrid and relaxed on the Costa Brava.

12. He went by bus from Madrid to Toledo.

13. Then he visited Granada for three days.

14. At the Alhambra he saw how the Moorish rulers lived during the Middle Ages.

15. Moorish influence is also evident in the architecture of Seville.

Language and Sentence Skills Practice

for **CHAPTER 4: THE PHRASE AND THE CLAUSE**   pages 79–84

Adjective and Adverb Phrases A

4c.   A prepositional phrase that modifies a noun or pronoun is called an **adjective phrase.**

ADJECTIVE	**Wooden** carvings lined the shelves.
ADJECTIVE PHRASE	Carvings **of wood** lined the shelves.

4d.   A prepositional phrase that is used to modify a verb, an adjective, or an adverb is called an **adverb phrase.**

ADVERB	She goes **there** often.
ADVERB PHRASE	She goes **to the cove** often.

EXERCISE A   Identify each underlined prepositional phrase as an adjective phrase or an adverb phrase. Above the phrase, write *ADJ* for *adjective phrase* or *ADV* for *adverb phrase.*

                    ADJ

Example 1. People <u>throughout Alaska</u> are concerned with the issue of oil production and

drilling.

1. Ecologists study relationships <u>between living things and their environments.</u>

2. Ecologists worry that oil will have negative effects <u>on Alaskan wildlife.</u>

3. <u>In the future</u>, more safeguards should be required for oil tankers.

4. Some <u>of the Alaskan people</u> depend on oil for employment.

5. Many Alaskans fear the loss <u>of wildlife and natural resources.</u>

EXERCISE B   Underline the prepositional phrase in each sentence. Then, above the phrase, write *ADJ* if the phrase is an adjective phrase or *ADV* if it is an adverb phrase.

                    ADV

Example 1. A train ran <u>through the mountains.</u>

6. At Delhi we changed trains.

7. When the train pulled up, I stared at the steam engine.

8. The smoke from the engine was thick and white.

9. The view from the little window sometimes took my breath away.

10. The dining car on the train was open.

11. However, we had already bought some food at the station.

12. Friendly servers brought beverages to people's seats.

13. The water in my glass was fresh and cool.

14. The rhythm of the rails soothed me.

15. Soon I rested my head against the seat and fell asleep.

Adjective and Adverb Phrases B

4c.   A prepositional phrase that modifies a noun or pronoun is called an **adjective phrase.**

ADJECTIVE	A **wire** fence surrounded the garden.
ADJECTIVE PHRASE	A fence **of wire** surrounded the garden.

4d.   A prepositional phrase that is used to modify a verb, an adjective, or an adverb is called an **adverb phrase.**

ADVERB	He read the instructions **silently.**
ADVERB PHRASE	He read the instructions **to himself.**

EXERCISE A   Circle each prepositional phrase in the following sentences and draw an arrow to the word it modifies. Then, on the line provided, write *ADJ* if the phrase is an adjective phrase or *ADV* if it is an adverb phrase.

Example ___*ADV*___ **1.** Four knights galloped toward the castle.

_____ **1.** The knights rode across the drawbridge.

_____ **2.** Several of the king's attendants greeted them.

_____ **3.** Inside, the knights knelt before the king.

_____ **4.** They explained that they had ridden from a distant country.

_____ **5.** They had seen a dragon with long red claws.

_____ **6.** They had shot arrows at this fierce dragon.

_____ **7.** During the battle, one knight had been injured.

_____ **8.** Respectfully the knights asked the king for help.

_____ **9.** To his attendants, the king said, "Give these fine men our strongest bows, our sharpest arrows, and our swiftest horses."

_____ **10.** Each of the knights smiled and thanked the generous king.

EXERCISE B   For each of the following sentences, write an appropriate adjective phrase or adverb phrase to complete the sentence.

Example 1. The puppy was digging _____*in the garden*_____. (*adverb phrase*)

11. A mosquito was buzzing _____. (*adverb phrase*)

12. The new school will be located _____. (*adverb phrase*)

13. My dog King is the best dog _____. (*adjective phrase*)

14. _____, the Freemans went camping. (*adverb phrase*)

15. The discussion _____ will only take half the period. (*adjective phrase*)

Language and Sentence Skills Practice

The Clause

4e. A *clause* is a word group that contains a verb and its subject and that is used as a sentence or as part of a sentence.

            S   V

EXAMPLES   **Children crowded onto the sidewalks.** [This clause is used as a sentence.]

           S   V   S   V

            As children crowded onto the sidewalks, the parade began. [This sentence contains two different clauses.]

                    S   V   S   V

            The community band was first, and **it was followed by a group of clowns.** [This sentence contains two different clauses.]

EXERCISE A   Each of the following sentences contains an italicized clause. Underline the subject of the italicized clause once, and underline the verb of the italicized clause twice.

Example 1. *While my <u>brother</u> and <u>I</u> <u>are washing</u> the dishes,* my sister is drying them.

1. *Three trees grow in the Wagners' front yard.*

2. When I swim, *I always wear goggles.*

3. *The Big Dipper,* which is made up of seven stars, *forms part of Ursa Major.*

4. Alexander the Great, *who was tutored by Aristotle,* became king at the age of twenty.

5. *Aaron knows the lyrics to that song by heart.*

6. My dog, *whose name is Buster,* loves to fetch.

7. *After several long delays, the movie finally began.*

8. *Manuel has now read three books* that were written by J.R.R. Tolkien.

9. Bill and Michelle performed the skit *that Kevin and Jane had written.*

10. *When you finish that book,* will you lend it to me?

EXERCISE B   Above the underlined word group in each of the following sentences, write *C* if the word group is a clause or *NC* if the word group is not a clause.

Examples 1. *C* <u>Next time you go for a walk,</u> look carefully at the rocks all around you.

          2. *NC* Most people don't often stop to think <u>about rocks.</u>

11. The wide variety of rocks <u>can make them an interesting subject for study.</u>

12. <u>Diamonds and other gems come from rocks.</u>

13. <u>Some people search for rocks</u> that contain fossils.

14. People <u>who collect rocks and minerals as a hobby</u> are called "rockhounds."

15. <u>Many rocks of interest</u> can be found near your home.

Independent Clauses

4f. An *independent* (or *main*) *clause* expresses a complete thought and can stand by itself as a sentence.

 S   V
EXAMPLE   **Leta plays the violin and the guitar.**

An independent clause does not always stand alone. It can be joined with another clause.

EXAMPLE   Although both instruments sound beautiful, **Leta prefers the violin.**

EXERCISE A   Identify the underlined word group in each of the following sentences by writing above it *I* for *independent clause* or *NI* for *not an independent clause*.

                                    NI
Example 1. As the sun set, the temperature dropped.

1. The hikers walked until they were exhausted.

2. Has John met the family who moved in next door?

3. Gerry needs the book that is on his shelf.

4. If you see Charlotte, please give her this message.

5. We cannot leave yet because the play is not finished.

EXERCISE B   Underline the independent clause or clauses in each of the following sentences.

Example 1. The Great Wall of China, which is about four thousand miles long, is the longest

structure ever built.

6. It was built entirely by hand.

7. Parts of the wall were built as long ago as 2,500 years, but the different sections were connected into the Great Wall about 2,200 years ago.

8. Several Chinese states began to build walls for protection.

9. Emperor Shi Huangdi united China when he ordered the walls to be connected.

10. The Great Wall protected the northern border; it was the first line of defense.

11. The wall worked, and invasions succeeded only if the Chinese leaders were weak.

12. Much of the wall was in ruins when the Ming dynasty took power in A.D. 1368.

13. The Ming government began rebuilding the crumbling ruins in the fifteenth century, and much of their work remains today.

14. The Great Wall is no longer needed for defense, but it has become a major tourist attraction.

15. The wall is as high as thirty-five feet, and the width can reach twenty-five feet.

Subordinate Clauses

4g.   A *subordinate* (or *dependent*) *clause* does not express a complete thought and cannot stand by itself as a complete sentence.

                                     S   V

SUBORDINATE CLAUSE   **if the coaches agree**

A subordinate clause must be joined with at least one independent clause to make a sentence and express a complete thought.

                  SENTENCE   **If the coaches agree,** the game will be rescheduled.

EXERCISE A   Identify the underlined clause in each of the following sentences by writing *SUB* for *subordinate clause* or *IND* for *independent clause* above the clause.

                                                             SUB

Example **1.** Shannon's sister is majoring in marine biology, <u>which she has loved since childhood</u>.

1. The marks <u>that indicate the suit</u> on playing cards are called "pips."

2. The referee was blowing his whistle, but <u>the players didn't hear it</u>.

3. The pyramids, <u>which were built as tombs</u>, are among the Seven Wonders of the World.

4. Aaron had to walk with crutches <u>while his sprained ankle healed</u>.

5. <u>Whenever the wind blew</u>, we had to rake more leaves in the yard.

6. Janet said she would study for the math test <u>after she finishes eating lunch</u>.

7. <u>Whoever has the missing copy of the book</u> should return it to Room 302 this afternoon.

8. Heather would like to go camping, but <u>Gail would rather see a play</u>.

9. <u>After she talked with the foreign-exchange student</u>, Marisa wanted to visit Italy.

10. The sand <u>that trickled through the hourglass</u> showed that Mario had little time left.

EXERCISE B   Underline the subordinate clause in each of the following sentences.

Example **1.** The month of August is named for Augustus Caesar, <u>who was the first emperor of Rome</u>.

11. When the Roman Senate renamed the month in his honor, they also added a day to it.

12. The month of July was named for Julius Caesar, who was the great-uncle of Augustus.

13. Before the Senate named him Augustus, he was called Octavian.

14. While Augustus was emperor, Roman architecture and literature reached new heights.

15. Augustus' reign was the period that came to be called the Augustan Age, and his influence continued for nearly two hundred years.

Adjective Clauses

4h. An *adjective clause* is a subordinate clause that modifies a noun or pronoun.

> **EXAMPLES** The plant **that is hanging by the window** needs more water. [The adjective clause *that is hanging by the window* modifies the noun *plant*.]
>
> The team leader will be Carmen, **whose math skills are excellent**. [The adjective clause *whose math skills are excellent* modifies the noun *Carmen*.]

EXERCISE A Underline the adjective clause in each of the following sentences.

Example 1. Algebra I, which is my favorite class, starts right after lunch.

1. A parable is a short story that teaches a lesson.

2. Patrick, who was born in Ireland, is spending the summer with his cousins.

3. Julia very gently cleaned the clock that had been made by her great-grandfather.

4. The secondhand shop where Teresa bought her guitar has many good values.

5. Are the fish that you catch in this lake safe to eat?

6. The squirrel, which had scared off all the birds, ate the food in the bird feeder.

7. The person whose number is called should join us on the stage.

8. Toshi, whom I had not yet called, had already heard about the study session.

9. Buildings that have stood for centuries can provide valuable knowledge.

10. Jared was showing everyone the photo in which Sean and Lori were making funny faces.

EXERCISE B Write adjective clauses to complete the following sentences.

Example 1. The football game, *which we won by three points* , was very exciting.

11. This type of rock, _____, is very

rare in this part of the country.

12. Evan was busy working on his research paper, _____

_____.

13. The tree _____ needs trimming.

14. Mr. Turner is the sort of person _____

_____.

15. The test, _____, was easier than

Michele expected it to be.

Language and Sentence Skills Practice

Adverb Clauses

| **4i.** | An *adverb clause* is a subordinate clause that modifies a verb, an adjective, or an adverb. |

> **EXAMPLES** **After I cleaned my room,** I went to the pool with friends. [The adverb clause *After I cleaned my room* modifies the verb *went*.]
>
> I never go swimming **unless I have a buddy with me.** [The adverb clause *unless I have a buddy with me* modifies the verb *go*.]

EXERCISE A Underline the adverb clause in each of the following sentences.

Example 1. <u>As soon as I get home,</u> I change into more comfortable clothes.

1. As the rain stopped, a beautiful rainbow could be seen in the distance.

2. Will you lend me that book when you have finished it?

3. If you enjoy sports, you should come to my martial arts class.

4. Because the lead actor was ill, the understudy played the role.

5. The candidate shook hands until her fingers were numb.

6. Who is taking care of your cat while you're out of town?

7. Always proofread your work before you turn it in.

8. The dog looks silly when it chases its tail.

9. Whenever I get a lot of exercise, I sleep well at night.

10. Emily can run one hundred meters faster than her brother can.

EXERCISE B Write five sentences using the following word groups as adverb clauses.

Example 1. when it's raining _____ *When it's raining, we wait inside for the bus.* _____

11. because the class was taking a test _____

_____

12. until all the leaves have fallen _____

_____

13. when the geese fly south _____

_____

14. if Marshall will type the final draft _____

_____

15. as soon as the airplane lands _____

_____

Adjective and Adverb Clauses A

4h.	An *adjective clause* is a subordinate clause that modifies a noun or pronoun.
4i.	An *adverb clause* is a subordinate clause that modifies a verb, an adjective, or an adverb.

> **ADJECTIVE CLAUSE**   The game, **which went into overtime,** lasted three hours.
>
> **ADVERB CLAUSE**   Please mow the lawn **before you leave.**

EXERCISE   For the following sentences, identify each underlined clause by writing above it *ADJ* for *adjective clause* or *ADV* for *adverb clause*.

Example 1. We will begin rehearsals as soon as you have learned your part. [ADV]

1. Claudia took almost two hundred pictures while she was on vacation.

2. The book that Jeff just finished reading is being made into a movie.

3. The person whom you need to see is not available right now.

4. As long as the team keeps winning, the coach will be in a good mood.

5. I'll meet you at the tennis courts after I finish fixing my bike.

6. Everyone watched in silence as the moon passed in front of the sun.

7. You can't earn extra credit until you've completed your regular assignments.

8. The movie, which was about twenty minutes too long, could have been more exciting.

9. Road crews are making repairs on Willow Street, where Jeremy lives.

10. If that tree does not recover soon, it will have to be cut down.

11. According to some people, when the sky is red in the evening, the weather will be nice the next day.

12. Sometimes, gum is easier to remove from clothing if the gum is hardened first with ice.

13. Racquetball is a fast, exciting game that can be played by two, three, or four people.

14. Because earthworms break down decaying matter and loosen soil, they can help plants grow.

15. Sherlock Holmes, who is probably the best-known fictional detective in the world, solved cases by observing the clues carefully.

16. Since we moved into this neighborhood, the power has gone out three times.

17. Sometimes, Daniel finishes his test faster than he should.

18. The fans were cheering as though they had just won the national championship.

19. With a cool, silent determination that seemed to be instinctive, the kitten stalked and pounced on the ball of yarn.

20. As the sun set, a feeling of peace came over the campers.

Language and Sentence Skills Practice

GRAMMAR

Adjective and Adverb Clauses B

4h. An *adjective clause* is a subordinate clause that modifies a noun or pronoun.

4i. An *adverb clause* is a subordinate clause that modifies a verb, an adjective, or an adverb.

ADJECTIVE CLAUSE The man **who bought lunch for us** is my uncle.
ADVERB CLAUSE Look on this shelf **before you call the library.**

EXERCISE A For each of the following sentences, underline each adjective clause and adverb clause and label it *ADJ* for *adjective clause* or *ADV* for *adverb clause.*

Example 1. The battle of the Alamo was important to the people fighting for Texas indepen-
                        ADV
               dence, <u>even though they lost.</u>

1. The Alamo was originally a Roman Catholic mission that was called San Antonio de Valero.

2. When Texas declared itself independent from Mexico, General Santa Anna brought in the

Mexican Army.

3. A small group, which included such famous men as James Bowie and Davy Crockett, defend-

ed the city of San Antonio.

4. Lieutenant Colonel William Barret Travis and his men retreated to the Alamo, which is in the

center of San Antonio.

5. One hundred eighty-nine men held off the Mexican Army for thirteen days before General

Santa Anna's army stormed the mission and killed all the men there.

EXERCISE B Write an appropriate adjective clause or adverb clause to complete each of the following
sentences as indicated in parentheses.

Example 1. _When it started to rain_____, everyone at the picnic ran to the shelter.
                        (adverb clause)

6. The principal, _____, introduced herself at the assembly.
(adjective clause)

7. _____, they all enjoyed a good laugh. *(adverb clause)*

8. The Washingtons spent a lot of time cleaning their house _____.
(adverb clause)

9. Katrina just bought the new album by her favorite singer, _____.
(adjective clause)

10. _____, the puppy curled up in its box for a nap. *(adverb clause)*

Simple and Compound Sentences

4j. A *simple sentence* has one independent clause and no subordinate clauses.

A simple sentence may have a compound subject or a compound verb or both.

                      S   V

EXAMPLES   **Jamyce has** no brothers or sisters.

               S   S   V

           The **tacos** and **burritos are** ready. [compound subject]

           S   V   V

           Damon auditioned for the play and **got** the lead role. [compound verb]

4k. A *compound sentence* consists of two or more independent clauses, usually joined by a comma and a connecting word.

      EXAMPLE   I like hot-and-sour soup, **but** won-ton soup is my favorite.

EXERCISE A Decide whether each of the following sentences is simple or compound. On the line provided, write *S* for *simple* or *C* for *compound.*

Example _____S_____ **1.** Japan took control of the Marshall Islands during World War I.

_____ **1.** The Marshall Islands consist of thirty-four small islands in the Pacific Ocean.

_____ **2.** The area is called Micronesia, and the people are known as Micronesians.

_____ **3.** Farming is vital to the economy, but many islanders work at a military base.

_____ **4.** The Republic of the Marshall Islands and the United States signed an agreement.

_____ **5.** The agreement allows for self-government, but the United States provides for defense.

EXERCISE B Combine each pair of simple sentences to create one compound sentence. Write your new sentence on the lines provided.

Example 1. I will draw the map. Ed will color it. *I will draw the map, and Ed will color it.*

6. Keeshawn worked on the puzzle for hours. He did not finish it. _____

_____

7. My brother practices the drums every day. He is improving. _____

_____

8. Frozen orange juice is good. I prefer fresh-squeezed. _____

_____

9. Please proofread your essay. Then, turn it in. _____

_____

10. Nari held the kitten. Kevin checked its paws for thorns. _____

_____

GRAMMAR

Compound and Complex Sentences

4k.   A *compound sentence* consists of two or more independent clauses, usually joined by a comma and a connecting word.

SENTENCE	Daryl was reading the paper, and Jolene was writing a letter.
INDEPENDENT CLAUSE	Daryl was reading the paper
INDEPENDENT CLAUSE	Jolene was writing a letter

4l.   A *complex sentence* contains one independent clause and at least one subordinate clause.

SENTENCE	Yori raised his arms as he crossed the finish line.
INDEPENDENT CLAUSE	Yori raised his arms
SUBORDINATE CLAUSE	as he crossed the finish line

EXERCISE   On the line provided, identify each of the following sentences as *compound* or *complex*.

Example   *compound*   **1.** The sun twinkled on the new-fallen snow, and a light breeze was blowing.

_____ **1.** A megawatt is a unit of power that is equal to one million watts.

_____ **2.** Edgar Allan Poe's poem "The Raven" was scary, but his story "The Pit and the Pendulum" was downright terrifying.

_____ **3.** I think this singer, whose newest album is my favorite, deserves a Grammy Award.

_____ **4.** Now that I can use e-mail, I write to my cousins much more often.

_____ **5.** The sun was setting, so we had to end the game with a tie score.

_____ **6.** Whenever the tide goes out, an island reappears in the canal.

_____ **7.** Tommy plays bass, Karen plays drums, and Chris plays the keyboard in our new band.

_____ **8.** The main ship stayed in orbit around the distant planet, but the probe plunged toward the surface.

_____ **9.** Books on every conceivable subject surrounded and towered over Mario; he couldn't have been happier.

_____ **10.** We can't use that photograph because Maria blinked while it was taken.

Complex and Compound-Complex Sentences

4l. A *complex sentence* contains one independent clause and at least one subordinate clause.

COMPLEX SENTENCE	Before I left for school, I re-read the letter that Grandpa had sent me.

4m. A sentence with two or more independent clauses and at least one subordinate clause is a *compound-complex sentence*.

COMPOUND-COMPLEX SENTENCE	Hopes soared when Erica stepped to the plate, and the crowd cheered.
INDEPENDENT CLAUSE	Hopes soared
INDEPENDENT CLAUSE	the crowd cheered
SUBORDINATE CLAUSE	when Erica stepped to the plate

EXERCISE   Underline the independent clauses in the following sentences once and underline the subordinate clauses twice. Then, identify the sentence by writing *CX* for *complex sentence* or *CD-CX* for *compound-complex sentence* at the end of the sentence.

Example   1. Although he is often thought of as one of England's worst kings, King John signed one of the most important documents in the history of democracy. *CX*

1. Richard the Lion-Hearted and John, who were both sons of Henry II, lived interesting lives.

2. Richard was king for ten years, but he spent only about six months of his reign in England because he was fighting in the Crusades and with France.

3. While Richard was out of the country, John tried to take power.

4. The legendary Robin Hood was supposedly one of the men who fought to keep the crown from John.

5. After Richard died in 1199, John became king.

6. King John argued both with his barons, who thought he was too dictatorial, and with church leaders, and in 1209, Pope Innocent III excommunicated him.

7. After John made concessions to the church, he won back the support of the pope.

8. The barons still decided to rebel, after John could not regain lost territory.

9. If he wanted to remain king, John would have to give his barons certain rights and limit his own power, so he signed the Magna Carta in June 1215.

10. Eventually, the Magna Carta served as a model for countries that wanted to protect individual rights.

Identifying Kinds of Sentences

A *simple sentence* has one independent clause and no subordinate clauses.

EXAMPLE   The fans waited outside for a glimpse of the singer.

A *compound sentence* has two or more independent clauses.

EXAMPLE   The fans waited outside, and they got a glimpse of the singer.

A *complex sentence* has one independent clause and at least one subordinate clause.

EXAMPLE   The fans waited outside because they wanted a glimpse of the singer.

A *compound-complex sentence* has two or more independent clauses and at least one subordinate clause.

EXAMPLE   The concert was over, but the fans waited outside because they wanted a glimpse of the singer.

EXERCISE   Underline each of the independent clauses in the following sentences once, and underline each of the subordinate clauses twice. Then, on the line provided, identify the sentence as *S* for *simple sentence, CD* for *compound sentence, CX* for *complex sentence,* or *CD-CX* for *compound-complex* sentence.

Example _CD-CX_ **1.** Just before the bell rings, Mr. Feldman assigns our homework, and we gather up our books.

_____ **1.** Lightning flashed, and thunder rumbled.

_____ **2.** After dinner, we played a game in the living room.

_____ **3.** The varsity team will play as soon as the junior varsity is finished.

_____ **4.** The noise from the ducks in the pond was soothing.

_____ **5.** Thirty laps is the most that I have ever swum.

_____ **6.** When Stephanie calls, tell her that I'll meet her in front of the movie theater.

_____ **7.** My sister was going to take me to dinner, but her car wouldn't start.

_____ **8.** Is that a new jacket, or did you borrow it from Chris?

_____ **9.** The movie that I want to see was at the video store, but I won't have time to watch it this weekend.

_____ **10.** Did the package that you were expecting arrive yesterday?

for **CHAPTER 4: THE PHRASE AND THE CLAUSE** pages 74–103

Review A: **Phrases and Clauses**

EXERCISE A In the following sentences, underline each prepositional phrase and draw an arrow to the word or words it modifies.

Example 1. At age ten, Cesar Chavez traveled with migrant farmers.

1. As a child, Cesar Chavez lived near Yuma, Arizona.

2. He lived with his parents, brothers, and sisters.

3. In 1937, Cesar Chavez's family did not have enough money for the taxes on their farm.

4. Those in this small Mexican American community were worried and frightened.

5. In California there was work for farmworkers if they could go from one farm to another.

6. That was the time when Cesar Chavez first lived among the migrant workers.

7. Chavez became a spokesperson for poor farmworkers.

8. In 1962, he established the National Farm Workers Association.

9. He organized several boycotts of grapes and lettuce.

10. Throughout his life, Chavez focused on nonviolent action.

EXERCISE B For each of the following sentences, identify the underlined clause by writing above it *IND* for *independent clause* or *SUB* for *subordinate clause*.

                              SUB

Example 1. As the team ran onto the court, the band played the school fight song.

11. When you pack the dishes, be sure to use enough padding.

12. Some whales can hold their breath for up to two hours, but they still must come to the surface to breathe.

13. The ball went through the hoop just as the buzzer sounded.

14. The book that April was waiting for is available now.

15. *Mark Twain*, which was a riverboat term meaning "two fathoms" (twelve feet), was the pen name of Samuel Clemens.

16. If those plants aren't covered tonight, the frost may kill them.

17. A bird picked the crocodile's teeth clean while the crocodile sat patiently with its mouth open.

18. All of the receivers were covered, so the quarterback had to run with the ball.

19. Because a storm was predicted, the fair was postponed.

20. The play, which the students had rehearsed for six weeks, was a huge success.

Review B: Phrases and Clauses

EXERCISE A Underline the prepositional phrase in each of the following sentences. On the line provided, identify the phrase by writing *ADJ* for *adjective phrase* or *ADV* for *adverb phrase*.

Example _ADV_ **1.** Our town gets its drinking water <u>from a nearby river</u>.

_____ **1.** A professor from the university will be the next guest speaker.

_____ **2.** Just take a little off the top.

_____ **3.** A cat was napping on the car's hood.

_____ **4.** Where did Jared find the information about political cartoonists?

_____ **5.** Turn left at the next stop sign.

_____ **6.** Nick heard and then saw three helicopters fly over his house.

_____ **7.** The first of the band's five albums is Stacy's favorite.

_____ **8.** Who is the new president of the student council?

_____ **9.** One in five students will retake the test.

_____ **10.** After the party we all cleaned the house.

EXERCISE B Underline the subordinate clause in each of the following sentences. On the line provided, identify the clause by writing *ADJ* for *adjective clause* or *ADV* for *adverb clause*.

Example _ADV_ **1.** <u>Even though the rain had stopped</u>, the field was too muddy for the game to

be played.

_____**11.** The movie theater that is being built on this site should open in the fall.

_____**12.** If Mother calls, please give her this message.

_____**13.** Did you scream when the monster was finally shown?

_____**14.** Algebra, which was already Cesar's favorite class, was getting even more interesting.

_____**15.** Jerri set the ball to Teresa, who slammed it down for a point.

_____**16.** This car is hard to start if the temperature is below freezing.

_____**17.** The robin that nests in our backyard just laid its eggs.

_____**18.** Wherever Maria goes, her new kitten wants to follow.

_____**19.** Mr. Contreras has worked for the same company since the day that he graduated from

college.

_____**20.** Jeremy, whose reading of Lincoln's "Gettysburg Address" amazed us all, will represent

the school at the state competition.

Review C: **Sentences**

EXERCISE A On the line provided, identify each of the following sentences as *S* for *simple* or *CD* for *compound*.

Example __*S*__ **1.** The children broke the piñata and lunged for the toys.

_____ **1.** My arm is better, but it is still quite stiff.

_____ **2.** Katya and her mother washed the windows and dusted the furniture.

_____ **3.** In the future I will be more cautious on the soccer field.

_____ **4.** The movie was starting, so we found our seats quickly.

_____ **5.** Lori cleaned out the garage, and Stu rearranged the sports equipment.

EXERCISE B Combine each of the following word groups into the type of sentence indicated in parentheses. You may need to add words. Be sure to use correct capitalization and punctuation.

Example 1. the class was divided into groups / the groups were to make posters / the posters

would illustrate life in the 1800s   (complex sentence)

The class was divided into groups that were to make posters illustrating life in the 1800s.

6. Franklin was assigned to a group / Mario was assigned to the same group / Vince was

assigned to the same group   (simple sentence) _____

_____

7. Franklin spent summers on a farm / Mario agreed to study nineteenth-century farm life /

Vince agreed to study nineteenth-century farm life   (compound sentence) _____

_____

8. Mario looked in the history section / Vince looked in the history section / Franklin checked

the reference books   (complex sentence) _____

_____

9. we found many descriptions / we found many drawings / we could not find many

photographs   (complex sentence) _____

_____

10. Franklin collected the pictures / Mario pasted them in place / Vince wrote the captions

(compound-complex sentence) _____

_____

for **CHAPTER 4: THE PHRASE AND THE CLAUSE** `pages 74–103`

Literary Model: Description

> Miyax pushed back the hood of her sealskin parka and looked at the Arctic sun. It was a yellow disc in a lime-green sky, the colors of six o'clock in the evening and the time when the wolves awoke. Quietly she put down her cooking pot and crept to the top of a dome-shaped frost heave, one of the many earth buckles that rise and fall in the crackling cold of the Arctic winter. Lying on her stomach, she looked across a vast lawn of grass and moss and focused her attention on the wolves she had come upon two sleeps ago.
>
> —from *Julie of the Wolves* by Jean Craighead George

EXERCISE A List ten of the prepositional phrases in the above excerpt from *Julie of the Wolves*.

1. _____   6. _____

2. _____   7. _____

3. _____   8. _____

4. _____   9. _____

5. _____   10. _____

EXERCISE B Underline the prepositional phrases in the paragraph; then, read the passage aloud, leaving out all the prepositional phrases. How is the paragraph different when you leave out the prepositional phrases? Is it as easy to picture the scene? Explain your answer.

_____

_____

_____

_____

_____

_____

_____

_____

_____

_____

Literary Model (continued)

EXERCISE C Write the opening paragraph of a story about a young boy or girl having an adventure. Use prepositional phrases to add details that help your reader see the place and character you are describing.

_____

_____

_____

_____

_____

_____

_____

_____

_____

_____

_____

_____

EXERCISE D Read your paragraph aloud. Does it contain enough details for your reader to be able to see the scene as you do? Are the details interesting? Revise your paragraph, using additional prepositional phrases to provide details or replacing prepositional phrases with ones that are more vivid and precise. When you are finished, answer the following questions:

1. What kind of information did you include in your prepositional phrases?

_____

_____

2. Would it be hard to write an interesting opening paragraph if you could not use any preposi-tional phrases? Why or why not?

_____

_____

_____

Writing Application: Personal Narrative

Writers rely on adverb phrases and clauses to add details about *how, when, where, why, how often,* and *how long.*

CLAUSE	**As soon as it began to snow,** children rushed from every house to dance among the drifting flakes.
	Because they had not seen snow for months, the children could hardly wait to make a snowman.
PHRASE	**For the next three nights,** a deep blanket of white hushed every street.
	The icicle fell off the roof and landed on the ground **with a loud crash.**

WRITING ACTIVITY

For your English class, students are writing personal narratives about a time when they were able to help a friend or family member. You will write two paragraphs. In the first, recall when and why you had the chance to help. In the second, write about how helping someone else affected you and what you learned from the occasion. In both paragraphs, use adverb phrases and clauses to tell *how, when, where, why, how often,* and *how long.*

PREWRITING The first step in this exercise, of course, is to decide what to write about. You may recall right away a time when you helped someone else; otherwise, you will need to spend some quiet time thinking about a time when you helped. Once you have the occasion in mind, brainstorm to recall all the details that you can: Who was involved? What was the problem? How did you help out?

WRITING Because this personal narrative recalls an event, you can easily organize the paragraphs chronologically, telling the first action first and moving through time till you reach the last action. After you write your first draft, check it to be sure that you have not left out any important actions. Have you used adverb phrases and clauses to explain the *how, when, where, why, how often,* and *how long* of this event?

REVISING In a personal narrative, you can use first-person pronouns: *I, me, my, mine,* and *myself.* Although you should write complete sentences, you need not use very formal language. Think of this exercise as a chance to tell a story about yourself—on paper. Readers would like to hear your voice speaking in the words you write. Read your narrative to a friend and ask whether it sounds like you.

PUBLISHING Check your paragraphs for mistakes in spelling and punctuation. Then, follow your teacher's requirements for getting the narrative ready to turn in.

EXTENDING YOUR WRITING

This exercise could lead to a more extended writing project. Taking the two paragraphs you have written as an introduction, you could write a longer essay in which you think deeply about why helping others, not only ourselves, is good for us. What do we gain when we help others? What kind of society would we live in if we never helped others? For a speech class, you could prepare an inspiring speech on helping others.

Choices: Fishing for Complements

Here's your chance to step out of the grammar book and into the real world. You may not notice complements, but you and the people around you use them every day. The following activities challenge you to find a connection between complements and the world around you. Do the activity below that suits your personality best, and then share your discoveries with your class. Have fun!

WRITING

Happiness Is . . .

What person, place, situation, event, or object makes you happy? Whoever or whatever it is, that's what happiness is to you. Identify the people or things you associate with happiness. Write sentences in which each functions as a predicate nominative.

GAME

Think Fast!

Got a beanbag? If your answer is yes, you could be in charge of this project. Make a list of twenty or more verbs that take direct objects. Be sure to include several verbs that can function as either action verbs or linking verbs, such as *sound*; these special verbs will cost your classmates points! Then, get your beanbag and arrange your classmates in a circle. Call out a verb, and throw the beanbag to the person of your choice. This person must complete your verb with a direct object. Then, he or she throws the beanbag to the next person. If somebody gives a predicate nominative or a predicate adjective, he or she is eliminated from the game. Have a prize (how about a beanbag?) for the winner!

TECHNOLOGY

Put Your Right Foot In

Do you remember the song called "The Hokey Pokey"? The lyrics of the song are full of direct objects. This song would be just the thing to help younger students understand direct objects. Create a slide show or animation (complete with soundtrack, of course) of this song and its lyrics. Your purpose is to teach direct objects, so be sure to identify them in some way. When you're done, show your creation to the class. Then, pass your work along to an elementary teacher.

DISCUSSION

I'd Like to Give the World . . . ?

Would you like to give the world a song? Perhaps you have something else in mind. What is it? Lead a discussion of what you and your classmates would like to contribute to the world. On the chalkboard, write the sentence, "I'd like to give the world. . . ." Then, add each gift to complete the sentence. When you're done, you'll have one long sentence with one indirect object and a giant, compound direct object.

WRITING

I Am the Wind

You are a lot more than meets the eye. What places, things, ideas, or animals do you identify with? Write an "I Am" poem in which you use predicate nominatives to name these things.

DRAMA

One of Each

Write a dialogue for four people in which each character uses only one type of complement. For instance, every sentence that one character speaks will include a predicate adjective, another character will include a direct object in each of his or her sentences, and so on. Perform your dialogue for the class.

LINGUISTICS

The Object of the Game

Wait until you see the number of meanings for *object* in the dictionary! Check them out for yourself. Then, make a chart of the meanings. Include a sentence for each meaning. Your chart could be simply geometrical, or your chart could be more pictorial, such as a tree or an octopus, with each branch or arm representing a meaning. Pass out copies of your chart or make a poster so that everyone can get a good look at it.

Language and Sentence Skills Practice

GRAMMAR

for CHAPTER 5: COMPLEMENTS   *pages 105–106*

Complements

5a.   A *complement* is a word or word group that completes the meaning of a verb.

> **EXAMPLES**   Mr. Fernandez planted **tulips**. [*Tulips* completes the meaning of the verb *planted*.]
>
> Uncle Terrell brought **us** some fresh **fruit**. [*Us* and *fruit* complete the meaning of the verb *brought*.]
>
> Shanda will be the **captain**. [*Captain* completes the meaning of the verb *will be*.]
>
> The night air felt **cold** to Gerald. [*Cold* completes the meaning of the verb *felt*.]
>
> An adverb cannot be a complement. A complement is also not part of a prepositional phrase.
>
> **EXAMPLES**   Bobby Jo plays **well**. [adverb]
>
> She is employed by the **hospital**. [object of a preposition]

EXERCISE   For each sentence in the following paragraph, underline the complement or complements of the verbs.

Example   **[1]** Tien's family gave <u>him</u> a big <u>party</u> for his twelfth birthday.

[1] Many of Tien's friends brought him birthday presents.   **[2]** Tien's favorite present was a surprise from his father.   **[3]** Tien's father gave him a new violin.   **[4]** Tien's sister was already a talented violinist.   **[5]** She could offer lessons.   **[6]** She bought Tien a shoulder rest.   **[7]** A shoulder rest supports the violin.   **[8]** Tien's sister showed him the correct posture.   **[9]** Tien held the bow correctly.   **[10]** Tien's best friend brought him some rosin for the bowstrings.   **[11]** Tien's sister was patient with him.   **[12]** Tien learned the name of each string.   **[13]** Tien practiced every morning and grew confident.   **[14]** Scales were not difficult for him.   **[15]** Soon he could play a simple melody.

[16] Classical music sounded beautiful to Tien.   **[17]** A neighbor became Tien's violin teacher.

[18] The teacher and Tien played duets.   **[19]** The teacher taught Tien his part in each duet.

[20] One day Tien will become an accomplished violinist.

Direct Objects

5b. A **direct object** is a noun, pronoun, or word group that tells who or what receives the action of the verb.

A direct object answers the question *Whom?* or *What?* after a transitive verb.

> **EXAMPLES**   I like little **kittens.** [I like *what*? *kittens*]
>
> He helped **me** with the drawing. [He helped *whom*? *me*]

A direct object may be a compound of two or more objects.

> **EXAMPLE**   They made **soup** and **sandwiches.**

A direct object cannot follow a linking verb because a linking verb does not express action.

> **EXAMPLE**   She is a great doctor. [The linking verb *is* does not express action. Therefore, *doctor* is not a direct object.]

EXERCISE A   Underline the direct objects in the following sentences. Remember that a direct object may be compound. If a sentence does not contain a direct object, write *none* above the sentence.

Example   1. Have you ever used oils or pastels in art class?

1. In her free time Rosalinda studies art.

2. Many artists prefer certain colors.

3. They repeat them in their paintings.

4. Van Gogh often used yellows in his paintings.

5. He painted many portraits and landscapes.

6. Van Gogh's collection of Japanese prints influenced his work.

7. Many people admire Thomas Gainsborough's paintings.

8. Blue was one of his favorite colors.

9. He used the word in the title of one of his paintings.

10. The title is *The Blue Boy.*

EXERCISE B   Underline each direct object in the following paragraph. Remember that a direct object may be compound. Not every sentence contains a direct object.

Example   [1] Roberto read a book about Piet Mondrian.

[11] Piet Mondrian was a famous Dutch artist. [12] Throughout his career Mondrian refined his geometric style. [13] He used black lines and white backgrounds in many of his paintings. [14] The lines formed rectangles or grids of various sizes. [15] Mondrian's work influenced modern architecture and graphic design.

Indirect Objects

| **5c.** | An *indirect object* is a noun, pronoun, or word group that usually comes between the verb and the direct object. An indirect object tells *to whom* or *to what* or *for whom* or *for what* the action of the verb is done. |

> **EXAMPLES** I sent **Carmen** a letter. [*To whom* did I send a letter? *Carmen*]
> Luis bought **Ted** a birthday gift. [*For whom* did Luis buy a gift? *Ted*]
>
> An indirect object may be compound.
> **EXAMPLE** Mom gave **Kim** and **me** a ride to school.

EXERCISE A Each of the following sentences contains both a direct object and an indirect object. Underline each direct object once and each indirect object twice. Remember that direct objects and indirect objects can be compound.

Example 1. Aunt Rosa made me some delicious tamales.

1. Mr. Franklin will give Carmelita his old baseball glove.

2. Tomás showed his aunts and uncles his pictures.

3. The manager gave his employees an extra day of vacation.

4. Mrs. Williams left the waiter a tip.

5. Amherst College sent my brother an application form.

6. Did Tamisha offer you some rice?

7. The director handed them their scripts for the play.

8. For Mother's Day I bought Mom a pair of earrings.

9. Coach Brooks has taught us the drill.

10. Mr. Liu sent Daryl and Mishi a CD of jazz music.

EXERCISE B For each of the following sentences, write *DO* above the underlined word if the word is a direct object or *IO* if it is an indirect object. If the word is neither a direct object nor an indirect object, write *N*.

Example 1. The museum guide showed our group some Indian pottery.

11. The principal introduced our guest at the assembly.

12. I quickly handed the tray to Alicia.

13. The worker fed the penguins some fish.

14. Did Rita lend Jonah a pencil?

15. The kindergarten teacher assigned each child a partner.

for **CHAPTER 5: COMPLEMENTS**   pages 107–10

Direct Objects and Indirect Objects A

5b. A **direct object** is a noun, pronoun, or word group that tells *who* or *what* receives the action of the verb.

5c. An **indirect object** is a noun, pronoun, or word group that usually comes between the verb and the direct object. An indirect object tells *to whom* or *to what* or *for whom* or *for what* the action of the verb is done.

If a sentence has an indirect object, it must also have a direct object.

EXAMPLE   Shelter workers bought the **animals** more **food.** [The direct object is *food*. The indirect object is *animals*.]

EXERCISE   In the following sentences, underline each direct object once and each indirect object twice. Remember that both direct and indirect objects may be compound.

Example 1. The worker brought the giraffes and elephants some food.

1. Please don't feed the birds popcorn.

2. We gave the visitors a map of the wildlife park.

3. The park workers sent us information about the animals.

4. The director mailed my family a membership packet.

5. We sent her our application.

6. They offered free train rides for children.

7. A store clerk gave my sister and me some postcards.

8. My sister mailed a postcard to our grandmother.

9. I made my aunts and uncles gifts.

10. The dolphin trainer showed us some training methods.

11. My mother lent me her camera.

12. The clerk sold my mother some film.

13. Will you hand me the camera, please?

14. Please teach my brother and me the proper feeding techniques.

15. May I give the geese and swans food pellets?

16. The jaguar showed us its teeth.

17. The park worker offered the monkeys fruits and vegetables.

18. Will the toucan build her young a nest?

19. Our trip to the wildlife park gave me an idea for a school project.

20. My report will give the class information about endangered species.

Direct Objects and Indirect Objects B

5b. | A *direct object* is a noun, pronoun, or word group that tells *who* or *what* receives the action of the verb.

5c. | An *indirect object* is a noun, pronoun, or word group that usually comes between the verb and the direct object. An indirect object tells *to whom* or *to what* or *for whom* or *for what* the action of the verb is done.

If a sentence has an indirect object, it must also have a direct object.

EXAMPLE   Please send the **newspaper** several **copies** of our flier. [The direct object is *copies*. The indirect object is *newspaper*.]

EXERCISE   In each of the following sentences, identify the underlined word by writing above it *DO* for *direct object* or *IO* for *indirect object*.

Example 1. The composer wrote her <u>daughter</u> a new song.   *IO*

1. The pianist practices the commonly used <u>scales</u> daily.

2. She can play numerous <u>songs</u> from memory.

3. A professional tunes her <u>piano</u> every month.

4. The piano tuner shows the <u>pianist</u> the hammers and strings inside the piano.

5. The pianist cleans the <u>keys</u> with a soft cloth.

6. She takes <u>lessons</u> once a week.

7. Her teacher gives <u>her</u> advice.

8. He also shows her proper <u>technique</u>.

9. The pianist writes down <u>ideas</u> for new songs.

10. She sends her <u>teacher</u> the new compositions.

11. Her teacher studies the <u>music</u> closely.

12. Sometimes he offers <u>her</u> suggestions for improvement.

13. The pianist might make some <u>changes</u> to the music.

14. She makes each <u>decision</u> thoughtfully.

15. Some of her compositions express <u>sadness</u>, but others are joyful.

16. She gives each <u>piece</u> her full attention.

17. The pianist records each new <u>composition</u> on tape.

18. In addition, she writes every <u>note</u> on special paper.

19. She offers other <u>pianists</u> copies of the music.

20. Her hard work brings <u>her</u> great satisfaction.

Subject Complements

5d. A *subject complement* is a word or word group that is in the predicate and that identifies or describes the subject.

A linking verb connects a subject complement to the subject.

EXAMPLES Ms. Echohawk is a dedicated **teacher.** [The subject complement *teacher* identifies the subject *Ms. Echohawk.* The linking verb *is* connects *Ms. Echohawk* and *teacher.*]

The neighborhood seems **peaceful** late at night. [The subject complement *peaceful* describes the subject *neighborhood.* The linking verb *seems* connects *neighborhood* and *peaceful.*]

EXERCISE A Underline the subject complement in each of the following sentences.

Example 1. Running long distances at a fast pace seems <u>difficult</u>.

1. Many types of athletes must become fast runners.

2. Interval training is a method of improving a runner's speed.

3. Intervals are short distances.

4. The athletes grow weary, but they must run the intervals as fast as possible.

5. A track is a good place to practice intervals.

6. Distance markers are usually visible on the track.

7. Although fairly short, the distance can seem quite lengthy to a beginner.

8. To new runners, interval training looks difficult.

9. The training sessions are intense.

10. However, most runners who use this method become faster.

EXERCISE B In each of the following sentences, underline the linking verb once. Then, underline the subject complement twice.

Example 1. The view from that tower <u>will be</u> <u><u>beautiful</u></u>.

11. Your younger sister looks sleepy today.

12. She is the captain of her soccer team.

13. Was she very busy this weekend?

14. Her team seemed invincible on the field.

15. They became the champions of the league.

for **CHAPTER 5: COMPLEMENTS** | *pages 112–13*

Predicate Nominatives

5e. A *predicate nominative* is a word or word group that is in the predicate and that identifies the subject or refers to it.

A predicate nominative may be a noun, a pronoun, or a word group that functions as a noun. A predicate nominative is connected to the subject by a linking verb.

EXAMPLES Yesterday was the first **day** of spring. [The noun *day* is a predicate nominative following the linking verb *was*. *Day* identifies the subject *Yesterday*.]

Will the winner be **she**? [The pronoun *she* is a predicate nominative completing the meaning of the linking verb *Will be*. *She* identifies the subject *winner*.]

EXERCISE A Underline the linking verb in each of the following sentences. Then, underline the predicate nominative twice. Remember that a predicate nominative may be compound.

Example 1. Was the speaker Toni Morrison or Amy Tan?

1. The elm is a large tree.

2. Alaska became a state in 1959.

3. Stamp collecting was my grandmother's hobby.

4. The highest scorers in the game were Lucy and she.

5. *The Incredible Journey* is my favorite book.

6. Latoya became a skilled gardener in no time.

7. Is your cousin a mechanic?

8. The two goalies this season are Juwan and he.

9. My hamster is the one in the exercise wheel.

10. Is he your friend?

EXERCISE B For each of the following sentences, identify the underlined word by writing above it *PN* if the word is a predicate nominative or *DO* if the word is a direct object. If the word is neither a direct object nor a predicate nominative, write *N.*

Example 1. The best sprinters are Yoko and she. *(PN)*

11. Today we watched a movie in school.

12. Your wet clothes are in the dryer.

13. Pablo Picasso became a great artist.

14. Long-distance running requires much training.

15. Ms. Johnson remains our choice for mayor.

Predicate Adjectives

5f. A *predicate adjective* is an adjective that is in the predicate and that describes the subject.

> **EXAMPLES** The rabbit's fur feels **soft.** [The adjective *soft* describes the subject *fur.*]
>
> The river was **wide** and **deep** there. [The adjectives *wide* and *deep* describe the subject *river.*]

EXERCISE A Underline the linking verb in each of the following sentences. Then, underline the predicate adjective twice. Remember that a predicate adjective may be compound.

Example 1. The baby seems sleepy today.

1. Is the music too loud?

2. The director seemed content with our performance.

3. We felt proud and happy after the game.

4. The corn from your garden was delicious.

5. Suddenly the sky became cloudy.

6. That game is too difficult for a young child.

7. Was Vanessa happy with her test scores?

8. At first the puppy seemed healthy and energetic.

9. The seafood gumbo tastes spicy to me.

10. That Navajo blanket is beautiful!

EXERCISE B For each of the following sentences, identify the underlined word by writing above it *PA* if the word is a predicate adjective or *PN* if the word is a predicate nominative.

Example 1. Many of Lane's ancestors were Norwegian.

11. Norway is a country in northern Europe.

12. The country is long and narrow and is shaped almost like a spoon.

13. Northern Norway is quite remote.

14. In the summer, the night sky is sunny.

15. The sun stays bright all night long.

16. Then, in the winter, the daytime skies are dark.

17. Dairy products and fish are the leading products of Norway.

18. Lumber and oil are important, too.

19. Norway's seacoast is very rocky.

20. The water in the Norwegian Sea is cold.

Language and Sentence Skills Practice

Predicate Nominatives and Predicate Adjectives A

Predicate nominatives and predicate adjectives are the two kinds of subject complements. Both are connected to the subject by a linking verb. A *predicate nominative* identifies the subject. A *predicate adjective* describes the subject.

| PREDICATE NOMINATIVE | Richard Wright became a great **writer.** |
| PREDICATE ADJECTIVE | I have grown **tired** of skating. |

EXERCISE For each of the following sentences, identify the underlined word by writing above it *PA* if the word is a predicate adjective or *PN* if the word is a predicate nominative.

Example 1. My new hobby is <u>fun</u> and exciting. *(PA)*

1. In-line skating can be <u>strenuous</u>.

2. For many people, skating seems <u>difficult</u>.

3. Newly purchased skates should be <u>comfortable</u>.

4. In-line skating is a fun <u>exercise</u> for many people.

5. Skate rental fees are not very <u>expensive</u>.

6. A person who practices can become a good <u>skater</u>.

7. Skaters who grow <u>tired</u> might fall more often.

8. Therefore, practice sessions should remain <u>short</u>.

9. Indoor rinks are safe <u>places</u> to practice.

10. Skating on the street can be <u>dangerous</u>.

11. An experienced skater might be a good <u>teacher</u>.

12. Balance is very <u>important</u> in skating.

13. Practicing drills helps skaters feel more <u>confident</u>.

14. Some drills may look almost <u>impossible</u>, especially to beginners.

15. Squatting is one <u>method</u> of braking.

16. Braking quickly is a <u>skill</u> that requires practice.

17. Skaters feel more <u>confident</u> as they gain more control.

18. Some drills help skaters remain <u>balanced</u>.

19. Well-drilled people often become fast <u>skaters</u>.

20. A helmet is essential safety <u>equipment</u>.

Predicate Nominatives and Predicate Adjectives B

Predicate nominatives and predicate adjectives are the two kinds of subject complements. Both are connected to the subject by a linking verb. A *predicate nominative* identifies the subject. A *predicate adjective* describes the subject.

> PREDICATE NOMINATIVE   Garrett is my best **friend.**
> PREDICATE ADJECTIVE   She felt **confident** about the test.

EXERCISE A In each sentence in the following paragraph, underline the subject complement.

Example [1] The children looked nervous this morning.

   [1] Miguel and his sister, Angelina, visited their aunt's farm in a neighborhood that was quite friendly. **[2]** Only the small cottage at the edge of the property was empty. **[3]** The cottage seemed different because no one had lived in it for eight years. **[4]** The neighborhood children were afraid of the cottage. **[5]** Some people said it was spooky. **[6]** Many children had heard noises that sounded eerie. **[7]** One day Miguel and Angelina became curious and decided to investigate the cottage. **[8]** The old door seemed heavy as they slowly opened it. **[9]** The old kitchen smelled musty. **[10]** Suddenly, they heard a clicking noise that sounded odd. **[11]** The children remained still and listened. **[12]** They felt anxious, but they walked toward the noise. **[13]** The rooms were very dark. **[14]** Angelina heard a noise that sounded loud. **[15]** The children walked past the old, damp sofa, which smelled moldy. **[16]** When they saw the source of the noise, they were no longer afraid. **[17]** In the middle of a pile of shells sat a large gray squirrel who appeared quite upset. **[18]** The squirrel was the source of the noise. **[19]** The clicking noise no longer seemed so mysterious. **[20]** The story of the "ghost" squirrel is still funny to them.

EXERCISE B Complete each of the following sentences by writing a predicate adjective or a predicate nominative on the lines provided. Be sure to include any other words that are necessary for your sentence to make sense.

Example 1. My mother is *an architect*_____.

21. Fatima seems especially _____ today.

22. A brisk walk can be _____.

23. We are still _____ even though we argue sometimes.

24. In a short time, the cocoon will become _____.

25. I think the piano sounds _____.

Review A: **Complements**

EXERCISE A   In each of the following sentences, identify the underlined word by writing above it *DO* if the word is a direct object or *IO* if it is an indirect object. If a word is neither a direct object nor an indirect object, write *N*.

Example 1. Did Lien give you that <u>magazine</u>? *[DO]*

1. Eartha brought <u>oranges</u> and water to the soccer game.

2. We bought Dad a book about the <u>Civil War</u>.

3. Has Rachel mailed the <u>invitations</u> to her friends?

4. You owe <u>Ray</u> and me an apology.

5. Mr. Rodriguez taught <u>us</u> some magic tricks.

6. Will the quarterback ever throw Julio the <u>ball</u>?

7. We pulled the little children on the <u>sled</u>.

8. The dentist cleaned my <u>teeth</u>.

9. Joyce showed <u>Tanya</u> and Peg her new dress.

10. Parvis paid the <u>clerk</u> ten dollars.

EXERCISE B   In each of the following sentences, identify the underlined word by writing above it *PN* if the word is a predicate nominative or *PA* if the word is a predicate adjective. If a word is neither a predicate nominative nor a predicate adjective, write *N*.

Example 1. My dog has always remained <u>faithful</u> to me. *[PA]*

11. Captain William Kidd became a <u>pirate</u>.

12. This fresh milk tastes <u>cold</u> and creamy.

13. Will this poodle be a loyal <u>pet</u>?

14. Dad makes delicious blueberry <u>muffins</u>.

15. The small village looked <u>peaceful</u> in the moonlight.

16. That evergreen tree has long, sharp <u>needles</u>.

17. Wasn't Thomas Edison a talented <u>inventor</u>?

18. We were <u>tired</u> and hungry after raking the leaves.

19. Ada May became the president of our <u>club</u>.

20. The two leading agricultural products in our region are <u>corn</u> and wheat.

Review B: **Complements**

EXERCISE A Identify the underlined complement in each sentence by writing above it *DO* for *direct object*, *IO* for *indirect object*, *PN* for *predicate nominative*, or *PA* for *predicate adjective*.

Example 1. Mr. Levine gave <u>Antonio</u> and me a hint. *IO*

1. The kitchen felt <u>warm</u> and cozy.

2. My aunt bought Ricardo and me two <u>tickets</u> to a play.

3. Two popular sports in the United States are football and <u>baseball</u>.

4. Collecting coins has been my <u>hobby</u> for several years.

5. Will you give <u>me</u> a ride to the stadium?

6. The workers have painted the fence and the <u>barn</u>.

7. The first two speakers were Harold and <u>she</u>.

8. Karen has passed the <u>sandwiches</u> to Earl.

9. Grandma has told <u>us</u> many stories about the history of our family.

10. My new sweater has pink and green <u>stripes</u>.

EXERCISE B Underline the complement or complements in each of the following sentences. Then, identify each complement by writing above it *DO* for *direct object*, *IO* for *indirect object*, *PN* for *predicate nominative*, or *PA* for *predicate adjective*.

Example 1. Denzel Washington is the <u>director</u> and <u>star</u> of that film. *PN   PN*

11. The elephant is a very large animal, but the giraffe is the tallest animal of all.

12. Yesterday I gave the dog and her puppy new rubber toys.

13. The pizza has too much sauce and seems too hot to me.

14. Nicolas Cage is a popular actor.

15. Maisie has sent my sister and me many cards and letters.

16. The performer will end the show with a beautiful song.

17. The audience became silent when the conductor raised her arms above her head.

18. The students in my class seemed happy with their test scores.

19. Roberto's pet rabbit is white and brown.

20. I am the captain of the baseball team and the co-captain of the basketball team.

Review C: Complements

EXERCISE A Identify the underlined complement in each sentence by writing above it *DO* for *direct object*, *IO* for *indirect object*, *PN* for *predicate nominative*, or *PA* for *predicate adjective*.

                                                   PA

Example 1. Does the soup taste too <u>salty</u> to you?

1. Two large cities in Pennsylvania are <u>Philadelphia</u> and Pittsburgh.

2. My uncle has taken his <u>car</u> to a garage for repairs.

3. The workers will give the town hall a fresh <u>coat</u> of paint.

4. The family threw my <u>cousin</u> a surprise birthday party.

5. The apple looked <u>ripe</u> and juicy.

6. Doesn't Bernice seem <u>cheerful</u> today?

7. Gina gave the <u>cat</u> a saucer of milk.

8. Please put your dirty <u>clothes</u> in the washing machine.

9. I had a ham <u>sandwich</u> and a glass of milk for lunch.

10. Diego showed Kimberly and <u>me</u> his stamp collection.

EXERCISE B Underline the complement or complements in each of the following sentences. Then, identify each complement by writing above it *DO* for *direct object*, *IO* for *indirect object*, *PN* for *predicate nominative*, or *PA* for *predicate adjective*.

                                          IO   *DO*

Example 1. Has Mr. Hughes assigned the <u>students</u> their <u>parts</u> for the play yet?

11. Danny Glover had the lead role in the movie.

12. Is today really your birthday?

13. Will our class visit the science museum or the natural history museum this year?

14. Michael has brought Tyrone and me our books and homework assignments.

15. Irving Berlin is the composer of many beautiful songs.

16. We should have left our coats and hats in the front hall.

17. Claude McKay was an important poet and novelist.

18. Mr. and Mrs. Sanchez gave each child a book and a bookmark.

19. The soil in the flowerpot seemed very dry.

20. The steamed vegetables look attractive and taste fresh and flavorful today.

for **CHAPTER 5: COMPLEMENTS**   pages 112–15

Literary Model: Biography

Abraham Lincoln wasn't the <u>sort</u> of man who could lose himself in a crowd. After all, he stood six feet four inches tall, and to top it off, he wore a high silk hat.

His height was mostly in his long, bony legs. When he sat in a chair, he seemed no <u>taller</u> than anyone else. It was only when he stood up that he towered above other men.

At first glance most people thought he was <u>homely</u>. Lincoln thought so too, referring once to his "poor, lean, lank face." As a young man he was <u>sensitive</u> about his gawky looks, but in time he learned to laugh at himself. . . .

Today it's hard to imagine Lincoln as he really was. And he never cared to reveal much about himself. In company he was <u>witty</u> and <u>talkative</u>, but he rarely betrayed his inner feelings. . . .

Lincoln struggled hard to rise above his log-cabin origins, and he was <u>proud</u> of his achievements. By the time he ran for president he was a wealthy <u>man</u>, earning a large income from his law practice and his many investments. . . .

He was certainly . . . <u>famous</u> for his rollicking stories. But he was also <u>moody</u> and <u>melancholy</u>, tormented by long and frequent bouts of depression.

—from "The Mysterious Mr. Lincoln" by Russell Freedman

EXERCISE A   Which of the underlined words in the above passage are predicate nominatives and which are predicate adjectives?

Predicate Nominatives

_____

_____

Predicate Adjectives

_____

_____

_____

EXERCISE B   Why is an author likely to use several predicate nominatives and predicate adjectives when writing about a person?

_____

_____

_____

From "The Mysterious Mr. Lincoln" from *Lincoln: A Photobiography* by Russell Freedman. Copyright © 1987 by Russell Freedman. All rights reserved. Reprinted by permission of **Clarion Books/Houghton Mifflin Company.**

for **CHAPTER 5: COMPLEMENTS**   *pages 112–15*

Literary Model (continued)

EXERCISE C   Imagine that someone you know has recently achieved fame and that you have been asked to write a short biographical article about him or her. Write two or three paragraphs of the article. Use several predicate nominatives and predicate adjectives. In addition to the verb *be*, use other linking verbs such as *appear, become, remain, look,* and *seem.*

_____

_____

_____

_____

_____

_____

_____

_____

_____

_____

_____

_____

_____

_____

EXERCISE D

1. Make a list of the predicate nominatives and predicate adjectives that appear in your paragraphs. After each one, write the subject that is being referred to, described, or identified.

_____

_____

2. Read your list of predicate nominatives and predicate adjectives. Make sure they identify and describe your subject accurately. If they don't, go back now and revise your paragraph to better describe the person.

_____

_____

_____

_____

Writing Application: Personal History

Subject complements complete a sentence's meaning any time you use a linking verb. Without the complement, the sentence leaves readers guessing what the writer meant.

    INCOMPLETE   The rain felt as it slipped inside the collar of my parka.

    COMPLETE   The rain felt icy as it slipped inside the collar of my parka.

Readers of the first sentence may wonder how rain can feel anything! Of course, it's not the rain that is feeling—it's the person wearing the parka.

WRITING ACTIVITY

In your history class, you are talking about personal histories, or "family trees." Your teacher has asked you to choose a relative older than you—a grandparent, great-grandparent, great-uncle or great-aunt—to research. Before you come to class, you will ask other family members what they remember or know about this person. You can also talk to the person if he or she is still living. Bring the information to class to write a paragraph about your personal history. Use linking verbs and subject complements to describe this relative.

PREWRITING   Ask people in your family about the relative you have chosen. When was this person born? What was this person like? Where did he or she live, work, and play? Write down as many details as you can; then you can choose the most interesting facts from your collection.

WRITING   Just listing interesting facts about a person does not make a well-organized paragraph. Now that you know which facts you want to include, sketch out several possible plans. You might want to start with the person's birth and work forward. You could take the opposite and unusual course, starting with the latest events in the person's life and working backward! You could even start in the present and write flashbacks to the past. Sketch out several patterns, and decide which one you like best.

REVISING   When you jotted down information during the prewriting stage of this exercise, you probably wrote quickly in fragments and even single words. Now that you are revising your latest draft, be sure that every sentence is complete and that every linking verb has a descriptive subject complement.

PUBLISHING   Check your paragraph for mistakes in grammar, usage, spelling, and punctuation. With your teacher's permission, take turns in class reading your family tree paragraphs. If possible, bring a picture of the relative you wrote about with you.

EXTENDING YOUR WRITING

This exercise could lead to a more developed writing project. In the same way that you learned about one relative, find out more about other older members of your family. Write a short paragraph for each; then, assemble your paragraphs with photographs in a book about your family. Not only will this book be special to your family, but you could also enter it in photo-essay competitions, which many schools and fairs hold yearly.

Language and Sentence Skills Practice

Choices: Exploring Agreement

Here's your chance to step out of the grammar book and into the real world. You may not notice agreement, but you and the people around you use it every day. The following activities challenge you to find a connection between agreement and the world around you. Do the activity below that suits your personality best, and then share your discoveries with your class. Have fun!

DISCUSSION

Indigestion

Some foods just don't go together. Lead a discussion of foods that don't necessarily agree with each other (or with you!). For starters, consider the effects of chilies and strawberries together. Then, ask the class what might be the effects of subjects and verbs that don't agree with each other.

ETYMOLOGY

Antipasto, Anyone?

You've been reading about antecedents, but what does the word really mean? Find out about the prefix *ante-*. What does it mean? What's the difference between *ante-* and *anti-*? What are five other words that use the prefix *ante-*? What are the meanings of these words? Prepare a handout or poster featuring this information.

GAME

Scissors Cut Paper

One way to remember that words like *scissors* are plural is to recall the old game Rock, Paper, Scissors. If you know this game, teach it to the class. Then, everyone can just remember that "scissors cut (not cuts) paper." Think of at least three other common agreement problems, and invent games or sayings that will help your classmates remember the rules.

DISCUSSION

Square Pegs

Grammar isn't the only discipline that demands that elements match. Sometimes, instead of being said to *agree*, these elements are said to be compatible. For instance, in computer science, a program must be compatible with an operating system in order to work. What other systems demand that their components match? Lead a discussion of these points.

BUILDING BACKGROUND KNOWLEDGE

The Three Bears

Hearing titles that seem to be plural paired with singular pronouns can sound strange at first. However, the more you hear them, the faster you'll get used to them. Brainstorm a list of at least ten book, story, and poetry titles that are plural in form. You might want to check the indexes of some literature books and a few best-seller lists or ask your friends and classmates for some of their favorites. Pass out copies of your list to your classmates. Then, lead the class in writing sentences that use pronouns to refer to each of these titles.

MUSIC

Song and Dance

Break out the tap shoes, your hat, and your cane. It's time for a trip down memory lane. You'll need a song. You can use existing music or make up a tune, but you'll need to write new lyrics. Your lyrics should be about the agreement issues in this chapter. Make them easy to remember. Then, with your teacher's permission, perform your song and dance for the class.

TECHNOLOGY

Acid Test

Can a computer grammar checker really catch those pesky subject-verb agreement errors and pronoun-antecedent agreement errors? Before you rely on one of these programs, find out if it can do the job. Write a paragraph or two that include a number of such errors, or simply type in an exercise or two from this chapter. Then, run the grammar checker. Did it catch every error? Did it identify errors that aren't really errors? Score the program, and give it a grade. Then, present your data to the class. Point out which errors were corrected and which were missed.

Number

USAGE

6a. Words that refer to one person, place, thing, or idea are generally **singular** in number. Words that refer to more than one person, place, thing, or idea are generally **plural** in number.

SINGULAR	lake	he	puppy	wife	bench
PLURAL	lakes	they	puppies	wives	benches

EXERCISE A   On the line before each word, write *S* if the word is singular or *P* if it is plural.

Example ___S___ **1.** reality

_____ **1.** flowers   _____ **11.** planet

_____ **2.** storm   _____ **12.** windows

_____ **3.** clocks   _____ **13.** children

_____ **4.** we   _____ **14.** country

_____ **5.** valley   _____ **15.** it

_____ **6.** geese   _____ **16.** idea

_____ **7.** taxes   _____ **17.** strawberries

_____ **8.** people   _____ **18.** doctor

_____ **9.** diaries   _____ **19.** freedom

_____ **10.** England   _____ **20.** I

EXERCISE B   On the line provided, write a singular word or a plural word to complete each word group correctly. Use the italicized words as hints.

Example 1. a *few* _____coins_____

21. *a* big _____   **31.** *several* important _____

22. *four* exciting _____   **32.** *one* rare _____

23. *many* interesting _____ **33.** *some* different _____

24. *one* green _____   **34.** *three* more _____

25. a *few* tiny _____   **35.** a *bunch* of _____

26. *an* excellent _____   **36.** a *single* _____

27. *those* wonderful _____ **37.** too *many* _____

28. *twenty* old _____   **38.** *fewer than ten* _____

29. *another* lucky _____ **39.** *millions* of _____

30. *a* funny _____   **40.** just *one* _____

Language and Sentence Skills Practice

USAGE

Subject and Verb Agreement A

6b. A verb should agree in number with its subject.

(1) Singular subjects take singular verbs.

    EXAMPLE   **She plays** softball every weekend.

(2) Plural subjects take plural verbs.

    EXAMPLE   **They play** softball once a month.

If a sentence has a verb phrase, the first helping verb in the phrase agrees with the subject.

    EXAMPLES   **Sophie has** been practicing every day.

                The **runners have** been practicing all week.

EXERCISE A In each of the following sentences, the verb agrees with its subject. On the line before each sentence, write *S* if the subject and verb are singular or *P* if the subject and verb are plural.

Example _____*S*_____ **1.** Dad is cooking dinner.

_____ **1.** The door slams.

_____ **2.** He has been painting the fence.

_____ **3.** Our forests need rain.

_____ **4.** Belize is a small country.

_____ **5.** My uncles bowl on Wednesdays.

_____ **6.** The radios are too loud.

_____ **7.** Dr. Rodriguez is writing a letter.

_____ **8.** The dogs were barking.

_____ **9.** The twins are swimming.

_____ **10.** Earl has been practicing.

EXERCISE B Each of the following sentences contains two verb forms in parentheses. For each sentence, underline the verb form that agrees with the subject.

Example 1. Justine (*plays*, *play*) the clarinet in the school band.

11. The clarinet (*is*, *are*) a musical instrument.

12. Most clarinets (*is*, *are*) made of wood.

13. A clarinet (*has*, *have*) a long, hollow tube and a bell-shaped opening.

14. The mouthpiece (*is*, *are*) located at the other end of the tube.

15. A flat reed (*fits*, *fit*) into the back of the mouthpiece.

16. These reeds (*comes*, *come*) from cane plants.

17. The clarinet player (*blows*, *blow*) air into the mouthpiece.

18. The air (*makes*, *make*) the reed vibrate.

19. The vibrations (*creates*, *create*) sound.

20. A player (*controls*, *control*) the sound with keys on the clarinet's tube.

for **CHAPTER 6: AGREEMENT**   *pages 124–25*

Subject and Verb Agreement B

6b.   A verb should agree in number with its subject.

(1) Singular subjects take singular verbs.

EXAMPLE   **He rides** his bicycle in the park.

(2) Plural subjects take plural verbs.

EXAMPLE   **We collect** newspapers for the paper drive.

If a sentence has a verb phrase, the first helping verb in the phrase agrees with the subject.

EXAMPLES   **Janet has** played clarinet for three years.
              The **ducks are** flying south.

EXERCISE A   Each of the following sentences contains two verb forms in parentheses. For each sentence, underline the verb form that agrees with the subject.

Example [1] Maria (*loves, love*) her new bicycle.

[1] Maria (*rides, ride*) her bicycle almost every day. **[2]** She (*knows, know*) how to take care of her bike. **[3]** Maria (*oils, oil*) the chain whenever it gets wet. **[4]** She (*pumps, pump*) up the tires once a week. **[5]** Sometimes the brakes (*wears, wear*) down. **[6]** Her cousins (*knows, know*) how to adjust the brakes. **[7]** Maria (*has, have*) a new helmet, too. **[8]** At night, she (*uses, use*) a headlight. **[9]** Reflectors (*makes, make*) her more visible to motorists. **[10]** Maria (*enjoys, enjoy*) riding her bicycle safely.

EXERCISE B   Each of the following sentences contains two verb forms in parentheses. For each sentence, underline the verb form that agrees with the subject.

Example 1. Camping (*is, are*) a fun family event.

11. Many campers (*carries, carry*) a tent.

12. The tent (*keeps, keep*) the campers dry when it rains.

13. It also (*protects, protect*) them from insects.

14. Campers (*uses, use*) poles to hold up the tent.

15. The poles (*supports, support*) the tent and give it its shape.

16. Stakes (*helps, help*) anchor the tent during strong winds.

17. Tents (*is, are*) often made of nylon.

18. Nylon (*is, are*) a light material.

19. A rubber coating (*makes, make*) the tent waterproof.

20. Campers (*wants, want*) to stay dry and comfortable.

Language and Sentence Skills Practice

Phrases Between Subject and Verb

| **6c.** | The number of a subject is not changed by a phrase following the subject. |

EXAMPLES Our **hike** in the mountains **was** fun.

The **hands** on my watch **glow** in the dark.

The **tomatoes** from your garden **are** delicious.

EXERCISE A Underline the subject in each of the following sentences. Then, underline the form of the verb in parentheses that agrees with the subject.

Example 1. A box of old photographs (*was, were*) found in the attic.

1. The sneakers in the closet (*belongs, belong*) to me.

2. A fan in the bleachers (*was, were*) waving a large banner.

3. A pile of dirty dishes (*is, are*) in the sink.

4. Many paintings by Vincent van Gogh (*hangs, hang*) in the art museum.

5. The teacher of my science class (*was, were*) writing a book.

6. Many houses in my neighborhood (*has, have*) wooden porches.

7. The capital of the United States (*is, are*) Washington, D.C.

8. The author of these short stories (*has, have*) written a play, too.

9. The players on our team (*works, work*) hard.

10. Five students in my school (*plays, play*) in a band.

EXERCISE B The following paragraph contains errors in agreement of subject and verb. Correct each error by crossing out the incorrect verb form and writing the correct form above it. If a verb is already correct, write *C* above it.

includes
Example [1] The history of the Irish people ~~include~~ many hardships and struggles.

[11] A popular name for Ireland is "the Emerald Isle." [12] The green rolling hills and pastures of Ireland was the source of this name. [13] Many farmers in Ireland raises cattle, horses, and sheep. [14] Other farm products from the Emerald Isle include dairy products, wheat, and potatoes. [15] Shallow waters along Ireland's coastline gives the country a rich supply of fish, too.

Agreement with Indefinite Pronouns A

6d. The following indefinite pronouns are singular: *anybody, anyone, anything, each, either, everybody, everyone, everything, neither, nobody, no one, nothing, one, somebody, someone,* and *something.*

6e. The following indefinite pronouns are plural: *both, few, many, several.*

6f. The indefinite pronouns *all, any, more, most, none,* and *some* may be either singular or plural, depending on their meaning in a sentence.

EXERCISE Each of the following sentences has an indefinite pronoun as a subject. On the line before each sentence, write *S* if the indefinite pronoun is singular or *P* if it is plural. Then, underline the correct form of the verb in parentheses.

Example ___*P*___ **1.** Some of the pages (*is, are*) torn.

_____ **1.** Each of these apples (*is, are*) ripe.

_____ **2.** During the play, someone (*was, were*) whispering.

_____ **3.** All of the actors (*knows, know*) their lines.

_____ **4.** One of my favorite songwriters (*is, are*) Paul Simon.

_____ **5.** A few from the other class (*needs, need*) new textbooks.

_____ **6.** Some of my cousins (*has, have*) come to my party.

_____ **7.** Both of my parents (*works, work*) at the hospital.

_____ **8.** All of the bread (*was, were*) eaten.

_____ **9.** Neither of my two uncles (*speaks, speak*) French.

_____ **10.** This morning several (*was, were*) late.

_____ **11.** Most of the plants (*needs, need*) water.

_____ **12.** Now more of the waiters (*seems, seem*) busy.

_____ **13.** One of my cousins (*is, are*) on vacation.

_____ **14.** In the past month several in that department (*has, have*) gotten raises.

_____ **15.** Something about those people (*seems, seem*) suspicious to me.

_____ **16.** No one in the bleachers (*cheers, cheer*) more loudly than Jason.

_____ **17.** Most of the field (*needs, need*) mowing.

_____ **18.** Everyone in the club (*has, have*) read this book.

_____ **19.** None of the guests (*has, have*) left.

_____ **20.** Many of his classes (*requires, require*) daily homework.

Agreement with Indefinite Pronouns B

USAGE

6d. The following indefinite pronouns are singular: *anybody, anyone, anything, each, either, everybody, everyone, everything, neither, nobody, no one, nothing, one, somebody, someone,* and *something.*

6e. The following indefinite pronouns are plural: *both, few, many, several.*

6f. The indefinite pronouns *all, any, more, most, none,* and *some* may be either singular or plural, depending on their meaning in a sentence.

EXERCISE Each of the following sentences has an indefinite pronoun as a subject. For each sentence, underline the verb that agrees with the subject.

Example 1. Each of the planets in our solar system (*orbits, orbit*) the sun.

1. One of the planets (*has, have*) visible rings.

2. Nobody (*has, have*) observed moons around Mercury.

3. All of the students (*uses, use*) telescopes.

4. Everyone (*is, are*) able to see the moon tonight.

5. Some of the stars (*seems, seem*) to twinkle.

6. Most of the stars (*is, are*) invisible to us.

7. Each of the visible stars (*is, are*) a huge ball of gas.

8. None of the planets (*escapes, escape*) the gravitational pull of the sun.

9. No one (*knows, know*) how many stars there are.

10. Neither of the astronomers (*needs, need*) a microscope.

11. Most of the researchers (*has, have*) many questions.

12. Everyone (*needs, need*) to learn more.

13. One of the constellations (*resembles, resemble*) a hunter.

14. Several of the books (*contains, contain*) photographs.

15. Some of the scientists (*works, work*) high up on mountaintops.

16. Neither of the inner planets (*has, have*) moons.

17. (*Is, Are*) either of the inner planets visible tonight?

18. A few of the planets (*is, are*) not visible to the naked eye.

19. Someone (*is, are*) asking about comets.

20. (*Does, Do*) anyone know if comets orbit the sun?

Compound Subjects

6g.	Subjects joined by *and* generally take a plural verb.
6h.	Singular subjects that are joined by *or* or *nor* take a singular verb.
6i.	Plural subjects joined by *or* or *nor* take a plural verb.
6j.	When a singular subject and a plural subject are joined by *or* or *nor*, the verb agrees with the subject nearer the verb.

EXAMPLES   **Raoul** and **Mark have been playing** tennis all day.

Either **Julio** or his **brother is singing.**

Flowers or **balloons make** a nice gift for a sick friend.

Neither **rain** nor **ants are spoiling** our picnic.

Neither **ants** nor **rain is spoiling** our picnic.

EXERCISE A Each of the following sentences contains two verb forms in parentheses. For each sentence, underline the verb form that agrees with the subject.

Example 1. An adult or two children *(fits, fit)* inside this bumper car.

1. Two rabbits and a gerbil *(lives, live)* in big cages in our science classroom.

2. Either my brother or my sister *(is, are)* waiting for me.

3. One maple and three elms *(stands, stand)* in the yard.

4. Lentils or beans *(is, are)* are used in the stew.

5. Neither my sister nor my parents *(knows, know)* the answer to the riddle.

6. A car and three buses *(was, were)* involved in the accident.

7. Neither my cousins nor my aunt *(wants, want)* the apple.

8. Either Mr. Brooks or his son *(washes, wash)* the car.

9. Damont or his parents usually *(helps, help)* us.

10. He and his dogs *(is, are)* going for a hike.

EXERCISE B Each of the following sentences contains two verb forms in parentheses. For each sentence, underline the verb form that agrees with the subject.

Example 1. Fruits and vegetables *(contains, contain)* many nutrients.

11. Spinach and kale *(is, are)* green, leafy vegetables.

12. Neither a plum nor a pear *(is, are)* a citrus fruit.

13. Either an orange or a grapefruit *(is, are)* good for dessert today.

14. Lemons and limes *(provides, provide)* vitamin C.

15. Neither harsh winds nor rain *(affects, affect)* this tree.

USAGE

Subject After the Verb

6k. When the subject follows the verb, find the subject and make sure the verb agrees with it.

The subject usually follows the verb in questions and in sentences that begin with *there* and *here.*

EXAMPLES **Were** the **players** tired?

There **are** six **floors** in this building.

The contractions *there's* and *here's* contain the verb *is.* These contractions are singular and should be used only with singular subjects.

EXAMPLE **Here's** the **answer** to your question.

EXERCISE Underline the subject in each sentence. Then, underline the correct word or words in parentheses.

Example 1. *(There's, There are)* some sponges in that drawer.

1. *(Has, Have)* your neighbors moved to Phoenix yet?

2. There *(is, are)* fifty states in the United States.

3. *(Here's, Here are)* the train to Culver City.

4. *(Is, Are)* the loaves of bread in the oven?

5. *(Here's, Here are)* the cans of paint for your project.

6. *(There's, There are)* more bananas in the fruit basket.

7. *(Was, Were)* your parents born in Sweden?

8. Where *(has, have)* they gone for their picnic?

9. *(Has, Have)* Marie and Nina looked at the map?

10. *(There's, There are)* a library and a bus stop near my house.

11. *(Has, Have)* Hiromi opened her birthday presents?

12. *(Here's, Here are)* a gift for Hiromi.

13. *(Is, Are)* you going to guess what it is?

14. Where *(has, have)* she put the other gifts?

15. *(Does, Do)* you like your new doll?

16. *(Is, Are)* they going to give the doll a name?

17. *(There's, There are)* an extra dress for the doll.

18. *(Has, Have)* her friends seen her other presents yet?

19. *(Has, Have)* I shown you how to play this game?

20. *(Was, Were)* we late for the party?

USAGE

Don't and Doesn't

6l. The word *don't* is the contraction of *do not*. Use *don't* with all plural subjects and with the pronouns *I* and *you*.

> **EXAMPLES** These **kittens don't** have homes yet.   **I don't** want any salad.

6m. The word *doesn't* is the contraction of *does not*. Use *doesn't* with all singular subjects except the pronouns *I* and *you*.

> **EXAMPLES** **Doesn't he** know the answer?   That **bird doesn't** look healthy.

EXERCISE On the blank in each sentence, write *don't* or *doesn't* to complete the sentence correctly.

Example 1. My mother ____*doesn't*____ get home until 7:00.

1. You _____ have my new address.

2. Tanya _____ like spaghetti.

3. Howard's gloves _____ fit me.

4. Earl and Janice _____ want any more cereal.

5. I _____ dance very well.

6. Ms. Lowe _____ play badminton.

7. He _____ visit us often.

8. Jeff's grandparents _____ stay home much.

9. The baby _____ have any blue booties.

10. That program _____ come on until 8:00 tonight.

11. Mauricio _____ live near us anymore.

12. We _____ get to see him often.

13. His brother _____ go to our school.

14. They _____ play soccer on our team.

15. _____ Miriam play softball?

16. Miriam and Colleen _____ study with us.

17. _____ they usually study with Julie?

18. I _____ like to study alone.

19. _____ you prefer to study in the library?

20. The library _____ stay open late on weekends.

Language and Sentence Skills Practice

USAGE

Agreement of Pronoun and Antecedent A

| **6n.** | A pronoun should agree in gender with its antecedent. |

> **EXAMPLES** **Anthony** said **he** had done **his** homework.
> **One** of the **girls** has lost **her** book.
> **Someone** in the band left **his or her** uniform on the bus.

| **6o.** | A pronoun should agree with its antecedent in number. |

> **EXAMPLES** You may have the last **muffin** if you want **it**.
> The **puppies** will thrive if **they** are cared for well.

EXERCISE A In the following sentences, underline the pronoun or pronoun group in parentheses that agrees in gender and number with its antecedent.

Example 1. Scurrying across the yard, the chipmunk headed for (*their*, *its*) burrow.

1. Derrick asked his neighbor to take care of (*his*, *their*) cat for the weekend.

2. Each member of the girls' volleyball team received (*her*, *his or her*) own medal.

3. In the evening the raccoons climbed down from (*its*, *their*) nest in the trees.

4. The cat stalked the ball of yarn and then pounced on (*it*, *them*).

5. The new keyboards in the computer lab are still in (*its*, *their*) boxes.

6. Tanya enjoyed working at the restaurant because (*she*, *he or she*) met new people there.

7. The three children made breakfast for (*his or her*, *their*) dad on his birthday.

8. Every day, one student in the class would describe (*his or her*, *their*) progress on the research report.

9. Ms. Jackson called the boys into her office and gave (*him*, *them*) a lecture on responsibility.

10. The house was old but clean, and (*she*, *it*) seemed to welcome the new family.

EXERCISE B For each sentence, underline the pronoun form that agrees with the antecedent.

Example 1. The instruments will last longer if you take care of (*it*, <u>*them*</u>).

11. My doctor carries (*her*, *their*) notepad and pen with her.

12. They brought a tuba with (*it*, *them*) to the parade.

13. The plants will grow if you water (*it*, *them*).

14. I remember that tree from when (*it*, *they*) first sprouted.

15. The vegetables taste better with a little seasoning on (*it*, *them*).

Agreement of Pronoun and Antecedent B

6n. A pronoun should agree in gender with its antecedent.

> **EXAMPLES** **Betsy** can't leave the house until **she** has finished cleaning **her** room.
>
> **Each** of the **boys** must carry **his** own equipment.
>
> **Everyone** in the play knew **his or her** lines.

6o. A pronoun should agree with its antecedent in number.

> **EXAMPLES** May I borrow that **book** when you finish **it**?
>
> Each year the **flowers** bloomed, **they** seemed more colorful.

EXERCISE A In each of the following sentences, circle the antecedent. Then, underline the pronoun or pronouns in parentheses that agree in gender with the antecedent.

Example 1. (Karen) left *(her, its)* jacket at school.

1. Uncle Dave had an extra ticket, so *(he, she)* gave it to Marshall.

2. The oak tree in the backyard had lost most of *(his, its)* leaves.

3. Sharon was eating lunch with *(her, his or her)* friends.

4. The wasp returned to *(her, its)* nest.

5. Each student brought *(his, his or her)* poster to the game.

EXERCISE B On the blank in each sentence, write one or more pronouns that agree in gender and number with the antecedent.

Example 1. One girl wrote _____*her*_____ name on the board.

6. Neither boy remembered to bring _____ textbook.

7. Both coaches brought _____ whistles.

8. After two weeks off, the girls were glad _____ were playing a game Monday.

9. Did either of the men tell us _____ name?

10. Jeremy had dropped his hat, but he found _____ the next day.

11. Students who are attending the field trip must turn in _____ forms today.

12. My brother lent me _____ umbrella.

13. Each performer must bring _____ own costume.

14. When Diego got home, _____ began preparing dinner.

15. The lizard must have injured _____ leg.

USAGE

Indefinite Pronouns as Antecedents

6o. A pronoun should agree with its antecedent in number.

(1) Use a singular pronoun to refer to the indefinite pronouns *anybody, anyone, anything, each, either, everybody, everyone, everything, neither, nobody, no one, nothing, one, somebody, someone,* and *something.*

(2) Use a plural pronoun to refer to the indefinite pronouns *both, few, many,* and *several.*

(3) The indefinite pronouns *all, any, more, most, none,* and *some* may be singular or plural, depending on their meaning in a sentence.

EXERCISE For each of the following sentences, underline the pronoun form that agrees with the antecedent.

Example 1. Most of the actors remembered *(his, their)* lines.

1. Anyone who needs help may consult *(his or her, their)* script.

2. One of the lines loses *(its, their)* meaning when taken out of context.

3. A few of the dancers brought *(her, their)* shoes.

4. One of the paintings is losing *(its, their)* sharpness.

5. Everyone is wearing *(his or her, their)* costume tonight.

6. Neither of the dancers wore *(her, their)* hat.

7. Did anyone forget to bring *(his or her, their)* notes?

8. I don't know if either of the girls will sing *(her, their)* lines tonight.

9. Everything on the stage has *(its, their)* own place.

10. Somebody left *(his or her, their)* uniform behind the stage.

11. Most of the costumes are missing *(its, their)* buttons.

12. All of the furniture was put in *(its, their)* proper place.

13. Everyone sold *(his or her, their)* tickets last week.

14. More of the material needs to have *(its, their)* edges trimmed.

15. Some of the fabric is losing *(its, their)* stitching.

16. One of the costume designers needs *(his, their)* sewing kit.

17. Do any of the costumes need *(its, their)* zippers replaced?

18. Only a few of the actors need *(his, their)* full costumes tonight.

19. One of the set designers brought *(her, their)* paintbrush.

20. Is one of the scripts missing *(its, their)* cover?

USAGE

Antecedents Joined by *Or, Nor,* or *And*

6o(4).	Use a singular pronoun to refer to two or more singular antecedents joined by *or* or *nor*.

EXAMPLES   **Carmela or Sindey** will present **her** speech today.

Neither the **maple nor** the **oak** has lost all **its** leaves.

6o(5).	Use a plural pronoun to refer to two or more antecedents joined by *and*.

EXAMPLES   When **Jeremy and** his **brother** got home, **they** practiced with their guitars.

The **coach and** the **players** reviewed **their** game plan.

EXERCISE A   Each of the following sentences contains an underlined pronoun that agrees with its antecedent. Above each underlined pronoun, write *S* if the pronoun is singular or *P* if it is plural.

Example   1. Neither Myla nor Margaret has had <u>her</u> lunch.

1. Amelia or Amanda will read <u>her</u> report first.

2. Yolanda and Jaime found <u>their</u> dictionaries.

3. Neither my mother nor my aunt brought <u>her</u> umbrella.

4. The bus driver and the students clapped <u>their</u> hands.

5. Neither Bill nor Todd used <u>his</u> baseball glove today.

EXERCISE B   For each of the following sentences, underline the pronoun or pronouns that agree with the antecedent.

Example   1. If the game is played well, (<u>*it*</u>, *they*) is very interesting to watch.

6. When Henry and Noriyuki arrived, (*he, they*) set up the chess pieces.

7. The chessboard and pieces were placed so that (*it, they*) could be seen well.

8. A beginning player or an experienced player sometimes loses (*his or her, their*) concentration.

9. The players and the observers looked at (*his or her, their*) watches.

10. Either the bishop or the knight will lose (*its, their*) powerful position.

11. Neither Yuri nor Stan brought (*his, their*) rule book.

12. Neither the players nor the observers expressed (*his or her, their*) opinions.

13. A marble chess set or a wooden chess set will retain (*its, their*) value.

14. If either Timothy or Hiroshi plays, (*he, they*) will expect to use the marble chess set.

15. Natalie or Olga will give (*her, their*) advice first.

USAGE

Review A: Subject-Verb Agreement

EXERCISE A In each of the following sentences, the verb agrees with its subject. On the line before each sentence, write *S* if the subject and verb are singular or *P* if the subject and verb are plural.

Example ___*S*___ **1.** Chuck or Tyrell takes out the trash.

_____ **1.** They have been cheering for the team.

_____ **2.** A letter from your aunt and uncle is on the table.

_____ **3.** All of the water in the pail was leaking onto the floor.

_____ **4.** A woman and two men were sharing a taxi.

_____ **5.** Here's your ticket to the game.

_____ **6.** An after-school snack for your friends is in the refrigerator.

_____ **7.** Eartha and you have been working hard all afternoon.

_____ **8.** There's a green coat in the closet.

_____ **9.** Jefferson's plans don't make sense to us.

_____ **10.** Most of the beach has been cleaned.

EXERCISE B Underline the subject in each of the following sentences. Then, underline the form of the verb in parentheses that agrees with the subject.

Example 1. *(Is, Are)* there any beans left for me?

11. Most of my work *(is, are)* finished.

12. Songs from the movie *(has, have)* been on my mind all day.

13. Either his grandparents or his father *(comes, come)* from Japan.

14. *(There's, There are)* two big trucks parked out front.

15. Our trip to the western states *(begins, begin)* tomorrow.

16. Lucia and Marcus *(lives, live)* on a farm.

17. Many of the citizens *(agrees, agree)* with the mayor.

18. *(Is, Are)* there some empty seats up front?

19. It *(doesn't, don't)* really matter.

20. Either the Germans or the Italians *(is, are)* playing soccer tomorrow.

Review B: **Pronoun-Antecedent Agreement**

EXERCISE For each sentence below, underline the pronoun or pronouns that agree with the antecedent.

Example 1. The children and their parents went to (his or her, _their_) neighborhood supermarket.

1. Does anyone have (his or her, their) grocery list?

2. One of the grocery carts is missing (its, their) rear wheels.

3. Most of the shoppers brought (her, their) lists.

4. Neither the mother nor her daughter brought (her, their) purse.

5. I see the laundry detergent, but I can't find (its, their) price.

6. There are twelve eggs here, but some of (its, their) shells are broken.

7. Did someone lose (his or her, their) calculator yesterday?

8. The cottage cheese or the yogurt will be fine if (it, they) is refrigerated.

9. Several of the bananas have brown spots on (its, their) peels.

10. One of the jars has a dent in (its, their) lid.

11. All of the items were put back on (its, their) shelves.

12. Neither my sister nor my mother brought (her, their) pen.

13. Both of the frying pans are missing (its, their) handles.

14. Is anyone carrying (his or her, their) backpack?

15. Barbara and Alina found (her, their) favorite spices.

16. Some of the silverware has lost (its, their) shine.

17. Most of the kitchen utensils have (their, its) prices clearly marked.

18. Do any of the customers bring (his or her, their) own shopping bags?

19. Spinach or cabbage will retain (its, their) freshness better if sealed and refrigerated.

20. Most of the vegetables keep (its, their) sharp colors when steamed.

21. Darryl and Kyle found (his, their) school supplies in aisle three.

22. Either Connie or her brother will select (his or her, their) favorite breakfast drink.

23. A father and his son split (his, their) list in two so they could find things twice as fast.

24. One of the checkers needed a manager to help (her, them) fix the till.

25. The manager asked the family if (she, they) had found everything all right.

Review C: Agreement

USAGE

EXERCISE A Underline the subject in each of the following sentences. Then, underline the form of the verb in parentheses that agrees with the subject.

Example 1. *(Was, Were)* any of the animals injured?

1. The bowl of strawberries *(looks, look)* delicious.

2. Neither you nor he *(is, are)* strong enough to move that boulder.

3. Members of the club *(writes, write)* stories for the newspaper.

4. Two cars and a bus *(was, were)* stopped at the traffic light.

5. Some of the dancers *(is, are)* in the show.

6. Most of the apartment *(needs, need)* cleaning.

7. The play about the gods and the goddesses of Greece *(opens, open)* today.

8. Everybody in the two competing schools *(was, were)* eager for the game.

9. The fenders and the bumper *(was, were)* dented.

10. The colors in the material *(has, have)* faded.

EXERCISE B For each sentence below, underline the pronoun or pronouns that agree with the antecedent.

Example 1. Health clubs offer many benefits to *(its, their)* members.

11. An exercise bike or a rowing machine requires maintenance to keep *(it, them)* running well.

12. One of the health clubs offers free classes to *(its, their)* members.

13. Both weightlifting machines and free weights have *(its, their)* advantages.

14. My sister or my aunt will find the individual exercise program that serves *(her, them)* best.

15. The track and the swimming pool both have *(its, their)* appeal.

16. One of the women left *(her, their)* towel behind.

17. Neither my mother nor my sister is wasting *(her, their)* time here.

18. Can each of the swimmers find *(his or her, their)* goggles?

19. Most of the bicyclists wore *(his, their)* cycling shoes.

20. A club can expand when *(its, their)* membership increases.

Review D: **Agreement**

EXERCISE A   In each of the following sentences, underline the word or word group in parentheses that correctly completes the sentence.

Example 1. *(Has, Have)* most of the guests arrived?

1. *(Has, Have)* everybody finished the chapter?

2. A few of the students *(knows, know)* computer programming.

3. *(There's, There are)* two reasons for my opinion.

4. Her uncle *(doesn't, don't)* have a driver's license.

5. None of the kittens *(has, have)* been adopted yet.

6. *(Has, Have)* any of the milk spilled?

7. *(Does, Do)* most of your friends play football?

8. One of my gloves *(is, are)* missing.

9. All of the birds *(are, is)* singing.

10. Some of the color *(has, have)* faded.

EXERCISE B   For each sentence below, underline the pronoun or pronouns that agree with the antecedent.

Example 1. A new playground gives the park *(its, their)* appeal.

11. Does anyone know how the park got *(its, their)* name?

12. Parents like to bring *(her, their)* children to the park.

13. A child can use *(his or her, their)* imagination in the park.

14. Some of the swings have had *(its, their)* seats repaired.

15. My mother brings *(her, their)* books to the park.

16. Neither of the fountains has *(its, their)* water turned on yet.

17. The squirrels hide *(its, their)* pecans under the leaves.

18. One of the squirrels made *(its, their)* home inside a shack.

19. Do all of the pigeons build *(its, their)* nests under this bridge?

20. One of the girls saw *(her, their)* favorite kind of bird.

Language and Sentence Skills Practice

for **CHAPTER 6: AGREEMENT**   *pages 124–40*

Proofreading Application: Speech

Good writers are generally good proofreaders. Readers tend to admire and trust writing that is error-free. Make sure that you correct all errors in grammar, usage, spelling, and punctuation in your writing. Your readers will have more confidence in your words if you have done your best to proofread carefully.

Proofreading speeches is especially important. If you make mistakes in agreement, your listeners will not have a chance to go back and re-read a passage in order to understand it. Instead, your audience may just sit there, not listening, but trying to figure out what you meant in prior sentences. Errors in agreement can confuse your listeners and even give them the wrong idea.

PROOFREADING ACTIVITY

Find and correct the errors in subject-verb and pronoun-antecedent agreement. Use proofreading symbols to make your corrections.

Example   *Lazy Days* ~~were~~ was a play by the sixth-grade class.

Thanks to our sponsor, we has a first-class production for you tonight. I and the entire cast of *Lazy Days* offers our thanks to our sponsor. Flappy Fabrics have donated all the cloth for our costumes. Mr. Clement and his daughter Lisa have given us his and her assistance throughout the production. Either Lisa Clement or her assistant Mary shared their design skills with our students. Moreover, Mr. Clement and Lisa Clement have graciously given his or her time to us. The ones who made this production possible was they. All of the costumes in this play is the product of our sponsor's hard work. Each of us gives our thanks to Flappy Fabrics. Several of the cast have created an award for Flappy Fabrics, and he or she would like to present it now.

Literary Model: Poetry

The Sea
by James Reeves

The sea is a hungry dog,
Giant and gray.
He rolls on the beach all day.
With his clashing teeth and shaggy jaws
Hour upon hour he gnaws
The rumbling, tumbling stones,
And "Bones, bones, bones!"
The giant sea dog moans,
Licking his greasy paws.

And when the night wind roars
And the moon rocks in the stormy cloud,
He bounds to his feet and snuffs and sniffs,
Shaking his wet sides over the cliffs,
And howls and hollos long and loud.

But on quiet days in May or June,
When even the grasses on the dune
Play no more their reedy tune,
With his head between his paws
He lies on the sandy shores,
So quiet, so quiet, he scarcely snores.

EXERCISE A In his poem "The Sea," what pronouns does James Reeves use to refer to the sea? (You do not need to write repeated pronouns more than once.)

_____

EXERCISE B

1. What personal pronouns would you usually use to refer to the sea?

_____

2. Is the author trying to get readers to look at the sea differently by using the pronouns he does? How do you think the author wants us to see the sea? Explain your answers.

_____

_____

"The Sea" from *Complete Poems for Children* (Heinemann) by James Reeves. Copyright © by James Reeves. Reprinted by permission of **The James Reeves Estate.**

for **CHAPTER 6: AGREEMENT** | pages 124–40

Literary Model (continued)

EXERCISE C Think of something in nature that most people think of as an *it* but that you can see as being like a person or an animal. Write a poem in which you use the pronouns *he, him,* and *his* or the pronouns *she, her,* and *hers* to refer to something that people would usually refer to as *it* and *its*.

_____

_____

_____

_____

_____

_____

_____

_____

_____

_____

EXERCISE D Re-read your poem. Is the comparison you are making between something in nature and a person or an animal clear? Will your reader be able to see how one is like the other? Revise your poem to better show how your subject is like a person or an animal. Then, answer these questions:

1. What topic did you choose to write about? _____

2. How is it like a person or an animal? _____

_____

_____

_____

_____

_____

_____

Writing Application: Bulletin Board Display

In speech, it's acceptable to use plural third person pronouns like *they, them, their,* and *themselves* to agree with indefinite pronouns like *everybody, anyone, somebody,* and *no one.* In fact, it almost sounds strange to hear formal pronoun usage with indefinite pronouns! Read these sentences aloud.

SOUNDS NORMAL   *No one* noticed the absence of pepperoni on *their* pizza slices.

SOUNDS ODD   *No one* noticed the absence of pepperoni on *his or her* pizza slices.

The second sentence is correct in formal English, although it is not what we expect to hear, so be sure to use the singular pronouns when you write formally. On the other hand, if you want to avoid the odd sound, you could replace the indefinite pronoun with a plural noun that fits the sentence's meaning: "The *guys* watching the Super Bowl didn't notice the absence of pepperoni on *their* pizza slices."

WRITING ACTIVITY

You and several other students are putting together a bulletin board display on good study skills. The bulletin board display will be in the library, where all students can read and benefit from it. Your job is to describe two good study skills. You will explain each skill in a brief paragraph. Use indefinite pronouns to describe what students should do; and set a great example in your writing by using formal, correct pronoun-antecedent agreement.

PREWRITING   Work together with the other students on the project to brainstorm a list of important study skills. Then choose the two that you will describe. For each skill, come up with a mini-lesson on how to develop the skill and put it into action. What materials are required to carry out the skill?

WRITING   You are basically writing two tiny sets of instructions as you tell students how to develop the skill. Remember that students need not only help in learning the skill but also information on common problems or pitfalls that may temporarily stop their progress. Help them learn from others' mistakes rather than having to make the mistakes themselves!

REVISING   Because your information will be presented on a bulletin board, students will not have copies of the paragraphs to keep with them. They are unlikely to stand in front of the bulletin board and write down your good advice, either. So write very directly, and try to make your sentences memorable. You might even create a memory helper for students, to help them recall the most important information from the paragraphs. Indefinite pronouns like *everyone* and *anyone* will help you stress the idea that all students can benefit from your advice.

PUBLISHING   Be sure that no mistakes in spelling, punctuation, or agreement go up on that bulletin board for everyone to see! Then, combine your efforts with those of the other students, add illustrations, and, with your teacher's permission, assemble your bulletin board.

EXTENDING YOUR WRITING

This exercise could lead to a more developed writing project. For a class that is studying possible careers, you could explore how getting into the habit of using strong study skills now will help you succeed later in life, in whatever career you pursue.

Choices: Exploring Verbs

Here's your chance to step out of the grammar book and into the real world. You may not notice verbs, but you and the people around you use them every day. The following activities challenge you to find a connection between verbs and the world around you. Do the activity below that suits your personality best, and then share your discoveries with your class. Have fun!

GAME

Hot Potato

Does all this talk about tenses make you and your friends yawn? Wake everybody up! Grab an eraser, a beanbag, or just a ball of paper to serve as the "hot potato." Then, call out a tense and hand the "hot potato" off to a classmate who must give a sentence with a verb in the tense you named. The classmate should then pass the "hot potato" to the next person. The game is complete when everyone has had the "hot potato" once.

PUBLISHING

On Safari

Go on a scavenger hunt for irregular verbs. Look in newspapers, magazines, and other published sources to find places where an irregular verb might be hiding. Then, bring home your trophies—your irregular verbs. Photocopy or cut them out, and paste them to poster board. Be sure to note whether the irregular verb has been used correctly or incorrectly.

STUDY AIDS

Jet Fuel

Some people remember the different tenses easily, and some people take longer. Speed up the process. Write a poem or rap, or devise some other kind of study aid to help your classmates master these tenses.

TIME LINE

Then, Now, and Ever After

Create a time line on poster board that shows each of the different tenses. You might want to make the tenses stand out by printing them in different colors. Add a line or two of explanation and an example for each tense. Finally, with your teacher's permission, hang the time line in your classroom.

TECHNOLOGY

Horse of a Different Color

Choose twenty of the peskiest verbs in Chapter 7 of your textbook. Type them into a word processor. Then, change the color of the letters that change for each form. For instance, for the past participle of the word *swim*, you would see the letters *s*, *w*, and *m* in black and the letter *u* in, perhaps, red. Pass out copies of your list to your classmates. If you don't have a computer, you can still do this project; just print neatly on poster board. Then, with your teacher's permission, hang the poster in the classroom.

ART

Raise the Flag

Create small posters illustrating the proper use of the troublesome verbs *rise* and *raise*. Find or draw pictures that illustrate these actions. Write sentences that describe what's happening in the pictures. (Make sure you use the correct verbs in your sentences!) Hang the posters around the classroom so your classmates can learn from your efforts.

ART/WRITING

Most Wanted

You are surrounded by people who have no respect for the laws of English usage. Your mission is to aid in the capture of these outlaws. Create "wanted" posters, complete with portraits of each lawbreaker, his or her description, and an account of the crime. (No, you may not use real people.) Make these characters low-down, mean, and nasty. Write example sentences that show how they break the laws. Of course, you'll also want to show how these sentences should be corrected. Make sure that your verb tenses are consistent.

Identifying the Principal Parts of Verbs

7a. The four principal parts of a verb are the **base form,** the **present participle,** the **past,** and the **past participle.**

BASE FORM	PRESENT PARTICIPLE	PAST	PAST PARTICIPLE
receive	[is] receiving	received	[have] received
go	[is] going	went	[have] gone

The principal parts of a verb are used to express present, past, and future times.

PRESENT   Nakeesha **washes** her hands before dinner.

John and his father **are washing** the dog.

PAST   Last night, we **washed** the car.

Van and I **have washed** all the windows.

FUTURE   Annie **will wash** the dishes after the party.

He **will have washed** the floor by the time you arrive.

EXERCISE A   A principal part of a verb is underlined in each of the following sentences. Identify the underlined verb form by writing *base form, present participle, past,* or *past participle* in the space above it.

                                past participle
Example 1. Rama has taken the test already.

1. All of the balloons on the string popped except two.

2. Do you want to buy those books?

3. Daniel's dog is following the trail to the river's edge.

4. For thirty years the noon whistle has blown exactly on time.

5. The players have challenged their parents to a game of soccer.

EXERCISE B   Decide what kind of time each of the following verbs expresses. On the line provided, write *present* if the verb expresses present time, *past* if it expresses past time, or *future* if it expresses future time.

Example   _____*future*_____ **1.** will have driven

_____ **6.** reported   _____ **11.** have looked

_____ **7.** will write   _____ **12.** chooses

_____ **8.** will have played _____ **13.** is taking

_____ **9.** happened   _____ **14.** has called

_____ **10.** sees   _____ **15.** will swim

Language and Sentence Skills Practice

Using Regular Verbs

USAGE

| **7b.** | A *regular verb* forms its past and past participle by adding –*d* or –*ed* to the base form. |

BASE FORM	PRESENT PARTICIPLE	PAST	PAST PARTICIPLE
look	[is] looking	looked	[have] looked
shop	[is] shopping	shopped	[have] shopped
suppose	[is] supposing	supposed	[have] supposed

Remember that some regular verbs, such as *shop* and *suppose,* double the final consonant or drop the final *e* when adding –*ing* or –*ed.*

EXERCISE A   On the blank in each of the following sentences, write the correct form (present participle, past, or past participle) of the verb given in parentheses.

Example 1. One of the elephants has _____*wrapped*_____ its trunk around a tree. *(wrap)*

1. The plane has _____ in Nepal. *(land)*

2. The scientists from the museum are _____ to track rhinos in the jungle. *(plan)*

3. The government officials of Nepal _____ the project. *(support)*

4. The workers are _____ elephants for the scientists to ride. *(saddle)*

5. Yesterday, the trackers _____ a female rhino and her calf. *(spot)*

EXERCISE B   On the blank in each of the following sentences, write the correct form (present participle, past, or past participle) of the verb given in parentheses.

Example 1. Every day last winter, Christine _____*watched*_____ the squirrels. *(watch)*

6. Last year, Christine _____ watching the squirrels gather food. *(enjoy)*

7. One day, Christine _____ to build a feeder for the squirrels. *(decide)*

8. Christine has _____ several books about squirrels. *(purchase)*

9. Through her reading she has _____ that squirrels like sunflower seeds. *(learn)*

10. She _____ some pine wood to build the feeder. *(collect)*

11. Christine then _____ the feeder to a strong tree. *(nail)*

12. Christine's brother _____ to her more about squirrels. *(explain)*

13. From listening to him, Christine has _____ that squirrels also like fruit. *(discover)*

14. She is still _____ new things each day as she watches the squirrels. *(notice)*

15. Now Christine is _____ her friends to build feeders for squirrels. *(encourage)*

Using Irregular Verbs A

7c. An *irregular verb* forms its past and past participle in some other way than by adding *–d* or
–ed to the base form.

BASE FORM	PRESENT PARTICIPLE	PAST	PAST PARTICIPLE
swim	[is] swimming	swam	[have] swum
go	[is] going	went	[have] gone
catch	[is] catching	caught	[have] caught
hurt	[is] hurting	hurt	[have] hurt

EXERCISE A Underline the correct verb form in parentheses in each of the following sentences.

Example 1. We (*drove, driven*) along the Big Sur coast of California.

1. Some biologists have (*came, come*) here to collect peregrine falcon eggs.

2. Many eggs have (*broken, broke*) because their shells have been damaged by pesticides.

3. Lee, one of the biologists, had (*began, begun*) to gather the eggs.

4. He showed me the eggs, but I (*knew, known*) not to touch them.

5. The adult peregrine had (*flown, flew*) from the nest.

6. Lee (*began, begun*) to climb down the cliff to the nest.

7. Suddenly, I (*seen, saw*) a large bird in the sky.

8. Everyone (*froze, frozen*).

9. The peregrine dived at Lee's head and then (*went, gone*) away.

10. The huge, fierce bird (*given, gave*) us quite a scare.

EXERCISE B On the blank in each of the following sentences, write the correct form (past or past participle) of the verb given in parentheses.

Example 1. Mrs. Larkin has _____*taught*_____ the class about endangered species. (*teach*)

11. Sofia has _____ a report about peregrine falcons. (*write*)

12. Pollutants have _____ these fierce, fast-flying birds. (*hurt*)

13. The peregrine falcon has _____ endangered. (*become*)

14. To help increase the peregrine falcon population, biologists _____ eggs from a
peregrine nest. (*take*)

15. They _____ the falcon eggs to a laboratory. (*bring*)

Language and Sentence Skills Practice

USAGE

Using Irregular Verbs B

7c. An *irregular verb* forms its past and past participle in some other way than by adding –*d* or –*ed* to the base form.

BASE FORM	PRESENT PARTICIPLE	PAST	PAST PARTICIPLE
win	[is] winning	won	[have] won
draw	[is] drawing	drew	[have] drawn
begin	[is] beginning	began	[have] begun
write	[is] writing	wrote	[have] written

EXERCISE   Each of the following sentences contains a verb with an irregular past form. In the blank in each sentence, write the past form of the verb.

Example 1. The kitten _____*drank*_____ the milk from its favorite bowl. *(drink)*

1. She _____ to Boston last summer. *(drive)*

2. Tonya _____ a solo last night. *(sing)*

3. The bus driver _____ her time when crossing the bridge. *(take)*

4. The artist _____ her paintbrush to the studio. *(bring)*

5. When Jaime was ill, his stomach _____ all day. *(hurt)*

6. My sister _____ me her favorite sweater. *(give)*

7. What _____ your mom tell you yesterday? *(do)*

8. My shoes _____ out during the long hiking trip. *(wear)*

9. I _____ my name for the teacher. *(write)*

10. The mother _____ the baby in her arms. *(hold)*

11. She _____ the photo so she would always remember her vacation. *(keep)*

12. They _____ that they would arrive before noon. *(say)*

13. We _____ the comet last night. *(see)*

14. She _____ her little brother a paint set for his birthday. *(get)*

15. The wind _____ in from the north. *(blow)*

16. The puppy _____ me my slippers this morning. *(bring)*

17. She _____ a new bike for her son. *(buy)*

18. The orange juice _____ in the ice chest. *(freeze)*

19. He _____ in the rain for twenty minutes. *(stand)*

20. I _____ the baseball and threw it to second base. *(catch)*

Using Irregular Verbs C

7c. An *irregular verb* forms its past and past participle in some other way than by adding *–d* or *–ed* to the base form.

BASE FORM	PRESENT PARTICIPLE	PAST	PAST PARTICIPLE
grow	[is] growing	grew	[have] grown
hold	[is] holding	held	[have] held
cut	[is] cutting	cut	[have] cut
break	[is] breaking	broke	[have] broken

EXERCISE On the blank in each of the following sentences, write the past participle of the verb in parentheses.

Example 1. Has she _____*driven*_____ that far by herself before? *(drive)*

1. She has _____ a lawyer. *(become)*

2. Have they _____ to read their reports yet? *(begin)*

3. I have _____ a new book to read. *(choose)*

4. We have already _____ five laps. *(run)*

5. Has she _____ a letter to her pen pal yet? *(send)*

6. The dog has _____ some food from the table! *(steal)*

7. Have you _____ the book that inspired this movie? *(read)*

8. We have already _____ the movie. *(see)*

9. Have you _____ me your name? *(tell)*

10. I think I have _____ my keys. *(lose)*

11. Bill has _____ two inches since I last saw him. *(grow)*

12. Have the team members _____ their warm-up laps yet? *(swim)*

13. She has _____ the same bus for three years. *(ride)*

14. I have _____ many times while ice-skating. *(fall)*

15. The teacher has _____ the sketch already. *(draw)*

16. Vivian has _____ away her old clothes. *(give)*

17. Have you _____ to your mother yet? *(write)*

18. Has Mrs. Carter _____ to the class today? *(speak)*

19. The man has _____ his shirt on the fence. *(tear)*

20. We have _____ this song in choir many times. *(sing)*

Using Irregular Verbs D

7c.   An *irregular verb* forms its past and past participle in some other way than by adding *–d* or *–ed* to the base form.

BASE FORM	PRESENT PARTICIPLE	PAST	PAST PARTICIPLE
tear	[is] tearing	tore	[have] torn
freeze	[is] freezing	froze	[have] frozen
know	[is] knowing	knew	[have] known
get	[is] getting	got	[have] gotten *or* got

EXERCISE A   For each of the following sentences, write the correct form of the verb in parentheses.

Example 1. The sixth-graders have _____*eaten*_____ lunch already. *(eat)*

1. Franco and Marc have _____ each other for two years. *(know)*

2. They _____ best friends in the fourth grade. *(become)*

3. Franco _____ attending the school that year. *(begin)*

4. Marc has _____ to the same school since first grade. *(go)*

5. He has _____ the bus to school every year. *(ride)*

6. One day, he _____ a new student on the bus. *(see)*

7. The boy _____ that his name was Franco. *(say)*

8. The two boys have also _____ many movies together. *(see)*

9. They _____ to six movies last summer. *(go)*

10. Franco's mother _____ them to the movies. *(drive)*

EXERCISE B   For each of the following sentences, write the correct form of the verb in parentheses.

Example 1. The two brothers have _____*left*_____ the house already. *(leave)*

11. The pitcher _____ a no-hitter yesterday. *(throw)*

12. Have you ever _____ a cowboy hat? *(wear)*

13. The *Titanic* had _____ by the time the rescue boats arrived. *(sink)*

14. After practice, they _____ us to dinner. *(take)*

15. The cartoon character had _____ to the size of a mouse. *(shrink)*

Using Irregular Verbs E

7c. An **irregular verb** forms its past and past participle in some other way than by adding –*d* or –*ed* to the base form.

BASE FORM	PRESENT PARTICIPLE	PAST	PAST PARTICIPLE
leave	[is] leaving	left	[have] left
stand	[is] standing	stood	[have] stood

EXERCISE A   For each of the following sentences, underline the correct form of the verb in parentheses.

Example 1. The girls have (*went*, *gone*) camping twice before.

1. Sue and Imelda (*drive*, *drove*) to the mountains last summer.

2. The same guides (*lead*, *led*) the expedition last year.

3. Imelda has (*went*, *gone*) to the mountains many times.

4. She has (*saw*, *seen*) the sunset from atop the mountains.

5. Sue and Imelda (*chose*, *chosen*) to go hiking.

6. They (*began*, *begun*) their hike near their campsite.

7. Sue has (*run*, *ran*) long distances and is in good physical shape.

8. However, Imelda (*find*, *found*) the hike difficult.

9. Evening (*drew*, *drawn*) near, and they were both very tired.

10. Sue and Imelda (*fell*, *fallen*) asleep beneath the stars.

EXERCISE B   For each of the following sentences, write the correct form of the verb in parentheses.

Example 1. When comets _____*get*_____ close to the sun, they begin to evaporate. (*get*)

11. In the past, some people _____ that comets were signs of bad things to come. (*feel*)

12. People have not always _____ what comets really are. (*know*)

13. Scientists have _____ many articles about comets. (*write*)

14. Long ago, people _____ pictures of the mysterious comets they had seen. (*draw*)

15. At that time many people _____ that comets foretold wars or plagues. (*say*)

16. Today scientists _____ much more than they used to about comets. (*know*)

17. For example, scientists have _____ that comets contain ice and rock. (*teach*)

18. Many people have _____ of Hale-Bopp, one of the brightest comets ever seen. (*hear*)

19. Comets _____ long tails that people can see from Earth. (*have*)

20. Many people _____ these magnificent celestial objects to be quite interesting. (*find*)

Language and Sentence Skills Practice

Identifying Tense

7d.   The *tense* of a verb indicates the time of the action or the state of being that is expressed by the verb.

PRESENT	The boy **runs.**	**PRESENT PERFECT**	The boy **has run.**
PAST	The boy **ran.**	**PAST PERFECT**	The boy **had run.**
FUTURE	The boy **will run.**	**FUTURE PERFECT**	The boy **will have run.**

Each of the six tenses also has a form called the *progressive form.*

EXAMPLE   The boy **is running.** [present progressive]

EXERCISE   On the line provided before each of the following sentences, write the tense of the underlined verb *(present, past, future, present perfect, past perfect, future perfect).* Also indicate whether the tense is in the progressive form.

Example   _*present perfect progressive*_   **1.** Jenny has been learning how to use the computer.

_____ **1.** Jenny had never used graphics software on the computer.

_____ **2.** She was writing a report about the Ohio River.

_____ **3.** Jenny wanted photographs in her report.

_____ **4.** She has been taking many pictures of the Ohio River.

_____ **5.** Jenny has scanned the photographs with the new scanner.

_____ **6.** She uses a viewer program to look at the photographs.

_____ **7.** The new software helps Jenny modify the photographs.

_____ **8.** Jenny now knows how to make changes to her pictures.

_____ **9.** Jenny had taken one of the photographs at sunset.

_____ **10.** The picture was too dark.

_____ **11.** Jenny was using the software to change the photo.

_____ **12.** The software allows the user to brighten the photograph.

_____ **13.** Jenny made the photo lighter and clearer.

_____ **14.** Jenny had taken a photograph of the bank of the Ohio River.

_____ **15.** She wanted to use only a small portion of the photo.

_____ **16.** Jenny cropped the photo using the new software.

_____ **17.** Jenny had photographed birds with her zoom lens.

_____ **18.** She has always loved pictures of birds in flight.

_____ **19.** She will use the software to zoom in on the birds.

_____ **20.** Jenny will have improved her photographs.

Using Tense Consistently

| **7e.** | Do not change needlessly from one tense to another. |

To write about events that take place at about the same time, use verbs in the same tense. To write about events that occur at different times, use verbs in different tenses.

| INCONSISTENT | The squirrel stuffed the pecan into its mouth and scampers up the tree. [The events happened at about the same time, but *stuffed* is in the past tense, and *scampers* is in the present tense.] |
| CONSISTENT | The squirrel **stuffed** the pecan into its mouth and **scampered** up the tree. [Both verbs are in the past tense.] |

EXERCISE Underline the correct form of the verb in parentheses in each of the following sentences.

Example 1. Jaime made a sandwich and (*puts*, <u>*put*</u>) it in his lunchbox.

1. Every morning they got up early and (*run, ran*).

2. She wrote a letter and (*sends, sent*) it to her grandmother.

3. I have eaten and (*drank, drunk*) too much today.

4. The armadillo ran across the yard and (*hides, hid*) behind a log.

5. The sun rose and the sky (*turns, turned*) pink.

6. Every autumn the leaves turn brown and (*fall, fell*) off the trees.

7. The river flows down the valley and (*empties, emptied*) into the lake.

8. The wind changed directions and (*becomes, became*) stronger.

9. The volcano erupted and (*destroys, destroyed*) the tiny island.

10. A robin catches worms and (*feeds, fed*) her young.

11. The nurses checked on their patients and (*give, gave*) them their medicine.

12. All of the students studied hard and (*learn, learned*) the material.

13. The puppets sang and (*dance, danced*) to the music.

14. One of the horses kicked the fence and (*runs, ran*) toward the woods.

15. The skater tripped and (*falls, fell*) on the ice.

16. Have you read the book and (*discuss, discussed*) it with the teacher?

17. The violinist listens carefully and (*imitates, imitated*) her teacher.

18. The kitten hides under the bed and (*sleeps, slept*).

19. Last night the wind blew hard and (*knocks, knocked*) down the fence.

20. The rider got off her horse and (*removes, removed*) the saddle.

Using *Sit* and *Set*

The verb *sit* means "to be seated" or "to rest." *Sit* seldom takes a direct object. The verb *set* means "to put (something) in a place." *Set* usually takes a direct object.

BASE FORM	PRESENT PARTICIPLE	PAST	PAST PARTICIPLE
sit	[is] sitting	sat	[have] sat
set	[is] setting	set	[have] set

EXAMPLES Harry **will sit** in the front row. [no direct object]

Harry **will set** the tools on the bench. [*Tools* is the direct object.]

The children **have sat** down. [no direct object]

The children **have set** their books there. [*Books* is the direct object.]

EXERCISE A Underline the correct form of the verb in parentheses in each of the following sentences.

Example 1. She (sat, *set*) the crystal bowl on the end table.

1. The woman (sit, sat) on the bench.

2. The children are (sitting, setting) the puzzle pieces on the table.

3. Have you (sat, set) the table yet?

4. She had (sat, set) in the waiting room for thirty minutes.

5. We (sat, set) the cactus beside the window.

6. I will (sit, set) your trophy on the top shelf.

7. The men (sat, set) down after a hard day's work.

8. A large gray cat is (sitting, setting) on top of the piano.

9. That boy (sits, sets) in the desk next to mine.

10. My aunt had (sat, set) the aquarium on the large table.

EXERCISE B Write the correct form of either *sit* or *set* on the blank provided in each of the following sentences.

Example 1. I wish I hadn't _____ *sat* _____ on the cactus!

11. Mom always _____ her glasses down somewhere and then can't find them.

12. The dog is _____ underneath the porch where it is cool.

13. I _____ still during the entire three hours of the opera.

14. _____ down that backpack and rest for a while.

15. No one could believe that Carol had been _____ near the dog the entire time.

Using *Rise* and *Raise*

The verb *rise* means "to go up" or "to get up." *Rise* does not take a direct object. The verb *raise* means "to lift (something) up" or "to cause (something) to rise." *Raise* usually takes a direct object.

BASE FORM	PRESENT PARTICIPLE	PAST	PAST PARTICIPLE
rise	[is] rising	rose	[have] risen
raise	[is] raising	raised	[have] raised

EXAMPLES   The president **rose** for her speech. [no direct object]

The dog **raised** its head and yawned. [*Head* is the direct object.]

Throughout the day the temperature **has risen.** [no direct object]

The pilot **has raised** the lever. [*Lever* is the direct object.]

EXERCISE A   Underline the correct form of the verb in parentheses in each of the following sentences.

Example 1. He *(rose, raised)* early in the morning and made oatmeal.

1. The guard *(rose, raised)* the flag every morning at sunrise.

2. Is the city *(rising, raising)* its property taxes again?

3. The farmers *(rise, raise)* early in the morning.

4. Have they *(risen, raised)* prices?

5. A student in the second row quickly *(rose, raised)* his hand.

6. Has she *(risen, raised)* from bed yet?

7. The balloon slowly *(rises, raises)* as the air heats up.

8. The bread dough is *(rising, raising)* in the pan.

9. The sun *(rose, raised)* above the horizon.

10. The landlord *(rose, raised)* the rent earlier this year.

EXERCISE B   Write the correct form of either *rise* or *raise* on the blank provided in each of the following sentences.

Example 1. Whoever climbs the hill first will ___*raise*___ the flag.

11. My grades have _____ a little each semester.

12. Chi _____ her hand to wave goodbye.

13. My father jokes that he _____ at dawn each morning and walked ten miles to school.

14. The tale was so scary that the hairs on the back of her neck _____.

15. Have you ever _____ a young animal?

Language and Sentence Skills Practice

Using *Lie* and *Lay*

The verb *lie* generally means "to recline," "to be in a place," or "to remain lying down." *Lie* does not take a direct object. The verb *lay* generally means "to put (something) down" or "to place (something)." *Lay* usually takes a direct object.

BASE FORM	PRESENT PARTICIPLE	PAST	PAST PARTICIPLE
lie	[is] lying	lay	[have] lain
lay	[is] laying	laid	[have] laid

EXAMPLES The baby **lay** in the crib. [no direct object]

The father **laid** the baby in the crib. [*Baby* is the direct object.]

His coat **is lying** on the floor. [no direct object]

He **is laying** his coat on the floor. [*Coat* is the direct object.]

EXERCISE A Underline the correct form of the verb in parentheses in each of the following sentences.

Example 1. Memphis *(lies, lays)* on the Mississippi River.

1. Please *(lie, lay)* the box on the table.

2. The fawn *(lay, laid)* down in the undergrowth.

3. She must have *(lain, laid)* her house keys on the dresser.

4. Does the mountain range *(lie, lay)* in the eastern part of the country?

5. The woman *(lay, laid)* on the hot sand and fell asleep.

6. The bike was *(lying, laying)* in the middle of the driveway.

7. Does your dog always *(lie, lay)* its head on your foot?

8. Every night this week, the cat has *(lain, laid)* on the piano bench to sleep.

9. She *(lay, laid)* the blanket across the foot of the bed.

10. I have *(lain, laid)* here in the grass all morning.

EXERCISE B Write the correct form of either *lie* or *lay* on the blank provided in each of the following sentences.

Example 1. Sam _____*laid*_____ her head on the desk.

11. When she left, the key was still _____ on the table.

12. Greg has _____ in the hammock all afternoon.

13. Before I pack, I always _____ all my clothes out on the bed.

14. The storm had _____ a blanket of snow over the fields.

15. The workers have been _____ sod all afternoon.

HOLT HANDBOOK | Introductory Course

Six Confusing Verbs

SIT, SET	*Sit* means "to be seated" or "to rest." *Sit* seldom takes a direct object.
	Set means "to put (something) in a place." *Set* usually takes a direct object.
RISE, RAISE	*Rise* means "to go up" or "to get up." *Rise* does not take a direct object.
	Raise means "to lift (something) up." *Raise* usually takes a direct object.
LIE, LAY	*Lie* means "to recline," "to be in a place," or "to remain lying down." *Lie* does not take a direct object.
	Lay means "to put (something) down" or "to place (something)." *Lay* usually takes a direct object.

EXERCISE Underline the verb in parentheses that correctly completes each of the following sentences.

Example 1. The conga drums are (*lying*, *laying*) on the floor.

1. Juana (*sit*, *set*) the table for dinner.

2. Carl, please (*rise*, *raise*) the blinds.

3. Every afternoon Uncle Angelo (*lies*, *lays*) down for a short nap.

4. After he (*lay*, *laid*) the board on the sawhorses, Aaron carefully sawed it in half.

5. We forgot to add the yeast, and the dough didn't (*raise*, *rise*).

6. Rebecca was (*sitting*, *setting*) on the front steps to wait for her friends.

7. The reporters have (*risen*, *raised*) some interesting questions.

8. That book has (*laid*, *lain*) on that shelf ever since I can remember.

9. I think you have been (*laying*, *lying*) in the sun too long.

10. Cody (*set*, *sat*) down with a plop and a deep sigh.

11. I have been (*sitting*, *setting*) here for thirty minutes.

12. People usually (*raise*, *rise*) when the national anthem is played.

13. Parvati thought she had (*lain*, *laid*) the book on the counter, but it wasn't there.

14. Grandpa is (*lying*, *laying*) on the living room couch, watching the football game.

15. The kite (*rose*, *raised*) quickly in the brisk wind.

16. The baker had carefully (*sit*, *set*) the loaves on the counter.

17. A slight mist has (*raised*, *risen*) over the meadow.

18. A strange metal object was (*laying*, *lying*) in the cornfield.

19. He (*sit*, *set*) the clock for 6:00 A.M.

20. The public (*rose*, *raised*) many objections to the mayor's latest plan.

Review A: **Using Regular and Irregular Verb Forms**

EXERCISE A   For each of the following sentences, choose the correct form (present participle, past, or past participle) of the regular verb given in parentheses. Write the correct verb form on the line provided.

Example 1. Has Felicia _____*started*_____ her sketches for art class? (*start*)

1. The audience _____ with laughter at the opening scene. (*roar*)

2. The curators are _____ old farm tools for the exhibit. (*collect*)

3. Latisha is _____ the directions carefully. (*follow*)

4. I had _____ to pick up milk on my way home. (*plan*)

5. Alexander _____ lemonade on the patio yesterday. (*serve*)

6. Hamilton is _____ the fliers for the show. (*create*)

7. Many farmers have _____ against the new tax laws. (*rebel*)

8. Before moving here, we _____ in Wichita, Kansas. (*live*)

9. Many pioneers _____ west by boat and wagon train. (*travel*)

10. Is Dr. Cullar _____ into a new office? (*move*)

EXERCISE B   For each of the following sentences, decide on the correct form (past or past participle) of the irregular verb given in parentheses. Write the correct verb form on the line provided.

Example 1. Has anyone _____*heard*_____ any news about the hurricane? (*hear*)

11. Have you _____ tomorrow's math assignment? (*do*)

12. At the track meet, Judy _____ the record for the 50-yard dash. (*break*)

13. Some leaves have already _____ from the trees. (*fall*)

14. Coretta has _____ to research her topic at the library. (*go*)

15. The concert has not _____ yet. (*begin*)

16. Larry _____ lunch for the whole football team. (*make*)

17. The committee has _____ a patriotic theme for the February party. (*choose*)

18. On Sunday, our family _____ to the lake for a picnic. (*drive*)

19. She has _____ her knee on the corner of the desk. (*hurt*)

20. Has anyone _____ my running shoes? (*see*)

Review B: Tense

EXERCISE A   On the line provided before each of the following sentences, write the tense of the verb (*present, present perfect, past, past perfect, future,* or *future perfect*). Also indicate whether the tense is in the progressive form.

Example ___*present perfect progressive*___ **1.** Has Jutaro's family been planning a trip to Japan?

_____ **1.** Jutaro's family moved here from Japan last year.

_____ **2.** His father has been working for a railroad.

_____ **3.** At the open house, the entire family bowed to us.

_____ **4.** They always show traditional Japanese hospitality.

_____ **5.** I have tried sushi and teriyaki at their house.

_____ **6.** Have Japanese children always gone to school on Saturday?

_____ **7.** Summer vacation in Japanese schools will last only six weeks this year.

_____ **8.** On special occasions, Japanese women sometimes wear kimonos.

_____ **9.** In just a few weeks, Jutaro and his family will have been in the United States exactly one year.

_____ **10.** Will they be celebrating the anniversary?

EXERCISE B   On the line provided in each sentence, write the form of the verb described in parentheses.

Example 1. Some Chinese citizens ___*have struggled*___ for greater freedom. (present perfect of *struggle*)

11. In June 1989, Chinese troops _____ their tanks into Tiananmen Square in Beijing, China. (past tense of *drive*)

12. Chinese students _____ a pro-democracy demonstration. (past perfect of *begin*)

13. Soon shots _____ out, and people fled the square. (past tense of *ring*)

14. Throughout history, people _____ to speak out against unfair government practices. (present perfect of *choose*)

15. By the time the school year ends, my history class _____ several of these struggles for freedom and justice. (future perfect of *study*)

Review C: Writing Correct Verb Forms

EXERCISE For each of the following sentences, decide on the correct form (present participle, past, or past participle) of the verb in parentheses. Write the correct verb form on the line provided.

Example 1. Rosalinda has never _____*ridden*_____ on the trolley. *(ride)*

1. I have often _____ of becoming a great writer. *(dream)*

2. What have you _____ Jeremy for his birthday? *(buy)*

3. I _____ two glasses of orange juice at breakfast today. *(drink)*

4. Weren't you _____ to help me wash the dishes? *(suppose)*

5. Abdul is _____ today on the afternoon train. *(arrive)*

6. Their new boat had _____ in six feet of water. *(sink)*

7. Generations have _____ wood and food from the rain forests. *(take)*

8. Kam Shing _____ with a local ballet company. *(dance)*

9. The canal has _____, and the ferry can't get through. *(freeze)*

10. Our new puppy is _____ my English paper to shreds. *(chew)*

11. In one year my little brother has _____ two inches. *(grow)*

12. We _____ tropical fish in the warm waters surrounding the island. *(see)*

13. Have you _____ to your parents about the field trip? *(speak)*

14. The boys have _____ a surprise for us. *(plan)*

15. Teresa has _____ the smallest piece of chicken. *(choose)*

16. For three years, Sam Houston _____ in a Cherokee village. *(live)*

17. Someone _____ all the leftover sandwiches last night. *(eat)*

18. As soon as she got it, Haru _____ half of her allowance in the bank. *(put)*

19. What has _____ to your homework paper? *(happen)*

20. Is he _____ to hunt and fish as they did? *(learn)*

21. Last year my aunt _____ to South Africa. *(go)*

22. Yesterday someone on the radio _____ a song about Brazil. *(sing)*

23. Collectors once _____ many parrots into this country. *(bring)*

24. Mrs. Bishop and her husband are _____ a bakery downtown. *(open)*

25. Years ago, no one _____ how important the rain forests were. *(know)*

Review D: **Using Correct Verb Forms**

EXERCISE A Underline the verb form in parentheses that correctly completes each sentence.

Example 1. While Mom mixed the dressing, I *(lay, laid)* the tablecloth on the table.

1. I *(lose, lost)* the first race but won the next.

2. Yesterday the wind *(blew, blown)* so hard we could not sail.

3. Have the salmon always *(swam, swum)* in this river?

4. Where did Jerome *(sit, set)* his locker key?

5. After the sun had *(rose, risen)*, everyone felt better.

6. Grandfather *(lay, laid)* out a pair of clean pants for you.

7. Thank you, but I have already *(ate, eaten)* lunch.

8. After a short rest, we *(rose, raised)* and walked back into the jungle.

9. My mother and stepfather have always *(gave, given)* me good advice.

10. After splitting the logs, the farmer *(sat, set)* his ax on the ground.

EXERCISE B For each of the following sentences, decide on the correct form (present participle, past, or past participle) of the verb given in parentheses. Write the correct verb form on the line provided.

Example 1. I have not yet _____*written*_____ my book report. *(write)*

11. It was so cold that the water in the fountain had _____. *(freeze)*

12. Masato's bike has _____ on the sidewalk all day. *(lie)*

13. That old inflatable raft _____ last summer. *(burst)*

14. Someone has _____ on the freshly painted bench. *(sit)*

15. Randy _____ to see the seals at feeding time. *(go)*

16. Sheila has never _____ a mountain bike. *(ride)*

17. Last spring Urbi and Joe _____ every morning. *(swim)*

18. Neither sister had _____ a warm sweater to the game. *(bring)*

19. After a late night of studying, my cousin _____ just before noon. *(rise)*

20. Has the rider been _____ off the horse? *(throw)*

Language and Sentence Skills Practice

USAGE

for **CHAPTER 7: USING VERBS CORRECTLY** | *pages 147–68*

Proofreading Application: Lab Report

Readers admire and trust writing that is error-free. Make sure that you correct all errors in grammar, usage, spelling, and punctuation in your writing. Your readers will have more confidence in your words if you have done your best to proofread carefully.

Many times in school and later at work, you will need to describe a series of events. Whenever you describe a series of events, pay particular attention to the verbs you use. These verbs must be correct in form and in tense. If they are not, your description will not make sense. Your readers will not be sure what happened first and what happened second.

PROOFREADING ACTIVITY

The following excerpt from a science lab report contains several errors in verb usage. Find and correct these errors, using proofreading symbols to make your corrections.

Example Our team ᴧ~~choose~~ *chose* a biology experiment.

We taked bean seeds and planted them in three trays with soil and water. We putted one tray (X) in the freezer. However, we had gave the other two trays (Y and Z) a place in a warm closet. After two days, we seen that trays Y and Z all had seedlings. We maked a place in the freezer for tray Y and its tiny seedlings.

After five days, we will bring all the trays out. Apparently, the seeds in tray X had froze and had not grown at all. In tray Y, too much cold had hurted the growth of the seedlings. The growing seedlings had shrank. However, tray Z in the warm closet done quite well.

for **CHAPTER 7: USING VERBS CORRECTLY**   pages 160–61

Literary Model: Using Verb Tenses in Poetry

Legacy II
by Leroy V. Quintana

Grandfather never went to school
spoke only a few words of English,
a quiet man; when he talked
talked about simple things

planting corn or about the weather
sometimes about herding sheep as a
   child.
One day pointed to the four directions
taught me their names

         El Norte

Poniente   Oriente

     El Sur

He spoke their names as if they were
one of only a handful of things
a man needed to know

Now I look back
only two generations removed
realize I am nothing but a poor fool
who went to college

trying to find my way back
to the center of the world
where Grandfather stood
that day

EXERCISE A   In this poem the speaker uses the verbs *went, spoke, talked, pointed, taught,* and *stood* to tell you about someone and about various things that person did.

1. In what tense are these verbs?

_____

2. Who is it that went, spoke, talked, pointed, taught, and stood?

_____

3. In the last two stanzas of the poem, the speaker uses the verbs *look, realize,* and *am* to tell you about someone other than Grandfather. In what tense are these verbs?

_____

4. Who is it that looks, realizes, and is?

_____

EXERCISE B   Why do you think the author uses both past tense and present tense in the poem?

_____

_____

"Legacy II" by Leroy V. Quintana from *The Face of Poetry*, edited by L. H. Clark and Mary MacArthur. Copyright © 1979 by **Leroy V. Quintana.** Reprinted by permission of the author.

Literary Model (continued)

EXERCISE C   Using the above poem as a model, write a poem using the past tense to tell about one person and the present tense to tell about another person.

_____

_____

_____

_____

_____

_____

_____

_____

_____

_____

_____

_____

_____

_____

_____

_____

_____

_____

_____

EXERCISE D   How would it affect the meaning of your poem if you rewrote it entirely in the present tense? entirely in the past tense?

_____

_____

_____

_____

_____

Writing Application: Newspaper Article

Before you begin writing, you will want to think about your readers. Why are they reading what you have written? Readers of newspaper articles usually want to know what happened. In order to answer this question, you will need to use verbs correctly to describe the actions and states of being and to show the sequence of events.

WRITING ACTIVITY

Writers and speakers can't avoid irregular verbs because they describe so many daily happenings. For instance, many verbs describing motion, such as *go, run, fly, drive,* and *swim,* are irregular, as are many verbs that describe states of being, such as *be, become,* and *feel.* Imagine that you are a reporter writing about a school event. Write a short article of two paragraphs to be published in the school paper. Use five irregular verbs to describe states of being and actions that occurred during the event.

PREWRITING   First, you must choose an event to cover. Any event will do: A sports match, chess tournament, much-anticipated schoolwide standardized test, or musical concert are just a few possibilities. If the event has not happened yet, plan to attend and take notes on what you see. If it has already occurred, recall as clearly as you can the details of the event. Either way, answer these well-known reporter's questions: What? Who? Where? When? Why? How?

WRITING   Journalistic writing is brief and to the point. It often reports events chronologically, beginning with the first action and working through to the final event. Organize the facts and details you have gathered so that they cover the event quickly, while providing the information readers need. Since you are writing two paragraphs, you will have to find a logical point in the action to stop the first paragraph and begin the second. Is there a turning point in the action of the event?

REVISING   Ask a couple of friends who also attended the event to read your article. Can they remember anything that you left out? Have you used five irregular verbs as you reported on the event? Check the list of irregular verb forms. Have you used the correct forms?

PUBLISHING   Before you go public with your article, check the paragraphs for mistakes in spelling and punctuation. Ask the teacher who sponsors the newspaper what form you should use to submit your article, and follow his or her guidelines. Post your article on the class bulletin board or Web page.

EXTENDING YOUR WRITING

This exercise could lead to a more developed writing project. You could expand your reporting on the event to a full-page article. Combine the article with pictures of the event, and submit this photo essay as a one- or two-page spread in your school's yearbook. A yearbook is a much more permanent form of publication than a newspaper, so make it your best writing!

Choices: Pronouns in Everyday Life

Here's your chance to step out of the grammar book and into the real world. You may not notice pronouns, but you and the people around you use them every day. The following activities challenge you to find a connection between pronouns and the world around you. Do the activity below that suits your personality best, and then share your discoveries with your class. Have fun!

Inventing Sentences

Create a pronoun activity for your class—all you'll need is a pen, a few sheets of paper, and a shoe box. To create the activity, make a small paper strip for each of the subject and object pronouns, and put the strips in the shoe box. To start, a student draws a strip of paper from the box. After reading the pronoun written on the paper, the student goes to the chalkboard or overhead projector and writes a sentence that correctly uses the pronoun. In class, guess who gets to be the first volunteer? That's right—you.

The Hit Parade

Which pronoun is most popular in ordinary conversation? With permission, tape-record two or three conversations. Then, count the number of personal pronouns used. Which personal pronoun is used the most often in your experiment? Which ones are most often used incorrectly? Which ones are most often used correctly? Present the class with an organized visual that displays your results. Present, too, your opinions on why you obtained these results.

All Women Are Created Equal

Does writing *he or she* after an antecedent like *everyone* seem to be a lot of trouble to you? Maybe it just seems silly. When you are among those excluded by sexist language, though, such language is no joke. Rewrite the first half of the second paragraph of the Declaration of Independence. Change all the male references to female references. Read your revision to the class. Then, lead a discussion with your classmates about their reactions to the revision.

Close Examination

Before you put your trust in a computer's grammar checker, put the computer to the test. Take ten sentences with pronoun errors, and type them into a word processor. Then, run the grammar checker. How did it do? Did it find that sentence where *Steve* is referred to as *she*? Keep a detailed record of the grammar checker's performance, and report back to the class.

Pronouns in Print

Do you have any magazines or newspapers lying around your house or classroom? Well, it's time to get them out and start a pronoun search. Collect ten sentences that use pronouns and display them for the class. Paste your sentences onto poster board, using actual pages or photocopies. Don't forget to record your sources. Do any of the sentences use pronouns incorrectly? Here's your chance to catch someone else's mistakes!

Ella y Él

How do other languages handle pronouns? Do other languages have subject, object, and possessive pronouns? Are second- and third-person singular and plural forms used? Do more formal situations call for different pronoun uses than informal ones do? How are these or other rules handled in, say, Spanish? Explore pronoun use in the language of your choice, and be sure to discover at least three pronoun rules. When presenting your findings, you may want to let the class know which language's rules you think are easier to learn.

Forms of Personal Pronouns

The form of a personal pronoun shows how it can be used in a sentence. Pronouns used as subjects and predicate nominatives are in the *subject form* (*I, you, he, she, it, we, they*).

EXAMPLES   **She** and **I** sang two solos. [subjects]

The best singer was **she.** [predicate nominative]

Pronouns used as direct objects, indirect objects, and objects of prepositions are in the *object form* (*me, you, him, her, it, us, them*).

EXAMPLES   The audience applauded **her** and **me.** [direct objects]

Friends sent **her** flowers. [indirect object]

Marion gave a flower to **me.** [object of a preposition]

Possessive forms of pronouns (*my, mine, your, yours, his, her, hers, its, their, theirs, our, ours*) are used to show ownership or possession.

EXAMPLES   Ruben saved **his** ticket stub.

Is that **yours**?

EXERCISE A   Identify the form of each of the following personal pronouns. On the line provided, write *SUB* for *subject form,* *OBJ* for *object form,* or *POS* for *possessive form.*

Example 1. me _____*OBJ*_____

1. your _____   **6.** we _____

2. I _____   **7.** its _____

3. us _____   **8.** mine _____

4. she _____   **9.** them _____

5. him _____   **10.** they _____

EXERCISE B   Read each of the following sentences and identify the form of the underlined pronoun. Above each pronoun, write *SUB* for *subject form,* *OBJ* for *object form,* or *POS* for *possessive form.*

Example 1. The hero of today's game was <u>she</u>.   *SUB*

11. During the safety drill, the captain threw <u>them</u> life jackets.

12. <u>I</u> screamed loudly and then jumped for joy.

13. Did <u>they</u> search for gold all month?

14. <u>His</u> beard and eyebrows were flecked with gray hairs.

15. The cheers and applause, which came suddenly, pleased <u>her</u>.

USAGE

Using the Subject Form A

8a. Use the subject form for a pronoun that is the subject of a verb.

EXAMPLES   **He** studied for a test. [*He* is the subject of *studied*.]
Ed noticed that **she** and **I** agreed. [*She* and *I* are the subjects of *agreed*.]

8b. Use the subject form for a pronoun that is a predicate nominative.

EXAMPLES   The most confused person was **I**. [*I* is the predicate nominative of *was*.]
Are the best students **he** and **she**? [*He* and *she* are the predicate nominatives of *Are*.]

EXERCISE A   Underline the correct pronoun in parentheses in each of the following sentences.

Example 1. The first speakers will probably be LaShawn and (*I, me*).

 1. Did Shani and (*they, them*) watch the Dragon Boat Races in Naha, Japan?

 2. The people who had the most fun at the basketball game were (*they, them*).

 3. Later, my friends and (*I, me*) went to Moon Beach.

 4. After planning for weeks, (*we, us*) drove to the amusement park.

 5. Actually, those people in the photograph are (*we, us*).

 6. Taking advantage of the weather, Daryl and (*I, me*) took a long walk on the beach.

 7. My two closest friends from camp are Melissa and (*he, him*).

 8. (*They, Them*) and (*I, me*) go everywhere together.

 9. At the movie theater, the first ones in the ticket line were (*they, them*).

10. Was that really (*she, her*) in the mouse costume?

EXERCISE B   In each of the following sentences, cross out the underlined word or words and write an appropriate pronoun in the space above.

Example 1. Do Diego and ~~Janet~~ often sing together? *she*

11. The soldiers saddled their horses at once.

12. Before the race, Kara and her brother warmed up.

13. The owner of that cat is Davie or Susan.

14. Was that Clara and Salim in the black truck?

15. After lunch, Dad and my sister and I headed to the lake.

USAGE

Using the Subject Form B

| **8a.** | Use the subject form for a pronoun that is the subject of a verb. |

> **EXAMPLES** Does **he** want to try again?
>
> **She** and **we** would like to thank you.

| **8b.** | Use the subject form for a pronoun that is a predicate nominative. |

> **EXAMPLES** The proudest parent was **she.**
>
> The new yearbook photographer will be **he.**

EXERCISE A Cross out each incorrect pronoun in the following sentences. Then, write the correct pronoun above it. If a sentence is already correct, write *C* after the sentence.

Example 1. José, was your favorite elementary schoolteacher ~~him~~? *he*

1. The senders of these flowers were my cousin and me.

2. Mario and us are the best volleyball players.

3. Kendrick and her will be the team captains for the kickball game.

4. The first three chords in the book will be they, according to the guitar teacher.

5. The students who come first alphabetically are Nelson Abbott, Jill Abu-Rayyan, and him.

6. Yes, it is me, your loyal friend.

7. What could we possibly have done to deserve this good fortune?

8. The winner of the debate tournament will likely be him.

9. Was the woman at the next booth really her?

10. The lucky children who get to name our family's new dog will be them.

EXERCISE B Supply a pronoun to correctly complete each of the following sentences. Use a variety of pronouns, but do not use *you* or *it.*

Example 1. Much to their surprise, the first-place finishers were Armando, Shane, and _____*she*_____.

11. Were the first ones up this morning _____?

12. Ever since the first meet, the fastest runners have been Danika, Danielle, and _____.

13. Sometimes, the one with the best ideas is _____.

14. After lunch, _____ get to go on our long-awaited field trip.

15. The cashiers and _____ will have the night off, too.

Language and Sentence Skills Practice

157

Using the Object Form A

| **8c.** | Use the object form for a pronoun that is the direct object of a verb. |

> **EXAMPLES** The trainer helped **me** with my new dog. [*Me* is the direct object of *helped*.]
>
> The gift surprised **them** and **me**. [*Them* and *me* are the direct objects of *surprised*.]

| **8d.** | Use the object form for a pronoun that is the indirect object of a verb. |

> **EXAMPLES** Grandma gave **me** a hug. [*Me* is the indirect object of *gave*.]
>
> Loretta sent **her** and **me** postcards. [*Her* and *me* are the indirect objects of *sent*.]

| **8e.** | Use the object form for a pronoun that is the object of a preposition. |

> **EXAMPLES** Save one for **her**. [*Her* is the object of the preposition *for*.]
>
> Ann sat between **him** and **me**. [*Him* and *me* are the objects of the preposition *between*.]

EXERCISE A Read each of the following sentences and identify the underlined pronoun as *DO* for *direct object,* *IO* for *indirect object,* or *OP* for *object of a preposition.*

Example 1. Did Mother drive Mr. Chung and <u>her</u> to the store?   *DO*

1. I sold Willis and <u>them</u> my baseball cards.

2. The large bean burrito was shared by Lou and <u>her</u>.

3. Fiona will take <u>us</u> to the game.

4. We were thankful that the principal supported Susana and <u>me</u>.

5. The Red Cross worker wrapped a blanket around <u>him</u>.

EXERCISE B Underline the correct pronoun in parentheses in each of the following sentences.

Example 1. Lena will sit between Mother and (*I*, <u>me</u>) at the ceremony.

6. After our fund-raiser, Ms. Goldstein gave (*we, us*) all new uniforms.

7. Did the puppy from the park follow Ralph and (*he, him*) onto the bus?

8. The author read (*we, us*) a chapter of her wonderful new book.

9. The award was certainly a surprise to my family and (*I, me*)!

10. Above Ann and (*I, me*) hung an orange and yellow piñata.

11. The neighbors helped Jeremy and (*they, them*) with the car.

12. Grandmother sent our cousins and (*we, us*) a recipe for tamales.

13. The books for Rhonda and (*she, her*) are on the top shelf.

14. Do you think Dad will buy (*they, them*) all the new school supplies they want?

15. After seeing the report, Mr. Jee praised Ella and (*she, her*).

Using the Object Form B

8c. Use the object form for a pronoun that is the direct object of a verb.

> **EXAMPLE** The praise embarrassed **him** a little. [*Him* is the direct object of *embarrassed*.]

8d. Use the object form for a pronoun that is the indirect object of a verb.

> **EXAMPLE** Suzanne gave **us** a smile and a wink. [*Us* is the indirect object of *gave*.]

8e. Use the object form for a pronoun that is the object of a preposition.

> **EXAMPLE** Is the last helping for **him**? [*Him* is the object of the preposition *for*.]

EXERCISE A Read each of the following sentences and identify the underlined pronoun as *DO* for *direct object,* *IO* for *indirect object,* or *OP* for *object of a preposition.*

Example 1. I cannot believe I lent my favorite jacket to her! *(OP)*

1. The clerk directed them to the back of the store.

2. My birthday gift from Aunt Lulu and him was a new bike helmet.

3. Mr. Lopez gave Beth and me some fresh challah bread.

4. Will you apologize to them or not?

5. Last weekend Shara lent me her softball mitt.

EXERCISE B Supply pronouns to correctly complete the following sentences. Use a variety of pronouns, but do not use *you* or *it.*

Example 1. That photograph was the best image of ____*him*____ that I have seen!

6. After I walked through the door, an usher handed _____ a program for the play.

7. Wouldn't it be great if both of _____ get to be on the same soccer team again this year?

8. As the popcorn kernels started to pop, we watched _____ closely.

9. The audience gave _____ a standing ovation because the performance was magnificent.

10. Because I mowed the neighbors' lawn, they gave _____ enough money to buy a book.

11. The artist at the carnival drew the funniest picture of _____ and _____!

12. My sister won the spelling bee, and I am proud of _____.

13. The wind knocked those tree limbs onto the road, so we will have to drive around _____.

14. What happened to the painting you showed _____ earlier?

15. After Sonia gave _____ the present, the three-year-old boy squealed with delight.

USAGE

USAGE

Subject Form and Object Form Pronouns A

Use the *subject form* (I, you, he, she, it, we, they) for pronouns used as subjects or as predicate nominatives.

EXAMPLES   Did **they** meet you at the game? [subject]

Were the best players **he** and **she**? [predicate nominatives]

Use the *object form* (me, you, him, her, it, us, them) for pronouns that are used as direct objects, indirect objects, or objects of prepositions.

EXAMPLES   The principal thanked **him** and **me** for our help. [direct objects]

The master of ceremonies handed **them** their trophies. [indirect object]

Are those assignments for **them** or **us**? [objects of a preposition]

EXERCISE A   In the following sentences, replace the underlined words or word groups with correct pronouns.

Example   1. As soon as the gun went off, ~~the runners in the race~~ *they* leapt across the starting line.

1. At the park last weekend, both Kendra and Ian flew kites in the city competition.

2. My aunt enjoys cooking homemade lasagna and watching videos with Uncle Marshall and me.

3. My brother, my sister, my parents, and I got to camp at Yosemite National Park.

4. I have decided, Coach, that I would make a great partner for LaTonya in the tournament.

5. When will Jacob and Ginger be ready to turn in their report?

EXERCISE B   In each of the following sentences cross out the incorrect pronoun and write the correct form above it. If a sentence is already correct, write *C*.

Example   1. I was pleased when the quiet little boy offered to share his bread with ~~I~~ *me*.

6. Am I supposed to share this salad with he?

7. That company sends Sharon and I junk mail all the time.

8. Jenae, a talented ballerina, performs onstage even though she is only eleven years old.

9. After my brother and me got into an argument, Mom divided the food between us.

10. Our favorite movie personality is him.

11. The students who stood in line to get good seats are them.

12. His teacher brought Kim and he presents from the class.

13. After looking for fifteen minutes, Tasha found him under the bed.

14. The association hired Ali and she as interns for their outreach program.

15. Are your favorite songs from the soundtrack them?

USAGE

Subject Form and Object Form Pronouns B

Use the *subject form* (*I, you, he, she, it, we, they*) for pronouns used as subjects or as predicate nominatives.

> **EXAMPLES** Are **you** and **I** in charge of the party decorations? [subjects]
>
> The first fifth-grader to kick a home run was **she.** [predicate nominative]

Use the *object form* (*me, you, him, her, it, us, them*) for pronouns used as direct objects, indirect objects, or objects of prepositions.

> **EXAMPLES** I am relieved that I finally found **it.** [direct object]
>
> I will give either Maria or **her** the humorous book. [indirect object]
>
> May I go with **them** to the movie tonight? [object of preposition]

EXERCISE For each of the following sentences, underline the correct form of the pronoun in parentheses. Then, above the pronoun, write *SUB* if it is used as a subject, *PN* if it is used as a predicate nominative, *DO* if it is used as a direct object, *IO* if it is used as an indirect object, or *OP* if it is used as an object of a preposition.

Example 1. Will our summer camp have races, skits, and crafts for my friends and (*I*, <u>*me*</u>)? [*OP*]

1. After searching for five minutes, we found (*he, him*) in the literature section of the bookstore.

2. "Hello? Yes, this is (*she, her*)."

3. When Mia Hamm stole the ball, the crowd gave (*she, her*) a cheer.

4. It was an unknown scientist who discovered (*they, them*) in the ground.

5. Even Martina and (*we, us*) were surprised to hear about a special type of worm that lives in a cave and glows in the dark.

6. The drama club will be giving both Albert and (*I, me*) a prize for winning the dramatic interpretation contest.

7. The three of us who signed up for the computer class are Terry, Jen, and (*I, me*).

8. According to (*they, them*), we will get more snow than we did last year.

9. In *The Wizard of Oz,* she and (*they, them*) will play the flying monkeys.

10. About an hour ago, Mr. Ochoa came in and asked (*we, us*) an important question.

Who and *Whom*

The pronoun *who* has two different forms. *Who* is the subject form. *Whom* is the object form.

> **EXAMPLES** **Who** is that excellent dancer? [subject]
>
> You loaned your favorite book to **whom**? [object of a preposition]

EXERCISE A Underline the correct pronoun in parentheses in each of the following sentences.

Example 1. (Who, <u>Whom</u>) did they choose as their tour guide?

1. (Who, Whom) did you see at Lake Erie?

2. From (who, whom) did you learn about it?

3. (Who, Whom) will rent us a boat here?

4. (Who, Whom) do we give this money to, Georgina?

5. (Who, Whom) can take us on a tour of the lake?

6. (Who, Whom) knows where we can catch fish?

7. Tomorrow, (who, whom) will travel with us to the Island of the Sun?

8. To (who, whom) did you write this morning?

9. (Who, Whom) else will visit the Temple of the Moon?

10. With (who, whom) will you walk to the market?

EXERCISE B On the blank in each of the following sentences, write *who* or *whom* to correctly complete the sentence.

Example 1. ___*Whom*___ will you take to the dance?

11. _____ is that dancer in the blue costume?

12. _____ did you substitute for in the game?

13. _____ wrote *Black Beauty*?

14. Now, for _____ or for what was Michigan named?

15. _____ will you choose as your study partner?

Pronouns with Appositives

Sometimes a pronoun is followed directly by a noun that identifies the pronoun. Such a noun is called an *appositive*. To choose which pronoun to use before an appositive, omit the appositive and try each form of the pronoun separately.

> **EXAMPLE** *(We, Us)* goalies worked hard. [*Goalies* is the appositive identifying the pronoun. *We worked hard* or *Us worked hard*?]
>
> **ANSWER** **We** goalies worked hard.
>
> **EXAMPLE** Mrs. Rollins showed the routine to *(we, us)* dancers. [*Dancers* is the appositive identifying the pronoun. *Mrs. Rollins showed the routine to we* or *Mrs. Rollins showed the routine to us*?]
>
> **ANSWER** Mrs. Rollins showed the routine to **us** dancers.

EXERCISE A Underline the correct pronoun in parentheses in each of the following sentences.

Example 1. The neighbors asked *(we, us)* students for help.

1. At the hospital, *(we, us)* visitors had to wait until 3:00 P.M.

2. Please repeat the question for *(we, us)* students in the back.

3. Our group leader warned *(we, us)* campers about the poison ivy.

4. The happiest group was *(we, us)* lifeguards.

5. At the library, *(we, us)* students used the reference section.

6. Father gave *(we, us)* boys a hand with the boxes.

7. The guide shared some interesting details with *(we, us)* tourists.

8. Ms. Katz gave *(we, us)* three students study guides.

9. *(We, Us)* triplets are used to that question.

10. Mother will drive *(we, us)* fans to the game.

EXERCISE B In each of the following sentences, cross out each incorrect pronoun and write the correct form above it. If a sentence is already correct, write *C* after the sentence.

Example 1. A waitress offered ~~we~~ *us* visitors some sushi.

11. We travelers stayed in several small inns.

12. Mr. Hirota showed we teachers the game of Go.

13. Us plant lovers admired the beautiful garden.

14. After lunch, the host led we visitors around the grounds.

15. Someone left robes for us guests.

USAGE

Review A: **Using Pronouns Correctly**

EXERCISE A   In each of the following sentences, identify the underlined pronoun. Above each underlined pronoun, write *SUB* for *subject*, *PN* for *predicate nominative*, *DO* for *direct object*, *IO* for *indirect object*, or *OP* for *object of a preposition*.

Example 1. The team leaders will be Alicia and $\overset{PN}{\underline{\text{he}}}$.

1. My eyes were straining as I saw <u>him</u> in the crowd.

2. Grandma made Sara and <u>him</u> a quilt.

3. The best-prepared students should be <u>we</u>.

4. Do you know <u>them</u>?

5. Now Ted and <u>they</u> have colds.

6. Ann's father showed <u>her</u> the computer and software.

7. The tent fell on top of <u>us</u>.

8. In the afternoon <u>we</u> mowed the neighbors' lawn.

9. The bus left without Reiko and <u>me</u>.

10. The winners of the essay contest were Alice and <u>he</u>.

EXERCISE B   Underline the correct pronoun in parentheses in each of the following sentences.

Example 1. Please pass the tacos to Sabina and *(she, <u>her</u>)*.

11. My mother gave my sister and *(I, me)* some of Grandmother's jewelry.

12. The first people to speak were Tula and *(I, me)*.

13. Oh, I invited Marta and *(they, them)* to the party.

14. Monica and *(I, me)* enjoyed the film.

15. Please save seats for Rudy and *(she, her)*.

16. The guard asked Ms. Weston and *(we, us)* for identification.

17. The person at the door was not *(he, him)*.

18. On the stage, *(they, them)* all looked very impressive.

19. Melba and *(he, him)* can show you the experiment.

20. Sit here on the beach with the dogs and *(we, us)*.

HOLT HANDBOOK | Introductory Course

USAGE

Review B: **Using Pronouns Correctly**

EXERCISE A Underline the correct pronoun in parentheses in each of the following sentences.

Example 1. Has Tremain or *(he, him)* started the layout for the paper?

1. Uncle Roland will take Rickey and *(he, him)* to school.

2. Was *(she, her)* the person who designed the brightly colored stage decorations?

3. Did Justin and *(they, them)* learn Japanese?

4. Ms. Red Cloud told Edwina and *(we, us)* a fascinating story.

5. A secret agent gave *(she, her)* the message.

6. The teacher and *(we, us)* were working at the computer.

7. The dogs bark at everyone except Elena and *(I, me)*.

8. That woman and *(I, me)* are on the same bowling team.

9. Come and sit between Lonnie and *(I, me)*.

10. It was frustrating when neither Aaron nor *(I, me)* could find a better answer.

EXERCISE B Decide whether the underlined pronoun in each sentence is correct. If the pronoun is not correct, cross it out and write the correct form above it. If the pronoun is correct, write *C* above it.

Example 1. ~~Who~~ *Whom* does Maddie want on her team?

11. Please bring <u>we</u> runners some cool water.

12. From <u>who</u> did you receive that gift?

13. They often give material for costumes to <u>us</u> drama club members.

14. To <u>who</u> shall I give this package?

15. <u>Who</u> knows the answer to that question?

16. <u>Us</u> musicians can practice with them later.

17. The two remaining contestants were <u>we</u> students from Detroit.

18. <u>Whom</u> will you stay with during your vacation?

19. She gave <u>we</u> players our photographs.

20. <u>Who</u> can I ask for help?

Language and Sentence Skills Practice

Review C: **Using Pronouns Correctly**

EXERCISE Underline the correct pronoun in parentheses in each of the following sentences.

Example 1. The officer warned (*we, us*) skaters about thin ice.

1. My parents are proud of Mina and (*we, us*).

2. The wranglers gave (*he, him*) some roping lessons.

3. My sister and (*she, her*) stayed after school.

4. We are responsible for all of (*they, them*).

5. (*We, Us*) Simpsons love this movie.

6. (*Who, Whom*) will you meet at camp?

7. The driver handed (*I, me*) some change.

8. The counselor told (*we, us*) campers to be careful.

9. The winner of the essay contest was (*she, her*).

10. (*Who, Whom*) did you baby-sit for yesterday?

11. Next year, (*we, us*) students will go to the Museum of Natural History.

12. Mrs. Hsing made Lily and (*they, them*) new costumes.

13. The ball landed between Austin and (*I, me*).

14. It was (*she, her*) on the telephone.

15. Trish chose Emilio and (*he, him*) for her team.

16. (*Who, Whom*) wrote this poem about Knoxville, Tennessee?

17. The last soldiers to leave will be (*we, us*) officers.

18. Has anyone told Maya or (*she, her*) about the opera?

19. Eric and (*I, me*) watched his younger brother.

20. The coach was happy with (*we, us*) runners.

21. (*Who, Whom*) should I thank for these tickets?

22. Mr. Feldman showed Alicia and (*I, me*) the answer.

23. Please keep this information between you and (*I, me*).

24. Mr. Yu helped (*we, us*) students in the library.

25. (*Who, Whom*) will you march next to in the parade?

USAGE

for **CHAPTER 8: USING PRONOUNS CORRECTLY**   pages 177–90

Proofreading Application: Captions

Good writers are generally good proofreaders. Readers tend to admire and trust writing that is error-free. Make sure that you correct all errors in grammar, usage, spelling, and punctuation in your writing. Your readers will have more confidence in your words if you have done your best to proofread carefully.

Multimedia presentations offer a whole new way for students to express themselves. Photographs and illustrations can easily be scanned into a computer and captioned. When you do create a photo essay, cartoon, or electronic slide show, the captions that you write will stand out. One or two sentences will stand alone, often in large, boldface type. Proofreading these captions is especially important because they are highly visible.

Your captions will explain the action in the illustrations. Be particularly careful to use pronouns correctly when you write these captions. Incorrect pronoun usage will make readers wonder if the other information in the caption is incorrect as well.

PROOFREADING ACTIVITY

Find and correct the errors in pronoun usage. Use proofreading symbols to make your corrections.

Example   Lisa, Jerry, and ~~me~~ *I* go to see the mayor.

We meet her secretary and she.

Lisa explains to a council member and they the problems of student bus riders.

The mayor and them listen carefully.

Jerry and I give the mayor and they our letters.

The mayor asks Lisa and I a question or two.

Who will they listen to?

Whom is having a problem with the bus schedules?

The bus schedules could be more convenient for we students.

Thanks to the mayor and them, us students will not be late for school any more.

The answer to our problem was the mayor and him.

Language and Sentence Skills Practice

Literary Model: Poetry

Petals
by Pat Mora

have calloused her hands,
brightly colored crepe paper: turquoise,
yellow, magenta, which she shapes
into large blooms for bargain-hunting tourists
5 who see her flowers, her puppets, her baskets,
but not her—small, gray-haired woman
wearing a white apron, who hides behind
blossoms in her stall at the market;
who sits and remembers collecting wildflowers
10 as a girl, climbing rocky Mexican hills
to fill a straw hat with soft blooms
which she'd stroke gently, over and over again
with her smooth fingertips.

EXERCISE A   Write each personal pronoun that appears in the poem, even if it is repeated. After each pronoun, indicate the line in which it appears. Then, identify each pronoun as a *subject form*, an *object form*, or a *possessive form*.

_____

_____

_____

_____

_____

_____

EXERCISE B   The author has included personal pronouns without ever actually identifying the person to whom those pronouns are referring (called the antecedent). Why do you think she used this technique?

_____

_____

_____

_____

Literary Model (continued)

EXERCISE C   Using Mora's poem as a model, write a short poem about a person or animal that interests you—for example, a gymnast competing in a meet or a wolf howling in the woods. Be sure that your poem, like Mora's, uses personal pronouns to refer to your subject.

_____

_____

_____

_____

_____

_____

_____

_____

_____

_____

_____

_____

_____

EXERCISE D

1. Explain how you think readers of your poem will be affected by your use of personal pronouns.

   _____

   _____

   _____

   _____

2. Do you think it would be effective to use an excess of personal pronouns in other forms of writing—for example, in book reports, essays, or business letters? Explain your answer.

   _____

   _____

   _____

   _____

Writing Application: Letter

So often, pronoun problems happen because people can get away with incorrect usage in speech. Then they transfer the incorrect usage to their writing, where it is not acceptable. *Who* and *whom* present this problem, as do some pronouns used in appositives. Read the sentences below aloud.

INFORMAL	Who did we give the ski trip photo album to?
FORMAL	To whom did we give the ski trip photo album?

Which sentence would you probably say? Some day the first sentence may be more acceptable in writing; but for now, stick to the more formal usage when you write.

WRITING ACTIVITY

The library in your former elementary school plans to buy a number of children's books. They are asking former students to recommend books to buy. Write a letter to the librarians in which you recommend a favorite children's book for purchase. Explain why the library should spend part of its budget on this book. "Sell" the book to the librarians with enthusiasm. Use *who, whom,* and two appositives with pronouns in your letter as you describe this favorite book.

PREWRITING First, you will need to pick a book to recommend. Do you remember a book that you read and re-read as a child? You probably do, but if not, you may want to look through the children's section in a bookstore or public library to choose a book. Once you have your book, read it again. Then, brainstorm a list of positive traits about the book. The longer the list, the better.

WRITING With your list in hand, group together similar ideas. You may want to comment on the words in which the story is told, or on the story itself, or on the pictures that accompany the story. Keep like ideas together in your letter, and make comments on every element of the book. For children, beautiful or whimsical pictures are as important as well-written words!

REVISING You are writing a letter to busy librarians who will probably hear from many people. Be polite and direct. After a brief greeting, get right to your task: to persuade the librarians to choose your book! Use bits of quoted material from the story or describe the illustrations. Talk about the book's author if you like. All in all, write specifically, and don't waste time on vague comments. Use at least two appositives to describe the book, and watch those pronouns!

PUBLISHING Check your letter for mistakes in spelling and punctuation. Let your English teacher read over your letter—it's good to let a fresh set of eyes look for any problems you may have missed. Then write or print out the letter neatly and sign it. With your teacher's permission, post your letter on the bulletin board for your classmates to read.

EXTENDING YOUR WRITING

This exercise could lead to a more developed writing project. You could volunteer to read the children's book you are recommending to classes at your former elementary school. You would need to prepare an introductory speech on the book and its author and discussion questions to use with the children after reading the book. Work with the librarians to provide an entertaining half-hour for the children.

Choices: Exploring Modifiers

Here's your chance to step out of the grammar book and into the real world. You may not notice modifiers, but you and the people around you use them every day. The following activities challenge you to find a connection between modifiers and the world around you. Do the activity below that suits your personality best, and then share your discoveries with your class. Have fun!

CRITICAL THINKING

Face It

There's no point in denying it. Adverbs that modify adverbs can be as confusing as a house of mirrors. Face the problem head on. First, make a list of all kinds of adverbs. Then, find ones that can modify other adverbs. (Start with *so* and *quite*.) Make a list of these adverbs, and share your list with your classmates. They just might appreciate it.

GAME

Concentrate

Do you remember those memory games—the ones with the cards turned face down? Here's a new twist on those old games. Write appropriate words on four groups of cards: nouns, adjectives, verbs, and adverbs. Then, lay all the cards out face down. Each player takes a turn and turns over two cards. If one card cannot sensibly modify the other, turn the cards back over. After all possible matches have been made, the player with the most matches wins.

BUILDING BACKGROUND KNOWLEDGE

Friendly Persuasion

Some of your friends think only adverbs, not adjectives, end in *–ly*. Use a little friendly persuasion to show them the error of their ways. Not only do all adverbs not end in *–ly,* but some adjectives, such as *lovely*, do end in *–ly*. What are some others? Brainstorm a list of adjectives that end in *–ly*. Then, alphabetize your list and pass out copies of it to your classmates.

WRITING

To the Nth Degree

Every day, you make comparisons. For instance, you may check the temperature on one day to see whether it is different from the temperature

on the previous day. Can you think of other events, conditions, or qualities that are regularly compared on some sort of scale? What are these scales? What adjectives or adverbs do these scales use? What scales of measurement does science use? Economics? Fashion? Find out, and write up your findings to share with the class.

BUILDING VOCABULARY

Really and Truly?

Some people are really, really, really tired of hearing *really*. Are you one of them, or are you one of the offenders who would never utter the words *ever so* instead of *really*? Give yourself and your classmates some options. Brainstorm a list of words that could be used instead of *really*. You may want to use a thesaurus to start your list. Then, create a poster of these words to hang in your classroom, with your teacher's permission.

VISUAL

Go with the Flow

Sometimes a picture makes everything clear. If identifying adverbs and adjectives is easy for you, consider this project. Begin by making a list of the questions you ask yourself as you consider the possibilities. Then, make a flowchart detailing the steps in identifying a modifier as an adjective or an adverb. After you have finished, make copies of your flowchart and hand it out to your classmates.

WRITING

A Few of My Favorite Things

There are the things you like, the things you like better, and the things you like best. What are they? Write ten sentences about these things. In each sentence, use at least one of the forms of either *good* or *well.*

Language and Sentence Skills Practice

USAGE

One-Word Modifiers

A *modifier* is a word, a phrase, or a clause that makes the meaning of a word or word group more specific.

9a.   *Adjectives* make the meanings of nouns and pronouns more specific.

    EXAMPLES   **Mexican** food is served there. [The adjective *Mexican* modifies the noun *food*.]

                 Five players are **ill** today. [The adjectives *five* and *ill* both modify the noun *players*.]

9b.   *Adverbs* make the meanings of verbs, adjectives, and other adverbs more specific.

    EXAMPLES   The baby napped **peacefully.** [The adverb *peacefully* modifies the verb *napped*.]

                 The test was **rather** difficult. [The adverb *rather* modifies the adjective *difficult*.]

EXERCISE A   For each sentence in the following paragraph, underline the one-word modifier. Then, identify each modifier by writing above it *ADJ* for *adjective* or *ADV* for *adverb*. Do not underline the articles *a, an,* and *the.*

                                    ADJ

Example   **[1]** Su-Jan went to visit the beautiful city of Seattle.

   [1] Su-Jan and her family took a memorable vacation to Washington. **[2]** They bought a map and enthusiastically looked for places to visit. **[3]** Su-Jan wanted to see the tall Space Needle. **[4]** She took a photograph of the unique structure. **[5]** "We should take a ferry to Vancouver," said Su-Jan excitedly. **[6]** The family boarded a ferry and enjoyed the magnificent view of the water. **[7]** "If we return quickly, we can visit the markets," she thought. **[8]** After the visit to Vancouver, the family went to visit an outdoor market. **[9]** They bought beautiful souvenirs. **[10]** "We should visit Seattle often," remarked Su-Jan.

EXERCISE B   Supply the type of modifier specified in parentheses to complete each of the following sentences. Write the one-word modifiers on the lines provided.

Example 1. (*adverb*) They _____*noisily*_____ slurped the soup from large bowls.

11. (*adjective*)   Cecily gathered the _____ flowers in a basket.

12. (*adverb*)   My grandfather sprang _____ up the staircase.

13. (*adjective*)   I've known some _____ people.

14. (*adverb*)   My brother listens to _____ loud music.

15. (*adverb*)   The dog trotted _____ through the woods.

Phrases Used as Modifiers

A *modifier* is a word, a phrase, or a clause that makes the meaning of a word or word group more specific. Like one-word modifiers, phrases can also be used as adjectives and adverbs.

EXAMPLES   Jason chose the parakeet **with the green and white feathers.** [The prepositional phrase *with the green and white feathers* acts as an adjective that modifies the noun *parakeet.*]

After the play we attended the cast party. [The prepositional phrase *After the play* acts as an adverb that modifies the verb *attended.*]

EXERCISE   For each of the following sentences, indicate whether the underlined phrase is used as an adjective or an adverb. Above each, write *ADJ* for *adjective* or *ADV* for *adverb.* Then, circle the word each phrase modifies.

Example 1. Did you see the (dog) with the long ears?

1. The boy on the swing is my brother.

2. Where can we find a book of African folk tales?

3. They applauded after the performance.

4. We found the key to the chest.

5. A singer with a high voice is called a soprano.

6. She ate her meal with chopsticks.

7. The argument over the final score was finally settled.

8. They left this morning without me.

9. The opossum hid quietly behind the log.

10. My mom says, "Never eat snacks before dinner."

11. Everyone gasped as the horse galloped around the barrels.

12. The pig with the spots snorted several times.

13. Neither of us arrived before supper.

14. She cut the silhouettes from construction paper.

15. The player in the middle is the best.

16. They played outside in the rain.

17. Beneath the porch, the dogs lounged in the shade.

18. The girl in the picture is my sister.

19. Every song on the CD is fabulous.

20. Cactus was one of my favorite dishes.

Language and Sentence Skills Practice

Clauses Used as Modifiers

A *modifier* is a word, a phrase, or a clause that makes the meaning of a word or word group more specific. Like words and phrases, clauses can also be used as modifiers.

EXAMPLES   Jackie, **who plays guard,** is one of the team captains. [The adjective clause *who plays guard* modifies the noun *Jackie.*]

When you get home, please prepare the Greek salad. [The adverb clause *When you get home* modifies the verb *prepare.*]

EXERCISE   For each of the following sentences, identify whether the underlined clause is used as an adjective or an adverb. Above each, write *ADJ* for *adjective* or *ADV* for *adverb.* Then, circle the word or words each clause modifies.

Example 1. After we ate dinner, we cleared the table.

1. Before I went to the movie, I read the reviews.

2. Vicky, who just moved here, will be our pitcher.

3. The magazine that I was looking for was under the couch.

4. Since I have started studying each afternoon, I am making better grades.

5. We learned that the substitute teacher who was here last week is from Toronto.

6. Because he was tired, he took a long nap.

7. She exercises after she gets home from school.

8. The storm that we heard about is moving toward the west.

9. When Pablo won the tennis match, he was very happy.

10. Did you see the play that our class wrote?

11. After I dance, I usually feel better.

12. Annie, who won tickets to the rodeo, enjoyed seeing the horses.

13. Milk, which is a good source of calcium, helps strengthen bones.

14. Because he tried so hard, he usually succeeded.

15. Luzelle watched the stingray, which swam just below the surface of the water.

16. Since I learned how to do math, I've enjoyed it a lot more.

17. One of the pictures that he painted is hanging on the wall.

18. The woman who wore glasses was the one who made the muffins.

19. Spoons and plates clattered to the floor when she dropped the tray.

20. Ice hockey, which is popular here, soon became Paul's favorite sport.

Words, Phrases, and Clauses Used as Modifiers

A *modifier* makes the meaning of another word or word group more specific. A modifier can be a single word, a phrase, or a clause.

ONE WORD   Renee **carefully** sketched **red** and **yellow** tulips. [The adverb *carefully* modifies *sketched*. The adjectives *red* and *yellow* modify *tulips*.]

PHRASE   The squirrel jumped **onto the next tree**. [The adverb phrase *onto the next tree* modifies *jumped*.]

CLAUSE   The egg rolls **that were served with lunch** were delicious. [The adjective clause *that were served with lunch* modifies *egg rolls*.]

EXERCISE A   For each sentence in the following paragraph, indicate whether the underlined word or word group is used as an adjective or an adverb. Above each, write *ADJ* for *adjective* or *ADV* for *adverb*. Then, circle the word each word or word group modifies.

Example   [1] The girl chose the ⟨bird⟩ that seemed to be the friendliest.
                                      ADJ

[1] Jillian's father <u>kindly</u> gave her a wonderful gift.   [2] <u>Because she was very responsible</u>, he let her pick out a bird.   [3] Jillian preferred birds <u>that are very social</u>.   [4] <u>In a number of books</u>, she read about different types of birds.   [5] She chose a cockatoo <u>that was very intelligent and talkative</u>. [6] The cockatoo had a <u>yellow</u> crest.   [7] Jillian bought a cage <u>with several perches</u>.   [8] <u>When she returned with the bird</u>, her father gave her supplies that she would need.   [9] She fed the cockatoo a <u>nutritious</u> diet.   [10] The cockatoo, <u>which Jillian named Ludwig</u>, charmed everyone.

EXERCISE B   Supply the type of modifier specified to complete each of the following sentences. Write the words, phrases, or clauses used as modifiers on the lines provided.

Example 1. (*clause used as an adverb*) _____*Because I had slept late*_____, I was tardy.

11. (*phrase used as an adjective*)   The boy _____ won first place.

12. (*single-word adverb*)   Ernest stomped _____ through the house.

13. (*clause used as an adjective*)   The baby _____ has learned to crawl.

14. (*phrase used as an adverb*)   He scooted across the floor and _____ .

15. (*clause used as an adverb*)   I didn't tell her the story _____ .

USAGE

Regular Comparisons

9c.	The three degrees of comparison of modifiers are the *positive*, the *comparative*, and the *superlative*.

POSITIVE	COMPARATIVE	SUPERLATIVE
slim	slim**er**	slimm**est**
sandy	sand**ier** [*or* **more** sandy]	sandi**est** [*or* **most** sandy]
sweetly	**more** sweetly	**most** sweetly
wonderful	**more** wonderful	**most** wonderful

EXERCISE   Write the comparative and superlative forms of each of the following modifiers.

	Comparative	Superlative
Example 1. intelligent	*more intelligent*	*most intelligent*
1. careful		
2. bright		
3. colorful		
4. shiny		
5. slowly		
6. peacefully		
7. calm		
8. quickly		
9. loud		
10. cheerfully		
11. dedicated		
12. quietly		
13. rudely		
14. old		
15. honest		
16. loyal		
17. firmly		
18. rich		
19. sloppily		
20. dimly		

Irregular Comparisons

Some modifiers do not form their comparative and superlative degrees by using the regular methods.

POSITIVE	COMPARATIVE	SUPERLATIVE
good	better	best
well	better	best
bad	worse	worst
many	more	most
much	more	most

Notice that you don't have to add *–er/–est* or *more/most* to the irregular forms. For example, *better* is the comparative form of *well* or *good*. *More better* and *betterer* are nonstandard forms.

EXERCISE   On the line provided in each of the following sentences, write the form of the modifier described in parentheses.

Example 1. We all tell scary stories well, but Len tells them _____*best*_____. (superlative

form of *well*)

1. Jana is the _____ skater in her family. (superlative form of *good*)

2. Over the years, Mr. Hernandez has organized _____ blood drives than any

other teacher at our school. (comparative form of *many*)

3. In one story, the _____ villain of all time turns out to be a hero. (superlative

form of *bad*)

4. Howard makes _____ green chili stew than his mother does. (comparative

form of *good*)

5. Of all the high school teams, the Tigers have the _____ victories so far this

season. (superlative form of *many*)

6. Miguel plays basketball _____ than he did last year. (comparative form of

well)

7. Which band member raised the _____ money for the trip? (superlative form

of *much*)

8. Your mistake was bad, but mine was even _____. (comparative form of *bad*)

9. Toshi showed _____ kindness than her sister did. (comparative form of *much*)

10. Everyone in the play dances well, but I think Melissa dances _____ of all.

(superlative form of *well*)

Language and Sentence Skills Practice

Regular and Irregular Comparisons A

USAGE

| 9c. | The three degrees of comparison of modifiers are the *positive*, the *comparative*, and the *superlative*. |

POSITIVE	COMPARATIVE	SUPERLATIVE
tall	tall**er**	tall**est**
beautiful	**more** beautiful	**most** beautiful
good	better	best
bad	worse	worst
many	more	most

EXERCISE A   On the line provided in each of the following sentences, write the form of the modifier described in parentheses.

Example   1. This structure is the _____*sturdier*_____ of the two. (comparative form of *sturdy*)

1. My aunt thinks this is the _____ painting of all. (superlative form of *beautiful*)

2. Rhonda has _____ books than I do. (comparative form of *many*)

3. Esperanza is the _____ girl on the team. (superlative form of *tall*)

4. Jacqui gave Ellen the _____ necklace. (superlative form of *pretty*)

5. That last one was my _____ pitch of the day. (superlative form of *bad*)

6. Manuel did _____ than he expected on the test. (comparative form of *well*)

7. Tyugen is my _____ friend. (superlative form of *good*)

8. The news about the hurricane is _____ in this newspaper. (comparative form of *clear*)

9. Geoffrey and Keith were the _____ of all the runners. (superlative form of *fast*)

10. I think this poem is _____ than the other one. (comparative form of *good*)

EXERCISE B   For each of the following sentences, write the form of the modifier described in parentheses.

Example   1. Is that movie _____*longer*_____ than the other one? (comparative form of *long*)

11. Which film won the prize for _____ original score? (superlative form of *good*)

12. The voters thought that one film had _____ music than the others. (comparative form of *good*)

13. The film is about a young woman and a _____ monster. (positive form of *hairy*)

14. The beast looks scary at first, but he is _____. (positive form of *kind*)

15. My brother has seen this movie _____ than he has seen any other. (comparative form of *often*)

Regular and Irregular Comparisons B

9c.	The three degrees of comparison of modifiers are the *positive,* the *comparative,* and the *superlative.*

POSITIVE	COMPARATIVE	SUPERLATIVE
funny	funn**er**	funn**iest**
gently	**more** gently	**most** gently
well	better	best
bad	worse	worst
much	more	most

EXERCISE A   For each of the following sentences, write the form of the modifier described in parentheses.

Example 1. Who is the _____ *best* _____ female athlete on the United States team?

(superlative form of *good*)

1. Jackie Joyner-Kersee jumped the _____ distance of all the long-jump competitors in the 1988 Olympics. (superlative form of *great*)

2. In 1956, a Polish woman beat the 1952 Olympic record by jumping only slightly

_____. (comparative form of *far*)

3. In 1964, a British woman beat the record for the _____ jump. (superlative

form of *long*)

4. In 1980, a Soviet jumper leaped a little _____ than twenty-three feet. (comparative form of *much*)

5. A Romanian won in 1984, but her jump was _____ than the 1980 Soviet jump.

(comparative form of *short*)

EXERCISE B   For each of the following sentences, write in the form of the modifier described in parentheses.

Example 1. This umbrella is ____ *stronger* ____ than that one. (comparative form of *strong*)

6. These flowers are _____ than those. (comparative form of *bright*)

7. We were the _____ students in the school. (superlative form of *happy*)

8. This bread tastes _____ than the bread I ate yesterday. (comparative form of *bad*)

9. Are her math skills _____ than her writing skills? (comparative form of *good*)

10. Douglas thought his brother was _____. (positive form of *wise*)

USAGE

Use of Comparative and Superlative Forms A

9c. The three degrees of comparison of modifiers are the *positive*, the *comparative*, and the *superlative*.

(1) The ***positive degree*** is used when only one thing is being modified and no comparison is being made.

> **EXAMPLE**   That is a **cute** puppy.

(2) The ***comparative degree*** is used when two things are being compared.

> **EXAMPLE**   This puppy is **cuter** than the other one.

(3) The ***superlative degree*** is used when three or more things are being compared.

> **EXAMPLE**   This puppy is the **cutest** of all.

EXERCISE A   Underline the correct form of the modifier in parentheses in each of the following sentences.

Example 1. Of those two dancers, the second one dances (*more skillfully*, *most skillfully*).

1. African dancing is (*more popular*, *most popular*) at our school than basketball.

2. Our club has the (*more*, *most*) students of any special program at our school.

3. Of the two of us, Shamar is (*better*, *best*) at African dance.

4. Derrick used to think he was the (*worst*, *worse*) dancer in the class.

5. A good dancer listens (*more closely*, *most closely*) to the rhythms than to the words of the songs.

EXERCISE B   On the line provided in each of the following sentences, write the correct form of the modifier in parentheses.

Example 1. China is the only country with a _____*larger*_____ population than that of India. (*large*)

6. The Indian civilization is one of the _____ in the world. (*ancient*)

7. In 3000 B.C., the _____ villages in all India were in the Indus River Valley. (*large*)

8. India produced some of the _____ spices and teas in the world. (*fine*)

9. Great Britain had a _____ military than India had in the eighteenth century. (*strong*)

10. By 1947, it became apparent that India's desire for independence was _____ than the strength of the British. (*great*)

Use of Comparative and Superlative Forms B

9c. The three degrees of comparison of modifiers are the *positive*, the *comparative*, and the *superlative*.

(1) The *positive degree* is used when only one thing is being modified and no comparison is being made.

> **EXAMPLE**   That joke is quite **funny**.

(2) The *comparative degree* is used when two things are being compared.

> **EXAMPLE**   This joke is even **funnier**.

(3) The *superlative degree* is used when three or more things are being compared.

> **EXAMPLE**   This joke is the **funniest** of them all.

EXERCISE A   Underline the correct form of the modifier in parentheses in each of the following sentences.

Example 1. The trumpet was the (*louder, loudest*) instrument in the quintet.

1. Marcos always wanted to learn how to play (*more, most*) instruments.

2. He enjoys playing the clarinet the (*more, most*).

3. The clarinet's range is (*higher, highest*) than the trombone's.

4. Marcos also thought that the clarinet was (*easier, easiest*) than the flute.

5. The reed in the clarinet allows him to do (*more, most*) things with the instrument.

6. For example, Marcos can bend a note to make it slightly (*lower, lowest*).

7. Of course, the clarinet is not the (*easier, easiest*) instrument to play.

8. Some people think that percussion instruments are the (*more, most*) fun.

9. Percussion players often have (*better, best*) rhythm than other people.

10. Some think that percussionists must concentrate the (*harder, hardest*) of all the band members.

EXERCISE B   On the line provided in each of the following sentences, write the correct form of the modifier in parentheses.

Example 1. At the museum, Carla said that painters are some of the ____most creative____ people in

the world. (*creative*)

11. Mother thought that the Georgia O'Keeffe painting was the _____ of all. (*fine*)

12. Of the two paintings, the van Gogh was the _____. (*dark*)

13. Mother told us that van Gogh lived a _____ life than most artists. (*sad*)

14. Many of van Gogh's later paintings are _____ than his earlier ones. (*bright*)

15. The artist Monet lived to be _____ than van Gogh. (*old*)

Language and Sentence Skills Practice

USAGE

Good and Well

| **9d.** | The modifiers *good* and *well* have different uses. |

(1) Use *good* to modify a noun or a pronoun.

EXAMPLE   Our dog Brickle is a **good** swimmer. [The adjective *good* modifies the noun *swimmer*.]

(2) Use *well* to modify a verb.

EXAMPLE   Our dog Brickle swims **well**. [The adverb *well* modifies the verb *swims*.]

Well may also be used as an adjective meaning "in good health."

EXAMPLE   My grandmother is **well** now. [The adjective *well* modifies the noun *grandmother*.]

EXERCISE A   In each of the following sentences, draw an arrow from the underlined word to the word it modifies.

Example 1. Evan played <u>well</u> in today's game.

1. Twyla Tharp is a very <u>good</u> choreographer.

2. All the dancers move <u>well</u>.

3. Did you have a <u>good</u> sandwich for lunch?

4. Reuben writes <u>well</u> and wants to be a journalist.

5. Cotton is a <u>good</u> fabric for many types of clothing.

EXERCISE B   On the line provided in each of the following sentences, write either *good* or *well* to complete the sentence correctly.

Example 1. Did you do _____*well*_____ on the test today?

6. My great-grandmother has _____ eyesight.

7. Mr. Kwan was sick last week, but now he is _____.

8. Doesn't Emilia tell _____ stories?

9. Mrs. Park remembers her life in Russia _____.

10. How _____ does your father cook?

11. My little cousin Anna is a _____ baby.

12. Did your dog perform _____ at the obedience competition?

13. Marcus plays basketball _____, but he prefers soccer.

14. We have made a _____ start on our science project.

15. I can see _____ even in the dark.

Adjective or Adverb?

9e. Use adjectives, not adverbs, after linking verbs.

Linking verbs, such as *be, seem, become, feel, remain,* and *appear,* are often followed by predicate adjectives. These adjectives describe, or modify, the subject.

EXAMPLES   Venezuela became **independent** [not *independently*] in 1821. [The predicate
adjective *independent* modifies the subject *Venezuela*.]

Does Jonathan look **unhappy** [not *unhappily*] today? [The predicate adjective
unhappy modifies the subject *Jonathan*.]

EXERCISE A   For each of the following sentences, decide whether the verb is an action verb or a linking verb. Write *ACT* for *action verb* or *LINK* for *linking verb* on the line provided. Then, underline the correct form of the modifier in parentheses.

Example _____ **1.** The ice dancers looked (*happy, happily*) when they were dancing.

_____ **1.** One couple moved (*quick, quickly*) over the ice.

_____ **2.** They seemed quite (*light, lightly*) as they moved easily on the ice.

_____ **3.** The man seems (*strong, strongly*).

_____ **4.** He lifted his dance partner (*easy, easily*) over his shoulder.

_____ **5.** She landed (*light, lightly*) on the ice.

_____ **6.** He twirled her (*graceful, gracefully*).

_____ **7.** They moved so fast that the ice did not feel (*cold, coldly*).

_____ **8.** We learned that they practice (*regular, regularly*).

_____ **9.** Ice dancing seems very (*difficult, difficultly*).

_____ **10.** However, the skaters make it look quite (*simple, simply*).

EXERCISE B   In the following sentences, identify the form of the underlined word by writing *ADJ* for *adjective* or *ADV* for *adverb*. Then, draw an arrow from the modifier to the word modified.

ADJ
Example 1. The boys were <u>sleepier</u> than they had been the previous night.

11. The campers' bags were <u>heavier</u> when they were full.

12. The trail grew <u>steeper</u> as the boys continued.

13. The boys seemed <u>happier</u> after they had eaten.

14. They could now hike <u>farther</u> with less equipment to carry.

15. The skies soon turned dark, so they pitched their tents <u>early</u>.

Language and Sentence Skills Practice

Double Comparisons

9f.   Avoid using double comparisons.

A *double comparison* is the use of both *–er* and *more* (or *less*) or both *–est* and *most* (or *least*) to form a single comparison. When you make a comparison, use only one of these forms, not both.

> **NONSTANDARD**   Margarita is my most oldest friend.
>
> **STANDARD**   Margarita is my **oldest** friend.

EXERCISE A   Underline the correct form of the modifier in parentheses in each of the following sentences.

Example   1. Some of Nikki Giovanni's poems are about her (*most happiest,* <u>happiest</u>) childhood memories.

1. Clara thinks that yogurt is (*more better, better*) than ice cream.

2. Frances has a (*more softer, softer*) voice than Tonya has.

3. Last year was the (*most saddest, saddest*) year of my life.

4. Maya runs (*faster, more faster*) than her brother.

5. He is the (*kindest, most kindest*) man I have ever known.

6. This spring is (*warmer, more warmer*) than last spring.

7. The tulips bloomed (*more earlier, earlier*) than they did last year.

8. Right now my room is the (*most messiest, messiest*) it has ever been.

9. The (*worstest, worst*) day was the day I broke my arm.

10. Mr. Johnson feels (*better, more better*) today than he did yesterday.

EXERCISE B   In each of the following sentences, cross out any incorrect modifier and write the correct form above it. If the sentence is already correct, write *C* on the line provided.

Example _____ **1.** This sunset is the ~~most prettiest~~ ^{prettiest} I've seen this fall.

_____**11.** Isn't this weather the bestest we've had all year?

_____**12.** Ruth thought that Jacob was the most handsomest of the three brothers.

_____**13.** Which of the two plants do you think is more beautiful?

_____**14.** Jacqueline's house is more farther away than my house.

_____**15.** Mayumi claimed to have the worstest singing voice in the class.

Double Negatives

9g.   Avoid using double negatives.

A *double negative* is the use of two or more negative words to express one negative idea.

  NONSTANDARD   I do not have no computer at my house. [The negative words are *not* and *no*.]

      STANDARD   I do **not** have a computer at my house.

      STANDARD   I have **no** computer at my house.

EXERCISE   On the line provided, revise each sentence to eliminate the double negative. Although there is more than one possible answer, you need to write only one revision. If a sentence is already correct, write *C* on the line.

Example 1. This book doesn't have no index.   *This book doesn't have an index.* or *This book has no index.*

1. We didn't have no pears on our tree this year. _____

2. Rex hasn't told no one about his parents' trip. _____

3. Sheila never eats nothing between meals. _____

4. I have never found any arrowheads in this field. _____

5. I can't barely hear you. _____

6. Boris hardly said nothing. _____

7. Mr. Navarro's explanation didn't make no sense to me. _____

8. Darcy has made no plans for the Chinese New Year. _____

9. This pencil doesn't have no eraser. _____

10. Joe hadn't done nothing all day. _____

Language and Sentence Skills Practice

USAGE

Misplaced One-Word Modifiers

9h.   Place modifying words, phrases, and clauses as close as possible to the words they modify.

The placement of a one-word modifier may affect the meaning of a sentence. Place adjectives and adverbs so that they clearly modify the words you intend them to modify.

> **EXAMPLES**   **Later** Dad said we could go fishing. [Dad made the statement later.]
>
> Dad said we could go fishing **later**. [According to Dad, we may go fishing later.]
>
> **Only** two workers were sent to trim the maple tree. [Two workers and no more were sent.]
>
> Two workers were sent to trim **only** the maple tree. [The two workers will trim the maple tree and no other trees.]

EXERCISE   For each of the following sentences, insert the given modifier in the proper place. The intended meaning for each sentence is included in parentheses. To insert the modifier, place a caret ($_\wedge$) in the proper place and write the word above the caret.

Example **1.** Gabriel $\overset{frequently}{\wedge}$ dreams of going fishing with his father. (*frequently:* He has the dream often.)

1. Claire sang for the guests who had gathered around the piano. (*sweetly:* Her singing was sweet.)

2. Miriam invites her friends to eat dinner with her. (*often:* The invitation occurs often.)

3. Roberto lifted the bird and put it in a cage. (*carefully:* Roberto was careful when he put the bird in a cage.)

4. Mother said she wanted us to prepare lunch. (*early:* The preparation takes place early.)

5. The invited lecturer spoke, and the audience listened. (*clearly:* The lecturer's speech was clear.)

6. Mauricio finished the race and found some cold water. (*quickly:* He was quick to find water.)

7. Annie goes jogging in the park after she gets home from school. (*frequently:* Her going jogging is a frequent event.)

8. The mother whispered to her daughter and hugged her. (*lovingly:* Her hug was loving.)

9. The tennis player picked up her racket and served the ball. (*impatiently:* She was impatient to pick up the racket.)

10. The cat crept toward the toy and pounced on it. (*silently:* The creeping was silent.)

Misplaced Prepositional Phrases

9h.   Place modifying words, phrases, and clauses as close as possible to the words they modify.

Place a prepositional phrase so that it clearly modifies the word you intend it to modify.

   MISPLACED   The kitten was jumping into the little girl's arms in the picture.

       CLEAR   The kitten **in the picture** was jumping into the little girl's arms.

   MISPLACED   Mr. Chen explained how tornadoes form in science class.

       CLEAR   **In science class,** Mr. Chen explained how tornadoes form.

EXERCISE   Each of the following sentences has a misplaced prepositional phrase. Rewrite each sentence, placing the phrase near the word it modifies.

Example 1. She spoke to the boy who seemed troubled in a soft voice. *She spoke in a soft voice*
to the boy who seemed troubled.

1. Two robins kept a watchful eye on the dog in a tree. _____

_____

2. That dress was hemmed by my aunt with yellow lace. _____

_____

3. An engineer bought a new house from Seattle. _____

_____

4. The books belong to my brother in that box. _____

_____

5. The house was built by my uncle by the lake. _____

_____

6. All of the tourists visited the Empire State Building from Miami. _____

_____

7. Immanuel sang a song for Berta with a pretty melody. _____

_____

8. I bought a cactus from the store clerk with sharp stickers. _____

_____

9. Please put my umbrella in the car with the long handle. _____

_____

10. The cow watched us drive by in the pasture. _____

_____

Language and Sentence Skills Practice

Misplaced Adjective Clauses

9h. Place modifying words, phrases, and clauses as close as possible to the words they modify.

Adjective clauses should generally be placed directly after the words they modify.

MISPLACED	Our neighbor's dog howls all the time, which is a beagle.
CLEAR	Our neighbor's dog, **which is a beagle,** howls all the time.

MISPLACED	The print is by a famous Dutch artist that my aunt gave us.
CLEAR	The print **that my aunt gave us** is by a famous Dutch artist.

EXERCISE Each of the following sentences has a misplaced adjective clause. Rewrite each sentence, placing the adjective clause near the word it modifies.

Example   **1.** The teacher sent us a letter who had visited our school. *The teacher who had visited our school sent us a letter.*

1. Both of the chairs will go in the living room that you bought. _____

_____

2. I read the book during my vacation that you recommended. _____

_____

3. Carol says the painter demonstrated his technique whom she admired. _____

_____

4. The car needs new tires that you picked out. _____

_____

5. Is the vase still in a box that Grandmother sent us? _____

_____

6. A soccer player arrived on the field who was wearing a new uniform. _____

_____

7. The man wrote the article with whom she spoke. _____

_____

8. The chapter will be on the test that we read today. _____

_____

9. We photographed the flowers and developed the pictures that grew in her backyard. _____

_____

10. The boy has a new mountain bike whom you met. _____

_____

Placement of Modifiers A

9h.   Place modifying words, phrases, and clauses as close as possible to the words they modify.

MISPLACED WORD	We heard that the shuttle launch will be delayed yesterday.
CLEAR	We heard **yesterday** that the shuttle launch will be delayed.
MISPLACED CLAUSE	Uncle Felipe is going to teach me the tango, who is a professional dancer.
CLEAR	Uncle Felipe, **who is a professional dancer,** is going to teach me the tango.

EXERCISE Each of the following sentences has a misplaced modifier. Underline the entire misplaced modifier. Then, draw an arrow from the misplaced modifier to the place where the modifier should be. In some cases, there may be more than one way to correct a sentence.

Example 1. The students asked the teacher many questions who were preparing for the test.

1. Danielle woke up so she could get all her work done before sunrise earlier than usual.

2. The chair was built by my uncle in the corner.

3. Do you know the man next to the large dog who is walking with a cane?

4. The piano belongs to my sister, which is out of tune.

5. The dog barked with long, floppy ears at the guests.

6. Can you find the city on the map that we visited?

7. Gabriela went jogging after a long day through the trails.

8. Traci brushes her teeth after she wakes up always.

9. Dogs are great companions to take camping that like romping outdoors.

10. The review was not well written about the new movie.

11. Franco uses his typewriter since he got a computer rarely.

12. Did the tree blossom in the spring that you planted?

13. There are some peanuts on the table in a can.

14. The movie amused the audience, which was a romantic comedy.

15. Adela eats an apple after she finishes her homework occasionally.

16. The sleepy little boy climbed out of the comfortable bed with brown hair.

17. The apples are from the grocery store in that bag.

18. Sara opened the gifts in the kitchen that her friends brought.

19. The man is my neighbor at the door.

20. The cat rested in the chair with yellow eyes.

Placement of Modifiers B

9h. Place modifying words, phrases, and clauses as close as possible to the words they modify.

MISPLACED WORD	Dad says he likes to play tennis on Saturday always.
CLEAR	Dad **always** says he likes to play tennis on Saturday.
	Dad says he **always** likes to play tennis on Saturday.
MISPLACED CLAUSE	Ms. Ramirez just had a baby son, who teaches Spanish.
CLEAR	Ms. Ramirez, **who teaches Spanish,** just had a baby son.

EXERCISE Each of the following sentences has a misplaced modifier. Underline the entire misplaced modifier. Then, draw an arrow from the misplaced modifier to the place where the modifier should be.

Example 1. The leader looked at the crowd of listeners, who had just made a long speech.

1. The children played new games, who were at recess.

2. The bookcase was built by my sister that is painted green.

3. We met the actor and his wife with the gray beard.

4. The duck swam on the lake with the spoon-shaped bill.

5. My sister under the mat left an extra key.

6. The police officers took a lunch break who had just finished a call.

7. Friedrich said he goes to bed on school nights earlier.

8. The squirrel ran up the tree with the long tail.

9. Michelle goes with her father to work after she gets home from school sometimes.

10. We do our homework before going out to play always.

11. The oranges don't look ripe from that tree.

12. A student visited our school who is from Ecuador.

13. I put my sandwich in my lunchbox that I will eat at lunchtime.

14. The puppeteers finished the show who had been performing.

15. An athlete listened to the coach who is my teammate.

16. Did you find the skates that I mentioned to you with the sharp blades?

17. We watched the videotape yesterday morning about wildlife.

18. He said yesterday we would go.

19. The lion roared at the onlookers with the large mane.

20. The meal was the best I had ever eaten that you cooked for me.

Review A: **Forms and Comparisons**

EXERCISE   On the line provided in each of the following sentences, write the correct form of the modifier given in parentheses.

Example 1. This problem is _____*more difficult*_____ than the first. *(difficult)*

1. I feel _____ than I did yesterday. *(well)*

2. Both rugs are beautiful, but I think this one is _____. *(durable)*

3. That is the _____ thing anyone has ever said to me! *(nice)*

4. Next time, speak _____ onstage than you did today. *(slowly)*

5. This is the _____ storm I have ever seen. *(bad)*

6. Blue is a _____ color on you than green. *(good)*

7. This chemical is the _____ material in the factory. *(hazardous)*

8. You perform _____ on tests than you do on homework. *(well)*

9. Of those two flags, which one is _____? *(colorful)*

10. What was the _____ moment of your baseball career? *(exciting)*

11. Marco thinks this one is the _____ of the two curries. *(spicy)*

12. This is the _____ fruit I have ever tasted. *(sweet)*

13. She seemed to be the _____ girl in the world. *(happy)*

14. Sarah was flying the _____ of the two kites. *(large)*

15. This perfume smells _____ than that one does. *(strong)*

16. The _____ mountain in Africa is in Tanzania. *(tall)*

17. Of all our trees, the lime tree grew _____. *(well)*

18. Which of these two towels is _____? *(white)*

19. The starter on the car is getting _____ every day. *(bad)*

20. In the yard, a rake would be _____ than a broom. *(useful)*

Language and Sentence Skills Practice

USAGE

USAGE

Review B: Special Problems and Double Negatives

EXERCISE A Underline the correct modifier in parentheses in each of the following sentences.

Example 1. Many of the students shifted (*restless,* <u>*restlessly*</u>) in their seats.

1. My sister was sick, but now she is (*good, well*).

2. As the curtain rose, the dancers took the stage (*graceful, gracefully*).

3. Mina felt (*good, well*) about her grades.

4. This perfume will remain (*fragrant, fragrantly*) for many years.

5. Your chowder tastes as (*good, well*) as it smells.

6. After his talk with the coach, Joel appeared (*solemn, solemnly*).

7. Jason finished his chores (*more quickly, more quicklier*) than David.

8. You always do (*good, well*) in science.

9. Martin felt (*calm, calmly*) during the test.

10. The students did a (*good, well*) job on the science project.

EXERCISE B Most of the following sentences contain either double comparisons or double negatives. Correct each sentence by crossing out the incorrect form and writing the correct form above it. If a sentence is already correct, write *C* on the line provided.

Example 1. The dog's condition is ~~worser~~ *worse* today than yesterday.

_____ **11.** I think spinach tastes more better than lettuce.

_____ **12.** There isn't no milk in the refrigerator.

_____ **13.** To my surprise, I did not see anyone I knew at the game.

_____ **14.** She's the most fastest skater I know.

_____ **15.** The boys didn't do nothing wrong.

_____ **16.** Dad thinks the lead dancer is the bestest in the world.

_____ **17.** Those monkeys are the noisiest animals in the entire wildlife park.

_____ **18.** Maria hasn't never gone swimming in a lake.

_____ **19.** The little boy could not find his dog nowhere.

_____ **20.** This hat is more expensiver than the one at the other store.

Review C: Misplaced Modifiers

EXERCISE   Each of the following sentences has a misplaced modifier. Underline the entire misplaced modifier. Then, draw an arrow from the misplaced modifier to the place where the modifier should be.

Example   1. We were introduced to the girl who joined our team with long, red hair.

  1. I enjoyed the article about elephants that you sent me.

  2. Luigi played a composition for my friends by Bach.

  3. The building has several offices inside, which overlooks the highway.

  4. Mrs. Peterson recommended the book to all the children about African dances.

  5. The bird landed on a branch with white-tipped wings.

  6. Our relatives came over for Thanksgiving, who are living in Algeria.

  7. We studied Glinka and learned a great deal, who is a Russian composer.

  8. Mother makes us breakfast every morning with orange juice.

  9. The singers practiced the song who had just joined the choir.

 10. Have you met the principal already who will be speaking?

 11. Janet picked blackberries to use for the dessert from the vine.

 12. I watch the train go by before I go to school usually.

 13. They sent some flowers to my aunt with a nice card.

 14. The children tie their shoelaces carefully before riding their bikes always.

 15. Evan writes in cursive when taking notes rarely.

 16. The tree is nearly a hundred years old in our backyard.

 17. My favorite song was playing on the radio from the musical *Oliver!*

 18. The rope is not strong enough that you bought yesterday.

 19. He put the ring on her finger with several small diamonds.

 20. Su-Lin wrote a poem for the class about friendship.

Review D: **All Types of Problems**

USAGE

EXERCISE A   For each of the following sentences, underline the correct form of the modifier in parentheses.

Example 1. Miguel was the <u>(better,</u> best) of the two golfers.

1. Katerina had read the (more, most) books over the summer.

2. Kristen is (taller, tallest) than Jonathan.

3. We were the (fastest, most fastest) swimmers on the team.

4. Did Margarette write (more, most) pages than Colleen?

5. Of the two photographs, the darker one is (worse, worst).

6. Angelo was the (happiest, most happiest) child in the room.

7. This book is (better, more better) than the one I read last week.

8. Juanita can ride her bike (faster, more faster) than I can.

9. Georgia's last putt was her (worst, most worst) one all day.

10. Which of the two paintings do you like (better, best)?

EXERCISE B   Each of the following sentences has a misplaced modifier. Underline the entire misplaced modifier. Then, draw an arrow from the misplaced modifier to the place where the modifier should be.

Example 1. The roses are growing beside the house <u>that Mother planted.</u>

11. Peter's iguana got out of his cage with the long tail.

12. The violinist spoke to the audience, who was carrying her violin and bow.

13. Carl goes to a movie when he gets home from church occasionally.

14. The birthday party was fun for everyone that we had last week.

15. Sandy dropped her tray nearly on the floor.

16. Anita won the prize for best actress, who is the daughter of a famous singer.

17. A bird stood on a log with a long beak.

18. The senator delivered a speech who had just been elected.

19. This shirt needs to be washed with the tan collar.

20. My grandmother will be living with us, who just retired.

for **CHAPTER 9: USING MODIFIERS CORRECTLY** | pages 197–214 |

Proofreading Application: Art Critique

Good writers are generally good proofreaders. Readers tend to admire and trust writing that is error-free. Make sure that you correct all errors in grammar, usage, spelling, and punctuation in your writing. Your readers will have more confidence in your words if you have done your best to proofread carefully.

Whenever you make evaluations and comparisons, you use modifiers—adjectives and adverbs. Modifiers are the words that best express evaluations and comparisons. If you don't use modifiers correctly, people might not understand what you are saying. Correct use of modifiers will enable you to communicate your opinions clearly and effectively.

PROOFREADING ACTIVITY

Find and correct the errors in modifiers in the following classroom art critique. Use proofreading symbols to make your corrections.

Example Wow! This artist draws ⌃*well* ~~good~~!

    Of all the paintings in the class, this one is better. It uses
color quite good. The greens and reds are more colorfuller than
those I usually see. Certainly, the dragon theme is the most
excitingest theme in this group of art works. The dragon is made
more scarier by the fire's realism. However, the tail of the dragon looks badly and part of it is off the canvas. Why didn't the
artist plan more wiser? Why doesn't the dragon have no teeth? The
dragon actually seems alive to most viewers. In conclusion, this
painting is wonderful, but I hope that the artist plans more careful next time.

Literary Model: Folk Tale

Dog found a spot near the front of the cave, settled down and went to sleep.

Everybody knows that Dog has the best hearing of almost any animal in the world. Dog could hear a raindrop fall on cotton.

In the darkest part of the night, the time of night that's so scary even Moon wishes she had someplace to hide, Dog woke up suddenly. . . .

Dog ran back to the front of the cave and waited. The footsteps got louder and louder until out of the forest, holding a tree in each hand, came Gorilla.

Dog growled his growliest growl. He rushed at Gorilla and barked his barkiest bark. Gorilla looked down, picked Dog up, and threw him over his shoulder. . . .

—excerpt from "Why Dogs Chase Cats," retold by Julius Lester

EXERCISE A List ten of the one-word modifiers (adjectives and adverbs) used in the passage above. Beside each modifier, write the word it modifies.

	MODIFIER	WORD MODIFIED		MODIFIER	WORD MODIFIED
Example 1.	*best*	*hearing*			
1.			6.		
2.			7.		
3.			8.		
4.			9.		
5.			10.		

EXERCISE B

1. Which modifiers are superlative forms? Comparative forms?

_____

_____

2. Which two modifiers are invented words?

_____

From "Why Dogs Chase Cats" from *How Many Spots Does a Leopard Have? and Other Tales* by Julius Lester. Copyright © 1989 by Julius Lester. Reprinted by permission of *Scholastic, Inc.*

Literary Model (continued)

EXERCISE C Which animal species appeals to you? Write a short folk tale, or the beginning of a longer folk tale, that is a fantasy explanation of a typical behavior of that animal. Use several positive, comparative, and superlative forms of adjectives and adverbs in your folk tale, and underline each one. If you like, include a modifier that is an invented word.

_____

_____

_____

_____

_____

_____

_____

_____

_____

_____

_____

EXERCISE D Why are comparative and superlative forms of modifiers especially useful or dynamic in your folk tale?

_____

_____

_____

_____

_____

_____

_____

_____

_____

_____

_____

_____

_____

for **CHAPTER 9: USING MODIFIERS CORRECTLY** | *pages 197–214*

Writing Application: Using Modifiers in a Description

Putting modifiers in the wrong place can result in some funny sentences. Read each sentence aloud, and think about what the writer meant to say as opposed to what the sentence actually says.

INCORRECT   Walking down the neatly edged sidewalk, the capitol dome loomed in the distance.

Smothered with jalapeños, they gobbled up the enchiladas.

These sentences are amusing—as long as you didn't write them! Be sure that all modifiers are as near as possible to the word or words that they modify.

CORRECT   Walking down the neatly edged sidewalk, we saw the capitol dome looming in the distance.

Smothered with jalapeños, the enchiladas steamed on the plate.

WRITING ACTIVITY

In your social studies class, you are studying geography and are planning to put together a global map. Each student will write a well-developed paragraph about a city that he or she would like to visit some-day. Choose a city to write about, and learn a little about it from encyclopedias, online sources, or books—all sources that travelers turn to before they visit a city. As you write your paragraph, use at least five descriptive modifiers. Be sure to place each modifier as close as possible to the word it modifies.

PREWRITING   For this exercise, you will need to do a little advance work. Find out some details about your city: What's the best time of the year to visit? What are the city's most visited spots? Is the city valued for its beauty, its history, or perhaps for some special item that is made there? You are writing only one paragraph, but you should pack it full of tempting details.

WRITING   You will need to decide how to arrange your paragraph, and you have several organizational patterns to choose from. You could take readers on a tour through the city streets or spend some time talking about the city's history or mention why this city appeals to you. Outlining provides a quick method for experimenting with several plans. Try a few patterns, and choose your favorite.

REVISING   Once you have an organized draft of the paragraph, consider its overall tone. Think of it as a little travel brochure designed to interest readers visiting the city. Read the paragraph to several friends, and ask them if the paragraph interests them in the city and why. Use their responses as you tailor your paragraph for other students.

PUBLISHING   Check your paragraph for mistakes in grammar, usage, spelling, and punctuation. Find a picture of the city to post with the neatly written paragraph. Then, work with your class-mates to prepare a bulletin board with a world map. Learn from other students about cities they would like to visit someday.

EXTENDING YOUR WRITING

You could extend this assignment by making your paragraph part of a travel brochure that you create. Collect or draw pictures of the city you wrote about, and design a brochure encouraging others to visit that city.

Choices: Practicing Correct Usage

Here's your chance to step out of the grammar book and into the real world. You may not notice standard English usage, but you and people around you use it every day. The following activities challenge you to find a connection between usage and the world around you. Do the activity below that suits your personality best, and then share your discoveries with your class. Have fun!

ART

Road Signs

Create road signs cautioning against errors in usage. Begin by sketching the actual road signs you see every day. You can find many of these in a state-issued driver's manual or in a driver's education textbook. You may be surprised to learn that the shape of a road sign has a meaning. Incorporate these shapes into your designs, and show your sketches to the class.

GRAPHICS

Day by Day

Have you seen those calendars with a saying for every day on them? Make a week-long calendar with one usage word pair or entry on each page. Then, hang your calendar as a class display. Don't forget to turn the page each day.

ETYMOLOGY

One Little Word

As you read the glossary, did you notice the number of usage problems associated with the word *of*? This one little word certainly causes a lot of trouble. Look up the word *of* in a good dictionary. What is its etymology—its roots and their original meanings? From what languages did it emerge? Is there anything in its history that could explain why it is such a troublemaker? Report your findings to the class.

WRITING

In Your Own Words

The entries in your glossary cover only a few of the usage errors that you are likely to encounter. What errors would you like to add to this list? Keep a journal for five days. In your journal, make notes of usage errors that you think should be included. Feel free to include actual usage errors you hear in conversations or see in print. Then, write your own additions to the glossary.

DIALOGUE

Opposites Attract

How would conversations sound if half of us used our words correctly, while the other half made constant usage errors? Create a dialogue that involves one perfect speaker and one not-so-perfect speaker. Make sure that your first speaker makes no usage errors, while the other incorrectly uses at least one word or phrase in each sentence. Choose a partner, and perform your dialogue for the class.

DRAMA

Coming or Going?

Whether you are bringing or taking something to the picnic depends on your point of view. Get together with three or four classmates, and write a short skit in which you correctly use the word *bring* and the word *take*. Include several short scenes, so that everyone will have several chances to hear *bring* and *take* used correctly. You may want to include a telephone call or different locations to make your point clear. Then, perform your skit for the class.

ILLUSTRATION

Picture the Difference

Sometimes people have trouble learning something new until they see an example of what they are learning. Help your classmates learn the difference between *accept* and *except* by illustrating examples of these two words. Draw one picture that illustrates a sentence using the word *accept* and another that illustrates the word *except*. As the caption for each of your pictures, write out a sentence that includes the word you have illustrated. Share your knowledge by hanging your artwork in the classroom.

USAGE

Avoiding Usage Problems A

Review the glossary entries on pages 222–23 of your textbook for information on the correct usage of the following words and phrases:

a, an	*a lot*
accept, except	*already, all ready*
ain't	*anyways, anywheres, everywheres,*
all right	*nowheres, somewheres*

EXERCISE A For each of the following sentences, circle the word or word group in parentheses that is correct according to the rules of formal, standard English.

Example 1. Has Latisha (*already,* all ready) left for band practice?

1. Naomi Shihab Nye is (*a, an*) honest poet.

2. Megan has (*all ready, already*) told many people the big news.

3. Finally, after much preparation, the bathroom was (*all ready, already*) to be painted.

4. I have (*a, an*) hour until the library closes.

5. Nobody (*accept, except*) Desmond can sing that note.

6. The potato pancakes (*ain't, aren't*) ready yet.

7. Janelle can't find her new shoes (*anywhere, anywheres*).

8. After a few days, Kevin's wrist felt (*all right, alright*).

9. Did you use (*alot, a lot*) of curry powder in that dish?

10. You'll see yucca plants (*everywheres, everywhere*) in this part of the country.

EXERCISE B Each of the sentences in the following paragraph has an error in the use of standard, formal English. Cross out each error, and write the correct usage above it.

Example [1] I have ~~all ready~~ *already* bought some new ice skates.

[11] The sixth-grade class got an new aquarium for the classroom. [12] We looked everywheres for the best aquarium. [13] Our teacher even did alot of research. [14] She all ready knew about aquariums because she keeps fish at home. [15] We found a aquarium that was quite large. [16] All the students accept for two voted for the larger aquarium. [17] We knew we should put it somewheres safe. [18] Our teacher said we could put it anywheres in the back of the classroom, as long as we chose a strong surface. [19] Lu-Wan said that putting the aquarium on a strong table would be alright. [20] Carmelita excepted the job of feeding the fish daily.

USAGE

Avoiding Usage Problems B

Review the glossary entries on pages 223–26 of your textbook for information on the correct usage of the following words and phrases:

at	good, well
bad, badly	had ought, hadn't ought
between, among	hardly, scarcely
bring, take	hisself, theirself, theirselves
could of	how come
fewer, less	

EXERCISE A   For each of the following sentences, circle the word or word group in parentheses that is correct according to the rules of formal, standard English.

Example 1. My ankle hurts (bad, *badly*) when I put weight on it.

1. Where do you suppose I left (*my jacket at, my jacket*)?

2. After the earthquake, people had to (*bring, take*) their belongings and find new homes.

3. Grandmother could (*of, have*) taught us her American Indian language.

4. We have (*fewer, less*) money in the bank since we took our vacation.

5. The camp counselor distributed the mail (*between, among*) all the campers.

6. After passing the exam, Donovan felt very proud of (*himself, hisself*).

7. Did Mrs. Sanchez know (*why, how come*) Mishi was late?

8. Their quarterback doesn't play (*bad, badly*) for a rookie.

9. Van danced (*good, well*) at the recital.

10. Something in this refrigerator smells (*bad, badly*).

EXERCISE B   Each of the sentences in the following paragraph has an error in the use of standard, formal English. Cross out each error, and write the correct usage above it.

Example [1] No one ~~between~~ *among* the three of us had ever rowed before.

[11] The rowers are very proud of theirselves. [12] There's a strong friendship among the coach and the team captain. [13] Some people thought the team would row bad in their first race. [14] They said that the team hadn't ought to compete yet. [15] The team, however, did quite good. [16] There wasn't hardly a rower dissatisfied with the race. [17] With more practice the team could of been even better. [18] The new team expected to win less races than the other teams. [19] After the race, the rowers went home, bringing their trophies with them. [20] Even the coach wondered how come they did so well.

Language and Sentence Skills Practice

201

USAGE

Avoiding Usage Problems C

Review the glossary entries on page 228 of your textbook for information on the correct usage of the following words and phrases:

   its, it's   *kind of, sort of*   *learn, teach*

EXERCISE A For each of the following sentences, circle the word or word group in parentheses that is correct according to the rules of standard, formal English.

Example 1. I wonder if (*its*, ⟨*it's*⟩) going to rain this afternoon.

1. Will you (*teach, learn*) me how to play flute?

2. Carmen handed the puppy (*its, it's*) toy.

3. It's not easy to (*teach, learn*) someone how to scull.

4. I was (*kind of, somewhat*) tired by the end of the trip.

5. (*Its, It's*) time to do my homework.

6. After I bought the table, I saw that (*its, it's*) leg was broken.

7. We decided not to go to the beach because it was (*sort of, rather*) cold outside.

8. Mario wants to (*teach, learn*) about horses.

9. The professor (*teaches, learns*) English literature to college students.

10. The clock stopped when (*its, it's*) main spring broke.

EXERCISE B For each of the following sentences, cross out any usage errors and write the correction above the error. If a sentence is already correct, write *C* after the sentence.

Example 1. I think ~~its~~ *it's* a bit too cold in this room.

11. Michael told me he would learn me how to play classical guitar.

12. All the kids in my cabin were kind of sad when our camp session ended.

13. I am always in a good mood when it's the first day of spring.

14. My youngest brother thinks its fun to go to the grocery store and help Dad.

15. I want to take a photography class, but I am also sort of nervous about trying something new.

16. Chi, I wish you could teach me everything you know about fashion.

17. The tiny monkey at the zoo was looking for it's mother.

18. After the dramatic ending of the play, the audience sat kind of still for a few moments.

19. If you really want to learn to swim the butterfly stroke, I will learn you.

20. Be sure to put the pasta in it's pot as soon as the water is boiling.

Avoiding Usage Problems D

Review the glossary entries on pages 229–30 of your textbook for information on the correct usage of the following words and phrases:

of · *their, there, they're* · *than, then*
suppose to, supposed to · *them*

EXERCISE A Most of the following sentences contain an error in the use of standard, formal English. Cross out each error, and write the correct usage in the space above it. If a sentence is already correct, write *C* after the sentence.

Example 1. How long have people had fireplaces inside ~~they're~~ *their* homes?

1. We are suppose to read this African myth about how humans got fire.

2. The people on earth are cold, and their leader sends his son to the god Obassi Osaw.

3. Obassi Osaw refuses to show them humans how to make fire.

4. Than, the boy goes to Obassi Osaw's compound.

5. The people on earth welcome him as he brings fire to there homes.

EXERCISE B For each of the following sentences, circle the word or word group in parentheses that is correct according to the rules of standard, formal English.

Example 1. The swimmers listened to (*their,* they're) coach.

6. Maya is a better swimmer (*then, than*) she was last year.

7. She knows that she is (*suppose to, supposed to*) practice three times a week.

8. Maya swims at a pool (*inside, inside of*) the gym.

9. She warms up and (*then, than*) does drills.

10. Sometimes her coach is (*their, there*) when she is practicing.

11. Maya's coach has been with (*their, there*) team for six years.

12. I thought (*those, them*) exercises were harder than the last ones.

13. During one difficult drill, Maya accidentally swam (*outside, outside of*) her lane for a moment.

14. After practice, Maya jumps (*off of, off*) the diving board.

15. The team's first meet was (*supposed to, suppose to*) be in September.

16. Because of schedule changes, (*there, they're*) going to compete in October.

17. (*Then, Than*), they will have had an extra month to practice.

18. (*Their, There*) will be several other meets this year.

19. Are there more competitions in the spring (*than, then*) in the fall?

20. Maya's team hopes to do (*their, there*) best this season.

Language and Sentence Skills Practice

203

USAGE

USAGE

Avoiding Usage Problems E

Review the glossary entries on pages 231–32 of your textbook for information on the correct usage of the following words and phrases:

this here, that there	*when, where*
try and	*whose, who's*
use to, used to	*your, you're*
way, ways	

EXERCISE A For each of the following sentences, cross out the error in the use of standard, formal English and write the correction above the error.

Example 1. Roberto ~~use to~~ *used to* go skiing every winter.

1. I chose this here fish to go in my new aquarium.

2. I think your going to like the new library.

3. Class, do any of you know who's jacket this is?

4. Ravi will try and learn the new software.

5. The lady who gave us directions said we still have a long ways to go.

6. A good friendship is when both people trust each other.

7. The teacher said she enjoyed you're essay about the Civil War.

8. Is that there history book the one with the colorful, detailed maps?

9. The woman whose talking to my mother is the boss.

10. After much debate, the judges gave that there project first place in the science fair.

EXERCISE B Cross out each usage error in the following sentences, and write the correct form above the error. (Hint: Each sentence in the following paragraph contains at least one error in the use of formal, standard English.)

Example [1] Before we went on ~~this here~~ *this* vacation, we were disappointed about having to drive the whole ~~ways~~ *way* there.

[11] My brother and I were not use to car trips, but we enjoyed our family vacation. **[12]** We didn't mind traveling a long ways because Dad developed a silly game. **[13]** As we passed by houses or animals, we each made up a story about who's they were. **[14]** It can be fun to use you're imagination on car trips. **[15]** These here photos remind me of our best stories.

Review A: Common Usage Problems

EXERCISE A For each of the following sentences, circle the word or word group in parentheses that is correct according to the rules of formal, standard usage.

Example 1. Each story we read had (*its*, *it's*) own adventurous quest.

1. Coach Weinberg will (*learn, teach*) us the basics of softball.

2. Shana has limped (*bad, badly*) since her mishap in the soccer match yesterday.

3. Please limit your essays to five hundred words or (*fewer, less*).

4. We are (*all ready, already*) for the camping trip.

5. Please put (*those, them*) candles on the table.

6. It is a long (*way, ways*) to the river from here.

7. Hector is (*an, a*) honest man.

8. There (*are hardly, aren't hardly*) any people here today.

9. Justine and Toshiro were (*accepted, excepted*) into the new school.

10. Thank you for all (*your, you're*) hard work.

EXERCISE B Most of the following sentences contain errors in the use of standard, formal English. Cross out each error, and write the correct usage in the space above it. If a sentence is already correct, write *C* after the sentence.

Example 1. Nobody ~~accept~~ *except* the butler was in the room at the time of the crime.

11. Do you know where Mom's keys are at?

12. We would of had a picnic if it had not been raining.

13. Gerald asked us how come we did not join him at the park yesterday.

14. Take this message when you go to see the king.

15. We took a vote between the team members.

16. My grandmother wants to learn me about keeping track of my money.

17. A lobster pushes it's body backward through the water.

18. Antonia's hair is curlier then mine.

19. I am supposed to do my chores when I get home.

20. The boys combed there hair and walked out onto the dance floor.

Review B: **Common Usage Problems**

USAGE

EXERCISE A For each of the following sentences, circle the word or word group in parentheses that is correct according to the rules of standard, formal English.

Example 1. Aunt Matilda is (*suppose,* (*supposed*)) to arrive at six o' clock.

1. The girls were (*all ready, already*) for (*they're, their*) fishing trip at four o' clock in the morning.

2. Do you know (*how come, why*) the cat jumped (*off, off of*) the counter?

3. Always stretch (*your, you're*) muscles (*good, well*) before running in a race.

4. I will (*except, accept*) your apology because I (*ought not, hadn't ought*) to turn away a good friend.

5. Uncle Sid (*used, use*) to work at (*a, an*) animal shelter.

6. (*Them, Those*) boys saved (*themselves, theirselves*) some time by preparing so carefully.

7. The game went (*good, well*), but I still (*can't hardly, can hardly*) believe our team won first place.

8. I like all fruit (*except, accept*) pineapple, which I find (*rather, kind of*) unappetizing.

9. (*Whose, Who's*) recipe did you use for (*these here, these*) Vietnamese spring rolls?

10. I will try (*and, to*) find some origami paper at the craft store, but the last time I was there I didn't see origami paper (*anywhere, anywheres*).

EXERCISE B Most of the following sentences contain errors in the use of standard, formal English. Cross out each error, and write the correct usage in the space above it. If a sentence is already correct, write *C* after the sentence.

                                  already
Example 1. My brother has ~~all ready~~ graduated from high school.

11. Is there a doctor among the audience members?

12. You catch less flies with vinegar than you do with honey.

13. Jason has had an accident, but he will be alright.

14. We have put alot of time into our science project.

15. There were no harsh words among the two diplomats.

16. The alarm clock is over their.

17. I had ought to study for my math test.

18. Than, the Czechs declared their independence.

19. Golf may look easy, but its a hard sport to learn.

20. Both of the figure skaters lost there balance, but only one of them fell down.

HOLT HANDBOOK | Introductory Course

Review C: **Common Usage Problems**

USAGE

EXERCISE For each of the following sentences, cross out the error in the use of standard, formal English and write the correction above the error. If a sentence is already correct, write *C* after the sentence.

Example 1. Ben wants to try ~~and~~ ride a unicycle.
                                       to

1. If we had been in better shape, we might of won the game.

2. I think we ought to study harder for the next test.

3. The children looked at theirselves in the mirror.

4. Did you know that my mother use to be a concert pianist?

5. I hope that little boy will not hurt hisself while skiing.

6. Is that there book with the gold cover the one you'd recommend?

7. Do you know whose keys these are?

8. Interval training is an exercise where athletes train hard for short periods of time.

9. As soon as the sun came up, Marvin was inside of the treehouse.

10. There are less children in my neighborhood than in yours.

11. Where did you put you're favorite pen?

12. Jason ain't a member of this team anymore.

13. Because she loves to read and write poetry, Kali has collected alot of anthologies of

    contemporary poetry.

14. Going to the movies is alright with me.

15. On our camping trip, we felt as though we were a long ways from home.

16. This here is the most unusual poem in the collection.

17. It was raining in the morning, but we went hiking anyway.

18. Let's try and improve our tennis game before the tournament.

19. We can learn to write good if we practice.

20. I have no idea how come Gabrielle has decided to leave the volleyball team and join the

    soccer team.

Proofreading Application: Letter

Good writers are generally good proofreaders. Readers tend to admire and trust writing that is error-free. Make sure that you correct all errors in grammar, usage, spelling, and punctuation in your writing. Your readers will have more confidence in your words if you have done your best to proofread carefully.

The Internet can provide you with the opportunity to write to students from all over the world who are eager to try out their English skills on American students. When you are writing to a person who does not know English well, remember that correct usage is especially important.

PROOFREADING ACTIVITY

Find and correct the errors in standard English usage in the e-mail letter below. Use proofreading symbols to make your corrections.

Example Dear Gunther,

We ~~all ready~~ *already* know a lot about you.

However, you don't hardly know much about us. Thanks for you're questions. I'll try and answer them. Our teachers learn us about mathematics, history, science, social studies, and English. I like all my classes accept history. You might wonder how come I dislike history class. I don't remember dates too good. They're kind of confusing for me. However, I do like hearing them stories about historical events. Tell us more about your school; it seems to be harder then ours.

You asked about which sports I play good. Among my sister and me, we play almost every sport you can imagine. I'm good at most of them accept for basketball. I'm afraid I'm still pretty badly at shooting baskets. I am practicing alot, though. When I go to school, I bring my own basketball with me. The gym don't supply enough balls for all the teams. In fact, there are five less balls than teams. Anyways, the coach is going to order more next season. When you write me back, tell me about you're favorite sports.

Your friend,

for **CHAPTER 10: A GLOSSARY OF USAGE**   *pages 221–32*

Literary Model: Nonstandard Usage in a Folk Tale

Well, when God made de snake, he put him in de bushes to ornament de ground. But things didn't suit de snake so one day he got on de ladder and went up to see God.

"Good mawnin', God."

"How do you do, Snake?"

"Ah ain't so many, God, you put me down there on my belly in de dust and everything trods upon me and kills off my generations. Ah ain't got no kind of protection at all."

from an African American folk tale, retold by Zora Neale Hurston

EXERCISE A

1. Underline any examples of nonstandard usage in this **excerpt** by Zora Neale Hurston.

2. On the following lines, rewrite in standard English any sentence that includes nonstandard usage.

_____

_____

_____

_____

_____

_____

_____

_____

_____

_____

_____

EXERCISE B

1. Does the nonstandard usage make the story seem as though it is meant to be **spoken out loud** or read silently? Explain.

_____

_____

_____

_____

2. Why do you think Hurston might have chosen to retell the folk tale in nonstandard **English?**

_____

_____

_____

_____

From "How the Possum Lost the Hair Off His Tail" from *Mules and Men* by Zora Neale Hurston. Copyright 1935 by Zora Neale Hurston; copyright renewed © 1963 by John C. Hurston and Joel Hurston. Reprinted by permission of **HarperCollins Publishers, Inc.**

Language and Sentence Skills Practice

Literary Model (continued)

EXERCISE C Create your own folk tale about any kind of animal. Include at least three examples of nonstandard usage. After you have finished writing, underline the examples of nonstandard usage.

_____

_____

_____

_____

_____

_____

_____

_____

_____

_____

_____

EXERCISE D Re-read the folk tale that you wrote. How would it be different if you had used only standard English? Why do you think it is acceptable to use nonstandard English in some situations but not in others? Explain.

_____

_____

_____

_____

_____

_____

_____

_____

_____

_____

_____

Writing Application: Quiz Show

"When in doubt, spell it out!" is a good tip to remember when you're not sure when to use certain contractions. Remember that the apostrophe in *you're, they're, it's,* and *who's* stands for a letter or letters that have been left out. Add the letter or letters back in to see the words spelled out correctly. Then you will know for certain that you are using the correct spelling.

WRITING ACTIVITY

The end of the semester is just around the corner, and your science teacher has come up with a fun way to review the topics you've learned. To help students remember this semester's science chapters, your class is going to develop a quiz show. For the quiz show, each student will challenge the class by providing five clues about a topic he or she has chosen.

As you write your clues, you will need to use some of the words in the English textbook's glossary of usage. You may need to know when to use *its* rather than *it's,* for example, since your clues will probably include pronouns. Be sure to use all your words correctly—your clues will be on display for the whole class!

PREWRITING First, choose your quiz topic. Looking through your science textbook is an easy way to find a topic that interests you. From the textbook, pick out five important facts about the topic. Prewriting for this exercise is as easy as that!

WRITING The writing can be a bit trickier. Write five clues to help your classmates guess your topic. Each clue must correctly demonstrate at least one rule from the glossary of usage in *Elements of Language.* If your topic is *Saturn,* you might write, "*It's* the sixth planet from the sun." If you choose *genes* as your topic, you might give as your clue, "*They're* made up of mostly DNA and protein."

REVISING Once you have all five clues for your category, arrange them from easiest to hardest. Let the easiest question be worth ten points and the hardest be worth fifty points. Check your facts one more time against your science textbook—your facts must be correct! Also, check your clue sentences against the glossary of usage in your English textbook. When you use a contraction from the glossary of usage, remember this hint: When in doubt, spell it out!

PUBLISHING Check your clues for mistakes in spelling and punctuation. Then, give your clue sentences to your teacher, who will assemble all the clues for the game. Divide into teams, and have fun reviewing what you've learned!

EXTENDING YOUR WRITING

This exercise could lead to a more developed writing project. With several students, gather the most important clues from the quiz show and turn them into a set of review worksheets for the upcoming exam. Work with your teacher to prepare the worksheets for the whole class. You will know the material by heart when you have finished this exercise, and your classmates will appreciate the help!

Language and Sentence Skills Practice

Choices: Exploring Capital Letters

Here's your chance to step out of the grammar book and into the real world. You may not notice capital letters, but you and the people around you use them every day. The following activities challenge you to find a connection between capital letters and the world around you. Do the activity below that suits your personality best, and then share your discoveries with your class. Have fun!

BUILDING BACKGROUND KNOWLEDGE

A Picture Is Worth a Single Definition?

Use a dictionary to study the definitions of the word *capital.* Then, create a poster that illustrates the many meanings of this word. On your poster, be sure to illustrate the meaning of each definition. Do not include the definitions on your poster. When your poster is finished, show your classmates. Then, have them guess each of the meanings of the word *capital* by studying the illustrations on your poster.

RESEARCHING RESOURCES

Reading List

Compile a list of interesting books and articles about the English language. Include books and articles on slang, idioms, bloopers, and word history. Be sure to capitalize the titles on your list correctly. Then, with a special color or code, mark titles that are available in your school library. Make copies of your list available to anyone in the class who wants one.

INVENTION

Martians and Muscovites

Brainstorm a list of at least ten place names, such as Mars and Moscow. What suffix, or word ending, would you add to each of the proper nouns on your list to describe someone who lives in that place? If you need help, look in a dictionary or ask friends and family. When your list is complete, have some fun. Apply the suffixes you learned to ten other names. For instance, what would you call people who go to your school, people who live in your county, or people who share specific interests? When writing your list, remember to use capital letters where appropriate.

MUSIC

Before and After Beethoven

If you are interested in music, make a time line showing the proper names of famous musicians throughout history. If possible, include an illustration and a sentence or two identifying some of the musical selections that made each musician popular. Be sure to capitalize proper names and the titles of musical works.

TECHNOLOGY

Gadgets and Gizmos

It may not be too long before you will own a wristwatch that's much more than a clock. It may be a telephone, a miniature TV, and who knows what else. Check out some technical publications such as computing magazines to find out what gadgets and gizmos will be available in the near future. Make a list of these items. Be sure to use capitals correctly when writing the brand names of business products. Present your findings to the class, and give everyone a copy of your list.

GEOGRAPHY

The Grand Tour

In the eighteenth century, some young adults were sent on grand tours, or educational trips, throughout Europe. With the advancements in transportation over the last three hundred years, today's grand tour would probably be a bit different from those of the eighteenth century. Surely, cities and sites from all over the globe would now be included. In a few paragraphs, identify each city or site that you would like to visit if you could plan your own grand tour. Be sure to include reasons for your choices. Also, don't forget to use capital letters where needed.

for **CHAPTER 11: CAPITAL LETTERS** | *pages 239–40*

First Words and *I*

11a. Capitalize the first word in every sentence.

> **EXAMPLE**   **M**ost of the leaves have already fallen. **I**t is not too soon to start raking.

The first word of a direct quotation is capitalized, whether or not the quotation starts the sentence.

> **EXAMPLE**   Luis said, "**L**et's walk to the library."

11b. Capitalize the first word in both the salutation and the closing of a letter.

> **EXAMPLES**   **D**ear Montel,   **Y**ours truly,

11c. Capitalize the pronoun *I*.

> **EXAMPLE**   Before lunch **I** think **I** will walk the dog.

EXERCISE A For each of the following groups of words, circle any letters that should be capitalized but are not.

Example 1. ⓓear Pamelita

1. my brother came home.
2. Tomorrow i will leave early.
3. sincerely, David
4. Bill said, "my keys are missing."
5. Margaret and i are waiting for you.
6. yours truly, Myla
7. Libby said, "let's go home!"
8. dear Eddie,
9. did you see Fiona today?
10. Ruth asked, "where is Gail?"

EXERCISE B Each of the sentences in the following letter contains an error in capitalization. For each sentence, circle the letter that should be capitalized but is not.

Example [1] Before lunch, ⓘhad already finished my assignment.

[11] dear Mrs. Herrera,

  [12] i was in your fifth-grade class last year. **[13]** my family moved to Chicago after the school year had finished. **[14]** You used to tell me, "when you go to your new school, you will make many friends." **[15]** on the first day of school, I met a very nice boy. **[16]** He said to me, "you should join our soccer team." **[17]** he introduced me to the other players. **[18]** In a very short time, i had many new friends. **[19]** thank you for the encouragement you gave me, Mrs. Herrera!

                            [20] sincerely,

                            Carlos

MECHANICS

Proper Nouns A

11d(1).	Capitalize the names of persons and animals.

PERSONS	**M**ichael **J**ordan	**G**ary **S**oto
	Attila the **H**un	**K**atharine **H**epburn
ANIMALS	**W**ishbone	**S**neakers
	Buttons	**F**lipper

EXERCISE A Each of the sentences in the following paragraph contains an error in capitalization. For each sentence, circle the letter that should be capitalized but is not.

Example **[1]** Have you met ⌐janet before?

[1] Janet and becky went to visit their cousin in Hartford, Connecticut. **[2]** Their cousin's name is sally. **[3]** Sally has a horse named ichabod and a pony named Bluebonnet. **[4]** Sally also has a cow named katrina and several goats. **[5]** janet and Becky asked to ride the horses. **[6]** Sally's brother, jessie, helped them saddle the horses. **[7]** Janet chose to ride ichabod. **[8]** At first, neither Ichabod nor bluebonnet would budge. **[9]** jessie told the girls to be firmer with their commands. **[10]** Within a few minutes becky and Janet were riding with ease.

EXERCISE B For each of the following common nouns, write a corresponding proper noun. Be sure to use capital letters correctly.

Example ___*Abraham Lincoln*___ **1.** a former U.S. President

_____ **11.** a pet dog or cat

_____ **12.** an actor or actress

_____ **13.** a famous singer

_____ **14.** a pet horse

_____ **15.** a government official or mayor

_____ **16.** a pet bird

_____ **17.** a friend

_____ **18.** an animal from a book or movie

_____ **19.** a relative

_____ **20.** a famous poet

Proper Nouns B

11d(2). Capitalize geographical names.

CONTINENTS	South America	Africa	Asia
COUNTRIES	Finland	Peru	Italy
CITIES, TOWNS	Mexico City	Chicago	Tokyo
STATES	Nevada	New Hampshire	Alabama
BODIES OF WATER	Lake Erie	Red River	Panama Canal
STREETS, HIGHWAYS	Interstate 95	Highland Avenue	Sixth Street
SECTIONS OF THE COUNTRY	the Midwest	the Northeast	Sun Belt

EXERCISE A In the following sentences, circle each letter that should be capitalized but is not. If a sentence is already correct, write *C* after it.

Example 1. Brazil is the largest country in South america.

1. Many people in Brazil live in cities along the coast of the Atlantic ocean.

2. The city of brasília is the nation's capital.

3. Rain forests lie along the amazon river in Brazil.

4. Iguaçu Falls is a beautiful waterfall that is more than two miles wide.

5. It lies on the border between Brazil and argentina.

EXERCISE B Each of the following sentences contains an error in capitalization. For each sentence, circle the letter that should be capitalized but is not.

Example 1. The composer showed patriotism for his native country of finland.

6. The short story was set in japan.

7. Have you been to canada?

8. We heard that Portland, oregon, is a good city for bicycling.

9. Our family moved to a house on palmer Avenue.

10. The news anchor was from the midwest.

11. The bookstore that you're looking for has moved to Third street.

12. We drove down interstate 10 from Houston to Baton Rouge.

13. Georgia took some beautiful photographs at Lake tahoe.

14. Francesca traveled through europe last summer.

15. We will be staying with our uncle in indianapolis during the holidays.

MECHANICS

Proper Nouns C

11d(3). Capitalize the names of organizations, teams, institutions, and government bodies.

ORGANIZATIONS	**G**irl **S**couts of the **U**nited **S**tates of **A**merica	**T**he **H**umane **S**ociety of the **U**nited **S**tates
TEAMS	**H**ouston **C**omets	**G**lendale **P**umas
INSTITUTIONS	**T**ulane **U**niversity	**H**anover **H**igh **S**chool
GOVERNMENT BODIES	**C**entral **I**ntelligence **A**gency	**U**nited **N**ations

EXERCISE A Each of the sentences in the following paragraph contains an error in capitalization. For each sentence, circle the letter that should be capitalized but is not.

Example [1] Mrs. Nguyen belongs to the Parent-(t)eacher Association.

[1] Tien's school is called westdale Elementary. [2] Tien's sixth-grade class formed a baseball team called the Westdale cougars. [3] They will be competing against the eastman Elementary Bears next week. [4] The pitcher is Bobby, whom Tien first met during a Ranger scouts of America meeting. [5] Bobby and Tien went to a baseball training camp together at California State university. [6] Bobby used to go to fairview Elementary School in Sacramento. [7] His father works for the Federal aviation Administration and was transferred to San Francisco. [8] In San Francisco, Bobby practiced pitching and joined the westdale Cougars. [9] Next year, Bobby and Tien will attend Copperfield middle School. [10] They will then be old enough to join the Bay Area baseball League.

EXERCISE B Most of the following groups of words contain errors in capitalization. Circle all letters that should be capitalized but are not. If the group of words is already correctly written, write *C* after it.

Example 1. the New (O)rleans (S)aints

11. Federal bureau of investigation

12. the Happy gardeners club

13. Kingstown pottery association

14. the Johnson high school bobcats

15. the seattle wildflower association

16. lincoln high school

17. the St. Louis Rams

18. department of Transportation

19. the university of tennessee

20. the Compton middle school orchestra

Proper Nouns D

11d(4). Capitalize the names of special events, holidays, and calendar items.

SPECIAL EVENTS	**S**ummer **O**lympics	**C**otton **B**owl
HOLIDAYS	**P**residents' **D**ay	**F**ourth of **J**uly
CALENDAR ITEMS	**T**uesday	**A**ugust

11d(5). Capitalize the names of historical events and periods.

HISTORICAL EVENTS	**B**attle of **G**ettysburg	**I**ndustrial **R**evolution
HISTORICAL PERIODS	**S**tone **A**ge	**M**iddle **A**ges

11d(6). Capitalize the names of nationalities, races, and peoples.

EXAMPLES	**N**avajo	**A**frican **A**merican	**I**talian	**H**ispanic

MECHANICS

EXERCISE Each of the following sentences contains an error in capitalization. For each sentence, circle the letter that should be capitalized but is not.

Example 1. Was George Washington the general during the Battle of [y]orktown?

1. The figure skater retired after the Winter olympics in Nagano, Japan.

2. The book about the Roman Empire ended with the period of history known as the dark Ages.

3. Have you read about Martin Luther and the reformation?

4. The holiday of christmas is celebrated in many different ways.

5. Guadalupe wrote a report about the spanish-American War.

6. Connie always watches the Super bowl with her father.

7. The Rosenthal family invited their neighbors to join them for the religious holiday of passover.

8. She will be moving to Lincoln in february.

9. Our teacher, who is Asian american, is fluent in Korean, Japanese, and English.

10. I like to study the period of history known as the renaissance.

Language and Sentence Skills Practice

Proper Nouns E

11d(7). Capitalize the names of businesses and the brand names of business products.

BUSINESSES	**A**rnold's **D**og **G**rooming **S**hop
	Eatin' **R**ight **D**iner
BUSINESS PRODUCTS	**N**issan **P**athfinder

11d(8). Capitalize the names of ships, trains, aircraft, and spacecraft.

SHIPS	*Mayflower*	*Titanic*
TRAINS	*Orient Express*	*Rapido*
AIRCRAFT	*Silver Dart*	*Air Force One*
SPACECRAFT	*Challenger*	*Mariner 4*

EXERCISE   Each of the following sentences contains an error in capitalization. For each sentence, circle the letter that should be capitalized but is not.

Example 1. Yuri Gagarin orbited the earth in the spaceship ⓥostok.

1. The tourists visited the ship USS *constitution* when they traveled to Boston.

2. Charles Lindbergh's plane was called the *spirit of St. Louis*.

3. Javier wrote a report on the sinking of the ship *lusitania*.

4. Stacy got a job at computer World.

5. Our textbook has a picture of astronaut John Glenn inside the *friendship 7*.

6. The spectators gasped as the *hindenburg* exploded and fell from the sky.

7. The wedding party ate breakfast at the blackforest Cafe.

8. Pierre's family bought a chevrolet minivan.

9. The train that my grandmother rode was called the *scenic Limited*.

10. We bought a Fun time train at the toy store.

MECHANICS

Proper Nouns F

11d(9).   Capitalize the names of buildings and other structures.

BUILDINGS	Thompson Hall	Statue of Liberty
OTHER STRUCTURES	Space Needle	Mile High Stadium

11d(10).   Capitalize the names of monuments, memorials, and awards.

EXAMPLES   Washington Monument   Thomas Jefferson Memorial   Grammy

EXERCISE   Each of the following sentences contains an error in capitalization. For each sentence, circle the letter that should be capitalized but is not.

Example   1. When we were in New York, we saw the Empire ⃞state Building.

1. The children could easily recognize the Taj mahal in the photographs from India.

2. A well-known cathedral in Paris is Notre dame.

3. We took several photographs of the Golden gate Bridge.

4. A famous nobel Prize winner is Albert Einstein.

5. Can you identify the style of architecture used in the Chrysler building?

6. One of the temples we visited was Temple israel.

7. Our class went on a field trip to the lincoln Memorial.

8. The young writer was hoping to win the Pulitzer prize some day.

9. The college freshmen were told to meet their advisors in boyd Hall.

10. Did you know that the famous london Bridge is no longer in London?

11. The tourists booked several rooms at the fairview Hotel.

12. Earning the Medal of freedom is a great honor.

13. Can you name a stanley Cup winner?

14. My uncle visits the Vietnam veterans Memorial every winter.

15. The sewing classes will be held on the first floor of stephan Hall.

16. Our coach presented the team captain with the golden Athlete Award.

17. The Grover Elementary School Jaguars will play at holden Stadium next week.

18. Miki took a photograph of the St. Louis cathedral.

19. Stewart won the Outstanding achievement Award last year at Milgate High School.

20. We learned that eastridge Hall is being converted into a modern art gallery.

Language and Sentence Skills Practice

Proper Nouns G

MECHANICS

11d(11). Capitalize the names of religions and their followers, holy days and celebrations, sacred writings, and specific deities.

RELIGIONS AND FOLLOWERS	Islam	Buddhist	Christianity
HOLY DAYS AND CELEBRATIONS	Hanukkah	Easter	Lent
SACRED WRITINGS	Talmud	Koran	Old Testament
SPECIFIC DEITIES	Allah	God	Zeus

11d(12). Capitalize the names of planets, stars, constellations, and other heavenly bodies.

EXAMPLES	Venus	Little Dipper	Orion

EXERCISE A   Each of the following sentences contains an error in capitalization. For each sentence, circle the letter that should be capitalized but is not.

Example 1. The Muslims fasted during the holy month of (r)amadan.

1. Have you read the entire New testament?

2. The woman explained her belief in god.

3. Rabbi Feldman read a passage from the torah.

4. We studied the differences between saturn and Jupiter.

5. Prakash and his family practice hinduism.

6. Followers of Judaism celebrate rosh Hashana.

7. Did you see the Big dipper last night?

8. The studies were focused on the atmosphere of mars.

9. Our neighbors belong to a lutheran church.

10. The children dressed up in costumes to celebrate the holiday of purim.

EXERCISE B   In the following paragraph, circle any letter that should be capitalized but is not.

Example [1] We learned about (b)uddhism and (h)induism from our guest speakers.

[11] Our teacher invited several speakers to talk to our class about different religions such as islam and judaism. [12] The first speaker taught us that muslims worship allah. [13] We read several passages from the koran, the holy book of the muslims. [14] Another speaker taught us some of the jewish laws as they are defined in the book of leviticus. [15] Our most recent speaker, a hindu, taught us about brahma. Hindus believe that brahma created the universe.

School Subjects and Proper Adjectives

11e. Do not capitalize the names of school subjects, except course names followed by a numeral and the names of language classes.

> EXAMPLES   **h**istory   **C**omputer **S**cience I   **F**rench

11f. Capitalize proper adjectives.

> PROPER NOUN **S**hakespeare   PROPER ADJECTIVE **S**hakespearean actor

EXERCISE A   In the following sentences, circle each letter that should be capitalized but is not.

Example 1. british and italian soccer players went to a latin american tournament.

1. Nara knows many american indian legends.

2. At Ames High School, my brother studies spanish, art, and health.

3. Spanish, portuguese, french, and dutch ships came to the american coast.

4. The italian city of Venice has canals instead of streets.

5. My mother's evening courses are woodworking I and french cooking II.

6. In music class, we learned some greek songs and austrian folk dances.

7. The ethiopian people live on the african continent.

8. Many of the first european settlers in Australia were british prisoners.

9. That catholic church has a fresco painted by José Clemente Orozco, a great mexican artist.

10. The Puerto rican flag has one star on a blue triangle next to five stripes.

EXERCISE B   For each of the following sentences, circle the letter that should be capitalized but is not.

Example 1. Pearl bought a german cuckoo clock for her living room.

11. I learned the spanish word for *peace*.

12. We are learning a lot about african history this year.

13. There is a small baptist church near our house.

14. Lydia communicates using american Sign Language.

15. We got to taste belgian food at the exhibit.

16. I bought a book of Native american poetry.

17. Akbar taught us an iranian children's song.

18. Peter goes to a mormon church.

19. We bought a beautiful sculpture by a young nigerian artist.

20. Juan studies Spanish, Portuguese, and english.

Language and Sentence Skills Practice

MECHANICS

Proper Nouns and Proper Adjectives A

Capitalize proper nouns and proper adjectives.

EXAMPLES	**H**arold	**M**adison, **W**isconsin	**M**ars
	Friday	**F**ranciscan monk	**S**wiss watch
	Victorian furniture	**T**exas **S**tadium	**T**aoism

EXERCISE In the following sentences, circle each letter that should be capitalized but is not.

Example 1. Marta enjoys discussing (a)sian culture, the (t)itanic, biology, and (r)ussian literature.

1. My sister rita is writing a report on the great depression.

2. During the months of may and june, Carlos spends much of his time in alberta, canada.

3. Rosalinda's ancestors are spanish.

4. Mrs. Blair's lesson on shakespearean england thrilled her students.

5. Cecilia studies french and spanish at northside middle school.

6. Franco told us that jordan enjoys eating traditional turkish food.

7. The voyage of the *mayflower* is an important event in American history.

8. Every june, the teams compete in an event called the Little league world series.

9. The purpose of Memorial day is to honor those who died in war while serving the United States of America.

10. José admires italian art from the renaissance period.

11. Sharon's dog fritz was a christmas present.

12. In astronomy I, you will learn how stars, such as polaris, are formed.

13. Olga bought a skateboard from bikes and more, inc.

14. Yori and Greg found out that both of their birthdays were on February 14, which is also Valentine's day.

15. Scott gave an interesting report about scottish clans who lived during the middle ages.

16. After the school year, Julio's family moved to the midwest.

17. Each year, thousands of japanese people climb to the top of Mount Fuji.

18. Li's family invited Teresa to the beach at dauphin Island.

19. Mount rushmore national memorial honors four american presidents.

20. In the United States, Puerto rico, and canada, labor Day is celebrated in september.

Proper Nouns and Proper Adjectives B

Capitalize proper nouns and proper adjectives.

EXAMPLES **B**lue **R**idge **M**ountains   **B**uddhist   **L**assie

Canadian citizen   **R**oman history   **J**ewish holiday

EXERCISE In the following sentences, circle each letter that should be capitalized but is not.

Example 1. The trip from ⓙapan to ⓐmerica was quite an adventure for Takeo.

1. Takeo visited the united States this year.

2. His plane landed on Wednesday morning in Los Angeles, california.

3. Takeo rented a toyota van so that he could drive around the country.

4. He first drove to aspen, Colorado, to ski and to see the aspen music Festival.

5. In denver, colorado, Takeo met a german family who were also tourists.

6. The family invited Takeo to a lutheran church for easter services.

7. They photographed the beautiful church, which was built just after the great depression.

8. Takeo and his new german friends took a short trip together to boulder, colorado.

9. After leaving Colorado, Takeo headed for the grand canyon national park.

10. He then drove to the famous city of dallas to learn about texan culture.

11. While in texas, he drove to San antonio to visit the site where the battle of the alamo was fought.

12. Takeo then drove east to the french Quarter in New Orleans, louisiana.

13. On monday, he went for a long hiking trip in the Great smoky Mountains.

14. Of course, Takeo stopped to see the white house and the Washington monument in Washington, D.C.

15. After touring chesapeake bay, Takeo drove to new York on interstate 95.

16. He rode the elevator to the top of the empire state Building.

17. Takeo took a tour boat that circled the Statue of liberty and ellis island.

18. After touring the New england area, Takeo drove through the corn belt on his way to montana.

19. In Seattle, Takeo viewed the big dipper from high atop the Space needle.

20. Finally, he returned to California, watched the Los Angeles lakers play basketball, and then headed back to Tokyo.

MECHANICS

Abbreviations

11g. Most abbreviations are capitalized.

Capitalize abbreviations that come before and after personal names.

EXAMPLES   Mr., Ms., Mrs., Dr., Sen., Gen., Rep., **M.D., RN, Jr., Sr.**

Capitalize abbreviations of the names of organizations, businesses, and government bodies.

EXAMPLES   Inc., Co., Corp., **CIA, EEOC, UN, FDIC, NCAA**

Capitalize abbreviations used in addresses.

EXAMPLES   Ave., St., Dr., Rd., Apt., Rm., **P.O. B**ox

Capitalize abbreviations of geographical names.

EXAMPLES   St. Croix   S. America   Okla.   **USA**   **UK**   **NM**

Some abbreviations, especially those for measurements, are not capitalized.

EXAMPLES   etc., **e.g., v**ol., chap., in., lb, tsp, yd, cc, ml, mm

---

EXERCISE   Each of the following sentences contains an error in capitalization. For each sentence, circle the letter that should be capitalized but is not.

Example 1. Have you seen the zoo in ⓢt. Louis?

1. I read a biography about sen. Phil Gramm.

2. Phineas Newborn, jr., was a twentieth-century jazz pianist.

3. Dennis is an engineer for Technico, inc.

4. The woman was known for her superb photographs of st. Petersburg.

5. Joyce Day, Rn, spoke to our class today.

6. Our school competed in the choral contest in st. Paul, Minnesota.

7. The address on the envelope reads, "1100 Congress Ave., Austin, Tx 78701."

8. We learned that gen. Ulysses S. Grant became a U.S. president.

9. I visited the office of col. Helen Wright.

10. Have you met mrs. Evans, the new principal?

Personal Titles and Familial Titles

11h. Capitalize titles.

(1) Capitalize a person's title when the title comes before the person's name.

   EXAMPLES   **P**resident Carter   **Mr.** Sato   **Q**ueen Elizabeth

(2) Titles used alone or following a person's name generally are not capitalized.

   EXAMPLE   The club **s**ecretary will now read the minutes from last week's meeting.

(3) Capitalize a word showing a family relationship when the word is used before or in place of a person's name.

   EXAMPLE   We waited outside the store for **M**om and **A**unt **L**uisa.

EXERCISE In the following sentences, circle each letter that should be capitalized but is not.

Example 1. Mr. ⃝rivera is president of the neighborhood association.

1. My neighbor, who is a doctor, serves on a committee with mayor Pinelli.

2. Many people were saddened by the death of princess Diana.

3. Last week, mrs. Robinson was elected secretary of the local theater club.

4. The film was about president Roosevelt and Prime Minister Churchill.

5. For my birthday, aunt Lilith gave me a savings bond.

6. In history class, we studied the long reign of queen Victoria.

7. How many votes did mayor Phillips receive?

8. I visited uncle Robert at Thanksgiving.

9. Our teacher read us an article about lord Nelson's victories.

10. We asked about governor Long's nickname.

11. Colleen read one of president Lincoln's speeches.

12. The song was written for aunt Marguerita.

13. Our town was excited when mayor Romero was elected.

14. The book focuses on king Henry VIII's reign.

15. Gail commented on the sharp wit of captain Jones.

16. Some of the students chose to write their reports on president Mandela.

17. The sailors listened carefully to commander Foster.

18. The majority of voters chose representative Miller.

19. After church, I spoke with the reverend Allen Thompson.

20. father often plays checkers with either mom or Uncle Earl.

Language and Sentence Skills Practice   **225**

MECHANICS

Titles of Books and Other Works

11h. Capitalize titles.

(4) Capitalize the first and last words and all important words in titles and subtitles.

BOOKS	*Oliver Twist*	*Cheaper by the Dozen*
NEWSPAPERS	the *Boston Globe*	the *Chicago Tribune*
SHORT STORIES	"The Gift of the Magi"	"The Circuit"
MOVIES	*Return of the Jedi*	*Gone with the Wind*
WORKS OF ART	*The Peaceable Kingdom*	*The Old Guitarist*
MUSICAL WORKS	"Stir It Up"	*The Queen of Spades*

EXERCISE   Circle each letter that should be capitalized but is not.

Example 1. ⓐ ⓒhristmas ⓒarol

1. "the battle hymn of the republic"

2. *Little house on the prairie*

3. *the Phantom of the opera*

4. the *washington post*

5. "the moccasins of an old man"

6. *war and peace*

7. "the pit and the pendulum"

8. *pride and prejudice*

9. "moon river"

10. *The marriage of figaro*

11. *A man for all seasons*

12. *the muppets take manhattan*

13. *A tale of two cities*

14. *The starry night*

15. "petrified man"

16. *the phantom tollbooth*

17. "looking for mr. green"

18. *the Little Prince*

19. *the wizard of oz*

20. *the rite of spring*

MECHANICS

Abbreviations and Titles A

Capitalize titles and most abbreviations.

EXAMPLES	**M**r.	**M**rs.	**A**ve.
	Inc.	**P.O. B**ox	**N.** America
	Col. Juliet Parker	**FBI**	**J**r.
	Principal Owens	**K**ing David	**U**ncle Leo
	***S**tar **W**ars*	***T**he **C**all of the **W**ild*	***F**ahrenheit 451*

EXERCISE A Each of the following sentences contains one or more errors in capitalization. For each sentence, circle each letter that should be capitalized but is not.

Example 1. Has her mom spoken with ⃞captain Rogers or ⃞dr. Smith?

1. The soldiers saw gen. Norman Tiller approaching.

2. David is reading about queen Elizabeth I.

3. I sent a letter to aunt Margaret at p.o. box 42, San Antonio, Tx 78201.

4. Greg met dr. Mendoza, who is the author of *healthful diets in the age of fast food*.

5. Did you hear, mother, that I made an A in English?

6. My uncle used to work for the cia.

7. Today, professor Larsen gave a lecture on the short story "to build a fire."

8. We were happy to meet senator Caldwell.

9. I hope grandmother will enjoy her subscription to the magazine *dog fancy*.

10. Did you hear mayor Williams speak?

EXERCISE B Each of the following sentences has one or more errors in capitalization. For each sentence, circle each letter that should be capitalized but is not.

Example 1. Do you know, ⃞dad, that ⃞mayor Casterbridge reads *⃞mayor ⃞monthly* magazine?

11. Alicia Davis, m.d., has in her office a reproduction of the painting *american gothic*.

12. The senator from st. louis took his mother to see the play *the taming of the shrew*.

13. I didn't know that aunt Lisa and her mother enjoyed reading comic strips.

14. The scientist founded Research, inc.

15. Hector could not decide whether to research the history of the naacp, the fda, or the Un.

MECHANICS

Abbreviations and Titles B

Capitalize titles and most abbreviations.

EXAMPLES	**D**r.	**M**s.	**S**t.
	Co.	**A**pt.	**S**. Africa
	Gen. Rose Riley	**FDA**	**S**r.
	Senator Day	**Q**ueen Elizabeth	**U**ncle **P**at
	The Far Side	*Romeo and Juliet*	*Fantasia*
	Lord of the Flies	*Wishbone*	"**T**he **R**aven"

EXERCISE A Each of the following titles contains errors in capitalization. For each title, circle each letter that should be capitalized but is not.

Example 1. the ⓗouston ⓒhronicle

1. *tuck everlasting*

2. "kubla khan"

3. *great expectations*

4. "The ransom of red chief"

5. *The little mermaid*

6. "musetta's waltz"

7. *the lion king*

8. *marriage at cana*

9. "Unchained melody"

10. *Philosopher reading*

EXERCISE B Each of the following sentences contains one or more errors in capitalization. For each sentence, circle each letter that should be capitalized but is not.

Example 1. Has ⓐunt Paula read the book ⓐ ⓓay ⓝⓞ ⓟigs ⓦould ⓓie?

11. Stephanie read the review of *toy story 2* in *movie news* magazine.

12. My aunt loves the song "georgia on my mind."

13. Liz, did you know that mom was in the cia?

14. The game show *jeopardy!* is very challenging.

15. Have you seen Rodin's sculpture titled *the thinker*?

16. Write to me at 1410 west st., st. paul, mn 55101.

17. The committee gave president Hernandez, the founder of hernandez and co., an award.

18. Julie Jones, m.d., enjoys jogging down Jay street while listening to the song "eye of the tiger."

19. The writers of *national geographic* cover stories from around the world.

20. My sister said that the video *Play Piano like a pro in one day, guaranteed!* did not live up to the promise made in the title.

Review A: **Capital Letters**

EXERCISE A Each of the following sentences contains at least one error in capitalization. Circle each letter that should be capitalized but is not. Also, underline each letter that should be lowercased but is not.

Example 1. Tell uncle john about the Show you saw on thursday.

1. Last night i watched a great program on PBS.

2. it was a Play called *Anne of green Gables*.

3. My aunt Dolores, who lives in st. Croix, watched the Program with me.

4. After it was over, she said, "now let's read more about Anne."

5. She and I read L. M. Montgomery's Book *anne of Avonlea*.

6. I read a book about Charles drew, a famous Scientist.

7. He was an african american doctor who was born in Washington, d.c.

8. he was a Specialist in collecting and storing blood for transfusions.

9. During World war II, he helped develop blood banks.

10. The american Red Cross still uses his methods today.

EXERCISE B Each of the following sentences contains errors in capitalization. For each sentence, circle each letter that should be capitalized but is not.

Example 1. My mother likes to eat authentic chinese food at the restaurant China gate.

11. Jonah celebrated his birthday on the fourth thursday of November.

12. The professor studied the french paintings in the louvre.

13. according to mom, uncle pete is visiting spain.

14. The federal bureau of investigation is also known as the fbi.

15. the entire class sang "happy birthday" to dr. Proctor.

16. The cruise ship *voyager express* sailed to florida.

17. a russian scientist won the Nobel prize for his important work.

18. The class watched a video about gen. robert e. lee.

19. While sitting in a booth at salad sam's, Li looked up at the constellation orion.

20. dr. Small's history II class studied the life of president Truman.

MECHANICS

Review B: **Capital Letters**

MECHANICS

EXERCISE A In the following sentences, circle each letter that should be capitalized but is not.

Example 1. Did ⓘngrid ⓑergman ever win an ⓐcademy ⓐward?

1. we have a new stove made by Stay hot stoves.

2. Hans Christian andersen was born in the danish city of Odense.

3. the alamo is a historic spanish mission in san antonio, texas.

4. Mount kilimanjaro is in the african country of tanzania, near the kenyan border.

5. Seventh-graders at winthrop junior high school take art I, math, and english.

6. See dr. Sanchez if your cold isn't better by tuesday.

7. his grandfather works at henderson hardware.

8. i was born in new orleans on january 11.

9. Bill Cosby went to Temple university in philadelphia.

10. The 1992 olympics were held in Barcelona, Spain.

EXERCISE B Each of the following sentences contains errors in capitalization. For each sentence, circle each letter that should be capitalized but is not.

Example 1. ⓜs. ⓢchwartz observes the ⓙewish holiday ⓨom Kippur.

11. my history teacher said that i should study the french Revolution.

12. On the fourth of july, Eli went to the top of the Empire state building.

13. Leslie's father is part cherokee and part irish.

14. *Air force one* and the *spirit of St. Louis* are two famous planes.

15. The first five books of the bible are called the pentateuch.

16. According to grandmother, aunt Ramona knows much about the north star.

17. For breakfast, mom bought a brand of cereal called i can't believe it's wheat!

18. The council criticized president tate for his lack of leadership.

19. Last year, the doctor joined the American medical association, or AmA.

20. Washington irving, who was born the same year the American revolution ended, wrote short stories.

Review C: **Capital Letters**

EXERCISE A Each of the following sentences contains at least one error in capitalization. Circle each letter that should be capitalized but is not. Also, underline each letter that should be lowercased but is not.

Example 1. Is Mr. tyrone kersee, sr., the new Chair of the Committee?

1. Sixth-graders at our School take English, Spanish, math I, and Social Studies.

2. The sahara is an African desert, running from the atlantic ocean to the Red sea.

3. Yogi berra was a Great Catcher who played for the New York yankees.

4. The author joseph conrad was a polish immigrant to great britain.

5. My Elementary School was named after dr. martin luther king, jr.

6. Key West is an Island off the coast of Florida.

7. His Uncle Roberto runs a Gas Station that is across the street from the stokes Building.

8. Does dr. Ranelli see patients at phoenix General Hospital?

9. Muhammad, our class President, practices the religion of islam.

10. south African writer Nadine Gordimer won the nobel prize.

EXERCISE B Each of the numbered items in the following letter contains at least one error in capitalization. For each numbered item, circle each letter that should be capitalized but is not.

Example [1] Marta wrote a letter to aunt Carmelita.

[11] dear Aunt carmelita,

   [12] Do you remember that i am in the sixth grade at wilson elementary? **[13]** My teacher mrs. abel is swiss. **[14]** In english class, we are reading *The old man and the sea*. **[15]** In history, we are studying the revolutionary War. **[16]** I learned a lot about gen. george Washington. **[17]** In science class, we learned to identify the big Dipper. **[18]** We are going to learn about the space shuttle *discovery* after the thanksgiving holiday. **[19]** i will visit you and uncle jaime soon.

                                        [20] sincerely,

                                        Marta

Language and Sentence Skills Practice

Proofreading Applications: Directions

Good writers are generally good proofreaders. Readers admire and trust writing that is error-free. Make sure that you correct all errors in grammar, usage, spelling, and punctuation in your writing. Your readers will have more confidence in your words if you have done your best to proofread carefully.

Picture this: It is a hot summer day, and you have been walking eight blocks. You are now standing under a street sign that reads "Twelfth Street." In your hand is a crumpled page of handwritten directions. The directions say "Turn left at the twelfth street sign." What do you do? Do you turn left now? Or do you continue walking for another four blocks to the twelfth street sign? It's confusing, isn't it?

If the writer had capitalized *Twelfth Street*, you would know what to do. Proper capitalization makes a writer's meaning clear. Be particularly careful to use capital letters correctly whenever you write directions.

PROOFREADING ACTIVITY

Find and correct the errors in capital letters in the following directions. Use proofreading symbols to make your corrections.

Example I'm looking forward to seeing you on saturday Afternoon.

Our house is a little difficult to find, so i wrote these directions for you. Begin at Forrest elementary school. Get on the road that runs on the North side by the playground. Go past the little Store called Elmer's on the corner of Vine and elm. You'll go right past kaybean's coffee house.

You should now be on Ruskin drive. By the way, the pink house with the cement Rabbits out front belongs to Kelsey's Dad. Mr. Jackson always has a big thanksgiving day party for the whole neighborhood.

Next, you'll pass by a blue house where a south American macaw usually perches on the porch. His name is Pancho, and he actually speaks spanish and some portuguese. Our house is on the street next

Literary Model: Capital Letters in a Poem

> They [the Jumblies] sailed to the Western Sea, they did,
> To a land all covered with trees,
> And they bought an Owl, and a useful Cart,
> And a pound of Rice, and a Cranberry Tart,   60
> And a hive of silvery Bees.
> And they bought a Pig, and some green Jackdaws,
> And a lovely Monkey with lollipop paws,
> And forty bottles of Ring-Bo-Ree,
> And no end of Stilton Cheese.   65
>   Far and few, far and few,
>   Are the lands where the Jumblies live;
>   Their heads are green, and their hands are blue,
>   And they went to sea in a Sieve.

—from "The Jumblies" by Edward Lear

EXERCISE A   Write the words in the verse that do not follow the rules of capitalization covered in this chapter. (Hints: *Stilton* is the name of a place in England. *Western Sea* and *Jumblies* should be considered proper nouns. The words *jackdaws* and *sieve* are common nouns.)

_____   _____

_____   _____

_____   _____

_____   _____

_____   _____

EXERCISE B   What effect does the capitalization of the words you identified in Exercise A have on the poem? Before you answer, ask a classmate or your teacher to read aloud lines fifty-nine through sixty-five of "The Jumblies." Follow along in your workbook, highlighting the words from the poem that the reader stresses.

_____

_____

_____

_____

Language and Sentence Skills Practice

for **CHAPTER 11: CAPITAL LETTERS** | pages 238–61

Literary Model (continued)

EXERCISE C Write a poem that is at least eight lines long. It can be nonsense verse such as Edward Lear wrote, or it can be a serious poem. Use capital and lowercase letters either to create a distinct rhythm or to make the reader respond to certain words in a particular way.

_____
_____
_____
_____
_____
_____
_____
_____
_____
_____
_____
_____

EXERCISE D

1. Explain the effect you wanted to achieve by capitalizing (or not capitalizing) certain words in your poem. Give examples from your poem to support your response.

_____
_____

2. Do you think it would be effective not to follow standard conventions of capitalization in other forms of writing, such as book reports, essays, or business letters? Explain your answer.

_____
_____
_____
_____
_____
_____

Writing Application: Using Capital Letters in an Essay

A proper adjective is any adjective formed from a proper noun. For example, names of places and organizations very often give rise to proper adjectives.

EXAMPLES   The **Asian** restaurant around the corner has delicious food.

The **Rotarians** held a debate on recycling at the Rotary Club.

A proper noun is capitalized, and so is a proper adjective. Any time you use an adjective, determine whether it comes from a proper noun. If it does, the adjective probably needs to be capitalized. If you are not sure whether you should capitalize an adjective, check a dictionary.

WRITING ACTIVITY

Your school is planning an international culture day, with each grade level responsible for a certain part of the celebration. Sixth-graders are coming up with the menu for the event. Choose four foods from four cultures, and convince your class that your menu is the one students will enjoy most while learning about a new culture. Be sure to capitalize the proper nouns and adjectives you use.

PREWRITING   Because you are probably familiar with some cultures and their foods, you may already have menu suggestions in mind. If not, head for some cookbooks, which you can find in a public library, online, or perhaps in your own kitchen. Decide on four foods that would go together well. Don't forget a drink and perhaps a dessert!

WRITING   You will present a menu sheet—a list of the foods that you are suggesting—and two paragraphs describing the foods and the cultures of those who traditionally eat those foods. Persuade your class that the entire school needs to experience these cultures through the foods. You may wish to brainstorm a list of reasons that these cultures matter to students. Do people who belong to each culture live nearby? Have they made special contributions to our world? Is the culture mysterious or exotic? Does it have a long history? What interests you about the culture?

Organize your thoughts into two persuasive paragraphs, briefly discussing two cultures in each paragraph. Use transitional words and phrases to move readers smoothly from one food to the next so that their reading experience will be cohesive.

REVISING   After your paragraph is complete, think about the words that will best convince students to choose your suggested menu. Choose "appetizing" words that will make students want to taste these foods and learn about the culture from which the foods come.

PUBLISHING   Check your menu and paragraph for mistakes in spelling and punctuation. Be sure that you have capitalized all proper nouns and proper adjectives. Make your menu attractive by using illustrations or decorative fonts. Then, present your menu and paragraphs to the class and let them decide whether your menu should be adopted.

EXTENDING YOUR WRITING

This exercise could lead to a more developed writing project. For a social studies class, you could prepare a presentation about some of the traditions and beliefs of a culture that interests you. Write a speech that you will present to the class, choose pictures to illustrate your words, and try to bring some cultural items that students can see and handle. If you are able, top off your fine production with a sample of the culture's food.

for **CHAPTER 12: PUNCTUATION**   *pages 263–82*

Choices: Investigating Punctuation

Here's your chance to step out of the grammar book and into the real world. You may not notice punctuation marks, but you and the people around you use them almost every day. The following activities challenge you to find a connection between punctuation and the world around you. Do the activity below that suits your personality best, and then share your discoveries with your class. Have fun!

ART

Coming Soon!

What do commas look like to you? Maybe they make you think of tadpoles. Then again, commas might remind you of germinating seeds. Use your imagination to create posters advertising your vision. Then, with your teacher's permission, display the posters in the classroom.

ETYMOLOGY

Deep Roots

Look up the word *punctuate* in a dictionary. Find out its root and what it means. Then, find other words, such as *punctual*, that use this same root. When you're done, prepare a poster in which you illustrate how these words and their meanings grow out of a single root.

ORGANIZING INFORMATION

In a Nutshell

Make a two-column chart to help you and your classmates study end marks, commas, semicolons, and colons. List the rules from this chapter in the left-hand column and examples of the rules in the right-hand column. Then, make copies of your chart to give to your classmates. Now, everyone will have a quick reference listing of the rules on hand.

WRITING

Four by Four

Write a four-line poem. In your poem, end one sentence with a period. End another with a question mark and another with an exclamation mark. Finally, make the remaining sentence a command; end this sentence with either an exclamation mark or a period. Present your sentences in any order that you choose, but be sure that each sentence is correctly punctuated. With your teacher's permission, post your poem in your classroom.

GAME

Fun and Games

Make a list of at least ten mind-bending questions. Each question will ask contestants to name a set, such as all the planets, all the continents, or all seven wonders of the ancient world. For each question, two contestants must go to the chalkboard and write a sentence with a colon followed by the series that answers the question. The first contestant to get the correct answer with the correct punctuation wins a point for his or her team. The team with the most points at the end of the game wins!

WRITING

Obstacle Course

Write a paragraph in which you insert several unnecessary commas. Then, ask a brave classmate to read your paragraph to the class, but don't let him or her read the paragraph beforehand. Your classmate will probably stumble several times, so be sure to let him or her know that reading your paragraph will be a real obstacle course. When your classmate is finished, ask him or her to circle the commas that made reading the paragraph difficult. Did he or she circle every unnecessary comma?

INVENTION

Make Your Mark

It's a new century! Design a new mark of punctuation for our changing times. You'll need a shape, a name, and a purpose for your mark. Begin by considering what new situations or technologies, such as e-mail, might need such a mark. Once you have come up with a punctuation mark and a good reason for it, write five sentences using your new mark. Don't forget to share your invention with your classmates.

End Marks

12a. Use a period at the end of a statement (a declarative sentence).

12b. Use a question mark at the end of a question (an interrogative sentence).

12c. Use an exclamation point at the end of an exclamation (an exclamatory sentence).

12d. Use either a period or an exclamation point at the end of a request or a command (an imperative sentence).

EXAMPLES Fire safety is important for everybody.
Do you have a smoke detector in your house?
The movie was great!
Please help with the litter. [a request]
Pick up that litter. [a command]
Pick up that litter this instant! [a strong command]

EXERCISE A Insert periods, question marks, and exclamation points where they belong in the following sentences.

Example 1. What a beautiful seashell collection!

1. Leslie's mother collects driftwood

2. It's fun to collect things

3. Have you seen my shell collection

4. What a colorful collection it is

5. Please don't drop it

EXERCISE B Decide where each sentence in the following paragraph begins and ends. Then, insert punctuation marks where needed. Also, triple underline each lowercase letter that should be capitalized.

Example have you ever heard of Easter Island?

Easter Island is a small island in the South Pacific it is 2,300 miles west of South America the island was first settled about 1,600 years ago Easter Island is best known for its giant stone statues have you ever seen a picture of one the statues are called *moai* there are over six hundred of these statues on the island most of them are 11 to 20 feet tall some of them are as tall as 40 feet what a strange sight they are

Abbreviations

12e. Many abbreviations are followed by periods.

EXAMPLES	Dr. Ann Stern	James K. Polk	Diabetes Assn.	Feb.
	Springfield Ave.	Colo.	St. Louis	P.M.

Abbreviations for government agencies and some widely used abbreviations are written without periods. Each letter of such abbreviations (which are called *acronyms*) is capitalized.

EXAMPLES	UN (**U**nited **N**ations)	MLA (**M**odern **L**anguage **A**ssociation)
	ROTC (**R**eserve **O**fficers' **T**raining **C**orps)	OR (**o**perating **r**oom)

Abbreviations for units of measure are usually written without periods and are not capitalized.

EXAMPLES   cc   kg   ml   m   ft   lb   qt

EXERCISE A Insert periods where they belong in the following sentences.

Example 1. Didn't Dr. Wilson work for the FBI?

1. Is Mrs. Johnson's plane leaving at 10:00 AM. or 10:00 PM.?

2. The store's new address is 2800 S State St, Ann Arbor, MI 48104.

3. NASA's Johnson Space Center is in Houston, Tex, if I'm not mistaken.

4. The author of *The Hobbit,* my favorite book, is J R R Tolkien.

5. Patricia lives on Morning Glory Cir in Charleston, S Carolina.

6. My baby sister was born at 2:38 A.M. on Sat, Jan 9, 2000, at St Luke's Hospital.

7. Juanita Calderon, DDS, is my dentist.

8. Paul McIntyre, Jr, is 4 ft, 8 in tall.

9. Please drop off your old plastic bottles at M E Mayer Recycling, Inc, at 1423 Moscow Road.

10. During his TV lecture, Dr Olson said that the Battle of Hastings happened in AD. 1066.

EXERCISE B On the lines provided, spell out the words that are abbreviated.

Example 1. the U.S. of A. *the United States of America* _____

11. Dr. Robert Sanders _____

12. S. Anderson St. _____

13. Gen. Colin Powell _____

14. New Orleans, La. _____

15. Sun., April 15 _____

End Marks and Abbreviations

12a.	Use a period at the end of a statement (a declarative sentence).
12b.	Use a question mark at the end of a question (an interrogative sentence).
12c.	Use an exclamation point at the end of an exclamation (an exclamatory sentence).
12d.	Use either a period or an exclamation point at the end of a request or a command (an imperative sentence).
12e.	Many abbreviations are followed by periods.

EXERCISE Revise the following sentences, adding periods, question marks, and exclamation points where needed.

Example 1. If you're going to be home later than 6:00 P. M. , please call.

1. The British adventurer T E Lawrence is also known as Lawrence of Arabia

2. Did you know that my house is on N Peach St

3. Tonya grew up in St Augustine, Fla, but now she lives in Toronto.

4. Please be very careful with that box

5. My father is being treated by Dr John Kim

6. Where did you put the toaster

7. My mother left her job at Baxter, Baxter, and Assoc and went to work for the FBI

8. The dog snatched the bone off the kitchen counter

9. Please let me know if you and David, Jr , want to come to the movies with me

10. What a gorgeous sunset this is

11. Prof Pedro Ríos will speak to us about his research on black holes

12. Who bought the house at 2403 W Jefferson Lane

13. How nice our new neighbors are

14. Please call Mrs McConnell about this weekend's plans

15. Is Mr Patrick Leblanc, Sr, or his son going to the exhibit

16. I believe Timothy S Palmer published a new book last year

17. What nerve she has to say such a thing

18. The new community center will be on Kerr Ave next to the library

19. How much does that book by D H Lawrence cost

20. Betsy has just moved to Flagstaff, Ariz, with her family

Commas with Items in a Series

12f.	Use commas to separate items in a series.

12g.	Use commas to separate two or more adjectives that come before a noun.

WORDS IN A SERIES	Our parrot talks, whistles, and sings.
WORD GROUPS IN A SERIES	Every day I uncover the cage, pour the seed, and change the water.
TWO OR MORE ADJECTIVES	Italy is a beautiful, fascinating country.

EXERCISE A   Insert commas where they are needed in the following sentences.

Example   1. Mrs. Sanchez stood up, closed the book, and walked away.

1. Tracy made her bed hung up her clothes and took out the trash.

2. Dale has the following jobs: drying dishes walking the dog and ironing.

3. The plane stops at Chicago Atlanta and Miami.

4. Nick Tom and Molly walk to school together.

5. They hike swim and play volleyball on Friday.

6. Do you live near the school the park or the factory?

7. The flower show had lilies orchids and violets.

8. Mrs. Olson Mr. Ginsburg and Dr. Pratt spoke at the assembly.

9. Oregano adds flavor to sauces soups and pasta.

10. Would you prefer to eat bagels omelets or cereal?

EXERCISE B   Some of the following sentences need commas and some do not. If a sentence needs a comma, insert one. If a sentence is already correct, write *C* next to the number.

Example   1. Did you see the tall, quiet stranger?

11. Old worn tires may be recycled.

12. Yeast in warm moist dough makes bread rise.

13. This is the reddest roundest tomato in the pail.

14. We gathered tiny purple flowers.

15. Some children sang a jolly carefree tune.

16. They played in a cool spacious treehouse.

17. Have you learned the new soccer rules?

18. The fast exciting game was fun to watch.

19. What a colorful soft jacket that is!

20. Mountain goats and antelopes have powerful hind legs.

Commas in Compound Sentences

12h.	Use a comma before *and, but, for, nor, or, so,* or *yet* when it joins independent clauses in a compound sentence.

EXAMPLE Bicycle helmets are important**,** for they protect us.

EXERCISE A Add commas where they are needed in the following sentences.

Example 1. This helmet is well constructed**,** so it will probably last a long time.

1. Bicycle safety is important so learn the rules.

2. Drivers can't always see you but you can usually see them.

3. Pilar owns a helmet yet she sometimes forgets to take it.

4. Are you going to carry it to the park or will you wear it?

5. Most helmets have reflectors yet drivers may not see you.

6. My reflectors are shiny but they're small.

7. Helmets can be light and they should be comfortable.

8. Air vents are helpful for you may perspire.

9. There's a bicycle club at school so why don't we join it?

10. Jake did not race this week nor did he race last week.

EXERCISE B On the line provided, combine each pair of short sentences to form a compound sentence. Use *and, but, for, so,* or *yet.* Include commas as needed.

Example 1. We're very tired right now. We can rest soon.

We're very tired right now, but we can rest soon.

11. This is a long trip. We packed plenty of food.

_____

12. I'm wide awake. I'm not afraid.

_____

13. This backpack is bulky. It isn't heavy.

_____

14. It's foggy outdoors. We might start late.

_____

15. You prepare the camp stove. I will get the food ready.

_____

Language and Sentence Skills Practice

MECHANICS

Commas with Interrupters

| **12i.** | Use commas to set off an expression that interrupts a sentence. |

(1) Use commas to set off appositives and appositive phrases that are not necessary to the meaning of a sentence.

(2) Use commas to set off words used in direct address.

EXAMPLES   The first-place winner, Ricardo, can enter the finals.

Spaghetti, a thin pasta, can be served with different sauces.

Did you say, Mrs. Herbert, that you need a baby sitter?

Ted, will you take care of Dylan on Saturday?

EXERCISE A   Each of the following sentences contains at least one error in the punctuation of an appositive or an appositive phrase. Add commas to correct each error.

Example 1. Mr. Addison, our teacher, comes from Chicago.

1. The Jolly Tiger my father's favorite restaurant has a special this week on sandwiches.

2. I saw a special on television last night about cartography the science of mapmaking.

3. The organizers of the field trip Maya and Brenda prepared a guidebook for the class.

4. Have you met Dr. Santini our guest of honor?

5. Brendan a science fiction fan wrote a report about his favorite film.

6. I finally found a can of tomato sauce the last necessary ingredient for the recipe.

7. Whiskers our cat is fond of sleeping under the bed.

8. The story the funniest one I've read in a long time was the last one in the book.

9. The movie's music was written by Bernard Herrmann a well-known film composer.

10. A nutritionist Mr. Unruh will talk to us later about a balanced diet.

EXERCISE B   Add commas as necessary in the following sentences.

Example 1. Tom, will you bring me that wrench, please?

11. Tell me Dr. Morituri how long have you lived in San Francisco?

12. Carla are you finished reading the newspaper yet?

13. Ask your mother's permission before you turn on the television Nicoletta.

14. Try not to drop the ball next time Ernesto.

15. If you bring the plates Nedra I'll bring the silverware.

MECHANICS

Commas with Introductory Elements

12j. Use a comma after certain introductory elements.

(1) Use a comma after *yes, no,* or any mild exclamation such as *well* or *why* at the beginning of a sentence.

(2) Use a comma after two or more introductory prepositional phrases.

(3) Use a comma after an introductory adverb clause.

> **EXAMPLES** **Well,** can I expect you by two o'clock?
>
> **At the end of the tough practice,** the coach praised her players.
>
> **After you have finished eating your breakfast,** please help shovel the snow.

EXERCISE A Each of the following sentences is punctuated correctly. In the blank next to each sentence, write the number of the comma rule that applies to the sentence.

Example _12j, (2)_ **1.** At the top of the staircase, Ali stood with his arms folded.

_____ **1.** Before he went home, Michael had collected fifty seashells.

_____ **2.** On top of the workbench in the garage, you will find a claw hammer.

_____ **3.** As soon as Maria saw the moons of Jupiter through a telescope, she knew she wanted to study astronomy.

_____ **4.** Yes, that's exactly what I meant.

_____ **5.** In spite of the rain, we had a good time at the picnic.

EXERCISE B Add commas where necessary in the following sentences.

Example **1.** Before we left the house, we had locked all the doors and windows.

6. So are you ready to go?

7. In the trees around our house the birds make a loud racket every morning.

8. After the birthday party on Saturday Kyle and Lucita cleaned up the yard.

9. On behalf of the entire team the coach thanked Lakshmi for making the winning goal.

10. Say have you read today's newspaper?

11. Before you apply for a passport you will need to get your picture taken.

12. Once he was awake Paul no longer remembered the frightening dream.

13. In the yard behind the house a cat sleeps in a patch of sunlight.

14. Why here comes Katie!

15. Ten minutes after the fireworks display had ended smoke was still drifting across the lake.

Commas A

12f. Use commas to separate items in a series.

12g. Use commas to separate two or more adjectives that come before a noun.

12h. Use a comma before *and, but, for, nor, or, so,* or *yet* when it joins independent clauses in a compound sentence.

12i. Use commas to set off an expression that interrupts a sentence.

12j. Use a comma after certain introductory elements.

EXERCISE Add commas where necessary in the following sentences. Hint: Some sentences need more than one comma.

Example 1. Yes, the three winners of the spelling bee were Claudia, Latisha, and Benson.

1. I wish I could come to the movies with you but I have to mow the lawn.

2. No that book is not the one she read.

3. That long low mound of earth is called a barrow.

4. Isaac Newton was one of the founders of modern physics the study of matter and energy.

5. The three closest planets to the Sun Martin are Mercury Venus and Earth.

6. Hey is your dog a springer spaniel?

7. In the room at the top of the stairs I found an old photo album.

8. The small gray cat lapped milk from the saucer.

9. By the middle of the afternoon the snow had melted.

10. Ms. Ozu our next-door neighbor plays the violin.

11. What sort of apple is this Chester?

12. The short peppy song on the radio made us all laugh.

13. Last weekend we went to the park to the movie theater and to the museum.

14. The dog lay down and began to whimper so we gave it a treat.

15. Before you go Aimee tell us how you started writing songs.

16. Julio found an old faded picture of his grandfather.

17. Do you want to see a movie or would you rather see a concert?

18. Amelia has a dog a cat and a hamster.

19. The small fragile locket was a treasured heirloom and Kathryn wore it with pride.

20. Raphael read for three hours for he couldn't wait to find out what happened.

Commas B

12f.	Use commas to separate items in a series.
12g.	Use commas to separate two or more adjectives that come before a noun.
12h.	Use a comma before *and, but, for, nor, or, so,* or *yet* when it joins independent clauses in a compound sentence.
12i.	Use commas to set off an expression that interrupts a sentence.
12j.	Use a comma after certain introductory elements.

EXERCISE Add commas where necessary in the following sentences. Hint: Some sentences need more than one comma.

Example 1. Before he went out onto the basketball court, Michael made sure his shoes were tied.

1. The four Beatles were John Lennon Paul McCartney George Harrison and Ringo Starr.

2. Sarah do you know Mr. Elway the minister of our church?

3. Carlo does not like cold weather yet he enjoys skiing.

4. The happy energetic girl ran to meet her grandfather.

5. In the backyard of our old house we taught our dog to roll over.

6. Oh I suppose you're right Sue.

7. After lunch Mr. Pradesh raked the leaves mowed the lawn and trimmed the bushes.

8. Is someone coming to pick you up or are you walking home?

9. The main ingredients of bread are flour yeast and water.

10. In the box on the top shelf of the closet Mom's old ice skates are packed in tissue paper.

11. The man on the left is Dr. Salter a local dentist.

12. At the first sign of spring I start digging my garden.

13. The crafts project calls for a pine cone glue and some glitter.

14. Sara is interested in zoology the study of animals.

15. The thick dark mud pulled at the ankles of the horses but the horses kept going.

16. In the summer of 2000 Alicia went to Spain.

17. The dog had thick brown hair and large floppy ears.

18. Mr. Allen had won the lottery yet he continued to do most of his shopping at garage sales.

19. After she took a long peaceful nap Kerri felt rested and alert.

20. After the long cold winter we were thrilled when spring arrived.

Language and Sentence Skills Practice   **245**

Conventional Uses of Commas

12k. Use commas in certain conventional situations.

(1) Use commas to separate items in dates and addresses.

> **EXAMPLES** My grandmother was born on February 21, 1930, in Dayton, Ohio.
>
> Her first home was at 652 Deerfield Lane, Dayton, Ohio, ten miles from where she currently lives.

(2) Use a comma after the salutation of a personal letter and after the closing of any letter.

> **EXAMPLES** Dear Aunt Leilani,   Dear Oscar,
>
> Your nephew,   Sincerely yours,

EXERCISE Insert commas where they are needed in the following items.

Example 1. December 14, 1999, is the day Thomas was born.

1. Have you ever been to Charleston South Carolina?

2. We shopped at flea markets in Joliet Illinois last weekend.

3. Our family is moving to 335 Hopper Place Trenton New Jersey next month.

4. Her aunt moved to Dallas Texas on February 4 2001.

5. On October 26 1825 the first boat traveled the length of the Erie Canal.

6. They arrived in New York City on November 4 1985.

7. My cousin Morgan was born on January 12 1998.

8. Nicholas moved to 18 Maple Road Sacramento California.

9. Is the University of Iowa in Iowa City Iowa or in Des Moines Iowa?

10. Please send your request to Charing Cross Bookshop 323 S. State St. Ann Arbor MI 48104.

11. Mr. Thornhill took a train to Chicago Illinois on May 5 2000.

12. The senator's office in Washington D.C. accepts all her correspondence.

13. If you don't hear from me by August 23 2001 you should send me my trunk.

14. Dear Uncle Luis

15. Yours truly

16. We have lived in Roswell New Mexico ever since I was six.

17. Jason was born in Austin Texas.

18. My parents' twentieth wedding anniversary is on Monday February 7 2005.

19. Suzie has lived in Sacramento California and Seattle Washington.

20. Sincerely

MECHANICS

Comma Review A

12f.	Use commas to separate items in a series.
12g.	Use commas to separate two or more adjectives that come before a noun.
12h.	Use a comma before *and, but, for, nor, or, so,* or *yet* when it joins independent clauses in a compound sentence.
12i.	Use commas to set off an expression that interrupts a sentence.
12j.	Use a comma after certain introductory elements.
12k.	Use commas in certain conventional situations.
12l.	Do not use unnecessary commas.

EXERCISE   Add commas to the following items where necessary, and mark through unnecessary commas.

Example   1. This year the choir, is performing songs from *The Music Man*, a famous musical.

1. The primary colors of the spectrum, are blue red and green.

2. The cows came down the hill and the farmer led them into the barn.

3. You can recognize the gas station by its tall red sign.

4. This summer we passed through Denver Colorado on our vacation.

5. Ms. Marrazzo our English teacher recommended that we read *The Yearling*.

6. Before you get too caught up in your book bring me the newspaper.

7. Sincerely yours

8. Chelsea brought her CD player to the party and Bronwen brought some CDs.

9. Three of my favorite fruits are oranges apples and peaches.

10. The restaurant offers several specials on Tuesday evening the slowest night of the week.

11. Yes Virginia you can go to Sally's house.

12. During the last, fifteen minutes of every school day Ms. Long reads aloud to her class.

13. The cool clean water of the spring refreshed the weary hiker.

14. Preston comes from Albany New York and Blanche comes from New Orleans Louisiana.

15. I like your idea for a story Anya but let's ask Butler what he thinks.

16. Dear Dad

17. On a hook over the stove Joe you will find a long thin spoon.

18. Yes our new address is 1221 W. 57th St. New York NY 10001.

19. After July 12 2000 please forward my mail to 1400 S. Congress Ave. Austin TX 78704.

20. After the film, was over Nicci Laura and Michael walked out of the theater.

Language and Sentence Skills Practice

MECHANICS

Comma Review B

12f.	Use commas to separate items in a series.
12g.	Use commas to separate two or more adjectives that come before a noun.
12h.	Use a comma before *and, but, for, nor, or, so,* or *yet* when it joins independent clauses in a compound sentence.
12i.	Use commas to set off an expression that interrupts a sentence.
12j.	Use a comma after certain introductory elements.
12k.	Use commas in certain conventional situations.
12l.	Do not use unnecessary commas.

EXERCISE Add commas to the following letter where necessary, and mark through unnecessary commas.

Example [1] Leon is a funny, interesting, person.

[1] Dear Carla

[2] After I planned for college for years I am finally a freshman at the University of Michigan. [3] I am sharing a house near campus with my friends Carl Pete and Otto. [4] We don't always keep the house as orderly as we should but we all pitch in to help clean. [5] I am the dinner cook of the house so it's my job to provide a cheap nutritious, meal every evening. [6] If you could see me Carla you would hardly recognize me! [7] After class in the afternoon, I hurry home and start cutting up vegetables for a tasty healthy dish. [8] Yes I am quite the cook, although sometimes Otto the other cook in the house gives me a hand. [9] I would write more but it's time to start dinner!

[10] Your loving brother

Leon

Semicolons

MECHANICS

12m. Use a semicolon between the parts of a compound sentence if they are not joined by *and, but, for, nor, or, so,* or *yet.*

> **EXAMPLES** Rasheed wrote out his report; Jodi typed hers.
>
> The Indian rhinoceros has one horn; the African rhinoceros has two.

EXERCISE A Most of the following sentences have commas where there should be semicolons. If a sentence needs a semicolon instead of a comma, write the word before and the word after the comma. Then, insert the semicolon between the two words. If a sentence does not need a semicolon, write *C.*

Example ___*stopped; let's*___ 1. The rain has stopped, let's take a walk.

_____ 1. The open house is in February, the bowling party is in May.

_____ 2. My uncle loves peppers, he eats them on everything.

_____ 3. Trees were uprooted, and power lines swayed in the wind.

_____ 4. His mother is a lawyer, his father manages a store.

_____ 5. Kyle and Manuela are here early today, they are eager to complete their projects.

_____ 6. Jalen was on time, Kristen was late.

_____ 7. Bring a sweater, it will be cold tonight.

_____ 8. My parents' anniversary is next week, we are throwing a party for them.

_____ 9. Juan gave the dog a bath, and Maria cleaned up the mess.

_____ 10. Lydia plays soccer, Tamisha plays tennis.

EXERCISE B Most of the following sentences have commas where there should be semicolons. If a sentence needs a semicolon instead of a comma, write the word before and the word after the comma. Then, insert the semicolon between the two words. If a sentence does not need a semicolon, write *C.*

Example ___*bike; Anatole*___ 1. Jason rode his bike, Anatole walked.

_____ 11. My parents were born in Puerto Rico, they grew up in Chicago.

_____ 12. They lived in San Juan, it's the capital city.

_____ 13. In some areas, rain falls every day, but the showers are brief.

_____ 14. Some buildings are very old, others are modern.

_____ 15. Frost and snow are unknown, and hail is rare.

Language and Sentence Skills Practice

Colons

| **12n.** | Use a colon before a list of items, especially after expressions such as *the following* and *as follows*. |

| **12o.** | Use a colon between the hour and the minute when you write the time. |

| **12p.** | Use a colon after the salutation of a business letter. |

> **EXAMPLES** Bring the following items**:** math book, chart paper, ruler, and pencil.
>
> My team includes these students**:** Tanya, Boris, Sudi, and Roscoe.
>
> 7**:**00 A.M.   10**:**30 P.M.
>
> Dear Mr. McNally**:**   To Whom It May Concern**:**

EXERCISE A Insert colons where they are needed in the following items. If an item is already correct, write *C* before the item number.

Example 1. I packed the following.: books, tapes, and a radio.

1. Mrs. Yoshira will bring the following supplies a tent, two cots, and a camp stove.

2. The question is as follows "When does magma become lava?"

3. Uncle Jim ordered these items a shovel, a sled, and skates.

4. Diego begins his paper route at 515 A.M.

5. Utah's hills are rich in gold, silver, and copper.

6. At 740, we will leave for the airport.

7. Please bring the following crayons, art paper, and watercolors.

8. Mr. Itoh announced the winners Natalia Brooks, Teresa Cruz, and Jim Sheng.

9. Look for the following exhibits in the museum the Tyrannosaurus rex, the walk-through engine, and the mummy.

10. Dear Sir or Madam

EXERCISE B Insert colons where they are needed in the following items. If an item is already correct, write *C* before the item number.

Example *C* **1.** Tonya's favorite subjects are math, English, and history.

11. Show times are as follows 830, 930, and 1030.

12. Do you realize that it's 330 in the morning?

13. Every first-aid kit should contain bandages, an antiseptic, and a tongue depressor.

14. Dear Dr. Jackson

15. The following people should report to the cafeteria Brian, Karen, and Maria.

Review A: **End Marks and Abbreviations**

EXERCISE A Insert periods, question marks, and exclamation points where they are needed in the following sentences. Hint: Some items may need more than one mark of punctuation.

Example 1. Are you meeting us at the concert hall on Alameda Blvd.?

1. We're inviting Mrs Guevera to the concert

2. What a talented person she is

3. Her appointment is with Dr John R Peterson

4. Do we need to buy tickets now

5. I don't have enough money

6. Maybe Mr Goldman will lend you some

7. The Armstrong Corp is our sponsor

8. How nice they are

9. Ted now lives on Sunset Ave in San Diego

10. Please sit down

EXERCISE B Insert periods, question marks, and exclamation points where they are needed in the letter. Hint: Some items may need more than one mark of punctuation.

Example [1] Does Mrs. Rollins still live on Maple St.?

[11] Sept 6, 2001

[12] Dear Mrs Rollins,

[13] Did you know we moved to St Paul? [14] What a great apartment we have [15] Mom works at the Ames Co in town [16] She and Dad are usually home by 6:00 P.M [17] How are things in New Orleans [18] Are you still planning a trip to Seattle, Wash [19] Please call or write soon

[20] Yours truly,

Patrick R O'Malley

MECHANICS

Language and Sentence Skills Practice

Review B: **Commas**

EXERCISE A Insert commas where they are needed in the following sentences. Hint: Some items may need more than one comma.

Example 1. Beth, tell us about your uncle who lives in Dallas, Texas.

1. Uncle Milo was born in Skopje Macedonia but he moved when he was ten.

2. After a terrible earthquake in his homeland he immigrated to the United States.

3. If they get the chance they will return someday.

4. Before the sun rose that day he left to go fishing.

5. What horrible frightening sounds he heard!

6. Well what did he do then Emily?

7. The ground began to tremble and Milo rushed home.

8. When he got there the house had already collapsed.

9. Later he and his family gathered clothes food and other belongings to take with them.

10. It happened on July 26 1963.

EXERCISE B Insert commas where they are needed in the following letter. Hint: Some items may need more than one comma. If an item needs no commas, write *C* above the item number.

Example [1] After she had sold her house in California, my aunt moved to Arizona.

[11] July 18 2000

[12] Dear Yoko

[13] Well I'm spending the summer at my aunt's farm. [14] We're busy dyeing sheep yarn just as our Navajo ancestors did. [15] My aunt uses the yarn to weave rugs wall hangings and blankets. [16] You can see the bright colorful designs in this photo.

[17] If you have any free time I would love to hear from you. [18] My aunt's address is 22 County Line Road Pinedale AZ 82941.

[19] Your pal

[20] Lucy

Review C: Semicolons and Colons

EXERCISE A Most of the following sentences have commas where there should be semicolons. If a sentence needs a semicolon instead of a comma, write the word before and the word after the comma. Then, insert the semicolon between the two words. If a sentence does not need a semicolon, write *C*.

Example _____*music; she's*_____ **1.** Marisa loves music, she's always snapping her fingers to one tune or another.

_____ **1.** The snow has fallen pretty hard, we'll need to shovel the driveway.

_____ **2.** Take a look at Jennifer's new painting, isn't it colorful?

_____ **3.** Marko is usually a very careful cook, yet he forgot to add potatoes to the stew.

_____ **4.** The skyscraper was forty stories tall, from its observation deck the people on the street looked like ants.

_____ **5.** This next song is a waltz, it has three beats per measure.

_____ **6.** The horse did not want to leave, it was happy to stay where it was.

_____ **7.** Please hand me the wrench, this bolt needs to be tighter.

_____ **8.** We call the cat Tiger Lily, for she reminds us of the flower of that name.

_____ **9.** Jackson is the best sprinter on the team, he has won six races this year.

_____ **10.** I can't speak Dutch, but I can read it.

EXERCISE B Insert colons where they are needed in the following items. If a sentence is already correct, write *C* before the item number.

Example 1. Please bring the following on the day of the test: a number two pencil, a notepad, and a calculator.

11. These are the debaters who will attend the semifinals Bridget Humboldt, Anthony Pescecane, and Virginia Dunning.

12. Please bring the following for the field trip tomorrow a glass jar with a lid, a handkerchief, and a magnifying glass.

13. Our cat is affectionate, playful, and mischievous.

14. The combination for the safe is as follows right 21, left 15, right 7.

15. The train always arrives at 817 sharp.

Language and Sentence Skills Practice

Review D: **End Marks, Commas, Semicolons, and Colons**

EXERCISE A   Insert periods, question marks, exclamation points, and commas where they are needed in the following sentences. Hint: Some items may need more than one mark of punctuation.

Example 1. Yes, Justin, we are ready to begin cooking.

1. My favorite vegetables are peas squash and tomatoes

2. When you cook vegetables do you steam them or microwave them

3. Well I do both kinds of cooking

4. Wilford what goes into chow mein

5. You can use meat vegetables noodles and soy sauce

6. How delicious that sounds

7. Peg will bring the noodles and Samantha will bring the vegetables

8. We'll turn on the oven at 11:00 A.M

9. On the morning of the big feast Mrs Sanders will take us to the market

10. We will buy fresh crisp vegetables.

EXERCISE B   Insert commas, semicolons, and colons where they are needed in the following sentences. Hint: Some items may need more than one mark of punctuation.

Example 1. Veronica, what can you tell us about Laos?

11. Well I know that it's somewhere in Southeast Asia but I don't know its exact location.

12. Give a report about Asia's people land and animals.

13. There are a number of different cultures many have their own dialects.

14. Mr. Pollack tell us about the Plain of Jars.

15. It's an area with many large mysterious jars.

16. Are there wild animals roaming about or are the animals kept in zoos?

17. Monkeys elephants and leopards live in the forests.

18. What is the housing like Miranda?

19. Some houses are built of bamboo others are made with rattan.

20. The minerals in Laos include the following tin iron zinc and silver.

Proofreading Application: Poster

Good writers are generally good proofreaders. Readers tend to admire and trust writing that is error-free. Make sure that you correct all errors in grammar, usage, spelling, and punctuation in your writing. Your readers will have more confidence in your words if you have done your best to proofread carefully.

There's very little chance that you will avoid writing something that the public will see. Sooner or later, you will need to write a classified ad or a poster or a brochure, and you will want it to be easily understood. Whenever you place your writing before the public, pay particular attention to proofreading.

PROOFREADING ACTIVITY

In the following poster, find and correct the errors in end marks, abbreviations, and commas. Use proofreading symbols to make your corrections.

Example Have you heard about Cuddlies for Little Buddies**?**

Dear Kids

Do you have a bushel of stuffed animals just lying around your room.

The children at St. Joseph's Hospital need these warm cuddly

fuzzies! You have already enjoyed them so why not share them.

Puppies kitties bears lions and tigers are all needed Yes your

stuffed animals can comfort these kids and help them through a tough

time. At the end of this week we will be collecting stuffed animals

at two locations. Deliver your clean stuffed animals to: Otis T.

Higgens Elementary School. You can also place your animals in the

barrel in the lobby of the hospital at 54 N. Oakland St Dr Thelma

Thompson will make sure that your treasured friends find good homes.

Literary Model: Narrative

> The band began to play again. There was movement in the dense crowd at our end of the floor; it thinned rapidly. Boys came over, girls went out to dance. Lonnie went. The girl on the other side of me went. Nobody asked me. I remembered a magazine article Lonnie and I had read, which said *Be gay! Let the boys see your eyes sparkle, let them hear laughter in your voice!* . . . It was true, I had forgotten. My eyebrows were drawn together with tension; I must look scared and ugly. . . .
>
> Girls were still going out to the floor. Some, despairing, went with each other. But most went with boys. Fat girls, girls with pimples, a poor girl who didn't own a good dress and had to wear a skirt and sweater to the dance; they were claimed, they danced away. Why take them and not me? Why everybody else and not me? I have a red velvet dress, I did my hair in curlers, I used a deodorant and put on cologne. *Pray,* I thought. . . .
>
> —from "Red Dress" by Alice Munro

EXERCISE A

1. Circle all of the end marks used in the passage above.

2. Which end marks are used in this passage?

_____

EXERCISE B   The narrative is told in the first-person point of view. First-person point of view uses the pronoun *I* and includes clues about the author's feelings. What does the use of a variety of types of sentences—some punctuated with a period, others with a question mark, and still others with an exclamation point—tell you about the author's feelings concerning the events in the narrative? Include two sentences from the narrative to support your answer.

_____

_____

_____

_____

_____

_____

Literary Model (continued)

EXERCISE C   Using the excerpt as a model, write a brief narrative in first-person point of view that includes observations about a common situation. You can write about a situation that you have actually experienced, or you can write about a situation that you invent. Be sure that you include exclamations and questions and that they are punctuated correctly.

_____

_____

_____

_____

_____

_____

_____

_____

_____

_____

_____

_____

_____

EXERCISE D

1. Read your narrative aloud, pretending that you are someone reading it for the first time. What do the exclamations and questions reveal about the author's feelings concerning the events in the narrative? Write sentences from the narrative to support your answer.

_____

_____

_____

_____

2. Name at least one form of writing in which you would probably not expect the author to use exclamations and questions. Explain.

_____

_____

_____

Writing Application: Proposal Letter

The use of colons can make your writing look neat and professional. It can also help create variety and make your writing more interesting to read. However, some writers create sentence fragments by using colons incorrectly. You can avoid this problem if you remember this tip: Be sure that you have a complete sentence before the colon.

> **INCORRECT**   Thomas loves: watermelons, pears, and strawberries.
>
> **CORRECT**   Thomas loves many kinds of fruit: watermelons, pears, and strawberries.

WRITING ACTIVITY

Write a proposal letter to convince your family to let you have a sleepover. In your letter, you will have many opportunities to use colons. For example, you will introduce the guest list and the supply list with colons.

PREWRITING   Start with the basics. What information will your family need to know to decide whether to allow you to have a sleepover? Provide this information in the form of lists introduced with colons. For example, you could provide an activity list, a guest list, and an expense or supply list. Be sure that you introduce each list with a complete sentence and a colon.

WRITING   You now have a good deal of useful information, and you are ready to write it out as a letter. Begin the first paragraph by explaining why you want to have a sleepover. Also, give the date and time you want to have your sleepover. Then, include a separate paragraph for each list you brainstormed in prewriting. For example, your second paragraph could be about the activities you are planning. The first sentence in this paragraph could introduce your list; the next several sentences could elaborate on the items in the list or explain why the items are necessary. Use the last paragraph to restate why you want to have a sleepover. Be sure to maintain a polite, respectful tone throughout your letter.

REVISING   Once you have finished writing the body of your letter, have a friend read it to make sure the tone is polite. Then, make sure that you used colons correctly. Did you introduce each of your lists with a complete sentence and a colon?

PUBLISHING   Proofread your letter for errors in spelling and punctuation. Hand your letter to a member of your family. If you want to be more formal, you can ask a friend to send the letter through the mail from his or her home.

EXTENDING YOUR WRITING

This exercise could lead to a more developed writing project. For an English class you could practice writing a "how-to" essay by discussing the challenges involved in planning and pulling off the perfect party. Don't forget to warn students about things that can go wrong! You could illustrate potential problems with stories from your sleepover.

Choices: Investigating Punctuation

Here's your chance to step out of the grammar book and into the real world. You may not notice punctuation, but you and the people around you use it every day. The following activities challenge you to find a connection between punctuation and the world around you. Do the activity below that suits your personality best, and then share your discoveries with your class. Have fun!

GAMES

The Challenge

Can you write a sentence that contains an apostrophe in every single word? Can anyone? You'll never know until you try. Try it! Better yet, have a contest to see who can write the sentence that contains the most apostrophes. Questions and contractions are allowed. The prize is up to you.

ART

Inside and Out

First, draw an outline of a giant apostrophe. Then, inside the apostrophe, write as many contractions as you can. Naturally, you will want to include a few contractions that refer to your class, the students in it, and your projects. You may want to outline your giant apostrophe in a bright color and use the same color for the apostrophes in the contractions you use. You may have other ideas in mind. Whatever you do, be creative!

BUILDING BACKGROUND KNOWLEDGE

E-mail

Hyphenated words can be any of several parts of speech. For each part of speech, try to come up with an example of a hyphenated word. You won't find a hyphenated word for some parts of speech. Can you figure out which ones? Then, prepare a chart that lists each part of speech. Under or beside each part of speech, write a sentence that includes a highlighted example of a hyphenated word used as that part of speech. With your teacher's permission, hang your chart in the classroom.

ANALYZING SOURCES

Hyphen Detective

Think of five words with at least three syllables each. Then, look up each word in a different dictionary. Do all of the dictionaries agree on how to break each word into syllables? Do all of the dictionaries show where you may hyphenate each word? If so, do the dictionaries agree on where each word can be hyphenated? Take careful notes on each difference, if any, between dictionaries. Write a short paragraph, noting the results of your investigation.

HISTORY

In the Olden Days

Where did English get the word *italic*? There's an interesting story to discover. Start with a dictionary. Then, to find out more, move on to encyclopedias or whatever sources you need. Report to the class the story behind the word.

SURVEY

Top Twenty

Take a survey among your classmates. First, brainstorm a list of books and short stories with the class. Be sure that you correctly use quotation marks and underlining in your list. Then, ask each class member to choose the best book or story from the list. Arrange the results of your survey in order from the most popular book or story to the least popular. Then, post your list where everyone can see your class's top twenty books and stories.

Language and Sentence Skills Practice

Underlining (Italics) A

13a. Use underlining (italics) for titles and subtitles of books, plays, periodicals, films, television series, works of art, and long musical works.

BOOKS	*Treasure Island*	*The Joy Luck Club*
PLAYS	*A Raisin in the Sun*	*The Miracle Worker*
PERIODICALS	*Milwaukee Journal*	*Cricket*
FILMS	*Toy Story*	*Mulan*
TELEVISION SERIES	*Dr. Quinn, Medicine Woman*	*Sesame Street*
WORKS OF ART	*Mona Lisa* [painting]	*David* [statue]
LONG MUSICAL WORKS	*Nutcracker Suite*	*The Sound of Music*

13b. Use underlining (italics) for names of trains, ships, aircraft, and spacecraft.

EXAMPLES   USS *Nimitz*   *Spirit of St. Louis*   *Challenger*

EXERCISE A In the following sentences, underline the words that should be printed in italics.

Example 1. This fall my sister's theater group will present the play <u>Much Ado About Nothing</u>.

1. Uncle Ed gave me six copies of National Geographic.

2. Is there a travel section in the Miami Herald?

3. Fog Warning was painted by Winslow Homer.

4. My sister sang in The Mikado, an operetta.

5. Judy Garland starred in The Wizard of Oz.

EXERCISE B In the following sentences, underline the words that should be printed in italics.

Example 1. Have you ever read the book <u>The Hobbit</u> by J.R.R. Tolkien?

6. Every Sunday my aunt does the crossword puzzle in The New York Times.

7. The train City of New Orleans runs from Chicago to New Orleans.

8. My favorite old television show is Lost in Space.

9. Have you ever read Mark Twain's novel The Adventures of Huckleberry Finn?

10. Last night my sister took me to see the opera The Marriage of Figaro.

11. What year did the Titanic sink?

12. What year was the film Titanic released?

13. My young brother always reads the magazine Boy's Life from cover to cover.

14. The painting American Gothic is the work of the American artist Grant Wood.

15. Can anyone tell me who wrote the play Romeo and Juliet?

MECHANICS

Underlining (Italics) B

| **13a.** | Use underlining (italics) for titles and subtitles of books, plays, periodicals, films, television series, works of art, and long musical works. |

   EXAMPLES   *The Butter Battle Book*   *Touched by an Angel*   *Stone Soup*

| **13b.** | Use underlining (italics) for names of trains, ships, aircraft, and spacecraft. |

   EXAMPLES   *California Zephyr*   USS *Macon*   *Voyager 2*

EXERCISE A   In the following sentences, underline the words that should be printed in italics.

Example 1. The launch of the space shuttle <u>Endeavor</u> was a success.

1. Last night the orchestra played George Gershwin's long work Rhapsody in Blue.

2. What time does TV Guide say the program starts?

3. Mary Shelley's novel Frankenstein was published when she was only twenty-one years old.

4. The funniest movie I ever saw was Duck Soup, a Marx Brothers film.

5. My little sister enjoys watching reruns of The Andy Griffith Show.

6. Stuart is reading The Phantom Tollbooth, a book by Norton Juster.

7. How long is the play Hamlet?

8. When we were in Long Beach, California, we visited the old ocean liner the Queen Mary.

9. In the museum Maria spent a long time looking at Rembrandt's painting Night Watch.

10. This year the student musical will be The Music Man.

EXERCISE B   In the following sentences, underline the words that should be printed in italics.

Example 1. The ending of the film <u>Old Yeller</u> always makes me cry.

11. The song "I Could Have Danced All Night" appears in the musical My Fair Lady.

12. We learned about the Constitution, a warship.

13. Picasso's famous painting Guernica was painted in response to the Spanish Civil War.

14. Ms. Dominquez read aloud to her class from the book I Know Why the Caged Bird Sings.

15. For his birthday, Prentice's parents took him to see the film James and the Giant Peach.

16. The narrator for this recording of Peter and the Wolf is the actor Patrick Stewart.

17. Sondra read a profile of Denzel Washington in People magazine.

18. The Civil War battleships the Monitor and the Merrimack fought a battle on March 9, 1862.

19. Maria's sister enjoys watching the show 7th Heaven.

20. The song "Octopus's Garden" appears on the Beatles album Abbey Road.

Language and Sentence Skills Practice

MECHANICS

Quotation Marks with Direct Quotations

13c–h. Use quotation marks, other punctuation marks, and capital letters correctly to set off direct quotations.

EXAMPLES Janine said, "I like movies with surprise endings."
Patricia asked, "**M**ay I help with the decorations?"
"We will begin decorating the gym," said Roger, "**at** 5:30."
"I found the perfect hamster at the pet store**!**" cried Yoko.
"The game did not go well**,**" said Dean. "We lost by twenty points**.**"
Who said, "The play starts at 7:30"**?**

EXERCISE In the following sentences, add quotation marks and other punctuation marks where they are needed. Also, correct any errors in capitalization. If a sentence is already correct, write *C* before the item number.

Example 1. Viviana asked, "
M
may I have milk instead of tea?"

1. Mr. Lasky said, You can leave for the game.

2. Your dress looks like a costume, Mother remarked.

3. Thomas, will you buy the sandwiches? asked Coach Schultz.

4. Jake replied that he didn't mind at all.

5. Judith said, I'll bring paper plates.

6. Who borrowed my ruler Carmen asked.

7. I said that I might have left my book in math class.

8. Grandma cried out a tornado is coming!

9. Who said Each player will receive a prize

10. Renee said that she was joking about the iguana.

11. Can I have an apple, too? asked Fiona.

12. Yikes! shouted Annie. There's a snake on the trail.

13. Casey pulled her lips back over her gums and asked do I have anything on my teeth?

14. Wash the dishes, instructed Dad, and afterward we'll play chess.

15. Beauregard is the name of my new pet rabbit announced the girl proudly.

16. Sometimes, said Felipe, I go to the Tejano record store in my electric wheelchair.

17. Catch Fido before she catches that cat! screamed Greg.

18. Who said, I have your sweater?

19. I told him that I didn't want to be on the team.

20. I have learned the names of the constellations, said Ashley, but can't identify them yet.

Quotation Marks in Dialogue

13i. When you write dialogue (conversation), begin a new paragraph every time the speaker changes.

EXAMPLE   "How many laps did you swim in the pool this morning?" Tony asked his older sister, Millicent.

"Well," replied Millicent. "I swam forty laps."

13j. When a quotation consists of several sentences, put quotation marks only at the beginning and the end of the whole quotation.

EXAMPLE   "I just love my new sweater. It's so warm, and it fits perfectly," said Ruth.

13k. Use single quotation marks to enclose a quotation within a quotation.

EXAMPLE   "I'm sure Jason said, 'Meet me at the theater,'" said Elena.

EXERCISE A   Some of the quotation marks in the following dialogue are unnecessary. Cross out any quotation marks that should not appear. Also, insert single quotation marks where needed. Insert a paragraph symbol (¶) wherever a new paragraph should begin.

Example   **[1]** "I like using the computer to write papers." "I finish my papers faster, and they look better, too," said Rena. **[2]** ¶ "Yes, I agree," replied Sonia.

[1] Rena asked, "What are you doing here, Sonia?" "Do you need to use the school's computer?" **[2]** "Well, maybe," Sonia replied, "but I don't have anyone to show me how." **[3]** "I'll be glad to show you," said Rena." **[4]** "I don't really understand everything that Mr. Frank told us," Sonia said. **[5]** Rena laughed, "Who could understand everything about computers?" **[6]** Sonia said, "Well, let's get started." "I only have thirty minutes." **[7]** "Please hand me the mouse," Rena said. "Do you remember what Mr. Frank said?" **[8]** "He said," continued Rena, "Students, to open a document on a disk, you must double-click on the disk icon." **[9]** "Thanks for the tip," Sonia said. That sounds easy." **[10]** "No problem," said Rena.

EXERCISE B   Add quotation marks where they are needed in the following sentences.

Example   **1.** "I think that man said, 'Do you know the way to the library?'" said Becky.

11. Alice asked me, Have you already read the assignment? said Lewis.

12. Then Mr. Okonkwo said, Let's make a model of the catapult, continued Enrico.

13. Victor said, Why don't we all pitch in? We can finish the project early if we all work together.

14. I used to have a bicycle just like this one, said Sara.

15. It's such a gloomy day. Do you want to stay inside and play a board game? asked Tomas.

Quotation Marks with Titles

13l. Use quotation marks to enclose the titles of short works such as short stories, poems, newspaper or magazine articles, songs, episodes of television series, and chapters and other parts of books.

SHORT STORIES	"Petronella"	**SONGS**	"God Bless America"
POEMS	"The Sneetches"	**EPISODES OF TV SERIES**	"Moon Landings"
ARTICLES	"Improve Your Soccer Game"	**PARTS OF BOOKS**	"Spelling"

Titles that appear in quotation marks are set in single quotation marks when they appear within a quotation.

EXAMPLE Jerry said, "I enjoyed reading the short story 'The Tell-Tale Heart.'"

EXERCISE Add quotation marks and single quotation marks where they are needed in the following sentences.

Example 1. Please read the next chapter, "England in the Middle Ages."

1. Have you read Hector the Collector, a poem by Shel Silverstein?

2. That was in the chapter Reading Poetry.

3. Denise said, "The story Mufaro's Beautiful Daughters is an African tale."

4. How to Open a Savings Account is a good article.

5. The School Bus Mystery was a thrilling episode.

6. Did you find the article Caring for Your Puppy helpful?

7. We sang Row, Row, Row Your Boat all the way home.

8. The story The Three Billy Goats Gruff makes my cousin laugh.

9. "Next Monday you will each recite the poem Jimmy Jet and His TV Set," said Mr. Smith.

10. Over the Rainbow is a song from *The Wizard of Oz*.

11. The Lake Isle of Innisfree is a poem by W. B. Yeats.

12. We read Faulkner's short story Barn Burning.

13. Lisa read a story called The Darling.

14. The journalist wrote about his experiences on the job in the article How I Got That Story.

15. "Would you like to sing Don't Rain on My Parade?" asked Mary.

16. My favorite TV show featured an episode called Hush.

17. One section of our literature text is called Machine Mania: People and Technology.

18. Jason replied, "My favorite song is Bridge over Troubled Water."

19. The article Build Your Own Airplane ended with a list of necessary parts.

20. A Day in the Life is the last song on the album *Sgt. Pepper's Lonely Hearts Club Band*.

HOLT HANDBOOK | Introductory Course

Quotation Marks

Use quotation marks to enclose direct quotations as well as the titles of short works such as short stories and poems.

EXAMPLES   Gary exclaimed, "I hope that's not my sandwich you're eating!"

"I like the short story 'To Build a Fire,'" said Terry.

"Who would like to go first?" asked Mrs. Frasier.

Have you heard Beethoven's "Moonlight Sonata"?

EXERCISE A   In the following sentences, add quotation marks and other punctuation marks where they are needed. Also, correct any errors in capitalization.

Example 1. Kenneth asked, "How many books by Yoshiko Uchida are in our library?"

1. Who is your favorite author asked Miss Ray.

2. Blake read the short story The Lottery during the lunch period.

3. Those customs said Anna are interesting.

4. Have you heard Ray Charles sing America the Beautiful?

5. Sherri replied many people enjoy swimming. It is great exercise.

6. Danny Gatton plays an interesting version of the song Sleepwalk.

7. In Japan there is a holiday called Children's Day reported Xavier.

8. What is the point of the story? asked Lee.

9. Mr. Thompson said, if you study the chapter, you will do well on the test.

10. David will be in charge of lighting. Marie will handle the props said Laurie.

EXERCISE B   Add quotation marks and single quotation marks where they are needed in the following sentences.

Example 1. Mr. Lucas asked, "Did you see the episode 'The Trouble with Tribbles' on *Star Trek* last night?"

11. Where is the article I read? asked Dad.

12. Ricki said that the entire crowd sang the song Take Me Out to the Ballgame during the seventh-inning stretch.

13. Mrs. Lindenmayer said, I want you to read Isaac Asimov's story The Fun They Had.

14. Did Mr. Standish say, The science projects are due next week? asked Tracy.

15. Tonya said, You'd love the poem The Red Wheelbarrow!

MECHANICS

Language and Sentence Skills Practice   **265**

Underlining (Italics) and Quotation Marks A

Use underlining (italics) for the titles and subtitles of works such as books, plays, periodicals, and works of art and for the names of ships, trains, aircraft, and spacecraft. Use quotation marks to enclose direct quotations as well as the titles of short works such as short stories and poems.

EXAMPLES   The bronze statue *The Thinker* was first modeled in clay.

"Who wrote *Incidents in the Life of a Slave Girl*?" asked Amy.

"I believe," said Emile, "that this is the answer."

Tim asked, "Have you read the poem 'The Raven' by Edgar Allan Poe?"

EXERCISE In the following sentences, underline all words and phrases that should be in italics, and insert quotation marks and single quotation marks where necessary.

Example 1. "We are going to see the musical The Sound of Music tonight," said Keith.

1. Sergio did a book report on The Return of the Native, a novel by Thomas Hardy.

2. His favorite chapter of the book was The Custom of the Country.

3. Please come in! said Steve. It's so good to see you!

4. The plane that Charles Lindbergh flew across the Atlantic was called the Spirit of St. Louis.

5. Teresa's favorite poem is Things to Do If You Are a Subway by Bobbi Katz.

6. My aunt and uncle subscribe to Reader's Digest.

7. Did anybody else see the episode of 7th Heaven last night? asked Stacy.

8. Please pick up your songbooks, said the choir director, and turn to This Land Is Your Land.

9. My grandfather, said Claire, once rode the famous train the Orient-Express.

10. The last song on the CD is the Cole Porter classic Night and Day.

11. I have tickets for a performance of the opera La Bohème, announced Rodney.

12. Is the song Mona Lisa about the famous painting Mona Lisa?

13. Han Solo's spaceship in the film Star Wars is called the Millennium Falcon.

14. Which story would you like to read, asked Michele, The All-American Slurp or La Bamba?

15. All aboard for the Orange Blossom Special! cried the conductor from the railway platform.

16. I just read an article in the paper yesterday, said Elisabeth, called Raising Bigger Pumpkins.

17. Please open your copies of the book Black-Eyed Susans, said Ms. Akers, and turn to the story A Sudden Trip Home in the Spring.

18. Mr. Costello told us to turn to the second chapter, Introduction to Atomic Structure.

19. Someday, said Ronnie, I'd like to take a cruise on the Queen Elizabeth 2.

20. David Copperfield is an enjoyable novel, said Professor Humboldt.

Underlining (Italics) and Quotation Marks B

Use underlining (italics) for the titles and subtitles of works such as books, plays, periodicals, and for the names of trains, ships, aircraft, and spacecraft. Use quotation marks to enclose direct quotations as well as the titles of short works such as short stories and poems.

EXAMPLES   David titled his new song "Chalkboard Dust."

The space probes *Viking 1* and *Viking 2* landed on Mars in 1976.

"What time is the movie *Babe* playing?" asked his mother.

"Yes," replied David, "I wrote the poem 'Mood.'"

EXERCISE   In the following sentences, underline all words and phrases that should be in italics, and insert quotation marks and single quotation marks where necessary.

Example 1. "My favorite song from that show," said Faith, "is 'People Will Say We're in Love.'"

1. The ships Columbus sailed to America were the Niña, the Pinta, and the Santa María.

2. The professor assigned the third chapter, The Circulatory System.

3. How long has it been snowing? asked Chelsea.

4. The first Mark Twain book he ever read was A Connecticut Yankee in King Arthur's Court.

5. He told us that he wanted to set the Langston Hughes poem The Weary Blues to music.

6. Glendon said, The train to the ski resort is called the Snowbird Express.

7. A good book about Germany, said Mr. Boylan, is After the Wall: Eastern Germany Since 1989.

8. I don't know the lyrics to Chattanooga Choo-Choo, said the pianist, but I can play the tune.

9. We subscribe to several newsmagazines, said Meadow, including Time and Newsweek.

10. The music teacher asked her class if they had ever heard the song Baby Elephant Walk.

11. I read an article last night called How to Start a Garden in Your Backyard.

12. We've never read a story like Dragon, Dragon before, said Jeff.

13. When did Arthur Conan Doyle write the book A Study in Scarlet? asked the editor.

14. I hear you saw the film Toy Story last night, said Alison. What did you think of it?

15. I think you should call your short story The End of the Day, suggested Anthony.

16. Doesn't the song Sunrise, Sunset come from the musical Fiddler on the Roof? asked Pavel.

17. Carla's favorite episode of Star Trek, Paul explained, is The Enemy Within.

18. In the lounge car of the California Zephyr, Michael found a copy of National Geographic.

19. My father sailed from Bombay to London, said Parvati, on a ship called The Star of India.

20. You will find the information you need, said Mr. Waldrop, in the book Famous Disasters at

    Sea, in the chapter titled The Sinking of the Lusitania.

Language and Sentence Skills Practice

Apostrophes with Possessives

13m. To form the possessive case of a singular noun, add an apostrophe and an *s*.

EXAMPLES a child's wagon Robert's coat the kitten's food

13n. To form the possessive case of a plural noun that does not end in *s*, add an apostrophe and an *s*.

EXAMPLES the children's toys women's hats the mice's cage

13o. To form the possessive case of a plural noun ending in *s*, add only the apostrophe.

EXAMPLES two dogs' tracks the campers' tent three days' vacation

EXERCISE A On the line provided, rewrite each of the following expressions by using the possessive case. Be sure to add apostrophes where they are needed.

Example 1. cars of the students *the students' cars* _____

1. the temperature of the patient _____

2. a coat that belongs to Mona _____

3. nests of the ducks _____

4. the boats owned by the women _____

5. the doll that belongs to the child _____

6. the lid for that box _____

7. the health of the goose _____

8. the shells of the turtles _____

9. shoes that belong to men _____

10. coastline of Florida _____

EXERCISE B One word in each of the following sentences is missing an apostrophe. Underline the word that needs an apostrophe, and write it correctly on the line provided.

Example ___*traffic's*___ **1.** The traffics roar kept us awake.

_____ **11.** Mr. Smiths dogs are in the backyard.

_____ **12.** Velmas twin sisters attend preschool.

_____ **13.** Have you heard Jeffreys poem?

_____ **14.** Those candidates speeches were brief.

_____ **15.** The birds cages had been left open.

MECHANICS

Possessive Pronouns

13p. Do not use an apostrophe with possessive personal pronouns.

    EXAMPLES   **His** tacos are not as spicy as **hers.**   Are those **our** sleeping bags or **theirs**?

13q. To form the possessive case of many indefinite pronouns, add an apostrophe and an *s*.

    EXAMPLES   anybody's coat   someone's umbrella   one's choice

EXERCISE A   If the underlined pronoun is correct, write *C* on the line provided. If the pronoun is incorrect, write the correct form of the pronoun.

Example _____*yours*_____ **1.** Is this photograph your's?

_____ **1.** Is that soccer ball our's?

_____ **2.** Frank's handwriting is not as easy to read as her's.

_____ **3.** Which picture would you rather see, Paula's or his?

_____ **4.** Our offensive line is stronger than their's.

_____ **5.** Yes, that glove is mine.

EXERCISE B   On the line provided, rewrite each of the following expressions by using the possessive case. Be sure to add apostrophes where they are needed.

Example **1.** the prayers of everyone   *everyone's prayers*_____

  6. the cup of someone _____

  7. the task of them _____

  8. the fault of no one _____

  9. the friend of him _____

10. the desk of you _____

11. the shoes of anyone _____

12. the habits of one _____

13. the glasses of him _____

14. the project of you _____

15. the pencils of anybody _____

MECHANICS

Apostrophes in Possessives

Use apostrophes to form the possessive case of singular and plural nouns and to form the possessive case of many indefinite pronouns. Note that possessive personal pronouns do not have apostrophes.

EXAMPLES   the dog's bowl   the turtle's shell   the girls' lunches

America's athletes   **our** house   somebody's pencil

EXERCISE   On the line provided, rewrite each of the following expressions by using the possessive case. Be sure to add apostrophes where they are needed.

Example 1. the houses of the teachers   *the teachers' houses* _____

1. the dish of the dog _____

2. the poems of the women _____

3. the raincoat of someone _____

4. the cassette of him _____

5. the basketball team of the two girls _____

6. the games of the children _____

7. the computer of the principal _____

8. the driveways of them _____

9. the dreams of no one _____

10. the wings of the geese _____

11. the baby of Rosa _____

12. the patience of her _____

13. the backpacks of the soldiers _____

14. the votes of the people _____

15. the studios of the artists _____

16. the classes of everybody _____

17. the color of the wall _____

18. the mooing of the cow _____

19. the wheelbarrow of us _____

20. the flashlight of neither _____

Apostrophes in Contractions

13r. Use an apostrophe to show where letters, numerals, or words have been left out in a contraction.

EXAMPLES   they are—they're   I have—I've   where is—where's
               let us—let's   do not—don't   of the clock—o'clock
               you are—you're   cannot—can't   was not—wasn't

Do not confuse contractions with possessive pronouns.

CONTRACTIONS   **POSSESSIVE PRONOUNS**

It's [It is] a beautiful day.   **Its** left wing is healing.
Who's [Who is] ready to go?   **Whose** football is this?
You're [You are] a prince.   **Your** face is red.

EXERCISE A   On the lines provided, write the correct contractions for the underlined words.

Example _____*We're*_____   **1.** We are studying Latin American writers.

_____   **1.** I am reading a biography of Gabriela Mistral.

_____   **2.** Is not she a poet from Latin America?

_____   **3.** She is also known for her teaching.

_____   **4.** Gabriela Mistral is her pen name, is not it?

_____   **5.** That is right; her real name was Lucila.

_____   **6.** Max did not know she had won a Nobel Prize.

_____   **7.** Was not that in 1945?

_____   **8.** Let us read her poems to the class.

_____   **9.** Here is one about a beautiful valley.

_____   **10.** What a fine poem you have chosen!

EXERCISE B   Underline the correct word in parentheses to complete each of the following sentences.

Example 1. Will (*you're*, *your*) dad pick us up after skating practice?

11. (*Who's*, *Whose*) ice skates are on the bench?

12. (*They're*, *Their*) Melinda's figure skates.

13. (*It's*, *Its*) a shame that she left them.

14. Well, (*there's*, *theirs*) still time to call her.

15. We can tell her before (*it's*, *its*) too late for her to get them.

Apostrophes in Plurals

13s. Use an apostrophe and an *s* to form the plurals of letters, numerals, and symbols, and of words referred to as words.

> **EXAMPLES** Did you remember to cross your *t*'s and dot your *i*'s?
>
> Pavel's *7*'s look like *9*'s.
>
> Don't forget your *$*'s when you add your expenses.
>
> Use fewer *and*'s and *but*'s in your report.

MECHANICS

EXERCISE A Add apostrophes where they are needed in the following sentences.

Example 1. In my opinion, there are too many *then*'s in this paragraph.

1. Alex wrote *X*s in all of the boxes.

2. How many *c*s are in *necessary*?

3. Count to fifty by *10*s.

4. You forgot the dots in your *?*s and *!*s.

5. There are three *5*s in my telephone number.

6. Add commas after your *well*s and *why*s.

7. Write out your *and*s instead of using *&*s.

8. Iola makes fancy *G*s.

9. Make sure that your *too*s have two *o*s.

10. Ken's *V*s look like *U*s.

EXERCISE B On the line provided, correctly write the plural of each of the following items.

Example ___*yes's and no's*___ **1.** *yes* and *no*

_____ **11.** *to*

_____ **12.** *2*

_____ **13.** *

_____ **14.** *y*

_____ **15.** *uh huh*

_____ **16.** *K*

_____ **17.** *also*

_____ **18.** *75*

_____ **19.** *@*

_____ **20.** *if, and,* or *but*

Apostrophes Review

Use apostrophes to form the possessive case of singular nouns, plural nouns, and many indefinite pronouns. Also use apostrophes to form contractions and the plurals of letters, numerals, symbols, and words used as words.

EXAMPLES Carla's pen   men's clothing   foxes' paws

his bike   boxes' lids   somebody's book

I'm   she's   weren't

don't   *P*'s and *Q*'s   wouldn't

EXERCISE Add apostrophes where needed in the following sentences. If a sentence is already correct, write *C* on the line before the sentence. Some sentences may require more than one apostrophe.

Example _____ **1.** I can't remember if the scarf is Leslie's or if it's mine.

_____ **1.** Kathys scores from the ice-skating judges were all *9*s.

_____ **2.** The mens chorus sang an old Welsh hymn as their final number.

_____ **3.** Our science projects more complicated than theirs.

_____ **4.** How many *like*s do you count in Bretts essay?

_____ **5.** Three of the books covers were damaged.

_____ **6.** The cat is very protective of its territory.

_____ **7.** I cant say *no* to a good bargain.

_____ **8.** The mechanic tuned the cars engine.

_____ **9.** Everybodys hair got wet in the sudden rainstorm.

_____ **10.** The firefighters faces were streaked with soot.

_____ **11.** The mouses nest was lined with feathers and leaves for the winter.

_____ **12.** Eithers suggestion for a story would work just fine.

_____ **13.** That bicycle is not his; its hers.

_____ **14.** The childrens rooms were surprisingly tidy.

_____ **15.** There are too many *&*s in the books title.

_____ **16.** The radio announcers voice showed little emotion during the news bulletin.

_____ **17.** Nobodys house was damaged by the flood last week.

_____ **18.** Was the original idea for the story yours or mine?

_____ **19.** We shouldnt keep our friends waiting any longer.

_____ **20.** All the students votes were tallied by four oclock.

Language and Sentence Skills Practice

Hyphens

| **13t.** | Use a hyphen to divide a word at the end of a line. |

   EXAMPLE   My grandparents threw a surprise party for my sis-
                 ter Zena.

| **13u.** | Use a hyphen with compound numbers from *twenty-one* to *ninety-nine*. |

   EXAMPLE   Twenty-two invitations were sent out.

| **13v.** | Hyphenate a compound adjective when it comes before the noun it modifies. |

   EXAMPLE   a **world-famous** athlete

| **13w.** | Use a hyphen with the prefixes *all–, ex–, great–, self–,* and with the suffixes *–elect* and *–free*. |

   EXAMPLES   all-important   ex-coach   self-discipline   additive-free

EXERCISE A   On the line provided, rewrite each of the following words, using hyphens to show where the word may be divided at the end of a line. If a word should not be divided, write *do not divide* on the line.

   Example 1. meditation _____*med-i-ta-tion*_____

1. hiding _____
2. doorbell _____
3. open _____
4. friends _____
5. surprise _____

6. pumpkin _____
7. alone _____
8. apart _____
9. exercise _____
10. watch _____

EXERCISE B   Insert hyphens where they are needed in each of the following sentences.

   Example 1. My grandmother is sixty–two years old.

11. Thirty plus two equals thirty two.

12. My brother has a part time job.

13. In eleven years, I will be twenty three years old.

14. The secretary elect will attend the meeting.

15. The well planned party was a success.

16. My grandparents have lived in that house for forty one years.

17. The world famous actor signed autographs for three hours.

18. Does your camera have a wide angle lens?

19. Eighty four students have joined the Nature Club already.

20. Suki's self confidence grew with each speech she made.

MECHANICS

Parentheses

13x. Use parentheses to enclose material that is added to a sentence but is not considered of major importance.

> **EXAMPLES**   Ella Fitzgerald **(**1917–1996**)** is one of the bestselling vocalists in history.
> Pasta **(**my favorite food**)** is common in Italian cooking.

Material enclosed in parentheses may be as short as a single word or as long as a short sentence. A short sentence in parentheses may stand alone or be contained within another sentence. A parenthetical sentence within a sentence is not capitalized and has no end mark.

> **EXAMPLES**   My twin sister and I got new bicycles for our birthday. **(**They're both blue.**)**
> John's brother **(**he's a doctor**)** lives in a small town in Oregon.

EXERCISE   Insert parentheses where they are needed in the following sentences.

Example 1. Our house **(**we've lived there for two years**)** was built in 1971.

1. Descartes pronounced dā•kärt´ was a French philosopher and mathematician.

2. Will your sister bring Sally her best friend from fourth grade to the picnic?

3. At the age of three, Cameron a very energetic child learned to ride a bicycle.

4. Our dog he's a golden retriever loves to fetch sticks.

5. Sir Noel Coward 1899–1973 was a famous English playwright and songwriter.

6. The computer in our history class it's brand new has a direct connection to the Internet.

7. Suzi a two-year-old always enjoys playing in the backyard.

8. Ron takes a walk every afternoon after school. It's his time to relax.

9. Please find the information about the Civil War in your textbook pp. 203–224.

10. The song the choir performed I think it was called "Greensleeves" was beautiful.

11. Celia Cruz known as the "Queen of Salsa Music" was awarded the National Medal of Arts in 1994.

12. Some cooks use a roux pronounced ro͞o to thicken sauces and gravies.

13. W. C. Fields 1880–1946 is well known for the comedy films he made.

14. Is Patricia Henderson class of '99 now finishing college with a degree in advertising?

15. O. Henry the pseudonym of William Sydney Porter wrote short stories about ordinary people.

16. Thomas Allen do you know him? will be joining us for dinner.

17. How nice it is to live next to the Burtons a family of five!

18. The surgical procedure see description on page 153 takes about two hours.

19. Uncle Brent's new pet his name is Boggles is a calico cat.

20. Bob and Liz you may remember them from school are moving to Nevada.

MECHANICS

Language and Sentence Skills Practice

MECHANICS

Apostrophes, Hyphens, and Parentheses Review

Use apostrophes to form the possessive case of singular nouns, plural nouns, and many indefinite pronouns. Also use apostrophes to form contractions and the plurals of letters, numerals, symbols, and words used as words.

| EXAMPLES | Don's shoes | players' uniforms | someone's pencil |
| | I'm | *t*'s | can't |

Use hyphens to divide a word at the end of a line, with certain compound numbers, with a compound adjective that comes before the noun it modifies, and with certain prefixes and suffixes.

| EXAMPLES | well-known writer | self-discipline | sugar-free |

Use parentheses to enclose material that is added to a sentence but is not considered of major importance. Enclosed material may be as short as a single word or as long as a short sentence.

EXAMPLE   Randy **(**the boy from Sacramento**)** won the marathon.

EXERCISE   Add apostrophes, hyphens, and parentheses where they are needed in the following sentences.

Example 1. Eighty—seven people attended the author's lecture.

1. The third student in line the one in the yellow shirt will carry the classs sign.

2. Janes grandfather immigrated from Poland in 1926.

3. Jim an ex baseball player now coaches two high school teams.

4. Why wont you go to the movies with us on Saturday night?

5. The committee will sponsor a dinner in honor of the president elect.

6. Weve asked Donnas mother an architect to speak to our class.

7. Did they say we needed fifty five signatures or sixty five?

8. The creek is not very wide fifteen feet.

9. There are two *us* in the word *vacuum*.

10. The senators spouses will accompany them to the presidents speech.

Review A: Underlining (Italics) and Quotation Marks

EXERCISE Add underlining and quotation marks as needed in the following sentences.

Example 1. "How long did <u>The Sound of Music</u> run on Broadway?" Rosie asked.

1. Have you heard of the Discovery? Quentin asked. It's a space shuttle.

2. Our class sang This Land Is Your Land.

3. My favorite book is Sarah, Plain and Tall.

4. Watch out for that fence! yelled Lucas.

5. How many back issues of the magazine Cricket did you save?

6. You should read the article titled Remember the Space Shuttle Challenger.

7. My grandparents saw The King and I on Broadway.

8. Philadelphia Express, Jason explained, is the name of a train.

9. Meg asked, Did you check the reviews in The New York Times?

10. Bronco Buster is a painting by N. C. Wyeth.

11. Uncle Emil sailed for England on the Queen Elizabeth 2.

12. When I was younger, said Dad, I could run for miles.

13. Who has read the chapter called Enjoying Short Stories?

14. The spacecraft Giotto sent back images of a comet.

15. There's a list of summer camps in the June issue of Seventeen.

16. Josie boasted, My test score was the highest.

17. Seven Brides for Seven Brothers is a popular musical play.

18. Clara called her poem Wishing.

19. The article is called Making Friends with Your Parents.

20. What did you learn from it? Mom asked.

21. Is it hard to make? Angel wondered.

22. Kelly laughed and said, No, it's really easy.

23. I have tomatoes, Angel said, but no onions.

24. Robert asked, How much garlic should we use?

25. Angel said, Add lots. I love garlic!

MECHANICS

Review B: **Apostrophes**

EXERCISE A On the line provided, rewrite each of the following expressions by using the possessive case. Be sure to add apostrophes where they are needed.

Example ___*the boys' bikes*___ **1.** the bikes of the boys

_____ **1.** the gloves of someone

_____ **2.** the hats of the women

_____ **3.** the path of the deer

_____ **4.** the vacation of the Petersons

_____ **5.** the salaries of the employees

EXERCISE B On the line provided before each sentence, write the correct contraction for the underlined words.

Example _____*Here's*_____ **1.** <u>Here is</u> the book you wanted.

_____ **6.** If we <u>are not</u> ready, the others will wait.

_____ **7.** <u>Who is</u> that man waving a flag?

_____ **8.** I <u>cannot</u> tell from this far away.

_____ **9.** <u>Let us</u> get window seats.

_____ **10.** <u>That is</u> fine with me!

EXERCISE C Insert apostrophes where they are needed in the following sentences. If a sentence is already correct, write *C* on the line before the item number.

Example ___*C*___ **1.** Whose drawings were chosen for the exhibit?

_____ **11.** Mother says that I use too many *like*s when I tell a story.

_____ **12.** The cat licked its paws.

_____ **13.** Those movies plots are both predictable.

_____ **14.** Whos been eating my lunch?

_____ **15.** Theyre planning a trip to the beach.

_____ **16.** Are these water bottles yours or ours?

_____ **17.** The bean burritos seemed to be everybodys favorite dish.

_____ **18.** What do the +s and −s indicate on this chart?

_____ **19.** Two players mitts were left on the field.

_____ **20.** I found someones scarf on the floor.

Review C: Hyphens

EXERCISE A On the line provided, rewrite each of the following words, using hyphens to show where the word may be divided at the end of a line. If a word should not be divided, write *do not divide* on the line.

Example 1. nonfiction _____*non-fic-tion*_____

1. upward _____

2. bright _____

3. terrible _____

4. okay _____

5. today _____

6. baseball _____

7. brave _____

8. understand _____

9. elect _____

10. costume _____

EXERCISE B Add hyphens where necessary in the following items. If no hyphen is needed, write *C* next to the item number.

Examples *C* **1.** a vacation that is well deserved

2. a well–preserved fossil

11. a long standing argument

12. a friendship that is long standing

13. eighty six red balloons

14. the all seeing eye

15. my great grandmother Sarah

16. ex quarterback

17. up to date information

18. fat free yogurt

19. fifty one spoons

20. self help book

21. one hundred twenty five people

22. fifty two cards

23. a first rate book

24. a self made woman

25. an all inclusive list

26. an ex senator

27. a well made bicycle

28. a bicycle that is well made

29. television that is brand new

30. a brand new notebook

MECHANICS

Language and Sentence Skills Practice

279

Review D: Underlining (Italics), Quotation Marks, Apostrophes, Hyphens, Parentheses

EXERCISE Add underlining, quotation marks, single quotation marks, apostrophes, and hyphens as needed in the following sentences. Also, correct any errors in capitalization.

Example 1. "Many people," said Steve, "like the novel <u>Great Expectations</u>."

1. Marias oldest brother is studying the painting Mona Lisa.

2. There are, said Sally, two *m*s in *dilemma.*

3. The books fourteenth chapter is called Dr. Moreau Explains.

4. The womens basketball team is going to the state finals.

5. My favorite author, Ray Bradbury, wrote the book Something Wicked This Way Comes.

6. We subscribe to one newspaper, the Austin American-Statesman.

7. "Mark said, You should first preheat the oven," replied Helena.

8. Who knows about the ocean liner Queen Mary? asked her brother.

9. The long awaited pageant has speaking parts for thirty eight people.

10. Are any ex presidents going to comment on the election? asked Judge Thorpe.

11. I would have ridden my own bicycle in the race, but its being repaired.

12. Denzel Washington is my favorite actor. Ive seen all his movies, said Terri.

13. He didnt know that we subscribe to National Geographic magazine.

14. Many of the athletes parents were disappointed by the coachs decision.

15. Everybodys attention was diverted by the marching band.

16. She asked, Can you remember the first line of the William Blake poem The Tyger?

17. All of your permission slips, said Mr. Ghose, need to be returned by Thursday, the tenth.

18. My great grandfather knows all the words to the Irish folk song The Wild Colonial Boy.

19. I enjoy the long lasting flavor, announced Paul.

20. How many *if*s can you find in the story?

HOLT HANDBOOK | Introductory Course

Proofreading Application: Interview

Good writers are generally good proofreaders. Readers tend to admire and trust writing that is error-free. Make sure that you correct all errors in grammar, usage, spelling, and punctuation in your writing. Your readers will have more confidence in your words if you have done your best to proofread carefully.

Whenever you interview a person and write about the conversation, you use quotation marks. You may find yourself using italics, apostrophes, and hyphens as well. Take special care to use quotation marks correctly. If you don't, readers may not be able to tell who said what. Moreover, the person whom you interviewed might be upset if you misquote him or her.

PROOFREADING ACTIVITY

Find and correct the errors in punctuation and paragraphing. Use proofreading symbols to make your corrections.

Example "Thank you for agreeing to this interview," I began.

Tell me, Ms. Peabody, when did you begin writing?" I asked, thrilled to be talking to the author of the famous series of childrens books.

"My mother tells me that I started writing at the age of three." "By the time I was eight, I was making small booklets of my stories," Ms. Peabody answered.

"When did you publish your first story? I persisted. "I was twenty three when I published the story 'Noogie, the Squirrel'." she recalled.

"Noogie," I smiled "how I loved him when I was younger."

Ms. Peabody laughed, "Yes, so many children loved Noogie and his mischievous antics that I wrote the novel "Noogie's Big Idea."

"Hollywoods making that book into a film now," I observed.

"Indeed, it is, dear. The working title is Frantic Antics. It'll be animated by computers, or so they tell me," Ms. Peabody answered.

"I can't wait to see how the film handles the grocery store scene and it's pandemonium," I remarked.

"Whatever the director does, it'll never beat the readers' imagi-

Language and Sentence Skills Practice

Literary Model: Dialogue in Fiction

"Will any kind friend inform a poor blind man, who has lost the precious sight of his eyes in the gracious defence of his native country, England, and God bless King George—where or in what part of this country he may now be?"

"You are at the 'Admiral Benbow,' Black Hill Cove, my good man," said I.

"I hear a voice," said he—"a young voice. Will you give me your hand my kind young friend and lead me . . . to the captain?"

"Sir," said I, "upon my word I dare not."

"Oh," he sneered, "that's it! Take me straight, or I'll break your arm."

And he gave it, as he spoke, a wrench that made me cry out.

"Sir," said I, "it is for yourself I mean. The captain is not what he used to be. He sits with a drawn cutlass. Another gentleman—"

"Come, now, march," interrupted he; ". . . Lead me straight up to him, and when I'm in view, cry out, 'Here's a friend for you, Bill.' If you don't, I'll do this"; and with that he gave me a twitch that I thought would have made me faint.

—from *Treasure Island* by Robert Louis Stevenson

EXERCISE A

1. Carefully read the excerpt again. Then, use information from the dialogue of each character to describe each character's personality.

   the boy (Jim): _____

   _____

   the blind man (Pew): _____

   _____

2. The manner in which a writer reveals a character's personality is called *characterization*. Characterization can be *direct*—such as when an author directly states what a character is like—or *indirect*—such as when an author uses dialogue and actions to suggest what a character is like. Think of it this way: An author can state directly that a character is wicked, or an author can show indirectly that a character is wicked through the character's words and actions. Which kind of characterization does Stevenson use in the excerpt? Explain.

   _____

   _____

Literary Model (continued)

EXERCISE B   Do you think the characters of Jim and Pew would be as rich and lively if Stevenson had used direct characterization? What effect does Stevenson's use of dialogue have on your understanding of the characters' personalities? Explain.

_____

_____

_____

_____

EXERCISE C   On the lines below, write a short dialogue between two fictional characters of your own creation. Before you write your dialogue, brainstorm two adjectives for each of your characters. You should not use these adjectives in your dialogue. Then, as you write your dialogue, use indirect characterization to make readers think of the adjectives you brainstormed. Be sure to use paragraph breaks and quotation marks correctly so that readers can easily follow your dialogue.

_____

_____

_____

_____

_____

_____

_____

_____

_____

_____

_____

_____

_____

_____

_____

_____

EXERCISE D   Re-read your dialogue, and make any revisions that will make your indirect characterization more effective.

Language and Sentence Skills Practice

283

for **CHAPTER 13: PUNCTUATION**   *pages 290–312*

Writing Application: Character Analysis

Rules 13a and 13l remind you that titles of longer works are underlined (italicized) while titles of shorter works go in quotation marks. Sometimes you may wonder whether a work is long or short. It may help you to remember that longer works are often subdivided into sections like chapters, songs, acts, articles, and so on. The subdivisions are placed in quotation marks, while the longer titles are underlined (italicized).

EXAMPLES   I read the article "On the Road with Buffy" in *People* magazine.

                Greta recited "The Mystic Trumpeter" from Walt Whitman's *Leaves of Grass.*

                Tao's favorite aria from Handel's *Messiah* is "Every Valley Shall Be Exalted."

WRITING ACTIVITY

People read and watch fiction for many reasons, one of which is that they often see themselves in a story's characters. They feel that they can relate to a character—that they almost know him or her. Write three paragraphs in which you discuss three characters to whom you relate or with whom you have much in common. The characters can come from books, TV shows, movies, musicals, or any other fictional works. In each paragraph, discuss two ways that you and one of the characters are alike. Then, talk about one important way in which you are not at all like the character.

PREWRITING   First, you must think about characters—human, animal, alien—that you feel are similar to you. Then, think deeply about traits that you share with each character and ways in which you are quite different from the character. Generate a list of similarities and a list of differences for each of the three characters.

WRITING   For each paragraph and character, choose the two strongest similarities and the most striking difference to discuss. Then, decide in what order to discuss the similarities. Think of how the similarities are related to each other. Courage, for example, might lead to an adventurous spirit, and compassion is clearly related to a willingness to help others. Let the relationship between the two similarities help you organize the paragraph. Use a transition that expresses contrast as you move into the sentences about how you and the character differ. Repeat this process for each character.

REVISING   The hard work is done—now it's time to have fun by adding details and examples to your paragraphs! What does the character say that makes your point? What does he or she do? Do you say and do similar things? Specifics bring writing to life, so rather than simply writing, "He's very smart," tell how the character used a gum wrapper and a dead flashlight to defeat the bad guys.

PUBLISHING   Check your paragraphs for mistakes in spelling and punctuation. Be sure that you have used underlining (italics) and quotation marks correctly. Then, share with your class what you have learned about character, and listen to what your classmates have learned.

EXTENDING YOUR WRITING

This exercise could lead to a more developed writing project. You could take these paragraphs several steps further by thinking deeply about how writers create such realistic characters. Make a how-to booklet that explains ways to create realistic characters, and distribute the booklet to classmates.

for **CHAPTER 14: SPELLING** | pages 317–38

Choices: Exploring Spelling

Here's your chance to step out of the grammar book and into the real world. You may not notice mechanics, but you and the people around you use examples of mechanics every day. The following activities challenge you to find a connection between spelling and the world around you. Do the activity below that suits your personality best, and then share your discoveries with your class. Have fun!

Sound Off

Homonyms—words that sound alike but are spelled differently—can be tricky. Make the best of a tricky situation. Have a contest to find who can name the homonym with the most spellings.

Ahead of the Game

There are a number of classic and new word games. Take a poll, and find out which word game seems to be the class favorite. When you've settled on a game, hold a tournament. When you have a winner or a winning team, challenge another English class.

Weigh Eight Neighbors

Take another look at the *ei* and *ie* rules. Then, add to the list in your textbook. With a group of friends, think of as many *ei* and *ie* words as you can. Then, divide them up into words that follow the rules and words that are exceptions. When you've got a long list for each category, put your lists on posters and ask to hang them in the classroom.

According to Webster

Did you know that the way you talk and write has a lot to do with Noah Webster? You may not know much about him, though. Find out what kind of person he really was. Read a biography or do other research on him. Tell your class about how this one man affected spellings in American English.

From Arabia to India to England

Show the class how American English has borrowed words from every continent in the world. Get or sketch a good-sized world map. Then, trace the path of ten or twenty words as they entered the English language.

Lightning in a Bottle?

Create a cartoon illustrating how using the wrong homonym can lead to a humorous misunderstanding. For example, you could illustrate a woman who, when trying to lighten her hair, buys a hair-lightning kit. What would her hair look like after the bottled lightning struck? Ask to post your cartoon in the classroom.

Nobody's Perfect

Spelling is the number-one error in writings of all kinds. Tackle this problem now! Design forms for your classmates to use to record their spelling errors. Your forms should include columns for proper spelling, syllabication, and any other information that you think would be helpful. Make sure everybody gets a copy.

It's All Greek to Me

Foreign words are often written with accent marks or other markings over or under certain letters. These marks are part of the spelling of the word. In fact, they are sometimes part of the letter. Find out the names of these marks, and write up a memo for your friends. Include each mark, its name, and its sound, if possible.

Language and Sentence Skills Practice

Good Spelling Habits

The following techniques can help you spell words correctly.

- To learn the spelling of a word, pronounce it, study it, and write it.
- Use a dictionary.
- Spell by syllables.
- Keep a spelling notebook.
- Proofread for careless spelling errors.

EXERCISE A Look up each of the following words in a dictionary. Circle the word that is spelled correctly.

Example 1. simlar   (similar)

1. recognize	recgnize		**11.** ilegal	illegal
2. defintion	definition		**12.** wonderfully	wonderfuly
3. awkard	awkward		**13.** evil	eval
4. temperature	temperture		**14.** bisciut	biscuit
5. probbly	probably		**15.** Roman	Romin
6. pespire	perspire		**16.** noval	novel
7. educationle	educational		**17.** enormous	enormis
8. modern	madern		**18.** transcripts	transcrips
9. legslature	legislature		**19.** comotion	commotion
10. excellent	excellnt		**20.** heights	hieghts

EXERCISE B Look up each of the following words in a dictionary. On the line provided, rewrite each word, using hyphens to divide it into syllables.

Example 1. multinational _____mul-ti-na-tion-al_____

21. pedestrian _____   **26.** extremely _____

22. rivalry _____   **27.** president _____

23. strawberry _____   **28.** library _____

24. vaporize _____   **29.** assistant _____

25. hospitable _____   **30.** mysterious _____

MECHANICS

ie and *ei*

14a. Write *ie* when the sound is long *e*, except after *c*.

EXAMPLES	n**ie**ce	p**ie**ce	bel**ie**ve	rec**ei**ve	perc**ei**ve
EXCEPTIONS	**ei**ther	n**ei**ther	prot**ei**n	s**ei**ze	

Write *ei* when the sound is not long *e*, especially when the sound is long *a*.

EXAMPLES	n**ei**gh	fr**ei**ght	r**ei**gn	f**ei**gn	h**ei**ght	for**ei**gn
EXCEPTIONS	anc**ie**nt	fr**ie**nd	misch**ie**f	f**ie**rce		

EXERCISE A Underline the correctly spelled word in each of the following pairs.

Example 1. <u>niece</u>   neice

1. field	feild		**6.** sleigh	sliegh
2. wieght	weight		**7.** theif	thief
3. riendeer	reindeer		**8.** reciept	receipt
4. shield	sheild		**9.** releif	relief
5. nieghbor	neighbor		**10.** achieve	acheive

EXERCISE B In each of the following sentences, a word is underlined. If the word is misspelled, rewrite it correctly on the line provided. If the word is spelled correctly, write *C* on the line provided.

Example _____*receive*_____ **1.** Did you <u>recieve</u> a package in the mail today?

_____ **11.** The color <u>beige</u> is grayish tan.

_____ **12.** Alice Gardner is the new fire <u>cheif</u> for this county.

_____ **13.** Lupe is not <u>concieted</u>, even though she is more intelligent than most

people.

_____ **14.** The FBI had several suspects under <u>surviellance</u>.

_____ **15.** Optical illusions prove that a person's eyes can be <u>deceived</u>.

_____ **16.** Quinine is a drug used to <u>releive</u> fevers caused by malaria.

_____ **17.** If you multiply two by itself and then by two again, you get <u>eight</u>.

_____ **18.** The ancient Inca <u>preists</u> wore beautiful robes made of fine woven cloth.

_____ **19.** The <u>cieling</u> collapsed under the weight of the water bed.

_____ **20.** In New Hampshire, we took an old-fashioned <u>sliegh</u> ride.

Language and Sentence Skills Practice

Prefixes

14b. When adding a prefix to a word, do not change the spelling of the word itself.

> **EXAMPLES**   mis + trust = mis**trust**
> dis + satisfied = dis**satisfied**
> un + named = un**named**
> re + assure = re**assure**

EXERCISE A   Combine each of the following prefixes and words to create a new word. Spell the new word correctly on the line provided.

Example 1. dis + agree = _____*disagree*_____

1. il + logical = _____

2. im + mobile = _____

3. mis + spell = _____

4. over + react = _____

5. un + feeling = _____

6. pre + view = _____

7. un + natural = _____

8. im + measurable = _____

9. dis + interest = _____

10. re + evaluate = _____

EXERCISE B   Create five different words by combining the prefixes given below with the words listed beside them. (You may not use a prefix or word more than once.) Check each of your new words in a dictionary. Then, on the line provided, use each word in a sentence.

Prefixes			Words			
dis–	inter–	un–	cover	state	connect	natural
semi–	in–	pre–	appropriate	darkness	sold	view

Example 1. *disconnect—Earl disconnected his computer.* _____

11. _____

_____

12. _____

_____

13. _____

_____

14. _____

_____

15. _____

_____

MECHANICS

Adding –*ness* and –*ly*

14c. When adding the suffix –*ness* or –*ly* to a word, do not change the spelling of the word itself.

> **EXAMPLES** quick + ness = **quick**ness careful + ly = **careful**ly
>
> **EXCEPTIONS** For most words that end in *y*, change the *y* to *i* before adding –*ly* or –*ness*.
> sleepy + ly = sleep**ily** steady + ness = stead**iness**

EXERCISE A Combine each of the following words and suffixes to create a new word on the line provided.

Example 1. sure + ly = _____*surely*_____

1. slow + ness = _____

2. quick + ly = _____

3. perfect + ly = _____

4. messy + ness = _____

5. sad + ness = _____

6. bland + ly = _____

7. silly + ness = _____

8. blunt + ly = _____

9. sudden + ly = _____

10. tender + ness = _____

11. friend + ly = _____

12. hard + ness = _____

13. hardy + ly = _____

14. quiet + ly = _____

15. high + ness = _____

16. soft + ly = _____

17. hungry + ly = _____

18. together + ness = _____

19. loud + ness = _____

20. short + ness = _____

EXERCISE B On the line in each sentence, write the word made by combining the word parts shown in parentheses.

Example 1. Offering that person your seat was an act of _____*kindness*_____. (*kind + ness*)

21. The team showed more _____ in the second half than it had in the first. (*tough + ness*)

22. The other driver was _____ sorry about the accident. (*sincere + ly*)

23. These dogs are known for their _____. (*friendly + ness*)

24. What kind of _____ have you kids been up to? (*silly + ness*)

25. I would _____ go to the movies with you. (*happy + ly*)

MECHANICS

Language and Sentence Skills Practice

Adding Suffixes to Words Ending in Silent *e*

14d. Drop the final silent *e* before adding a suffix that begins with a vowel.

EXAMPLES	make + ing = **mak**ing sincere + ity = **sincer**ity
EXCEPTIONS	Keep the silent *e* in words ending in *ce* and *ge* before adding a suffix beginning with *a* or *o*.
	trace + able = trac**eable** courage + ous = courag**eous**

14e. Keep the final silent *e* before adding a suffix that begins with a consonant.

EXAMPLES	instinctive + ly = instinctiv**ely** state + ment = stat**ement**
EXCEPTIONS	argue + ment = **argu**ment true + ly = **tru**ly

EXERCISE A Combine each of the following words and suffixes to create a new word on the line provided.

Example 1. cause + ing = _____*causing*_____

1. love + less = _____
2. spite + ful = _____
3. grudge + ing = _____
4. true + ly = _____
5. drive + er = _____
6. live + ing = _____
7. state + ly = _____
8. outrage + ous = _____
9. inflate + ed = _____
10. state + ment = _____

11. sponge + ing = _____
12. replace + ment = _____
13. service + able = _____
14. spine + less = _____
15. strange + ly = _____
16. immerse + ible = _____
17. argue + ment = _____
18. love + able = _____
19. hate + ful = _____
20. face + ing = _____

EXERCISE B On the line in each sentence, write the word made by combining the word parts shown in parentheses.

Example 1. Isn't that kitten _____*adorable*_____? (*adore + able*)

21. The mechanic ordered a _____ part for the engine. (*replace + ment*)

22. What do you think is _____ all this rain? (*cause + ing*)

23. The bite of this spider is _____. (*harm + less*)

24. How _____ is this necklace? (*value + able*)

25. Joey's _____ made his teacher proud. (*achieve + ment*)

Adding Suffixes to Words Ending in *y*

14f. For words that end in a consonant plus *y*, change the *y* to *i* before adding a suffix.

EXAMPLES	easy + er = eas**ier**	dry + est = dr**iest**
EXCEPTIONS	Keep the *y* if the suffix begins with an *i*.	
	fry + ing = fr**ying**	marry + ing = marr**ying**

Keep the *y* if the word ends in a vowel plus *y*.

EXAMPLES	play + ed = pla**yed**	prey + ing = pre**ying**
EXCEPTIONS	say + ed = said	day + ly = daily

EXERCISE A Combine each of the following words and suffixes to create a new word on the line provided.

Example 1. defy + ing = _____ *defying* _____

1. pry + ed = _____
2. marry + ed = _____
3. play + ing = _____
4. spy + ing = _____
5. lay + ing = _____
6. gay + ly = _____
7. try + ed = _____
8. pretty + ness = _____
9. stay + ed = _____
10. easy + est = _____

11. lonely + er = _____
12. delay + ing = _____
13. lazy + est = _____
14. rely + able = _____
15. rainy + er = _____
16. fly + ing = _____
17. display +ed = _____
18. play + er = _____
19. silly + ness = _____
20. steady + er = _____

EXERCISE B On the line in each sentence, write the word made by combining the word parts shown in parentheses.

Example 1. "Wait for me!" _____ *cried* _____ his little brother. (*cry + ed*)

21. Those flowers look even _____ than they did yesterday. (*pretty + er*)

22. The comic strip appears _____ in the newspaper. (*day + ly*)

23. He spent the day _____ the kids to their dance lessons. (*ferry + ing*)

24. That's the _____ moustache I have ever seen. (*phony + est*)

25. The team _____ very well last night. (*play + ed*)

Language and Sentence Skills Practice

Doubling Final Consonants When Adding Suffixes

14g. Double the final consonant before adding *–ing, –ed, –er*, or *–est* to a one-syllable word that ends in a single vowel followed by a single consonant.

EXAMPLES   trim + ing = tri**mming**   pat + ed = pa**tted**
           mad + er = ma**dder**   sad + est = sa**ddest**

When a one-syllable word ends in two vowels followed by a single consonant, do not double the consonant before adding *–ing, –ed, –er*, or *–est.*

EXAMPLES   read + ing = rea**ding**   pool + ed = poo**led**
           meek + er = mee**ker**   weak + est = wea**kest**

MECHANICS

EXERCISE A Combine each of the following words and suffixes to create a new word on the line provided.

Example 1. creep + er = _____creeper_____

1. speak + er = _____
2. bug + ed = _____
3. slim + ing = _____
4. red + est = _____
5. sleep + er = _____
6. mat + ed = _____
7. wear + er = _____
8. leak + ing = _____
9. big + er = _____
10. pet + ed = _____

11. glad + est = _____
12. sad + er = _____
13. fat + er = _____
14. school + ed = _____
15. bat + ed = _____
16. weep + ing = _____
17. bear + ing = _____
18. meek + est = _____
19. sit + er = _____
20. swim + ing = _____

EXERCISE B On the line in each sentence, write the word made by combining the word parts shown in parentheses.

Example 1. The evening is _____cooler_____ after a rainstorm. (*cool + er*)

21. Rover _____ in his tracks when he heard the noise. (*stop + ed*)

22. The _____ thing to do would be to divide the fruit equally. (*fair + est*)

23. One of the hikers seemed to be _____ behind the others. (*lag + ing*)

24. The pitcher _____ with the shortstop as they waited for the rain to stop. (*chat + ed*)

25. My left arm is _____ than my right arm. (*weak + er*)

Suffixes

14c.	When adding the suffix –*ness* or –*ly* to a word, do not change the spelling of the word itself.
14d.	Drop the final silent *e* before adding a suffix that begins with a vowel.
14e.	Keep the final silent *e* before adding a suffix that begins with a consonant.
14f.	For words that end in a consonant plus *y*, change the *y* to *i* before adding a suffix.
14g.	Double the final consonant before adding –*ing*, –*ed*, –*er*, or –*est* to a one-syllable word that ends in a single vowel followed by a single consonant.

EXERCISE A Combine each of the following words and suffixes to create a new word. Spell the new word correctly on the line provided.

Example 1. worry + ing = _____*worrying*_____

1. general + ly = _____

2. peace + able = _____

3. invite + ation = _____

4. merry + ment = _____

5. value + able = _____

6. entertain + ment = _____

7. ferry + ing = _____

8. employ + ing = _____

9. big + est = _____

10. roof + ing = _____

11. silly + ness = _____

12. study + ing = _____

13. play + er = _____

14. slug + er = _____

15. near + est = _____

16. hairy + ness = _____

17. inflate + ion = _____

18. courage + ous = _____

19. try + ed = _____

20. fate + ful = _____

EXERCISE B On the line in each sentence, write the word made by adding the word parts shown in parentheses.

Example 1. Dr. Martin Luther King, Jr., was an _____*admirable*_____ man. (*admire + able*)

21. Dr. King led _____ protests against segregation. (*peace + ful*)

22. He acted in a _____ manner. (*courage + ous*)

23. He offered an active, _____ plan for achieving civil rights for all people, regardless of color, creed, or ethnic origin. (*create + ive*)

24. Many people remember the powerful _____ that he made during the March on Washington in 1963. (*state + ment*)

25. Dr. Martin Luther King, Jr., was an _____ to many people. (*inspire + ation*)

Language and Sentence Skills Practice

Forming the Plurals of Nouns A

14h. Follow these rules for spelling the plurals of nouns:

(1) To form the plurals of most nouns, add *s*.

EXAMPLES   friend—friend**s**   piñata—piñata**s**   sneeze—sneeze**s**   Clark—Clark**s**

(2) Form the plurals of nouns ending in *s, x, z, ch,* or *sh* by adding *es*.

EXAMPLES   fax—fax**es**   brush—brush**es**   perch—perch**es**   Ruiz—Ruiz**es**

MECHANICS

EXERCISE A   Write the plural of each of the following words on the line provided.

Examples   1. glass _____*glasses*_____

          2. doctor _____*doctors*_____

1. apple _____

2. wax _____

3. car _____

4. boss _____

5. beach _____

6. science _____

7. sock _____

8. pinch _____

9. splash _____

10. snooze _____

11. eagle _____

12. umbrella _____

13. Paul _____

14. glitch _____

15. Jones _____

16. zebra _____

17. pill _____

18. mix _____

19. Gomez _____

20. beagle _____

EXERCISE B   On the line in each sentence, write the plural of the word shown in parentheses.

Example   1. How many _____*peaches*_____ are in a bushel? *(peach)*

21. The border town is usually full of _____ this time of year. *(tourist)*

22. My aunt got a refund on her _____ this year. *(tax)*

23. How many _____ did Beethoven write? *(sonata)*

24. Both _____ need to be shortened somewhat. *(sleeve)*

25. There are over forty _____ in our town. *(church)*

Forming the Plurals of Nouns B

14h. Follow these rules for spelling the plurals of nouns:

(3) Form the plurals of nouns that end in a consonant plus *y* by changing the *y* to *i* and adding *es*.

    EXAMPLES worry—worr**ies**   army—arm**ies**   pony—pon**ies**

(4) Form the plurals of nouns that end in a vowel plus *y* by adding *s*.

    EXAMPLES key—key**s**   attorney—attorney**s**   ray—ray**s**

(5) Form the plurals of nouns that end in a vowel plus *o* by adding *s*.

    EXAMPLES patio—patio**s**   video—video**s**   zoo—zoo**s**

(6) Form the plurals of nouns that end in a consonant plus *o* by adding *es*.

    EXAMPLES echo—echo**es**   potato—potato**es**   hero—hero**es**

EXERCISE A Write the plural of each of the following words on the line provided.

Examples **1.** cherry _____*cherries*_____

        2. tomato _____*tomatoes*_____

1. navy _____

2. boy _____

3. kangaroo _____

4. soprano _____

5. trolley _____

6. antihero _____

7. Tracy _____

8. story _____

9. tray _____

10. pistachio _____

11. tragedy _____

12. monkey _____

13. payday _____

14. ratio _____

15. auto _____

16. country _____

17. Mario _____

18. tornado _____

19. rodeo _____

20. melody _____

EXERCISE B On the line in each sentence, write the plural of the word shown in parentheses.

Example 1. The banks close for several _____*holidays*_____ this month. (*holiday*)

21. There were several _____ on display at the electronics store. (*stereo*)

22. The drama festival will feature a number of new _____. (*play*)

23. During the storm all of our _____ were tuned to the emergency channel. (*radio*)

24. The president was responsible for fourteen _____ this month. (*veto*)

25. We saw six _____ in the backyard last night. (*turkey*)

Language and Sentence Skills Practice

Forming the Plurals of Nouns C

14h. Follow these rules for spelling the plurals of nouns:

(7) The plurals of a few nouns are formed in irregular ways.

    EXAMPLES   tooth—t**ee**th   goose—g**ee**se   child—child**ren**   mouse—m**ice**

(8) Some nouns are the same in the singular and in the plural.

    SINGULAR AND PLURAL   trout   deer   aircraft   Chinese

(9) Form the plurals of numerals, letters, symbols, and words referred to as words by adding an apostrophe and *s*.

    EXAMPLES   1860—1860**'s**   A—A**'s**   &—&**'s**   however—however**'s**

EXERCISE A Write the plural of each of the following words, numerals, letters, and symbols.

Examples **1.** woman _____*women*_____

          2. *C* _____*C's*_____

1. reindeer _____   **11.** *7* _____

2. child _____   **12.** Vietnamese _____

3. *$* _____   **13.** 1900 (century) _____

4. species _____   **14.** man _____

5. foot _____   **15.** herring _____

6. Sioux _____   **16.** series _____

7. fish _____   **17.** *!* _____

8. 1960 (decade) _____   **18.** louse _____

9. spacecraft _____   **19.** *if* _____

10. *X* _____   **20.** fowl _____

EXERCISE B On the line provided, identify the underlined word in each of the following sentences as *singular* or *plural*.

Example _____*singular*_____ **1.** Last night we saw a <u>deer</u> at the side of the road.

_____ **21.** How many <u>aircraft</u> will be at the air show?

_____ **22.** Isn't that a nice-looking <u>trout</u>?

_____ **23.** We usually see several <u>deer</u> at the salt lick every evening.

_____ **24.** How many <u>Chinese</u> attended the trade conference?

_____ **25.** Several <u>fish</u> nibbled at the bait before one of them was hooked.

Forming Plurals: Review

14h. Follow these rules for spelling the plurals of nouns:

(1) To form the plurals of most nouns, add *s*.

(2) Form the plurals of nouns ending in *s, x, z, ch,* or *sh* by adding *es*.

(3) Form the plurals of nouns that end in a consonant plus *y* by changing the *y* to *i* and adding *es*.

(4) Form the plurals of nouns that end in a vowel plus *y* by adding *s*.

(5) Form the plurals of nouns that end in a vowel plus *o* by adding *s*.

(6) Form the plurals of nouns that end in a consonant plus *o* by adding *es*.

(7) The plurals of a few nouns are formed in irregular ways.

(8) Some nouns are the same in the singular and in the plural.

(9) Form the plurals of numerals, letters, symbols, and words referred to as words by adding an apostrophe and *s*.

EXERCISE A On the lines provided, write the plurals of the following nouns. Refer to a dictionary if necessary.

Example 1. turkey _____*turkeys*_____

1. 1980 _____
2. ox _____
3. ratio _____
4. stereo _____
5. delay _____
6. mess _____
7. lunch _____
8. fox _____
9. ditch _____
10. party _____

11. flurry _____
12. beach _____
13. wax _____
14. whoosh _____
15. lass _____
16. way _____
17. hero _____
18. veto _____
19. 1490 _____
20. Swiss _____

EXERCISE B On the line in each sentence, write the plural of the word in parentheses.

Example 1. The two _____*cats*_____ chased each other through the living room. *(cat)*

21. How many _____ can you find in that sentence? *(and)*

22. Three _____ passed the crossing in an hour. *(train)*

23. The hikers saw several _____ during their walk across Isle Royale. *(moose)*

24. The cook combined two _____ to make this tasty pasta sauce. *(mix)*

25. The tour bus crossed through three _____ in one afternoon. *(country)*

Language and Sentence Skills Practice

Words Often Confused A

Review the words often confused covered on pages 329–30 of your textbook for information on the correct usage and spelling of the following words:

already, all ready	*brake, break*
altar, alter	*capital, capitol*
altogether, all together	*choose, chose*

EXERCISE A Underline the correct word or words in parentheses in each of the following sentences.

Example 1. Jackie will (<u>choose</u>, *chose*) the theme for her birthday party.

1. The space shuttle has (*brakes, breaks*) that allow it to land just like an airplane.

2. The ambassadors from the European nations were (*altogether, all together*) in a large conference room.

3. The Aztecs made sacrifices on their (*altars, alters*).

4. By the time we arrived, the tickets to the game had (*already, all ready*) been sold.

5. Did Millie (*choose, chose*) the blue sweater or the white one?

6. Mexico City is the (*capital, capitol*) of Mexico.

7. This ancient Chinese vase is made of thin porcelain and can (*brake, break*) quite easily.

8. "Are you (*already, all ready*)?" asked the Ferris wheel attendant.

9. Lima, Peru, was the (*capital, capitol*) of the Spanish Empire in Latin America.

10. The jury decided that the defendant's story was (*altogether, all together*) unbelievable.

EXERCISE B In each of the following sentences, cross out each word that is misused and then write the correct word above it. If a sentence is already correct, write *C* on the line provided.

Example _____ **1.** The train's ~~breaks~~ *brakes* squealed all the way into the station.

_____ **11.** Do not altar a single word of my story!

_____ **12.** Is Lansing or Detroit the capitol of Michigan?

_____ **13.** Some students have all ready finished the test.

_____ **14.** It's not unusual to brake a bone playing hockey.

_____ **15.** They rode all together on the hay wagon.

MECHANICS

Words Often Confused B

Review the words often confused covered on pages 330–33 of your textbook for information on the correct usage and spelling of the following words:

cloths, clothes	hear, here
coarse, course	its, it's
desert, dessert	lead, led, lead

EXERCISE A In each of the following sentences, underline the correct word in parentheses.

Example 1. Who put the directions for the microwave oven in *(hear, here)*?

1. A fabric store sells *(cloths, clothes)* of many different types, patterns, and colors.

2. Sea salt is larger and more *(coarse, course)* than regular table salt.

3. What is the largest *(desert, dessert)* in the Southern Hemisphere?

4. Yes, this tiny device actually helps people to *(hear, here)* better.

5. The coach has *(lead, led)* her team to victory again!

6. Margarita wants to take a *(coarse, course)* in welding at a community college.

7. Maria has read her favorite book so many times that *(its, it's)* pages are wearing thin.

8. Wouldn't fruit salad make a nice *(desert, dessert)* for this meal?

9. "I don't see that mouse now," thought the cat, "but I know that *(its, it's)* been here."

10. Nolan said, "I like this pencil because the *(lead, led)* is not too soft."

EXERCISE B In each of the following sentences, cross out the word that is misused and then write the correct word above it. If a sentence is already correct, write *C* on the line provided.

Example _____ **1.** Kendra prides herself on the stylishness of her ~~cloths~~. *clothes*

_____ **11.** The film *Lawrence of Arabia* is set mainly in the dessert in Arabia.

_____ **12.** You may put that wet bathing suit anywhere but hear.

_____ **13.** Who will lead the group through the forest?

_____ **14.** Its a pity that Sean couldn't join us for the party.

_____ **15.** This woolen fabric is very course, isn't it?

Words Often Confused C

Review the words often confused covered on pages 333–36 of your textbook for information on the correct usage and spelling of the following words:

loose, lose	*plain, plane*
passed, past	*principal, principle*
peace, piece	*stationary, stationery*

EXERCISE A In each of the following sentences, underline the correct word in parentheses.

Example 1. You made me (loose, <u>lose</u>) my place.

1. The thunderstorm has shaken my (peace, piece) of mind.

2. The wide (planes, plains) at the center of the state are covered mainly with grass.

3. She is one of the (principal, principle) performers in the band.

4. My aunt writes me letters every week on very colorful (stationery, stationary).

5. You (passed, past) the boat launch a few miles back.

6. Freedom of speech is one of the basic (principals, principles) of our system of government.

7. The (plane, plain) turned slowly toward the airport.

8. The bus drove (passed, past) the bus stop without stopping.

9. A (piece, peace) of the bank's roof was blown off by the tornado.

10. The maypole itself is (stationery, stationary) while the dancers dance around it.

EXERCISE B In each of the following sentences, cross out the word that is misused and then write the correct word above it. If a sentence is already correct, write *C* on the line provided.

Example _____ **1.** The diplomat hopes to negotiate a ~~piece~~ ^{peace} treaty in Northern Ireland.

_____ **11.** What is the name of the principal at your school?

_____ **12.** I do most of my exercise on a stationery bicycle.

_____ **13.** Finally the wheel came lose and fell off the toy truck.

_____ **14.** Why, the real reason for Bob's answer is as plane as the nose on your face!

_____ **15.** I past the library on my way to the grocery store.

Words Often Confused D

Review the words often confused covered on pages 336–38 of your textbook for information on the correct usage and spelling of the following words:

their, there, they're	*weak, week*
threw, through	*who's, whose*
to, too, two	*your, you're*

EXERCISE A In each of the following sentences, underline the correct word in parentheses.

Example 1. *(Their, There, They're)* the ones who brought the music to the party.

1. After his surgery, our dog was too *(week, weak)* to walk for a few days.

2. Meanwhile, the other *(to, too, two)* acrobats were swinging from their knees.

3. That's the author *(who's, whose)* book was reviewed in the newspaper last week.

4. Bring me *(your, you're)* glass, and I'll pour you some more juice.

5. This tea is *(to, too, two)* hot for me.

6. We passed *(threw, through)* Stanwood on our way to Big Rapids.

7. *(Who's, Whose)* coming with us to the play?

8. *(Your, You're)* the magician my sister was telling me about yesterday.

9. Conrad *(threw, through)* a pass that led to a touchdown in the last seconds of the game.

10. Cleaning up after the meal is *(their, there, they're)* responsibility.

EXERCISE B In each of the following sentences, cross out the word that is misused and then write the correct word above it. If a sentence is already correct, write *C* on the line provided.

Example _____ **1.** Please send this check ~~too~~ *to* the gas company.

_____ **11.** The cat tumbled threw the branches of the tree but landed on its feet.

_____ **12.** The library book is due next weak.

_____ **13.** Do you know who's boots these are?

_____ **14.** Leave your muddy shoes there, and come into the kitchen.

_____ **15.** You're time is up.

Language and Sentence Skills Practice

Review A: **Spelling Rules**

EXERCISE A Underline the correctly spelled word in parentheses in each of the following sentences.

Example 1. The *(theif, thief)* has finally been caught.

1. My *(neice, niece)* is named Maika Vanessa Sanchez Huaman.

2. That woman is very beautiful, but she is not at all *(conceited, concieted)*.

3. Roland's *(neighborhood, nieghborhood)* is quite friendly.

4. There are *(eight, ieght)* churches within the next two blocks.

5. When I first heard the news, I couldn't *(beleive, believe)* it.

6. This *(piece, peice)* of music is very beautiful.

7. Did you *(recieve, receive)* the package that I sent?

8. England was a mighty empire during the *(riegn, reign)* of Queen Victoria.

9. What a good *(neighbor, nieghbor)* you are!

10. That's a *(wieght, weight)* off my mind!

EXERCISE B Combine each of the following word parts to form a new word. Write the new word on the line provided.

Example 1. argue + ment = _____*argument*_____

11. mis + spell = _____

12. ugly + ness = _____

13. educate + ion = _____

14. outrage + ous = _____

15. peace + ful = _____

16. cry + ed = _____

17. marry + ing = _____

18. hot + er = _____

19. neat + est = _____

20. pre + heat = _____

EXERCISE C Write the plural forms of the following nouns on the lines provided.

Example 1. alto _____*altos*_____

21. lunch _____

22. worry _____

23. fax _____

24. army _____

25. attorney _____

26. patio _____

27. potato _____

28. 100 _____

29. aircraft _____

30. 1650 _____

MECHANICS

Review B: **Words Often Confused**

EXERCISE A   Underline the correct word or word group in parentheses in each of the following sentences.

Example   1. E-mail has become the (<u>principal</u>, principle) means of communication between my cousin and me.

1. Annapolis is the (capital, capitol) of Maryland.

2. The guide (lead, led) the hikers to the river.

3. Marlo has (passed, past) the fitness test with flying colors.

4. (Its, It's) time to prepare the decorations for the Cinco de Mayo festival.

5. Mr. Wauneka hates to (loose, lose) at chess.

6. By the time we got to the store, it was (already, all ready) closed.

7. Honesty is just one of the (principals, principles) of Tamika's moral code.

8. One (brake, break) on the car had to be replaced because it had worn out.

9. I've almost finished the jigsaw puzzle, but I think there is a (peace, piece) missing.

10. World history is one (coarse, course) that Paulo really liked.

EXERCISE B   Cross out the word that is misused in each sentence below, and write the correct word on the line provided. If a sentence is already correct, write C.

Example _____*weak*_____ **1.** The baby was too ~~week~~ to pick up the ball.

_____ **11.** Do you here the robin singing?

_____ **12.** The letter was written on letterhead stationery.

_____ **13.** Your not going to believe what I just saw.

_____ **14.** We drove past the intersection and had to turn around.

_____ **15.** Mr. Takagi is the principle violinist in the orchestra.

_____ **16.** Whose going to bring the oranges in from the car?

_____ **17.** The workers on the new cathedral are known for there attention to detail.

_____ **18.** He threw the stick across the yard, and the dog brought it back.

_____ **19.** We returned the books too the library.

_____ **20.** Standing at the center of the vast, grassy plain, she could see all the way to the horizon.

Language and Sentence Skills Practice

Review C: Spelling Rules and Words Often Confused

EXERCISE A   Underline the correct word or word group in parentheses in each of the following sentences.

Example   1. (There, Their, They're) all coming to the game tonight.

1. Please take off (your, you're) coat, and sit down.

2. Joanne says she is at (peace, piece) whenever she goes camping.

3. At night, the (desert, dessert) air can become quite cold.

4. Who (choose, chose) the video we watched last night?

5. Of (coarse, course) you should take her class!

6. Finally, the parade moved (passed, past) the spot where we were standing.

7. London, the largest city in England, is also the (capital, capitol).

8. The gymnasium is (already, all ready) for the dance tonight.

9. In this campaign, I promise you will hear nothing from me but (plain, plane) speech.

10. (Its, It's) a long way to Tipperary.

EXERCISE B   Cross out the misspelled word in each sentence below, and write the word correctly on the line provided.

Example _____*children*_____ **1.** A group of ~~childs~~ played soccer in the front yard.

_____ **11.** The dog was beging for a snack.

_____ **12.** The management hopes that you are not disatisfied with the replacement.

_____ **13.** This room has quite a high cieling.

_____ **14.** The kitten left long scratchs in the table's legs.

_____ **15.** Victor watched a family of mouses move through the grass.

_____ **16.** Several of the countys near Detroit have large populations.

_____ **17.** All of the radioes in the store are on sale this week!

_____ **18.** Did you recieve your copy of the book?

_____ **19.** Do you think the arguement in this editorial is convincing?

_____ **20.** My opinion is changable, but I need some good reasons.

Review D: Spelling Rules and Words Often Confused

EXERCISE A Underline the correct word in parentheses in each of the following sentences.

Example 1. Pack your (*clothes, cloths*) carefully in the suitcase so that they won't wrinkle.

1. It's a good idea to deposit (*your, you're*) check as soon as possible.

2. The singer remained (*stationary, stationery*) while the dancers moved around her.

3. (*Who's, Whose*) going to make dinner this evening?

4. The trainer (*lead, led*) the dog around the ring by its leash.

5. (*Their, There, They're*) is the hammer I've been looking for.

6. If you (*choose, chose*) to attend the party, please wear a tie.

7. Passing (*threw, through*) the village, Mr. Herrmann noticed the handsome courthouse.

8. The shifting sands of the (*desert, dessert*) slowly covered the ruins.

9. Please make (*peace, piece*) with your little brother.

10. Rafiq made his final decision based on (*principal, principle*) rather than self-interest.

EXERCISE B Cross out the misspelled word in each sentence below, and write the word correctly on the line provided.

Example _____*neighbor*_____ **1.** Our ~~nieghbor~~ is a colonel in the National Guard.

_____ **11.** This sunset is truely the most beautiful one I have ever seen.

_____ **12.** Keepping your promises is a very important virtue.

_____ **13.** Every day, several ferrys run between the mainland and Toad Island.

_____ **14.** The air traffic controller was managing several aircrafts at once.

_____ **15.** No *buts* about it: This is the best carrot bread I've ever tasted.

_____ **16.** The canyon was suddenly filled with echos.

_____ **17.** Protien is an essential component in any diet.

_____ **18.** The dishs were left on the counter to dry.

_____ **19.** The new film is showing three times dayly.

_____ **20.** The Sanchezs are the proud owners of a new car.

MECHANICS

Proofreading Application: Business Letter

Good writers are generally good proofreaders. Readers tend to admire and trust writing that is error-free. Make sure that you correct all errors in grammar, usage, spelling, and punctuation in your writing. Your readers will have more confidence in your words if you have done your best to proofread carefully.

When you write a letter requesting information, take the time to check your spelling carefully. If you are not careful about your spelling, your reader may not take you seriously.

PROOFREADING ACTIVITY

Find and correct the errors in spelling in the following excerpt from a request letter. Use proofreading symbols to make your corrections.

Example We love to attend rodeoes.

Dear Sir or Madam:

   My family is planing a trip to your state later this summer.

My father has given me the task of chooseing our route. We will be

spending a weak traveling through your state.

   Our friends tell us that we simply must see the Painted Dessert.

We have therefore put that stop on our list all ready. We would also

like to drive threw the state capital. Of coarse, we would be inter-

ested in any other sites that you could recommend. For instance,

which of your great citys would be a good place for us to stay?

   I beleive that you offer some travel information free of charge. I

would be truely grateful if you would send me any information that

you feel would be helpful.

Sincerely,

Jay Wight

Jay Wight

for **CHAPTER 14: SPELLING** pages 319–38

Literary Model: Folk Tale

> Yes, he did have hair on his tail one time. Yes, indeed. De possum had a bushy tail wid long silk hair on it. Why, it useter be one of de prettiest sights you ever seen. De possum struttin' 'round wid his great big ole plumey tail. Dat was 'way back in de olden times before de big flood.
>
> But de possum was lazy—jus' like he is today. He sleep too much. You see Ole Nora had a son named Ham and he loved to be playin' music all de time. He had a banjo and a fiddle and maybe a guitar too. But de rain come up so sudden he didn't have time to put 'em on de ark. So when rain kept comin' down he fretted a lot 'cause he didn't have nothin' to play. So he found a ole cigar box and made hisself a banjo, but he didn't have no strings for it. So he seen de possum stretched out sleeping wid his tail all spread 'round. So Ham slipped up and shaved de possum's tail and made de strings for his banjo out de hairs. When dat possum woke up from his nap, Ham was playin' his tail hairs down to de bricks and dat's why de possum ain't got no hair on his tail today. . . .
>
> —from "How the Possum Lost the Hair Off His Tail" by Zora Neale Hurston

EXERCISE A After reading the excerpt aloud, write five of its words that do not fit standard spelling conventions. (Hints: Do not include words in which an apostrophe indicates that a letter has been left out. *Plumey* is an invented word.)

_____ _____

_____ _____

_____

EXERCISE B The author deliberately uses some nonstandard spelling conventions in this folk tale. Would the tale read differently if all of the words had standard spellings? Explain why the author might have used the spellings she did.

_____

_____

_____

_____

_____

_____

From "How the Possum Lost the Hair Off His Tail" from *Mules and Men* by Zora Neale Hurston. Copyright 1935 by Zora Neale Hurston; copyright renewed © 1963 by John C. Hurston and Joel Hurston. Reprinted by permission of **HarperCollins Publishers, Inc.**

for **CHAPTER 14: SPELLING** *pages 319–38*

Literary Model (continued)

EXERCISE C "How the Possum Lost the Hair Off His Tail" is a fanciful tale of how something came to be. Write your own folk tale. Invent a story of how something in nature came to be, such as how the giraffe got its long neck or how the sky became blue. As Zora Neale Hurston did, have your narrator speak in a dialect, which is a form of speech spoken by people of a particular region or group. Use a few nonstandard spellings to help represent the dialect. (It may help you to think of a dialect you have heard in a movie, on television, or in real life.) Attach additional pages if necessary.

_____

_____

_____

_____

_____

_____

_____

EXERCISE D

1. How does the use of nonstandard spellings help you to represent dialect? Explain your answer.

_____

_____

_____

_____

2. In what types of writing would the use of nonstandard spelling be appropriate? In what types would it be inappropriate? Explain your answers.

_____

_____

_____

_____

_____

Writing Application: Puns

Homonyms can be tricky to spell. Because these words sound alike but are spelled differently, they often cause writers to make mistakes. For this very reason, homonyms make great puns. Many jokes, especially those for children, depend on homonym mix-ups for their humor.

> **EXAMPLE**   Where did Lancelot go to learn how to become a knight? To knight school, of course!

Here's a perfect example of how important spelling can be. In order to understand the joke, a person has to know the difference between *knight* and *night*. If you are not sure how to spell a homonym, check the word in a dictionary.

WRITING ACTIVITY

Write two jokes that each depend on a pun—a mix-up of two homonyms— for their humor. Then, write a paragraph for each joke that explains why it is funny. Pretend you are writing to a person who is much younger than you are, who may need help understanding your jokes. In each paragraph, explain the meanings of the pair of homonyms that appear in each of your jokes. Be sure to spell your homonyms correctly, or you will only add to the confusion.

PREWRITING   It may take you a while to come up with two silly jokes. Before you start to write, you can get ideas by looking at a book of riddles or jokes. Then, put the joke books away, and write a list of homonyms that you think would make for a good joke. Jot down any ideas that you have about funny ways these homonyms could be confused.

WRITING   Now, turn your ideas into two jokes. Once you have written your jokes, write a paragraph explaining why each one is funny. Help your younger audience understand how the homonyms you chose gave rise to the humor. Don't forget to include both homonyms, along with a description of their meanings, in each of your paragraphs.

REVISING   Once you have your explanations written, you can turn your attention to word choice. You are writing to a younger audience, so use words that they will know and adjust the length of your sentences so that they can understand them easily. Do what you can to make this mini-lesson in spelling fun—your jokes are already fun!

PUBLISHING   Check your paragraphs for mistakes in spelling and punctuation, paying special attention to the homonyms. Get with a partner and make a poster. Choose one joke from each person and write these jokes on poster board. Attach a copy of each joke's explanatory paragraph. Illustrate your poster, and ask to hang it in the classroom.

EXTENDING YOUR WRITING

This exercise could lead to a more developed writing project. For a school talent show, you could write a comedy routine using puns that a middle school audience would find funny. If you are too shy to go onstage, write the routine for someone who's ready to get up there and ham it up.

Choices: Exploring Common Errors

Here's your chance to step out of the grammar book and into the real world. You may not notice them, but examples of grammar, usage, and mechanics appear in your life every day. The following activities challenge you to find a connection between common errors and the world around you. Do the activity below that suits your personality best, and then share your discoveries with your class. Have fun!

GRAPHICS

Neither Fish nor Fowl

Wow! Some of those indefinite pronouns really are indefinite. They go either way—singular or plural. You know the ones—*all, any, most, none,* and *some.* Help out your friends. Design a sticker for your classmates' notebooks. Your sticker should feature these pronouns in bold type. A caution sign might be a good format. What do you think?

PUBLISHING

From Soup to Nuts

By now your English notebook should be so big that it's too heavy to carry. Your classroom should be wallpapered with posters, drawings, cartoons, and lists. Don't let all your hard work go into the recycle bin! With your teacher's approval, take down the posters and other materials and bind them into one large book. Design a fabulous cover with the name of your class and the year written in big letters. Have everyone in the class sign the cover.

TEAM PROJECT

Silly Story

Write a short story (about ten sentences long) that helps you practice pronoun-antecedent agreement. You will write the story yourself, but will leave blanks for your classmates to fill. Each sentence must include three things: a pronoun, a blank line where its antecedent should be, and a prompt that explains how to fill in each blank. A sentence in your story might read, "Several *(plural noun—type of animal)* decided they needed a vacation." In the classroom, get permission to read each prompt out loud—but only the prompt!—recording on the blank each word your class provides. When all the blanks are filled in, share your story with the class!

WRITING

What a Plain Plane Trip!

Take this sentence-writing challenge, and improve your ability to remember certain tricky words. See if you can write a sentence that includes a pair of words that are easily confused. (For ideas, see the *Words Often Confused* chart that begins on p. 329 of your textbook). For example, you could write, "When the church members voted to change the color of the altar, the look of the sanctuary was forever altered." Write at least five sentences that include word pairs.

WORD GAME

Categories, Categories

To play this capitalization game, the class will need to sit in a large circle. Announce a category to the class—for example, *countries.* The person to your right has to name a country that begins with the letter *A.* The next person names a country that begins with *B,* and so on. When someone gets stumped, the person to his or her left (in other words, the last person to come up with an answer) picks a new category, and the game continues in the same direction. Don't forget this important rule: All categories must be common nouns (nouns that are lowercase) and all answers must be proper nouns (nouns that are uppercase).

READING

Punctuation Marks All Around

Once you look around, you'll realize that punctuation marks show up in all kinds of materials. Scan books, magazines, and newspapers to find one example of each of the following punctuation marks: apostrophe, quotation mark, question mark, exclamation point, colon, and semicolon. (Punctuation errors are worth extra points!) Cut out your sentences and paste them to poster board, or copy them down with a bold marker. Don't forget to document your sources!

Sentence Fragments

EXERCISE A   Identify each of the following word groups by writing on the line provided *S* if the word group is a sentence or *F* if the word group is a sentence fragment.

Example ___*F*___ **1.** When a fire broke out in the engine room.

_____ **1.** On the other side of the mountain.

_____ **2.** Because we stayed up late on Friday night.

_____ **3.** All that glitters is not gold.

_____ **4.** When the fireworks lit up the sky.

_____ **5.** Please find your gloves and boots before tomorrow morning.

_____ **6.** Polishing the brass candlesticks in the hallway.

_____ **7.** If Sarah calls me before seven o'clock on Saturday morning again.

_____ **8.** An old book my great-grandfather owned is on the table.

_____ **9.** Might not have received the invitation last week.

_____ **10.** The delay after we reached the airport made us late.

EXERCISE B   Some of the following word groups are sentence fragments. Rewrite each fragment to make a complete sentence by adding a subject, a verb, or both. You will need to change the punctuation and capitalization, too. If a word group is already a sentence, rewrite it, adding a capital letter at the beginning and an end mark at the end.

Example 1. thumping sound in the middle of the night.

The children heard a thumping sound in the middle of the night.
_____

11. puzzled by the strange sounds

_____

12. what could be making so much noise at this late hour

_____

13. switched on the porch light and looked outside

_____

14. trash and garbage everywhere in the front yard

_____

15. sitting on the overturned garbage can

_____

COMMON ERRORS

Run-on Sentences

EXERCISE A Identify each of the following word groups by writing on the line provided *R* if the word group is a run-on sentence or *S* if the word group is a complete sentence.

Example _____*R*_____ **1.** I enjoyed visiting my grandmother she tells such great stories.

_____ **1.** Jaime and Ramon grew up in the same neighborhood.

_____ **2.** Our team made the playoffs this year our final game is on Saturday.

_____ **3.** When we looked out the window, we saw our dog, it had gotten out of the yard again.

_____ **4.** Did you forget to set your alarm clock, or did you turn it off and go back to sleep?

_____ **5.** Come to my house today after school, we can work on math together.

_____ **6.** My sister always turns up the volume when that song comes on the radio.

_____ **7.** The sauce is almost finished, you can start cooking the pasta now.

_____ **8.** School was canceled because a thunderstorm knocked down some power lines.

_____ **9.** My shoelace came untied in the middle of the race I had to stop and tie it again.

_____ **10.** Turn left at the stop sign, my apartment building is the second one on the right.

EXERCISE B Identify which of the following word groups are run-on sentences. Then, on the line provided, rewrite each run-on sentence by (1) making two separate sentences or (2) using a comma and a coordinating conjunction. You may have to change the punctuation and capitalization, too. If a word group is already a complete sentence, write *S* on the line.

Example 1. My brother collects rocks, he wants to be a geologist when he grows up.

My brother collects rocks. He wants to be a geologist when he grows up.

11. We are going ice-skating tomorrow don't forget to wear warm clothes.

_____

12. Tangerines are my favorite fruit, I also like peaches and apples.

_____

13. What a great time we had last summer, we visited my mother's family in Ireland!

_____

14. Please let me borrow that book when you are finished with it.

_____

15. That bakery sells fresh bread, the baker wakes up at 4:00 A.M. to start the dough.

_____

Sentence Fragments and Run-on Sentences

EXERCISE A Identify each of the following word groups by writing on the line provided *F* if the word group is a sentence fragment, *S* if it is a complete sentence, or *R* if it is a run-on sentence.

Example ___*R*___ **1.** My cousin plays the harp, her teacher studied music in Paris.

_____ **1.** The movie that was recommended by the newspaper's reviewer.

_____ **2.** The curator showed our class the museum's collection of hand-woven carpets from India, he also demonstrated a loom and a spinning wheel.

_____ **3.** After the dress rehearsal next Tuesday afternoon.

_____ **4.** Turn out the lights and lock the door when you leave.

_____ **5.** The assembly has been rescheduled it will take place in the cafeteria.

_____ **6.** That street is really busy, be careful when you cross it.

_____ **7.** Your father can take you to the drugstore when he comes home from work tonight.

_____ **8.** We went to the wrong room we didn't hear the announcement.

_____ **9.** The newspaper tied in bundles and stacked neatly next to the garage door.

_____ **10.** When you have time, please explain this problem, I just don't understand it.

EXERCISE B On the line provided, identify each word group as a sentence fragment *(F)*, a run-on sentence *(R)*, or a complete sentence *(S)*. Then, rewrite each sentence fragment and run-on sentence to create complete sentences. You may have to change the punctuation and capitalization, too.

Example ___*R*___ **1.** The trumpet is not a new instrument its long history is remarkable.

The trumpet is not a new instrument. Its long history is remarkable.

_____ **11.** Early trumpets were often made from reeds the instruments made sorrowful sounds.

_____

_____ **12.** Played at the end of the day to invite the sun back by morning.

_____

_____ **13.** In early Africa, when people needed to send messages a long distance.

_____

_____ **14.** Aztecs and Incas made their trumpets of silver, copper, wood, and clay.

_____

_____ **15.** They called to the gods on trumpets Egyptians and Hebrews used trumpets similarly.

_____

Language and Sentence Skills Practice

Subject-Verb Agreement A

EXERCISE A In each of the following sentences, underline the form of the verb in parentheses that agrees with the subject.

Example 1. *(Hasn't, Haven't)* any of the musicians arrived yet?

1. The boys *(has, have)* brought snacks for the hike.

2. *(Do, Does)* the English alphabet have twenty-six letters?

3. Either Max or Neil *(know, knows)* the answer to that question.

4. All of us *(want, wants)* to see that movie next week.

5. My little sister already *(count, counts)* to one hundred.

6. Her aunt and uncle *(own, owns)* a ranch in Wyoming.

7. *(Was, Were)* you standing at the bus stop when the rain started?

8. One of these chairs *(has, have)* a broken leg.

9. Whenever we *(give, gives)* the dog a bath, everyone gets soaking wet.

10. Every camper *(need, needs)* a flashlight, a sleeping bag, and two sets of clothing.

EXERCISE B Most of the following sentences contain a subject-verb error. If the verb does not agree with its subject, cross out the incorrect verb and write the correct form above it. If the verb already agrees with its subject, write *C* after the sentence.

Example 1. In the South Pacific Ocean, one group of volcanic islands ~~are~~ *is* called Samoa.

11. One of the oldest cities in North America are Quebec City.

12. The brilliant blue waters of the Caribbean makes the area popular with vacationers.

13. The city of Casablanca remain the largest in Morocco.

14. Either Sydney, Australia, or Budapest, Hungary, were settled by the British.

15. Bangladesh lies between India and Myanmar.

16. Have anyone found a photo of Lake Victoria for the report on lakes in Africa?

17. In Bahrain is located important oil reserves.

18. More of the world's population are in Asia than anywhere else.

19. Some of the pupils remember that Ethiopia was formerly Abyssinia.

20. Citizens of the Ivory Coast in West Africa has enjoyed prosperity and peace.

Subject-Verb Agreement B

EXERCISE A For each of the following sentences, decide whether the underlined verb agrees in number with its subject. If the verb form is incorrect, write the correct form above it. If the verb form is already correct, write *C* above it.

Example 1. My grandmother ~~bake~~ *bakes* her own bread twice a week.

1. She is ninety-one, but she get up early to start her baking.

2. She don't like the taste of store-bought bread.

3. Her favorite parts of the process are kneading the dough and shaping the loaves.

4. The kitchen smells wonderful when the bread come out of the oven.

5. Her whole-wheat bread tastes especially good.

6. Each of the loaves are carefully formed and set in a warm place to rise.

7. Sometimes she choose a new recipe.

8. I likes the spaghetti she makes, too.

9. Each of us pick the ingredients for the sauce.

10. The spices in the sauce are hot and flavorful.

EXERCISE B Underline the verb in each of the following sentences. Be sure to underline any helping verbs, too. Then, if the verb does not agree with its subject, write the correct form above the incorrect verb. If the verb is already correct, write *C* above it.

Example 1. *Has* Have everyone had a turn yet?

11. All of my friends knows the directions to my house.

12. Only one of the houses on our street have a bright blue door.

13. A huge oak tree shades the front of the house.

14. Has they given you instructions for the science project?

15. The windows and the door was left open.

16. Either science or history are my favorite subject this year.

17. In the summer, my family and I usually goes to the beach.

18. My uncle and my cousins often join us there.

19. Does you play on your school's soccer team?

20. My twin nephews, Joshua and David, have just celebrated their second birthday.

Language and Sentence Skills Practice

Pronoun-Antecedent Agreement A

EXERCISE A In each of the following sentences, choose the pronoun in parentheses that agrees with its antecedent.

Example 1. She, Jack, and I want to visit the Natural History Museum on *(their, <u>our</u>)* spring break.

1. Nick, please ask your sister to put air in *(his, her)* bicycle tires.

2. Each of the squirrels has *(their, its)* store of acorns in a different tree.

3. You left your gloves and jacket at my house; you can get *(it, them)* tomorrow morning.

4. Three of the women in our apartment building volunteer *(her, their)* time every other month.

5. Could you please show Anna and me how to do that for *(herself, ourselves)*?

6. Jennifer gave the boys a detailed map, but *(they, he)* still got lost.

7. The fox raised *(their, its)* ears, sniffed the air, and ran into the bushes.

8. This drum set was not very expensive; I bought *(it, them)* at a secondhand store.

9. Put your coat in the closet so that you will know where to find *(them, it)*.

10. Neither one of my nieces likes to have *(their, her)* hair combed.

EXERCISE B Most of the following sentences contain a pronoun that does not agree with its antecedent. If a pronoun is incorrect, cross it out and write the correct pronoun above it. If a sentence is already correct, write *C* after it.

Example 1. Did either Jorge or Dennis bring ~~their~~ *his* coin collection to school?

11. All of the kittens spend a lot of time washing themselves.

12. Please ask Jessica and Ramona to pick up her clothes.

13. One of the boys has forgotten their uniform.

14. This radio may be broken, or it may only need new batteries.

15. My brother and sister tried to fix the flat tire ourselves.

16. Should we ask Mr. and Mrs. Sansone to autograph a copy of her new book?

17. Nina asked Sonia to bring the snacks to the party, but she hasn't brought it yet.

18. The members of the cast posed for publicity photographs when its dress rehearsal was over.

19. Either Cindy or Felicia wants to rearrange the desks so that they can sit by the window.

20. All of us want to finish their social studies project by Monday.

HOLT HANDBOOK | Introductory Course

Pronoun-Antecedent Agreement B

EXERCISE On the line provided, complete each of the following sentences by writing a pronoun that refers to an antecedent in the sentence.

Example 1. All of the actors have memorized _____*their*_____ lines in the play.

1. My new puppy certainly likes to chase _____ own tail.

2. When she reached the top of the hill, she gave _____ a few minutes to catch her breath.

3. Two boys in my class always visit _____ relatives in Mexico during the winter break.

4. Those CDs belong to my aunt; please be careful with _____.

5. We can't go skating today because neither Alicia nor Tess remembered to bring _____ skates.

6. Would you please bring me a glass of water when _____ come back outside?

7. My cousin got us to the airport on time, but _____ flight was delayed.

8. If you want to have a dog, you will have to learn to take care of _____.

9. Both of the horses jumped over the low fence between _____ corral and the field.

10. As we approached the house, one of the dogs began to wag _____ tail.

11. I worked for three hours last night because _____ report is due today.

12. No one could use the telephone in the office because _____ was out of service.

13. My great-great-grandparents left Ireland because _____ could not get enough food or find work.

14. Naomi is a talented writer; _____ won the essay contest last year.

15. Please dust the books and put _____ back on the shelves.

16. At what time should Jill and Amy's parents pick _____ up after the party?

17. My sister is three years older than I am, but _____ enjoy the same music.

18. Yazmin left a message for Tom, but _____ hasn't called back yet.

19. I'm going to take a nap; please wake _____ up in an hour.

20. We allowed _____ exactly thirty minutes to finish the practice test.

Language and Sentence Skills Practice

Verb Forms A

EXERCISE On the line provided, write the form of the italicized verb that will complete the sentence correctly.

Example 1. *watch* Last Saturday we ___watched___ a baseball game.

1. *complete* Jeremy will _____ his first-aid course this week.

2. *eat* My brother bought six apples and _____ two of them immediately.

3. *forget* I have to pay a library fine; I must have _____ to return a book on time.

4. *bring* Justine _____ her new CD to the party so that we could all hear it.

5. *sit* When he came into the room, he _____ in a chair near the door.

6. *say* Didn't she _____ that the concert started at eight o'clock?

7. *frighten* Don't do that again! You _____ me!

8. *fix* I'm sure I could _____ this toaster if I had the right kind of screwdriver.

9. *teach* Last year, my aunt _____ English at a high school in the Czech Republic.

10. *look* Dan is _____ everywhere for the instructions that came with the game.

11. *walk* We should have _____ to school this morning.

12. *keep* Tricia _____ the secret as long as she could.

13. *study* Last year, my class _____ the solar system and visited NASA.

14. *find* Have you _____ your scarf yet?

15. *come* Who _____ to the first meeting of the French Club?

16. *throw* Unfortunately, she had already _____ the map away.

17. *laugh* He was _____ so hard that he could not stop.

18. *call* I have _____ every bookstore, but not one of them has that book.

19. *do* What would you have _____ in that situation?

20. *sing* Joaquin will be _____ a solo in tonight's performance.

21. *drive* My uncle Jack has _____ a taxicab for over thirty years.

22. *slide* The children sat on flattened cardboard boxes and _____ down the hill.

23. *read* Has your sister _____ the new book in that mystery series?

24. *write* Noah has already _____ a letter to his grandfather.

25. *blow* He took a deep breath and _____ air into the balloon.

COMMON ERRORS

Verb Forms B

EXERCISE A On the line provided, write the correct past or past participle form of the italicized verb.

Example 1. *blow*   Heavy rains _____*blew*_____ across Houston one night last summer.

1. *begin*   By morning, water had _____ to cover the sidewalks.

2. *rise*   Bayou water _____ another inch before the rain stopped.

3. *make*   My new neighbor from Detroit and I _____ the best of a wet vacation day.

4. *see*   Sheree had never even _____ a crawfish before.

5. *go*   She had _____ lake fishing many times, however.

6. *catch*   From the street curb, we _____ crawfish as they swam by.

7. *break*   Catching six in her net, Sheree _____ my best record.

8. *know*   There were more in the bayou, but we _____ to stay away from fast-moving water.

9. *find*   I _____ some fish with slightly blue scales.

10. *choose*   After our fun, we _____ to let them all swim home.

EXERCISE B In each of the following sentences, decide whether the underlined verb form is correct or incorrect. If the verb form is incorrect, write above it the correct form of the verb. If the verb form is correct, write *C* above it.

Example 1. These stone walls must have been <u>builded</u> over a hundred years ago.
(above builded: *built*)

11. Henry and Liam made sure to set their alarm clock every night because neither of them <u>trusts</u> himself to wake up on time.

12. <u>Began</u> the project by collecting all the supplies and materials you will need.

13. Have you <u>gave</u> the school office your new address and phone number?

14. The mail carrier has already <u>put</u> the mail in the boxes, but I'm sure the post office is still open.

15. Cole has always <u>drew</u> animals; his horses are especially lifelike.

16. Hermione had <u>took</u> out the trash and swept the floor before her parents returned.

17. They must have <u>went</u> home earlier; we didn't see them at the meeting.

18. No one was injured when the ropes <u>broke</u> and the boards tumbled to the ground.

19. Where have I <u>heared</u> that music before?

20. She had <u>stand</u> at the station for an hour, waiting for the train to arrive.

COMMON ERRORS

Pronoun Forms A

EXERCISE A Underline the correct form of the pronoun in parentheses.

Example 1. Coach Torres awarded *(we, us)* certificates of merit.

1. Thad gave Jennifer and *(I, me)* some good ideas for the stage set design.

2. Either *(her, she)* or I will take pictures of the Ferris wheel at night.

3. The scarecrow was placed between Raymond and *(he, him)*.

4. From off the dusty ground, the magic carpet lifted our friends and *(we, us)*.

5. Dr. Shin and *(he, him)* calmed the restless audience.

6. Reggie and *(they, them)* tried to find homes for sixteen puppies.

7. Who could have guessed the surprise in store for Latrice and *(I, me)*?

8. One of the best mathematicians in the contest was *(she, her)*.

9. Ken nodded to *(we, us)* as we entered the ballroom.

10. Can you offer some advice to her and *(they, them)*?

EXERCISE B Most of the following sentences contain a pronoun that has been used incorrectly. If a pronoun is incorrect, cross it out and write above it the correct pronoun. If the sentence is already correct, write *C* after the sentence.

Example 1. For ~~who~~ *whom* did you make that beautiful card?

11. The finalists in the chess tournament were her and I.

12. Them and Jack want to go to the circus on Friday night.

13. Sara told him and I about the new restaurant.

14. Michael sent they pictures from his trip.

15. Did Lawrence read the article about volcanoes to she and her sister?

16. My mother waved to we from the window of the train.

17. Whom will bring the refreshments for the class party?

18. The most imaginative writer in my class is he.

19. Charles made sandwiches for all of they.

20. Anya told her friends that she would meet them at the skating rink.

Pronoun Forms B

EXERCISE A Underline the correct form of the pronoun in parentheses in each of the following sentences.

Example 1. Throw the ball to (he, _him_).

1. Neither (she, her) nor I will be at the assembly today.

2. Did the club elect (her, she) president?

3. (He, Him) and Matthew voted for her.

4. I hope she will thank (they, them).

5. To (who, whom) did you address that package?

6. He and (I, me) found the answer immediately.

7. We walk to school with Natasha and (she, her).

8. Please let (he, him) come with us to the carnival.

9. Mrs. Jamison and (he, him) were my favorite teachers last year.

10. (Who, Whom) remembered to bring a flashlight?

EXERCISE B Each of the following sentences contains a pronoun that has been used incorrectly. Cross out the incorrect pronoun and write above it the correct pronoun.

Example 1. Ben and ~~me~~ $\overset{I}{}$ put away the clothes and washed the dishes.

11. Him and I have had the same piano teacher for years.

12. Mr. Jimenes showed they how to operate the slide projector.

13. Should Corinna or me put up the posters in the hallway?

14. Them are the juiciest oranges that I have ever eaten.

15. My father divided the chores between my brother and I.

16. Whom was calling so late last night?

17. Shawna and Mitchell invited they to the graduation ceremony.

18. The teacher assigned that topic to he and me.

19. Jessica shared the information with Bao and I.

20. Are they or us responsible for publicizing the school play?

COMMON ERRORS

Comparative and Superlative Forms of Modifiers

EXERCISE A In each of the following sentences, underline the correct form of the adjective or adverb in parentheses.

Example 1. The math test we had this week was (easier, easiest) than the one we had last week.

1. This is the (worse, worst) cold I've had all year.

2. If you try (harder, hardest) the next time, you'll be more successful.

3. You will need to mix the eggs into the dough (better, best) before you put in the vanilla.

4. Was that summer the (warmer, warmest) on record?

5. The corn in those fields appears (taller, tallest) than it was last year.

6. The exhibit of gems and minerals was the (more interesting, most interesting) of all.

7. She was (happiest, happier) when the puppy came home than her sister was.

8. I wish the weather were (most predictable, more predictable) than it is.

9. In my opinion, *The Phantom Tollbooth* is one of the (better, best) books I've ever read.

10. He is a good baseball player, but he enjoys basketball (most, more).

EXERCISE B On the line provided, write the correct comparative or superlative form of the italicized word.

Example 1. *famous*   Rome's Trevi Fountain is the ___most famous___ one in the world.

11. *difficult*   Silver was much _____ to mine in ancient Egypt than gold.

12. *big*   Objects held on the other side of a magnifying glass look _____.

13. *common*   Cereal grains are the _____ foods of all.

14. *warm*   Wool is _____ than cotton because its bulky fibers trap air.

15. *bad*   Coastal towns are often the _____ hit by high winds during a hurricane.

16. *good*   Many say that laughter is the _____ medicine.

17. *old*   As we grow _____, the lenses in our eyes lose elasticity.

18. *high*   The _____ tides anywhere occur in Canada's Bay of Fundy.

19. *powerful*   In 1883, the island Rakata suffered the _____ volcanic eruption on record.

20. *well*   Was that movie _____ than the one you saw last week?

Misplaced Modifiers

EXERCISE A   In each of the following sentences, underline the prepositional phrase or adjective clause that is in the wrong place.

Example 1. The parrot squawked at the people in the cage.

1. The man lost his hat that was dancing.

2. The tall boy with glasses is my cousin in the picture.

3. The squirrel sat on a tree limb that had been hiding acorns all summer.

4. Did you drink the juice before breakfast that was in a pitcher on the table?

5. The girl stopped and patted the puppy who was skating on the sidewalk.

6. The trees were visible in the light of the moon that were below the mountain.

7. We left our map on the bus of the city.

8. Behind the stove, we read the old letters we had found in a box.

9. A hurricane slammed into the coastal resort town with 90-mph winds.

10. She gave the bread to the children that had just finished baking in the oven.

EXERCISE B   Rewrite each of the following sentences to correct any errors in the placement of modifiers.

Example 1. I forgot to tell the girl about the party who had just joined the club.

  I forgot to tell the girl who had just joined the club about the party.

11. Mrs. Jackson gives away the vegetables to her neighbors that she grows in her garden.

_____

12. I bought the book at a secondhand bookstore, on which that movie was based.

_____

13. Wrapped in aluminum foil, we placed the potatoes into the hot ashes.

_____

14. Please take the package to the post office that has already been wrapped.

_____

15. I put the log next to the fireplace that was cut from the fallen tree.

_____

Language and Sentence Skills Practice

Double Comparisons and Double Negatives

EXERCISE On the lines provided, rewrite each of the following sentences to correct any double comparisons or double negatives.

Example 1. I can't do no more homework until I rest my eyes.

I can't do any more homework until I rest my eyes.

1. The track team can't scarcely jog in place because of the mud.

_____

2. Miriam hates to turn in papers written in her most messiest handwriting.

_____

3. Your sandwich got even more soggier than mine!

_____

4. Ned's pony, Blue Tail, won't eat apples no more.

_____

5. There wasn't nobody at the ticket window at six o'clock this morning.

_____

6. The tree is no more taller than it was three years ago.

_____

7. My little sister said that was the most scariest movie she had ever seen.

_____

8. Please adjust the volume so that the music is more quieter.

_____

9. The children can't hardly wait until the parade begins.

_____

10. She couldn't find no shoes that she wanted to buy.

_____

COMMON ERRORS

Standard Usage A

EXERCISE A For each of the following sentences, decide whether the underlined word or phrase is correct according to formal, standard English usage. If the usage is incorrect, write the correct usage above the underlined word or phrase. If the usage is already correct, write *C* above it.

Example 1. Charlene wants to know how come ^{why} people snore.

1. You should of heard my aunt snoring away last night.

2. She use to snore even louder than she does now.

3. When your asleep, you can't hear yourself breathing.

4. Less people admit to snoring than complain about others.

5. Its not true that only older people snore.

6. It ain't as if it's anyone's fault.

7. My aunt felt bad that her snoring kept me awake.

8. Even if you try and quit snoring, you may not succeed.

9. Snoring is a long ways from being a crime.

10. We should learn each other to be more understanding.

EXERCISE B In each of the following sentences, cross out the word or word group that is incorrect according to formal, standard English usage. Then, write the correct usage above the crossed-out word or words.

Example 1. ~~There~~ *They're* going to meet us this afternoon after school.

11. I've looked, but my shoes are nowheres in the house.

12. The six children divided the raisins between themselves.

13. I had all ready finished my homework by four o'clock.

14. Doesn't he play the guitar good?

15. You could of borrowed that book from the library.

16. He assured me that he could do the job hisself.

17. Do you know how come we are having an assembly on Friday afternoon?

18. Everyone accept Jenny is going on the field trip.

19. Biographies are kind of interesting to me.

20. This sofa is softer then that one.

Language and Sentence Skills Practice

Standard Usage B

EXERCISE A For each of the following sentences, decide whether the underlined word or phrase is correct according to formal, standard English usage. If the usage is incorrect, write the correct usage above the underlined word or phrase. If the usage is already correct, write *C* above it.

Example 1. Now I know that we really <u>ought to of</u> studied harder. *(ought to have)*

1. <u>That there</u> dog likes to chase our mail carrier.

2. <u>Who's</u> going to ride with us in our car?

3. We'll have to leave at least <u>a hour</u> before the show starts.

4. History is my favorite subject, but I like geography <u>alot</u>, too.

5. Could you tell me where the office <u>is at</u>?

6. She thought she did <u>alright</u> in the math competition, but she was surprised to hear that she

   had won.

7. You should always <u>bring</u> extra water when you go hiking in the desert.

8. If I <u>had of</u> known you would be home for dinner, I would have set an extra place.

9. My dog can fetch <u>well</u>.

10. Jovita forgot that she was <u>suppose</u> to meet us at the bus stop.

EXERCISE B In each of the following sentences, cross out the word or word group that is incorrect according to formal, standard English usage. Then, write the correct usage above the crossed-out word or words.

Example 1. This winter has been warmer ~~then~~ the last one was. *(than)*

11. The children haven't found they're mittens yet.

12. How much do them apples cost?

13. I read in the newspaper where the governor would be visiting our school today.

14. If your late again today, we'll have to leave without you.

15. This here book is about a family that lived in England during World War I.

16. Would you please carry the groceries inside of the house?

17. The horse flicked it's tail and galloped away.

18. My cousin is learning me how to change a bicycle tire.

19. Kendra felt really badly about hurting her father's feelings.

20. I hope my application for the part-time job will be excepted.

COMMON ERRORS

Capitalization A

EXERCISE A In each of the following sentences, underline any word or words that should be capitalized but are not.

Example 1. last spring, my family visited washington, D.C.

1. We especially enjoyed the Washington monument and the Lincoln memorial.

2. We had to wait for an hour to see the declaration of independence at the national archives.

3. My sister met two japanese exchange students at one of the museums.

4. The exchange students were trying to find Constitution avenue.

5. they studied the city map that my sister gave them.

6. I wanted to tour the white house, but no tickets were available.

7. My parents took us to see president Kennedy's grave at Arlington national cemetery.

8. We also visited Mt. vernon, George Washington's home, which is in virginia.

9. Someday I would like to visit some of the nearby civil war battlefields.

10. I have heard that williamsburg and jamestown are also interesting places to visit.

EXERCISE B Most of the following sentences contain capitalization errors. On the line provided, write *C* if the sentence is correct. If the capitalization in the sentence is incorrect, circle any letters that should be capitalized or made lowercase.

Example _____ **1.** At age twelve, Alexander the (g)reat probably did not know he would rule an

(E)mpire.

_____ **11.** Only eight years later, however, he inherited the kingdom of macedon.

_____ **12.** His father, king Philip, had ruled that region of greece before.

_____ **13.** Unfortunately, wars from his Father's time left little money in the royal treasury.

_____ **14.** so Alexander decided to conquer the persian empire for its wealth.

_____ **15.** Soon, he controlled all of Asia Minor.

_____ **16.** Across the Mediterranean sea, Egypt became his next conquest.

_____ **17.** After that, he led his soldiers into India.

_____ **18.** Alexander's victories quickly spread the greek language.

_____ **19.** The influence of Greek culture can still be seen over a significant portion of the World.

_____ **20.** His career was short, but clearly Alexander the Great was one of the most successful

Generals in recorded history.

Language and Sentence Skills Practice

Capitalization B

EXERCISE A In the following sentences, circle any letters that should be capitalized or made lowercase.

Example 1. My sister won an academic (S)cholarship to Auburn (u)niversity.

1. Is your correct address 923 West Forty-Fifth street?

2. Last night, the planets Venus and saturn were near the moon.

3. My mother works for a company called J. Smithson and sons, inc.

4. The letter began, "dear Mr. Samuelson."

5. Is Australia both a continent and a Nation?

6. The lawyers requested a meeting with judge O'Hanlon.

7. Either Simon or Natalie will be elected President of the club this year.

8. I was born in Florida, but I grew up in the north.

9. Are you waiting to see dr. gomez or her Nurse?

10. Argentina, Peru, and Chile are countries in south America.

EXERCISE B In the following letter, circle any letters that should be capitalized or made lowercase.

Example [1] I wrote a letter to Ms. Jean Thompson-(g)arcia, the editor of the (N)ewspaper.

Ms. Jean Thompson-Garcia

[11] Braxton News-leader

[12] 419 Ninety-Eighth Avenue

[13] Braxton, Tx 75771

[14] Dear ms. Thompson-garcia:

[15] I recently read an article in your newspaper about my school, Hill Country middle school. [16] I think the Reporter, Jeff Masterton, did not get all the facts before he wrote, "students have nothing to do after school." [17] my school offers many extracurricular activities. [18] I am a member of the spanish club. [19] I also play on the school's Baseball team. [20] Other students participate in Band or the Drama Club, and many play on our Sports teams.

I think your newspaper should print a correction.

Sincerely,

Elena Whitson

Commas A

EXERCISE In each of the following sentences, draw a caret (∧) to show where any missing commas should be inserted.

Example 1. My younger sister was born on January 22∧1997∧in Topeka∧Kansas.

1. My soccer team practices on Monday Wednesday and Thursday.

2. Dr. Michaelson could I get a copy of my immunization record?

3. You will need flour yeast water and a little salt to make this bread.

4. No I don't want the other half of your sandwich.

5. When you reach the corner turn left.

6. The new curtains are made of a thin soft cotton fabric.

7. I would like to go to the beach this summer but a camping trip would also be fun.

8. On weeknights before dinner Alexis plays chess with her father.

9. Bongo and Conga the dogs that my grandparents gave me for my birthday sleep at the foot of my bed.

10. We can give you a ride to the theater or you can meet us there at six o'clock.

11. If you will vacuum the bedroom I will change the sheets.

12. On Sunday afternoons after lunch Denise's family always visits her grandfather.

13. When my father was a boy he lived on a ranch in Nevada.

14. He shared a room with his older brother his younger brother and a cousin who lived at their house.

15. The storm the first of the winter knocked down power lines all over town.

16. Before I left the museum I took one last look at the bold colorful brush strokes of the painting.

17. Hey isn't that Cynthia's mother?

18. The highway goes through the center of Baton Rouge Louisiana.

19. If Nala got up earlier she would have time to fix her own lunch.

20. Martín's father was born in Puerto Rico but he grew up in Sevilla Spain.

Language and Sentence Skills Practice

329

Commas B

EXERCISE A In each of the following sentences, draw a caret (∧) to show where any missing commas should be inserted.

Example 1. Students∧would you recognize any of the great building accomplishments of the nineteenth century?

1. People are familiar with the Statue of Liberty but many do not know it was a gift from France.

2. In Paris France the view from the top of the Eiffel Tower is fantastic.

3. That tower is 984 feet high took two years to build and is held together by 2.5 million rivets.

4. Mrs. Clark my music teacher told me that the opera house at Manaus is well known.

5. The opera house at Manaus was built in the nineteenth century a period during which the Brazilian rubber industry was flourishing.

6. Monuments railroad tunnels and bridges were constructed in the 1800's.

7. Yes the Forth Railway Bridge extended the railroad from England to Scotland.

8. The first major railway passage through the Swiss Alps the Mont Cenis Tunnel opened in 1890.

9. When one of the first suspension bridges opened in England in 1864 the people must have been excited.

10. Amy can you list other nineteenth-century building achievements?

EXERCISE B All of the necessary commas are missing from the following paragraphs. Draw a caret (∧) to show where each comma should be inserted.

Example [1] One of my neighbors∧Nancy Moore∧is a reference librarian at the public library.

[11] She helps people find information shows students how to use reference books and leads school tours of the library. [12] When she first started working at the library she catalogued and shelved books. [13] Nancy says that modern librarians especially reference librarians need good computer skills. [14] When Nancy is away from the reference desk she is usually helping someone with the computers. [15] Nancy's job has changed over the years yet she still enjoys being a librarian.

COMMON ERRORS

Semicolons and Colons

EXERCISE A Underline any word that should be followed by a colon and draw a caret (∧) to show where a semicolon should be. Hint: In some sentences, semicolons will replace commas.

Example 1. Their trip included visits to the following <u>cities</u> Dublin, Ireland ∧ London, England ∧ and Glasgow, Scotland.

1. My favorite music is jazz, my brother's is gospel.

2. Nelda is on the swim team, she also plays volleyball for our school.

3. The following students should go to the office Frank, Debra, and Diego.

4. My grandmother grew up in North Dakota her family moved there right after she was born.

5. Be sure your letter contains the following the date, a salutation, and a closing.

6. You can take the bus, I prefer to ride my bike.

7. Pack the following items for our trip a sleeping bag, a flashlight, and a jacket.

8. The recipe called for these spices cinnamon, ginger, allspice, mace, and nutmeg.

9. The tall boy with black hair is my brother the girl who is standing next to him is my cousin.

10. I have lived in Austin, Texas, Washington, D.C., Key West, Florida, and San Diego, California.

EXERCISE B Rewrite each of the following sentences using semicolons and colons where needed.

Example 1. English speakers have borrowed the following expressions from other languages, *mañana*, from Spanish, *ciao*, from Italian, and *bon voyage*, from French.

English speakers have borrowed the following expressions from other languages:
mañana, from Spanish; ciao, from Italian; and bon voyage, from French.

11. Here are some excellent sources of vitamin C oranges, grapefruits, tomatoes, and lemons.

_____

12. *Ecology* has become a common term recycling has developed into a common habit.

_____

13. If the timer is set for 3 05, our recorder will miss the first five minutes of the program.

_____

14. Some areas of the country need rainfall some areas must cope with flooding.

_____

15. The following ingredients are needed for a tuna sandwich tuna, bread, tomato, and mayonnaise.

_____

Quotation Marks and Other Punctuation A

EXERCISE A Rewrite each of the following sentences, adding quotation marks, other punctuation, and capital letters where needed.

Example 1. Anita said Malcolm would you please help me with this problem

"Anita," said Malcolm, "would you please help me with this problem?"

1. What is the name of the poem that begins once upon a midnight dreary

_____

2. The name of that poem is The Raven by Edgar Allan Poe

_____

3. Help she shouted into the darkness my flashlight is broken

_____

4. Do you know the second verse of America the Beautiful

_____

5. I will be at your house by four o'clock she said

_____

EXERCISE B In the following sentences, draw a caret (∧) to show where a hyphen should be inserted.

Example 1. We have at least forty∧five minutes before the bell rings.

6. You certainly have a well organized desk.

7. My great great grandfather was born in Romania.

8. When the governor elect arrives, the band will begin playing.

9. The ski trip will cost each student more than ninety five dollars!

10. I called the radio station to get up to date information about the concert.

EXERCISE C In each of the following sentences, underline each title or name that should be in italics, and insert quotation marks around each title or name that should be in quotation marks.

Example 1. <u>Stuart Little</u> and <u>Charlotte's Web</u> were written by E. B. White.

11. Have you read the book Rabbit Hill?

12. The Tempest is one of Shakespeare's best-known plays.

13. The best chapter in this book is The Mystery Deepens.

14. Have you heard the song Duke of Earl?

15. A replica of the Santa Maria is moored in the harbor.

332   HOLT HANDBOOK | Introductory Course

for **CHAPTER 15: CORRECTING COMMON ERRORS** `pages 290–309`

Quotation Marks and Other Punctuation B

EXERCISE A On the lines provided, rewrite each of the following sentences, adding quotation marks, commas, end marks, and capital letters where needed.

Example 1. In my opinion Claire said history is the most interesting subject

"In my opinion," Claire said, "history is the most interesting subject."

1. I'd like to write the invitations offered Maxine

_____

2. Will Jim ride his bike asked Nate or will he walk with us

_____

3. Dennis told us that his family is moving to Florida in June

_____

4. What a great movie Jonah exclaimed when they left the theater

_____

5. Carolyn asked us to give her a ride to the park

_____

EXERCISE B On the lines provided, rewrite each word, inserting hyphens to show where the word may be divided at the end of a line. If a word should not be divided, write *do not hyphenate* on the line.

Example 1. communication *com-mu-ni-ca-tion*

6. development _____ **9.** thorough _____

7. fascinating _____ **10.** alert _____

8. real _____

EXERCISE C In each of the following sentences, underline each title or name that should be in italics, and insert quotation marks around each title or name that should be in quotation marks.

Example 1. <u>Ramona the Pest</u>, by Beverly Cleary, is my sister's favorite book.

11. In the novel Sounder, a father steals to feed his family.

12. The Owl and the Pussy-Cat is one of Edward Lear's best-known poems.

13. My brother likes to sing I Know an Old Lady Who Swallowed a Fly.

14. In what year did the Lusitania sink?

15. Mr. Browning read to the class Robert Frost's poem Stopping by Woods on a Snowy Evening.

Language and Sentence Skills Practice

Apostrophes

EXERCISE In each of the following sentences, decide whether the underlined word is correct as written. Above each incorrect word, rewrite the word correctly. If the word is already correct, write *C* above it.

Example 1. Is this jacket <u>your's</u> or Tom's?   *(yours written above your's)*

1. I <u>cant</u> believe you left so early!

2. The <u>dogs</u> tails were wagging happily.

3. Jesse wakes up at <u>six o clock</u> every morning to practice piano.

4. The kitten finished the milk and cleaned <u>its</u> whiskers.

5. Camping in the snow isn't <u>everyones</u> idea of a good time.

6. Do you spell *Connecticut* with two <u>ns</u> or one?

7. <u>Lets</u> try to concentrate on our work.

8. Her <u>sisters</u> name is Lora, not Laura.

9. Bettina is the one <u>whos</u> always late.

10. I'm sure this is <u>Chuongs</u> notebook.

11. I think <u>its</u> worth repairing.

12. <u>Whats</u> in the refrigerator at your house?

13. We went to <u>Trish's</u> apartment to study.

14. Your computer <u>skill's</u> are better than they used to be.

15. The boy's jackets were purchased in the <u>mens</u> department.

16. The <u>rose's</u> in your garden are blooming early this year.

17. <u>Who's</u> books fell on the floor?

18. In that song, the <u>women's</u> voices are rich and powerful.

19. How old was he in <u>99</u>?

20. Have you picked up all the <u>childrens'</u> toys?

All Marks of Punctuation A

EXERCISE On the lines provided, rewrite each of the following sentences with correct punctuation.

Example 1. A visit to the open air market is almost as exciting as a trip around the world

A visit to the open-air market is almost as exciting as a trip around the world.

1. Early every Saturday the fruit and vegetable vendors begin setting up their stalls

_____

2. Fruits vegetables and herbs are carefully displayed on tables and in crates

_____

3. Buckets of flowers line one aisle baskets of bread line the next

_____

4. How appetizing all the wonderful smells are

_____

5. My little brother always wants to look at the fish for some of them are as big as he is

_____

6. Some of the vendors stalls are decorated with bright blinking lights

_____

7. We bought the following items peppers lemons and limes

_____

8. We never buy much but we always have a wonderful time

_____

9. My mother declared The market is the perfect introduction to other countries and cultures

_____

10. Do you think youd enjoy coming with us next time or would you rather stay home

_____

Language and Sentence Skills Practice

All Marks of Punctuation B

EXERCISE   On the lines provided, rewrite each of the following sentences with correct punctuation.

Example   **1.** What have you been doing all day asked the camp director

     "What have you been doing all day?" asked the camp director.

1. Yes Johns younger brother has a leading role in the school play

_____

2. How thrilling for him exclaimed my mother

_____

3. Next weekend shes going to visit her sister in Omaha Nebraska

_____

4. He said that he would clear the table wash the dishes and sweep the kitchen floor

_____

5. Lets eat a snack first then well study for an hour

_____

6. Because she is a diabetic my grandmother reads labels very carefully

_____

7. Theyre going to bring the following supplies to the meeting markers scissors and tape

_____

8. If you liked The Chronicles of Narnia series you might also enjoy C S Lewiss other books

_____

9. We will sing The Battle Hymn of the Republic on Tuesday January 18

_____

10. Why I know that youll do well on the test you've studied so hard

_____

COMMON ERRORS

Spelling A

EXERCISE A In each of the following sentences, two words are underlined. Write *C* above each underlined word that is spelled correctly. Above each misspelled word, write the word correctly.

Example 1. The team is relying ^C on his steadyness ^{*steadiness*} on the balance beam.

1. Please write a breif biography of the musician you studied.

2. Neil Armstrong photographed Buzz Aldrin stepping couragously onto the surface of the moon.

3. Unfortunatly, there are several scratches on the new piano.

4. Sometimes called the Sheild of David, the Star of David is an ancient symbol.

5. Turkies don't seem interested in eating tomatoes.

6. Native only in China, giant pandas have a diet consisting largly of bamboo shoots.

7. Earlier, the Joneses had asked for a table by the window.

8. Those monkeys are always getting into mischief!

9. There are two tubas and two celloes in this unusual quartet.

10. Leon regrets causeing the argument this morning.

EXERCISE B In each of the following sentences, underline the misspelled word or words. (Some sentences have more than one misspelled word.) Above each misspelled word, write the word correctly.

Example 1. My nieghbor's ^{*neighbor's*} dog thinks I am his new best friend; he followes ^{*follows*} me everywhere.

11. Niether Jeff nor Jason is related to Jeremiah.

12. Tonight we are supposed to read the foreword, introduction, and first two chapters of the book.

13. Aren't those the most adoreable kittens you've ever seen?

14. My homework is manageable, but I could have planed my schedule more carefully.

15. The captain's courage and calmness inspirred the sailors.

16. The gooses on my grandparents' farm are almost as large as the turkies.

17. Rod, Geraldo, and Dorothy are singing soloes in the performance tonight.

18. How many bushels of potatos did you harvest this year?

19. If I had three wishs, my first wish would be for piece on earth.

20. This is a fascinateing book; you should read it when I'm done.

Language and Sentence Skills Practice

Spelling B

EXERCISE A   On the lines provided, write the plural form of each of the following words.

Example 1. mouse _____ *mice* _____

1. woman _____
2. box _____
3. salmon _____
4. tomato _____
5. Chinese _____
6. radio _____
7. lens _____
8. itch _____
9. louse _____
10. deer _____

11. tax _____
12. strawberry _____
13. excess _____
14. begonia _____
15. 1960 _____
16. dictionary _____
17. video _____
18. Gonzalez _____
19. house _____
20. city _____

EXERCISE B   In the following sentences, underline each word that has *ie* or *ei* in it. Then, if the word is misspelled, write the word correctly above it. If the word is already spelled correctly, write *C* above it.

Example 1. Did some <u>ancient</u> people <u>believe</u> the sky was a bowl over the earth?
(above ancient: *C*) (above believe: *believe*)

21. My neighbor was releived when his dog came home.

22. I know that the human body needs protien, but I can't remember why.

23. We painted the cieling first, the walls next, and all the woodwork last.

24. For my last birthday, I recieved two CDs and a gift certificate.

25. Some cooks weigh thier ingredients; others use measuring cups.

26. Late last night we heard a wierd howling sound.

27. Everyone at my school is friendly to new students.

28. My three cats are always getting into mischeif of one kind or another.

29. The frieght trains are often hundreds of cars long.

30. Does anyone know what a "one-horse open sleigh" is?

for **CHAPTER 15: CORRECTING COMMON ERRORS**   *pages 329–38*

Words Often Confused

EXERCISE In each of the following sentences, underline the correct word in parentheses.

Example 1. For health reasons, my family often skips (*deserts,* *desserts*).

1. You may (*already, all ready*) know that Pelé is the nickname of an outstanding Brazilian soccer player.

2. Some Europeans mistakenly believe that Dallas is the (*capital, capitol*) of Texas.

3. The small (*cloths, clothes*) laid on the table were eventually called *place mats.*

4. Daniel and Marcia are first using (*course, coarse*) sandpaper on their bookshelves.

5. Chief Joseph (*led, lead*) many discussions in the interest of lasting peace.

6. A highway detour will (*alter, altar*) our route to town this week.

7. Sandra can't wait to (*brake, break*) a swimming record at the next summer Olympics.

8. Is fruit the (*principle, principal*) snack at schools in Italy, too?

9. This (*passed, past*) winter, the Rodriguez family went skiing in Canada.

10. (*They're, Their*) going to tennis practice this afternoon, so they can't meet us at the skating rink.

11. My sister went to a (*stationery, stationary*) store to order her wedding invitations.

12. In geometry, the intersection of two (*plains, planes*) is a line.

13. The rabbit wriggled (*it's, its*) nose and ears and hopped into the bushes.

14. I'm glad you enjoyed the movie; I liked it, (*to, too*).

15. Her parents are waiting over (*there, their*), on the corner.

16. (*Who's, Whose*) going on the field trip next Wednesday?

17. How did you (*loose, lose*) your house key?

18. Everyone has to (*choose, chose*) a partner for the next project.

19. Should we go to the concert (*altogether, all together*) or arrange a time to meet there?

20. The (*principle, principal*) reason I did so well on the test is that I studied hard.

COMMON ERRORS

Spelling and Words Often Confused

EXERCISE In the following passage, many of the underlined words are misspelled or are incorrectly used. If a word or usage is incorrect, write the correct spelling or word above it. If the word is already correct, write *C* above it.

Example You won't **[1]** ~~beleive~~ *believe* what happened to me this morning!

My sister and I were **[1]** <u>already</u> halfway out the door when **[2]** I <u>rememberred</u> that my home-

work was still lying on the table. What a **[3]** <u>releif</u> that I remembered! I knew Mr. Mehta, my math

teacher, wouldn't **[4]** <u>except</u> one more excuse from me.

"Hurry! **[5]** <u>Your</u> late! I'm late, **[6]** <u>too!</u>" my father called, as he rushed **[7]** <u>passed</u> us on his way

to work. Just at that moment, our dog sped **[8]** <u>through</u> the open door.

"Oh, no!" my sister moaned. "Now we'll be **[9]** <u>extremly</u> late!"

"**[10]** <u>Its</u> your turn to chase him," I said.

"No, it's not!" she **[11]** <u>argueed</u>. "It's yours, and I don't want to get my **[12]** <u>cloths</u> dirty."

"Is the dog **[13]** <u>lose</u> again?" called my mother. "That's the third time this **[14]** <u>weak</u>."

By that time, I knew we would both have to stop by the **[15]** <u>principle's</u> office before we went to

class. The second bell had probably **[16]** <u>all ready</u> rung. Just then our **[17]** <u>neighbor</u> came around

the corner, holding the dog by its collar. I **[18]** <u>lead</u> the dog into the house. Then I turned around

and started **[19]** <u>runing</u> toward school.

"**[20]** Don't <u>dessert</u> me!" my sister **[21]** <u>cryed</u>, but I didn't stop. All the way there, I practiced

excuses and **[22]** <u>apologies</u>. How could I ever expect anyone to **[23]** <u>beleive</u> that my **[24]** <u>tardy-

ness</u> really was the **[25]** <u>dogs'</u> fault?

Review A: Usage

EXERCISE A Rewrite the following sentences, correcting errors in the use of modifiers or negative words.

Example 1. The woman stopped to pick up her scarf who was pushing two children in a stroller.

The woman who was pushing two children in a stroller stopped to pick up her scarf.

1. We can't barely imagine a time when no one had radios or televisions.

_____

2. My friend Nita can run the 100-yard dash much more faster than I can.

_____

3. My brother had the worse case of flu in my family.

_____

4. "Don't tell no one about it!" warned Tom.

_____

5. We found the little boy on the slide who had been lost.

_____

EXERCISE B In each of the following sentences, underline the correct form of the verb in parentheses.

Example 1. Each of the children (*want, wants*) a turn on the swing.

6. Neither Hank nor Jesse (*remember, remembers*) the name of the movie.

7. All of the horses (*is, are*) in the corral.

8. The color of the new curtains certainly (*brighten, brightens*) the room.

9. Both Diana and Heidi (*has, have*) entered the essay contest.

10. Most of the apples (*has, have*) already been eaten.

EXERCISE C In the following sentences, underline the correct form of the pronoun in parentheses.

Example 1. If you don't want those grapes, may I have (*it, them*)?

11. She and (*they, them*) were studying in the library.

12. Either Felix or Mark wants to be a marine biologist when (*they, he*) grows up.

13. Was the author of that wonderful short story (*her, she*)?

14. When you're finished with the drawing, could you show it to her and (*I, me*)?

15. Each child must pick up (*their, his or her*) toys before snack time.

COMMON ERRORS

Review B: **Mechanics**

EXERCISE On the lines provided, rewrite each of the following sentences, using capital letters and punctuation where needed and correcting any misspelled or incorrect words.

Example 1. have you read my life with the polar bears the new book by sharons uncle

Have you read My Life with the Polar Bears, the new book by Sharon's uncle?

1. please schedule an appointment with dr thompson the nurse instructed

_____

2. the graduation ceremony is scheduled to begin at 7 30 pm on saturday june 15 2008

_____

3. frank and his two brothers dan and mike like board games movies and sports

_____

4. theirs no need for an argument simply divide the crackers between the two children

_____

5. you will need the following supplies string a candle a glass of water and a stopwatch

_____

6. i dont need to borrow carols book watership down ive brought my own

_____

7. accept for jerry, everyone can come to the party on Friday

_____

8. we shouldnt have forgoten to wear our jackets

_____

9. did she say dont sit on that chair

_____

10. your supposed to be their at six o clock

_____

HOLT HANDBOOK | Introductory Course

Review C: **Usage and Mechanics**

EXERCISE   In the following article for the school newspaper, most of the punctuation and capitalization has been left out. The writer has also made errors in usage and spelling. Correct each of the numbered sentences in the article by (1) inserting correct punctuation, (2) circling any letter that should be capitalized but is not, and (3) underlining any misspelled word or incorrect usage and writing the correct word or words above it.

Example [1] (t)he start of a new school year is all ways hectic.
                                                        always

[1] students have to cope with all of the following unfamiliar class schedules they're new teachers and more harder subjects [2] in addition to all those things the schools air conditioning system are broken [3] normaly, that wouldn't be much of a problem but its August and we are in the middle of a heat wave [4] the classrooms are so hot that we cant hardly concentrate [5] on tuesday August 19 the temperature were over 95 degrees at 8 00 AM [6] now that's hot

[7] coach smithson remind students that its really important to drink water in hot whether [8] the coach said everyone needs at least eight glass's of water every day [9] dr malkovich our principle has buyed and borrowed fans for the cafeteria and the gym [10] students may eat his or her lunches on the lawn she announced and teachers may hold her classes outside

[11] one of the science classes are all ready meeting outside [12] the students are conducting experiments about heat and light [13] the class even tryed to fry an egg on the sidewalk [14] the drama club will also be rehearsing outside [15] the club president is worried that the clubs opening performance of Youre a good man charlie brown may be delayed [16] she said that the auditorium is one of the hottest rooms in the school

[17] this reporter asked mr bolm the chief of the maintenance staff when will the air condition-ing be fixxed [18] mr bolm's answer was not a releif [19] the repairs will take a week or longer he said

[20] until the air conditioning system is fixed well all just have to try to keep cool and dream about snow

COMMON ERRORS

Proofreading Application: Public Announcement

Good writers are generally good proofreaders. Readers tend to admire and trust writing that is error-free. Make sure that you correct all errors in grammar, usage, spelling, and punctuation in your writing. Your readers will have more confidence in your words if you have done your best to proofread carefully.

Correct usage and punctuation is especially important when writing for the public. When your words will be seen by hundreds or even thousands of people, proofreading is critical. Errors that slip by you certainly will *not* slip by your readers. Errors drag down the reputation of a product, a company, a person, or an event.

Sooner or later, you'll write a classified ad, a poster for your club, or some other announcement. Proofread this type of document carefully so that errors cannot threaten your success.

PROOFREADING ACTIVITY

Find and correct the errors in usage and mechanics. Use proofreading symbols to make your corrections.

Example   ~~Your~~ *You're* invited!

> We're having the biggest and bestest Talent Show ever!
>
> Has you ever dreamed of being in the spotlight?
>
> Its your time to shine!
>
> Get out them dancing shoes!
>
> Dust off that old guitar and try and write a hit song!
>
> The Drama Club and the Student Council is accepting applications from performers.
>
> The Talent Show will be held in the auditorium of Lincoln Middle school.
>
> The show begins on March 1 at 7:00 P.M..
>
> Everybody in the school is welcome to audition their act at noon on Saturday, January 12.
>
> Parents and teachers let us hear or see your act!

Literary Model: Personal Essay

> This is my neighbor. Nice lady. Coming out her front door, on her way to work and in her "looking good" mode. She's locking the door now and picking up her daily luggage: purse, lunch bag, gym bag for aerobics, and the garbage bucket to take out. She turns, sees me, gives me the big, smiling Hello, and takes three steps across her front porch. And goes "AAAAAAAAAGGGGGGGGGGGGHHHHHHHHHH!!!!" *(That's a direct quote.)* At about the level of a fire engine at full cry. Spider web! She has walked full force into a spider web....
>
> Now a different view of this scene. Here is the spider. Rather ordinary, medium gray, middle-aged lady spider. She's been up since before dawn working on her web, and all is well.... She's out checking the moorings and thinking about the little gnats she'd like to have for breakfast. Feeling good. Ready for action. All of a sudden everything breaks loose—earthquake, tornado, volcano.
>
> —from *All I Really Need to Know I Learned in Kindergarten*
> by Robert Fulghum

EXERCISE A Underline each sentence fragment that appears in the above excerpt.

EXERCISE B Rewrite the first paragraph to eliminate all sentence fragments. That is, whenever you come to a sentence fragment, supply the words that would make it a sentence.

_____

_____

_____

_____

_____

_____

_____

_____

_____

_____

_____

From *All I Really Need to Know I Learned in Kindergarten* by Robert Fulghum. Copyright © 1986, 1988 by Robert L. Fulghum. Reprinted by permission of **Villard Books, a division of Random House, Inc.** Electronic format by permission of **Van der Leun Associates.**

Literary Model (continued)

EXERCISE C   Using the excerpt as a model, write the beginning of a first-person essay in which an event is portrayed from the perspective of two different living beings (either human or animal). As Fulghum did, use sentence fragments some of the time to make the essay seem more conversational.

_____

_____

_____

_____

_____

_____

_____

_____

_____

_____

EXERCISE D

1. Read your writing in Exercise C aloud. Listen carefully to the effect produced by the sentence fragments. Then, describe that effect.

_____

_____

_____

_____

_____

_____

2. Do you think sentence fragments would be effective in other forms of writing—for example, in book reports, essays, or business letters? Explain your answer.

_____

_____

_____

_____

_____

Writing Application: Debate

Using modifiers can help you communicate how a person, place, thing, or idea relates to something else. For example, if you were to write, "Shelly is the most creative person in the class," your readers would understand that no one else in the class is as creative as Shelly. However, you should be careful not to overuse modifiers, especially superlatives. Writers who overuse them run the risk of producing writing that may seem insincere. A proper balance of effective modifiers and vivid descriptions will help ensure good writing.

WRITING ACTIVITY

Your speech teacher has announced the topic for the next in-class debate: Is TV a good or bad influence in students' lives? Argue either that TV is a good influence or that it is a bad influence. As evidence for your points, select a TV show that you know well. Use at least two modifiers in comparative forms and at least two in superlative forms, but don't let the modifiers take the place of specific examples and reasons.

PREWRITING Choose your side in the debate. Then, think about the TV show you plan to use. List its characters. Recall episodes in which events happen that support your claim about TV's influence. Write a list of examples that you could use as evidence. Provide as much detail as you can in the prewriting stage so that you can choose the most convincing details for your speech. You may need to watch an episode or two of the show if memory isn't giving you the specifics you need.

WRITING In a debate, speakers usually state their claims immediately. They don't make listeners guess. Write a clear thesis statement about TV's influence. Then, organize your points. In what ways is TV a good or bad influence, and how does the show you have chosen support your points? How you order the points is your decision, but speakers know that listeners will remember longest the last point they hear. Therefore, speakers often save their best, most persuasive point for last.

REVISING Once you have a draft of your speech ready, work it over for strong, direct word choice. A debate is not the time to sound uncertain or apologetic! Write confidently, and get rid of words that weaken your points. Comparatives and superlatives will strengthen your points if you choose them carefully. At this point, you should also check punctuation of the show's title and of any quoted material.

PUBLISHING Check your speech for mistakes in spelling and punctuation. You don't want to trip over mistakes while speaking, and your teacher will expect a clean copy of your speech to read. Practice your speech several times so that you can deliver it smoothly.

EXTENDING YOUR WRITING

This exercise could lead to a more developed writing project. Take the other side of the debate, and find evidence to support the opposing viewpoint. This exercise will help you understand the topic more thoroughly; it could also lead to a strong essay on the pros and cons of TV.

Symbols for Revising and Proofreading

Symbol	Example	Meaning of Symbol
≡	I will see you on saturday morning.	Capitalize a lowercase letter.
/	My Ðog's name is Spot.	Lowercase a capital letter.
∧	Do not walk away from me.	Insert a missing word, letter, or punctuation mark.
ꝺ	After you go go home, give me a call.	Leave out a word, letter, or punctuation mark.
⌒	pelice	Change the order of letters or words.
¶	¶After you finish the first steps, continue on to the next.	Begin a new paragraph.
⊙	Dr⊙Chavez	Add a period.
∧	Yes⹁ I like strawberry smoothies.	Add a comma.

Recognizing Fragments

EXERCISE A Decide which of the following word groups are sentence fragments and which are complete sentences. On the line provided, write *S* for a complete sentence and *F* for a fragment.

Examples _____*F*_____ **1.** Like to travel to interesting places.

_____*S*_____ **2.** We had been planning this trip for a long time.

_____ **1.** Last summer my family went on an interesting vacation.

_____ **2.** Traveled to Portland, Oregon.

_____ **3.** Because of the city's Rose Festival in June.

_____ **4.** The festival was first held in 1907.

_____ **5.** Attended many sporting events.

_____ **6.** Several parades with amazing floats.

_____ **7.** Is also the location of the Rose Garden arena.

_____ **8.** Where the Portland Trail Blazers play basketball.

_____ **9.** Portland's nickname is the City of Roses.

_____ **10.** Why Portland is called the City of Roses.

_____ **11.** My brother suggested doing some research.

_____ **12.** Also had fun exploring downtown Portland.

_____ **13.** It was designed with pedestrians in mind.

_____ **14.** Many tree-lined streets.

_____ **15.** We crossed each of the city's eight bridges at least once.

_____ **16.** Enjoyed the warm days and cool nights.

_____ **17.** The weather much cooler than in our hometown of Phoenix.

_____ **18.** Could see Mount Hood from many places in Portland.

_____ **19.** The beautiful, snowcapped peak glistened.

_____ **20.** I hope we go back to Portland one day.

SENTENCES

Recognizing Fragments (continued)

EXERCISE B Decide which of the following word groups are sentence fragments and which are complete sentences. On the line provided, write *S* for a complete sentence and *F* for a fragment.

Examples __*S*__ **1.** I recently read an interesting book on woodcarving.

___*F*___ **2.** Learned many facts about the history of woodworking.

_____ **21.** The book describes how to carve practical items, such as furniture.

_____ **22.** Woodcarving also a form of artistic expression.

_____ **23.** Not by all cultures during all historical periods.

_____ **24.** Woodcarving was unknown in ancient Persia and Babylon.

_____ **25.** Common in ancient Egypt, for ordinary household items.

_____ **26.** Royal images and furniture in tombs.

_____ **27.** From about 700 to 480 B.C., the ancient Greeks sculpted in wood.

_____ **28.** Eventually came to use bronze and stone for fine works.

_____ **29.** The Romans also used bronze and stone for sculpting.

_____ **30.** In northern Europe, wood was used for sculpture.

_____ **31.** Prows of Viking ships were adorned with woodcarvings.

_____ **32.** Imaginary beasts and intricate patterns on ships and houses.

_____ **33.** From the eleventh to the seventeenth centuries, especially in churches.

_____ **34.** Wood was the most popular material for sculpture in Spain.

_____ **35.** Woodcarving an important part of Asian art as well.

_____ **36.** Especially in China, Japan, and Indonesia.

_____ **37.** Some cultures of the Pacific famous for their carved woodwork.

_____ **38.** Ceremonial wooden masks in many African cultures.

_____ **39.** Some American Indians also created wooden masks.

_____ **40.** Totem poles symbols of families and clans.

SENTENCES

Revising Fragments

EXERCISE A   Some of the following word groups are sentence fragments; some are complete sentences. If the word group is already a complete sentence, write *S* on the line provided. If the word group is a fragment, revise it by (1) adding a subject, (2) adding a verb, or (3) attaching the fragment to a complete sentence. You may also need to change the punctuation and capitalization in your revised sentence.

Example 1. Lisa's birthday coming soon.

Lisa's birthday was coming soon.

1. Sandra a surprise party for Lisa, her best friend.

2. Lisa's mother told Sandra that a party would be fun.

3. To celebrate her birthday with her new friends.

4. Sandra spent several days preparing the party.

5. Mailed out more than twenty invitations.

6. All but two people that they would be able to attend.

7. Promised to keep the party a secret.

8. The cake and decorations the day before the party.

9. Working on the day of the party.

10. Lisa truly surprised and happy.

SENTENCES

Language and Sentence Skills Practice

Recognizing Fragments (continued)

EXERCISE B   Some of the following word groups are sentence fragments; some are complete sentences. If the word group is already a complete sentence, write *S* on the line provided. If the word group is a fragment, revise it by (1) adding a subject, (2) adding a verb, or (3) attaching the fragment to a complete sentence. You may also need to change the punctuation and capitalization in your revised sentence.

Example 1. Lies about a thousand miles southeast of Florida.

Puerto Rico lies about a thousand miles southeast of Florida.
_____

11. Puerto Rico is a beautiful island.
_____

12. Puerto Rico in the West Indies.
_____

13. The mountain El Yunque in the Caribbean National Forest.
_____

14. Wild parrots live in a rain forest on El Yunque.
_____

15. If you have never seen a wild orchid.
_____

16. My uncle's farm only a two-hour drive from the national forest.
_____

17. Visited Puerto Rico in June of last year.
_____

18. Exploring the national forest with my aunt and uncle.
_____

19. Mahogany trees for the first time.
_____

20. I heard the song of the small tree frog called the *coquí*.
_____

SENTENCES

Identifying and Revising Run-on Sentences

EXERCISE A   Decide which of the following word groups are run-ons. Use proofreading marks to revise each run-on by (1) making it into two separate sentences or (2) using a comma and a coordinating conjunction. You may have to change the punctuation and capitalization, too. If the word group is already correct, write *C* on the line provided.

Examples _____ **1.** Choosing a career can be hard, *but* having a role model makes it easier.

_____ **2.** A role model might be a relative, mine is.

_____ **1.** When I was eight years old, most of my friends wanted to be firefighters I wanted to be an archaeologist.

_____ **2.** My grandmother inspired me, she is an archaeologist.

_____ **3.** She has worked on many sites, including the remains of the Jamestown settlement in Virginia.

_____ **4.** My grandmother is also a good storyteller, she has told some amazing stories about her work.

_____ **5.** She vividly described the team's discovery, the skeleton of a man in his twenties who had been buried at the settlement about four hundred years earlier.

_____ **6.** The team dug up more than 100,000 objects they found swords, jewelry, and seventeenth-century coins.

_____ **7.** History fascinates me, one day I would like to dig up something that has been buried for hundreds of years.

_____ **8.** Next summer, I'm going to be a volunteer at the excavation site of an early pioneer settlement.

_____ **9.** My grandmother arranged for me to be on the dig she will be there, too.

_____ **10.** The dig is in North Carolina the work will be great experience for me.

SENTENCES

Language and Sentence Skills Practice

Identifying and Revising Run-on Sentences (continued)

EXERCISE B Decide which of the following word groups are run-ons. Use proofreading marks to revise each run-on by (1) making it into two separate sentences or (2) using a comma and a coordinating conjunction. You may have to change the punctuation and capitalization, too. If the word group is already correct, write C on the line provided.

Examples _____ **1.** Fashions change with time⌃styles vary from place to place.

_____ **2.** Even human features are subject to fashion⌇the beard is a good example.

_____ **11.** Although men have always been able to grow facial hair, beards have not always been in fashion.

_____ **12.** Among many ancient peoples, the beard was looked upon as a sign of strength removing it was a form of punishment.

_____ **13.** Ancient Egyptian men, however, shaved their beards they let them grow only when they were mourning someone's death.

_____ **14.** During some periods of history, it was fashionable to be cleanshaven when the ruler was, this practice happened in both France and Spain.

_____ **15.** During other periods and in other countries, such as eighteenth-century Russia, the ruler dictated that men had to shave.

_____ **16.** While Queen Elizabeth I was on the English throne, beards were very popular the noblemen were especially fond of them.

_____ **17.** Facial hair continued to he fashionable in England until about 1660, by the eighteenth century beards were no longer popular.

_____ **18.** As the eighteenth century ended, beards once again gained popularity.

_____ **19.** Nowadays, fashion is more relaxed, being bearded and being cleanshaven are both fashionable.

_____ **20.** I prefer the cleanshaven look my father wears a beard because shaving irritates his skin.

SENTENCES

Identifying and Revising Stringy Sentences

EXERCISE A Decide which of the following sentences are stringy. Use proofreading marks to revise each stringy sentence by breaking it into two or more sentences. If an item is already correct, write *C* on the line provided.

Example _____ **1.** Bird-watching is a great way to see many kinds of birds in their

natural environment, and you don't have to go very far to do so, and I go

to a wildlife sanctuary just outside town.

_____ **1.** My uncle Raymond loves bird-watching, and once a month, I go on a nature walk

with him, and he tells me about the birds in our area.

_____ **2.** We don't take along much equipment because all we need is a pair of binoculars, a

field guide to the birds, and a notebook in which we write our sightings.

_____ **3.** We go to the bird sanctuary, and it's about three miles from my house, and it covers

forty square miles.

_____ **4.** The best time to go bird-watching is just after sunrise, and my uncle picks me up in his

truck, and most of the people in my neighborhood are still sleeping.

_____ **5.** Uncle Raymond is concerned about the environment, and bird-watching is just one

way that he shows his interest in the natural world.

_____ **6.** He goes backpacking in wilderness areas, and he goes cross-country skiing in the win-

ter, and he also belongs to four different environmental organizations.

_____ **7.** Birds respond to their environment, and a small change in their world can greatly

affect their habits.

_____ **8.** We watch animals other than birds, and one Saturday, Uncle Raymond spotted a chip-

munk, and another time, I noticed a doe and her fawn behind a tree, and we always

see a lot of butterflies and moths.

_____ **9.** Last time I saw baby robins in their nest, and there were four babies, and an adult bird

was feeding them.

_____ **10.** After our walk, Uncle Raymond and I go to my house, and we look up each bird in a

guide, and we show my parents pictures of the birds we saw.

SENTENCES

Language and Sentence Skills Practice

Identifying and Revising Stringy Sentences (continued)

EXERCISE B   Decide which of the following sentences are stringy. Use proofreading marks to revise each stringy sentence by breaking it into two or more sentences. If an item is already correct, write *C* on the line provided.

Example _____ **1.** Most people would not think that a diving suit could save a cathedral, and the truth is that such a thing has happened, and William Walker is to thank for it.

_____ **11.** A huge stone building does not seem likely to sink, and in 1905, England's Winchester Cathedral certainly looked solid, and it had stood for over nine hundred years.

_____ **12.** Christians had been worshipping in Winchester Cathedral since it was built more than nine hundred years ago in England.

_____ **13.** However, Winchester Cathedral was sinking into a bog, and the cathedral had been built on a bed of underwater peat, and the peat was formed from decaying plants.

_____ **14.** Someone needed to dig out the peat and replace it with something more solid, but underwater peat was difficult to reach, and an inventive approach was needed.

_____ **15.** William Walker was recruited, and Walker was an experienced deep-sea diver, and his diving suit allowed him to spend long periods of time underwater.

_____ **16.** For years, visitors to the cathedral saw a man wearing a diving suit, and Walker put on his 200-pound suit each day, and then he worked underwater for six hours.

_____ **17.** He dug out the peat and put in 25,000 sacks of concrete, 115,000 concrete blocks, and roughly a million bricks.

_____ **18.** Walker finished in 1912, and a service was held to give thanks for the restoration, and King George V then thanked Walker for his work.

_____ **19.** Walker's skill and hard work paid off, and he saved one of England's finest cathedrals, and now many more visitors can enjoy this historic monument.

_____ **20.** Now you know how a diving suit saved Winchester Cathedral.

SENTENCES

Active and Passive Voice

EXERCISE A On the lines provided, tell whether the verb in each of the following sentences is in the *active voice* or the *passive voice*. Then, revise each sentence that is in the passive voice so that it is in the active voice.

Example 1. Has that room been cleaned by Ruben?

passive—Has Ruben cleaned that room?
_____

1. The dog was given a bath by Dad.
_____

2. Was the lamp in the living room broken by Sally?
_____

3. Next week, Isabel will return the books to the library.
_____

4. The desk was moved by Mom yesterday.
_____

5. I have been reading this book for two weeks.
_____

6. Did you see the evening news?
_____

7. That drawing on the refrigerator was made by Claire.
_____

8. At the end of the year, the house will be painted by the family.
_____

9. The key has been on the table all day.
_____

10. Have the pictures been developed by the photo shop?
_____

SENTENCES

Language and Sentence Skills Practice

Active and Passive Voice (continued)

EXERCISE B   On the lines provided, tell whether the verb in each of the following sentences is in the *active voice* or the *passive voice*. Then, revise each sentence that is in the passive voice so that it is in the active voice.

Example 1. Has the project been discussed by the students?

passive—Have the students discussed the project?

11. A squirrel has been living in our oak tree for several years.

_____

12. Teresa was praised by Mrs. Johnson for her essay.

_____

13. Several old books were bought by the visitors at the used-book store.

_____

14. Have all of your friends been invited to the party by you?

_____

15. From the top of the hill, we were able to see our house and our school.

_____

16. Stacey was made captain of the team by the coach.

_____

17. Will Dena be taking Spanish next year, too?

_____

18. At the next class, the homework assignments will be collected by Mr. Tillman.

_____

19. The group was taken to the rose gardens by the tour guide.

_____

20. Have Carlton and Alex been chosen by the principal to represent the school?

_____

SENTENCES

HOLT HANDBOOK | Introductory Course

Review A: Fragments, Run-ons, and Stringy Sentences; Active and Passive Voice

EXERCISE A   The following word groups are sentence fragments, run-ons, stringy sentences, or passive voice sentences. On the lines provided, revise each fragment, run-on, or stringy sentence to make it clear and complete. Revise each passive voice sentence to make it an active voice sentence. Remember to add correct punctuation and capitalization. If a sentence is already correct, write *C* on the line.

Example 1. In Mexico many beautiful sites. _In Mexico there are many beautiful sites._

1. If you are in Mexico, be sure to visit Xochimilco it is near Mexico City. _____

_____

2. Famous for the floating gardens on Lake Xochimilco. _____

_____

3. On the lake, the Aztecs and other American Indians built these gardens, called *chinampas*.

_____

4. The gardens do not actually float they are small, artificial islands. _____

_____

5. They were made by farmers from layers of vegetation and mud taken from the lake. _____

_____

6. Farmers sprouted seeds on rafts made of rushes, and they moved the rafts where they needed

them, and the farmers then transplanted plants to the gardens. _____

_____

_____

7. No one watered the *chinampas* the gardens got all the water they needed from the lake. _____

_____

8. Vegetables, as well as flowers, were raised by the Aztecs on these fertile garden islands. _____

_____

9. Helped feed the growing population of an expanding empire. _____

_____

10. Some *chinampas* still exist, and flowers and other crops grow on them, and families enjoy them

as quiet places to picnic and relax. _____

_____

SENTENCES

Review A (continued)

EXERCISE B The following word groups are sentence fragments, run-ons, stringy sentences, or passive voice sentences. On the lines provided, revise each fragment, run-on, or stringy sentence to make it clear and complete. Revise each passive voice sentence to make it an active voice sentence. Remember to add correct punctuation and capitalization. If a sentence is already correct, write C on the line.

Example 1. Many cultures have fairy tales, and these fairy tales pass from one generation to the next, and they become important parts of the culture. _____

Many cultures have fairy tales, and these fairy tales pass from one generation to the next. They become important parts of the culture.

11. Fairy tales from two very different cultures sometimes surprisingly similar. _____

_____

12. "Cinderella" is a German fairy tale "Yeh-Shen" is a fairy tale from China. _____

_____

13. When one compares "Cinderella" and "Yeh-Shen," the two stories are quite similar. _____

_____

14. In the German fairy tale, a stepdaughter is not allowed by a stepmother to go to a ball. _____

_____

15. However, a fairy godmother grants the young woman's wish to attend, and she goes to the ball, and she wears the beautiful clothes and glass slippers that her fairy godmother gives her.

_____

16. She leaves the ball in a hurry and a slipper that she loses leads a prince to her. _____

_____

17. In "Yeh-Shen," a mistreated stepdaughter is not allowed to go to a festival an old man teaches her how to wish on magic fish bones. _____

_____

18. The fish bones give her beautiful clothes and slippers she wears them to the festival. _____

_____

19. Leaves in a hurry, and on the way home, she loses one slipper. _____

_____

20. The stories are very similar, and they are probably two versions of the same tale, and there are nearly seven hundred other versions of the tale. _____

_____

SENTENCES

Combining Sentences by Inserting Words

EXERCISE A   Each of the following items contains two sentences. Combine the two sentences by taking the underlined key word from one sentence and inserting it into the other sentence. The directions in parentheses will tell you how to change the form of the key word if you need to do so. Use carets to show where you are inserting words. When you are finished, draw a line through the unused sentence.

Example 1. I like to hear stories about ^historical^ places around the world. ~~I like stories about places with a history~~. (Change *y* to *i*, and add *–cal*.)

1. Last fall my aunt went on tours of palaces in England. The tours were <u>incredible</u>.

2. She was fascinated by the palace called Hampton Court in London. Her fascination was <u>extreme</u>. (add *–ly*.)

3. Cardinal Thomas Wolsey began construction on the palace in the 1500s. He began construction in the <u>early</u> part of the 1500s.

4. The palace later became the residence of King Henry VIII. It was his <u>favorite</u> residence.

5. Henry VIII began the garden at Hampton Court. The garden was a <u>showplace</u>.

6. One feature of Hampton Court is the garden hedge that forms a maze. This feature is <u>interesting</u>.

7. The maze was planted in 1702 by another king. His name was <u>William III</u>.

8. The maze is formed by hedges. The hedges are <u>clipped</u>.

9. The palace grounds are <u>magnificent</u>. A path called the Broad Walk runs for half a mile through the palace grounds.

10. The palace is a <u>beauty</u>. My aunt encouraged me to visit this palace one day. (Change *y* to *i*, and add *–ful*.)

SENTENCES

Combining Sentences by Inserting Words (continued)

EXERCISE B   Each of the following items contains two sentences. Combine the two sentences by taking the underlined key word from one sentence and inserting it into the other sentence. The directions in parentheses will tell you how to change the form of the key word if you need to do so. Use carets to show where you are inserting words. When you are finished, draw a line through the unused sentence.

Example 1. The United States has set aside ^*various* sites as national parks. ~~The sites vary.~~ (Change *vary* to *various*.)

11. In July I went to a national park. It was an <u>impressive</u> place.

12. Carlsbad Caverns National Park has a system of caves with rock formations on the floors and ceilings. The caves are <u>underground</u>.

13. The parklands in the National Park System include parks, monuments, and historic sites. All of these places—whether they are parks, monuments, or historic sites—are <u>noteworthy</u>.

14. An especially interesting national park, the Petrified Forest, has tree trunks that have turned to stone because they are millions of years old. The tree trunks are <u>multicolored</u>.

15. Known for its species of birds, Everglades National Park is a good place to visit. This park has <u>many</u> different bird species for visitors to see.

16. Mesa Verde National Park preserves ruins of hundreds of Pueblo dwellings, some of which are more than twelve centuries old. These ancient living quarters were built into <u>cliffs</u>. (Change *cliffs* to *cliff*.)

17. The environment of Death Valley is <u>extreme</u>. Scientists and visitors like to learn about the environment of Death Valley, which is the lowest, hottest, and driest part of North America.

18. Fort Sumter National Monument, which marks the fort where the Civil War began, can be reached by boat. The fort itself has been <u>modified</u>.

19. The Statue of Liberty's torch is <u>enormous</u>. One of America's most famous national monuments is the Statue of Liberty whose torch is nearly thirty feet tall.

20. Visited by French and Spanish health seekers in the 1700s, the springs of Hot Springs National Park have an average temperature of 143 degrees Fahrenheit. The springs are <u>natural</u>.

Combining Sentences by Inserting Word Groups

EXERCISE A Combine each of the following pairs of sentences by taking the underlined word group from one sentence and inserting it into the other sentence. Use a caret to show where you are inserting words. Then, add commas or change capitalization where needed. When you are finished, draw a line through the unused sentence.

Example 1. Marta ^*My best friend,*^ reported on a great story called "The People Could Fly. ~~Marta is my best friend.~~

1. She read the story in a book. It was a book <u>of American folk tales.</u>

2. Virginia Hamilton retold the tale. She is <u>the granddaughter of a man who had escaped slavery in Virginia.</u>

3. A young enslaved woman named Sarah is not permitted to stop working to feed her crying baby. This event happens <u>in the folk tale.</u>

4. Sarah is <u>exhausted and desperate.</u> She can no longer tolerate the harshness of her life.

5. Toby is <u>an older man who works with Sarah.</u> Toby helps her by chanting words that make her fly away with her baby.

6. The next day a young man who is working falls sick from the heat. He is working <u>in the fields.</u>

7. Toby repeats the chant, and the young man flies away. The chant is <u>from Africa.</u>

8. Marta told us that we had to read the story to find out whether all the enslaved workers fly away. They fly away <u>to freedom.</u>

9. Virginia Hamilton has written other books in which she retells American folk tales. The folk tales are <u>from the deep South.</u>

10. Marta and I are going to the library <u>this weekend.</u> Marta and I are going to the library to find folk tales similar to "The People Could Fly."

SENTENCES

Combining Sentences by Inserting Word Groups (continued)

EXERCISE B   Combine each of the following pairs of sentences by taking the underlined word group from one sentence and inserting it into the other sentence. Use a caret to show where you are inserting words. Then, add commas or change capitalization where needed. When you are finished, draw a line through the unused sentence.

Example   1.   I just read a book about _∧Vincent van Gogh. *my favorite artist,* ~~He is my favorite artist~~.

11.   Are you familiar with the paintings of Vincent van Gogh? He was a <u>nineteenth-century Dutch artist</u>.

12.   Vincent van Gogh was born near Brabant. He was the <u>son of a minister</u>.

13.   He expressed great emotion in his work. He did this <u>by using intense colors and exaggerated lines</u>.

14.   One of his most famous paintings uses deep blues and yellows. It is <u>called *The Starry Night*</u>.

15.   The stars are surrounded by heavy, circular brushstrokes. The stars are <u>above a quiet village</u>.

16.   Van Gogh painted *Potato Eaters* in 1885 when he was a preacher. He was <u>inspired by the Belgian peasants among whom he lived</u>.

17.   In 1886, he went to Paris to live. He lived <u>with his brother Théo, an art dealer</u>.

18.   From the time he left Paris until his death in 1890, he wrote more than 700 letters. He wrote the letters <u>to his brother</u>.

19.   The letters are <u>an art historian's dream</u>. These letters provide documentation of some 750 paintings and 1,600 drawings that van Gogh created in his short lifetime.

20.   His pictures were <u>not considered valuable in his lifetime</u>. His pictures are auctioned today at high prices.

SENTENCES

Combining Sentences by Joining Subjects and Verbs

EXERCISE A   Use *and*, *but*, or *or* to combine each of the following pairs of sentences. If the sentences have the same verb, make one sentence with a compound subject. If the sentences have the same subject, make one sentence with a compound verb. The hints in parentheses will help you. Write your answers on the lines provided.

Example 1. North Carolina borders Tennessee. Kentucky borders Tennessee. (Join with *and*.)   *North Carolina and Kentucky border Tennessee.*

1. Northern states have diverse environments. Southern states have diverse environments. (Join with *and*.) _____

2. You can explore a swamp in Florida. You can go to a beach in Florida. (Join with *or*.)

_____

3. Michigan is home to American Indian burial grounds. Illinois is home to American Indian burial grounds. (Join with *and*.) _____

_____

4. Visitors to Texas can walk through pine forests. Visitors to Texas can explore sand dunes. (Join with *or*.) _____

_____

5. Sequoia trees are found in California. Sequoia trees are not found in North Dakota. (Join with *but*.) _____

6. California borders the Colorado River. Nevada borders the Colorado River. (Join with *and*.)

_____

7. Tourists visiting Maine can ski in the winter. Tourists visiting Maine can go sailing in the summer. (Join with *or*.) _____

_____

8. Georgia has popular beaches. Texas has popular beaches. (Join with *and*.) _____

_____

9. Utah has deserts and ski resorts. Arizona has deserts and ski resorts. (Join with *and*.) _____

_____

10. You can fish through the ice in Minnesota in the winter. You can cross-country ski in Minnesota in the winter. (Join with *or*.) _____

_____

SENTENCES

Combining Sentences by Joining Subjects and Verbs (continued)

EXERCISE B Use *and*, *but*, or *or* to combine each of the following pairs of sentences. If the sentences have the same verb, make one sentence with a compound subject. If the sentences have the same subject, make one sentence with a compound verb The hints in parentheses will help you. Write your answers on the lines provided.

Example 1. To do well in school, you should stay healthy. To do well in school you should get enough sleep. (Join with *and*.) *To do well in school, you should stay healthy and get enough sleep.*

11. Getting enough exercise will help you stay healthy. Eating vitamin-rich foods will help you stay healthy. (Join with *and*.) _____

_____

12. Vitamin D regulates the absorption of calcium. Vitamin D helps prevent bone disorders. (Join with *and*.) _____

13. To get vitamin D, you can eat eggs, fish, and dairy products. To get vitamin D, you can enjoy a few minutes in the sunshine. (Join with *or*.) _____

_____

14. Vitamin C is essential. Vitamin C cannot be stored in the body. (Join with *but*.) _____

_____

15. Most fruits and vegetables contain vitamin C. Most fruits and vegetables lack vitamin B12. (Join with *but*.) _____

16. Tomatoes are a good source of vitamin C. Citrus fruits are a good source of vitamin C. (Join with *and*.) _____

17. A person with a vitamin A deficiency may have skin problems. A person with a vitamin A deficiency may develop night blindness. (Join with *or*.) _____

_____

18. Eggs are rich in vitamin A. Milk products are rich in vitamin A. (Join with *and*.) _____

_____

19. Nuts are good sources of vitamin E. Leafy vegetables are a good source of vitamin E. (Join with *and*.) _____

20. Deficiencies in vitamin K can cause problems with blood clotting. Such deficiencies rarely occur in humans. (Join with *but*.) _____

Combining Complete Sentences

EXERCISE A The following pairs of short, choppy sentences need improving. Use editing marks to combine each pair into one sentence by using the connecting word given in parentheses. Be sure to change the capitalization and punctuation where necessary.

Example **1.** Each student in our class is giving a report on a different country. I chose New

Zealand as my topic. (Join with *and*.)

1. New Zealand is made up of two main islands. It also includes many small islands. (Join with *and*.)

2. New Zealand has two kinds of native bats. It has no snakes. (Join with *but*.)

3. All New Zealanders between the ages of six and fifteen must attend school. Those who choose to attend school between the ages of sixteen and nineteen do not have to pay for this education. (Join with *and*.)

4. Visitors to New Zealand can see hot springs on the North Island. They can tour glaciers on the South Island. (Join with *or*.)

5. You might not expect a glacier and a rain forest to exist right next to each other. One place in New Zealand has a glacier that flows into a rain forest. (Join with *but*.)

6. Most places in this country are within view of hills or mountains. All places in New Zealand are within 80 miles of a coastline. (Join with *and*.)

7. If I were to visit New Zealand, I'd like to see a cricket game. Perhaps my first priority would be to see a rugby game. (Join with *or*.)

8. The majority of New Zealand's citizens are of European descent. The first settlers in the country were Polynesian. (Join with *but*.)

9. About four hundred earthquakes occur in New Zealand every year. Nearly three fourths of these earthquakes are so mild that they are not even felt. (Join with *but*.)

10. New Zealanders support equal rights for all citizens. In 1893, New Zealand became the first nation in the world to allow women to vote. (Join with *and*.)

SENTENCES

Language and Sentence Skills Practice

Combining Complete Sentences (continued)

EXERCISE B   The following pairs of short, choppy sentences need improving. Use editing marks to combine each pair into one sentence by using the connecting word given in parentheses. Be sure to change the capitalization and punctuation where necessary.

Example   **1.**   Lorenzo went to the library. A few other students from his science class were there.
(Join with *and*.)

1. Lorenzo was doing research on the scientist Dian Fossey. The librarian recommended that he read Fossey's book *Gorillas in the Mist*. (Join with *and*.)

12. Gorillas had long been considered violent and aggressive. Fossey's studies of them indicated that they are gentle and social. (Join with *but*.)

13. An American scientist's observations about gorillas had inspired Fossey. Fossey traveled to Africa in 1963. (Join with *and*.)

14. Fossey's observations required patience. Over time she came to know each gorilla that inhabited her study area. (Join with *but*.)

15. Fossey knew she had to observe the gorillas quietly and patiently. She might frighten them if she were impatient. (Join with *or*.)

16. Her study site became world famous. She established a research center there in 1967. (Join with *and*.)

17. Fossey earned a college degree in 1954 and worked at a children's hospital for several years. She later decided to earn a Ph.D. in zoology, the study of animals. (Join with *but*.)

18. The habitats of the only surviving mountain gorillas must be protected. These animals could become extinct. (Join with *or*.)

19. Lorenzo found these facts interesting. He included them in his report. (Join with *and*.)

20. Lorenzo could use drawings of gorillas in his research presentation. Photos of Fossey and the gorillas she studied might be more effective. (Join with *but*.)

SENTENCES

Combining Sentences by Using Subordination

EXERCISE A The following pairs of short, choppy sentences need improving. Use editing marks to make each pair into one sentence by using the connecting word given in parentheses. Be sure to change the capitalization and punctuation where necessary. When you are finished, draw a line through the unused sentence.

Example 1. My aunt Julia, *whose home is in North Carolina,* enjoys her job as an ecologist. ~~Aunt Julia's home is in North Carolina.~~

(*whose*)

1. I hope to be an ecologist one day. I joined my school's environmental club. (*because*)

2. Ecologists study the environment. People can live well without losing environmental resources. (*so that*)

3. Last fall the club's president organized several fundraisers. The club's president wanted to go on a three-day field trip. (*who*)

4. We chose Everglades National Park as our destination. Everglades National Park has a variety of plants and animals. (*which*)

5. We made the trip. Each member gave a presentation about some aspect of the park's ecology. (*before*)

6. On the bus trip I sat next to Rosa. Rosa is my lab partner. (*who*)

7. Some students took a canoe trip down the park's Wilderness Waterway. Others took long hikes. (*while*)

8. I had never seen one before. I immediately recognized the white heron when I saw it. (*although*)

9. I spent hours making sketches of birds. I created a series of watercolors. (*after*)

10. You are interested in joining a club. You should get involved. (*if*)

SENTENCES

Combining Sentences by Using Subordination (continued)

EXERCISE B The following pairs of short, choppy sentences need improving. Use editing marks to make each pair into one sentence by using the connecting word given in parentheses. Be sure to change the capitalization and punctuation where necessary.

Example 1. Ella's cousin enjoys learning facts about the Olympic games. Olympians often have
~~because~~
unusual and interesting stories. (*because*)

11. Carl Lewis is a particularly memorable athlete. He is the only man who has repeated as long jump champion. (*because*)

12. Romanian gymnast Nadia Comaneci won three gold medals at the 1976 Olympic games. She was the first competitor to receive a perfect score on an Olympic gymnastic event. (*who*)

13. The purpose of the Olympics is to allow individuals to compete. The International Olympic Committee does not keep official tallies of the medals won by different nations. (*because*)

14. Most Olympic sports divide competitions between men and women. Horseback riding and some yachting events can have men and women on the same team. (*although*)

15. Nearly 100 more nations compete in the Summer Games than compete in the Winter Games. The Winter Games is a smaller event. (*which*)

16. Each Olympics is held in its host city. Runners and volunteers from around the world spend four weeks carrying the Olympic torch from Greece to the host city. (*before*)

17. Alberto Juantorena of Cuba won the 400- and 800-meter races in the 1976 Olympics. No runner had ever achieved this feat. (*until*)

18. American Eric Heiden won all five men's speed-skating events at the 1980 Olympics. He also broke Olympic records in all five of these events. (*when*)

19. East German swimmer Kristin Otto won six gold medals in the 1988 Olympics. She broke a women's Olympic record. (*as soon as*)

20. Each Olympic athlete competes in a certain uniform. The uniform is provided by his or her country. (*that*)

SENTENCES

Review A: **Revising a Paragraph by Combining Sentences**

EXERCISE A The following paragraph sounds choppy because it has too many short sentences. Using the methods you have learned, combine some of the sentences to make the paragraph read more smoothly.

Example I have been studying the history of dog breeds. I have particularly been studying Saint

Bernards. *I have been studying the history of dog breeds, particulary Saint Bernards.*

_____

   The Saint Bernard is a breed of dog. It is a breed of working dog. The Saint Bernard stands about twenty-five inches high at the shoulder. The Saint Bernard weighs up to two hundred pounds. The dog was named. The dog was named for the monastery of Saint Bernard in the Alps. Since the 1600s, the dog has been used to rescue people. It has been used to help rescue people lost in snowdrifts in the Alps. The Saint Bernard has a keen sense of smell. It has a keen sense of direction. The dog uses these abilities to detect people buried in the snow. It uses these abilities to lead rescuers back to safety. Saint Bernards have helped rescue people in dangerous situations. They have helped rescue thousands of people.

_____
_____
_____
_____
_____
_____
_____
_____
_____
_____
_____
_____
_____
_____

SENTENCES

Language and Sentence Skills Practice

Review B: Revising a Paragraph by Combining Sentences (continued)

EXERCISE B The following paragraph sounds choppy because it has too many short sentences. Using the methods you have learned, combine some of the sentences to make the paragraph read more smoothly.

Example I have been reading an interesting book about John Muir. John Muir was one of the early supporters of the idea of a national park system. *I have been reading an interesting book abot John Muir, one of the early supporters of the idea of a national park system.*

Have you been to Yosemite National Park? Have you heard about Yosemite National Park? The U.S. Congress created this park in 1890. It is a magnificent park. It was created largely because of the efforts of John Muir. John Muir was the founder of the Sierra Club. Muir was born in Scotland in 1838. His family moved to Wisconsin. The family moved when he was eleven years old. In 1867, he suffered an eye injury. The eye injury left him temporarily blind. He regained his sight. He regained it after a month of blindness. Then he decided to devote his energies to enjoying nature. He walked a thousand miles. He walked from Indianapolis, Indiana, to the Gulf of Mexico. In 1868, he settled in California. He settled in the Yosemite Valley. He herded sheep in Yosemite. He :ame to love the region that he would later help to preserve.

SENTENCES

Review C: **Writing Clear Sentences**

EXERCISE A The paragraph below is hard to read because it contains at least one of each of the following errors: sentence fragment, run-on sentence, and stringy sentence. Rewrite the paragraph to correct these errors and make the paragraph read more smoothly.

Example A magnificent natural formation lies on the border between Canada and the United States, and it has heavy falling water that pummels the different kinds of stone beneath it, and it is a unique place called Niagara Falls. *A magnificent natural formation lies on the border between Canada and the United State. A unique place called Niagara Falls, this formation has heavy falling water that pummels the different kinds of stone beneath it.*

Between the borders of Canada and the United States. A famous and spectacular natural formation. Located on the Niagara River, Niagara Falls is a huge waterfall with sections that are over 150 feet high and 2,500 feet wide. Niagara Falls was probably created more than twelve thousand years ago when an immense sheet of ice melted and caused Lake Erie to overflow, and since then, Niagara Falls has developed into a pair of large falls that tumble into a steep gorge. Niagara Falls is made of a set of two waterfalls: American Falls, which is located in New York, and Horseshoe Falls, which is located in Ontario. The motion of water continuously crashing over the falls creates erosion, almost one inch of the rock ledge of American Falls wears away each year. Horseshoe Falls, which has much more water flowing over it, erodes its ledge at a rate of three inches to six feet every year. Ever since the 1800s, Niagara Falls has been a popular tourist destination, this fact is not surprising. This natural wonder a fascinating place.

_____

_____

_____

_____

_____

_____

_____

_____

_____

_____

_____

_____

_____

_____

SENTENCES

Review C: (continued)

EXERCISE B   The following paragraph is hard to read because it contains sentence fragments, run-on sentences, and choppy and stringy sentences. Rewrite the paragraph to correct these errors and make the paragraph read more smoothly.

Example   In the early part of the twentieth century, working conditions for many United States factory workers were unhealthy. The working conditions were dangerous. *In the early part of the twentieth century, working conditions for many United States factory workers were unhealthy and dangerous.*

Alice Hamilton is a prominent figure in the history of medicine in the United States, her efforts led to safer workplace conditions for Americans. Hamilton was born in 1869 in New York City into a well-to-do family. She was actually raised in Indiana. When her father's business failed. Hamilton realized she would have to earn her own living. She decided to study medicine. She became a professor of pathology, the study of diseases. She became a professor of pathology in 1897. In Chicago she worked at Hull House. Hull House was a famous settlement house where immigrants and poor people received assistance. Hamilton ran a clinic, and in the clinic she saw an increasing number of lead poisoning cases, and she became concerned. Because lead poisoning was a serious problem for many industrial workers, Hamilton began to investigate poisonous substances used in American factories. She conducted a statewide survey of industrial poisons in Illinois in 1908. In 1911, began a national survey of occupational diseases. As a result, by the late 1930s, all states had laws that required job-related safety measures. In 1919, Hamilton became the first woman faculty member of Harvard University, and she was named professor of industrial medicine, and while she was at Harvard, she worked with companies to correct workplace practices that were harmful to employees.

_____

_____

_____

_____

_____

_____

_____

_____

_____

_____

_____

SENTENCES